International Criminology

This book provides a clear, accessible yet critical introduction to how conventional criminologists in the UK, the USA and Australia think about and carry out research on crime. What do we mean by ideas like 'crime' or 'violence'? And is measuring crime rates actually possible? This book

- offers a thoughtful, comparative, historical account of how criminology has evolved into a modern social scientific discipline;
- provides a simple framework for anyone wanting to understand criminologists, showing how it is possible to think critically about the claims made and evidence used by criminologists;
- points out the value of checking the assumptions relied on by criminologists;
- shows how a combination of persistent social myths and preoccupations with scientific rigour have produced simplistic explanations like 'poverty causes crime';
- provides a lively, critical counterbalance to various beliefs that obstruct more practical approaches to crime.

Outlining the key ideas, vocabulary, assumptions and findings of the discipline in a highly accessible and clear way, while opening up a set of critical underlying issues and problems, *International Criminology* will prove to be a valuable introduction for undergraduate students of criminology and sociology worldwide, and will serve as a useful refresher for more experienced students.

Rob Watts is Professor of Social Policy at Royal Melbourne Institute of Technology University, Australia. He is an award-winning university teacher and the author and co-author of many books including *Sociology Australia* (2007) with Judith Bessant, and *States of Violence* (forthcoming).

Judith Bessant is Professor of Youth Studies and Sociology at Royal Melbourne Institute of Technology University, Australia, and is one of the most published social scientists in Australia. She publishes and teaches in the areas of youth studies, social policy, social history and sociology.

Richard Hil is Senior Lecturer in the School of Arts and Social Sciences at Southern Cross University, Australia. His main areas of interest are youth justice, child and family welfare, criminology, and peace and conflict studies. Richard is founder and director of the Bellingen Institute and associate director of the Centre for Peace and Social Justice at Southern Cross University.

International Criminology

A critical introduction

Rob Watts, Judith Bessant and Richard Hil

Routledge
Taylor & Francis Group

LONDON AND NEW YORK

First published 2008
by Routledge
2 Park Square, Milton Park, Abingdon, Oxon OX14 4RN

Simultaneously published in the USA and Canada
by Routledge
270 Madison Avenue, New York, NY 10016

Routledge is an imprint of the Taylor & Francis Group, an informa business

Typeset in Times New Roman by
Florence Production Ltd, Stoodleigh, Devon
Printed and bound in Great Britain by
MPG Books Ltd, Bodmin

British Library Cataloguing in Publication Data
A catalogue record for this book is available from the British
Library

Library of Congress Cataloging in Publication Data
Watts, Rob
    International criminology: a critical introduction/Rob Watts,
    Judith Bessant and Richard Hil
        p. cm
    1. Criminology. 2. Crime. I. Bessant, Judith.
    II. Hil, Richard, 1953– III. Title
    HV6025.W387 2007
    364–dc22   2007013330

ISBN10: 0–415–43178–6 (hbk)
ISBN10: 0–415–43179–4 (pbk)
ISBN10: 0–203–93430–X (ebk)

ISBN13: 978–0–415–43178–1 (hbk)
ISBN13: 978–0–415–43179–8 (pbk)
ISBN13: 978–0–203–93430–2 (ebk)

CONTENTS

PREFACE AND ACKNOWLEDGMENTS

In keeping with the intent of this book we will make our prefatory remarks brief. We are pleased that Routledge has seen merit in this book. It has been rewritten and revised in the light of helpful if sometimes trenchant criticism from several anonymous readers. We thank them.

We also thank the many groups of students who have been vocal critics of our 'road-testing' of ideas that have ended up here. Many of the chapters reflect, albeit often in considerably altered form, a variety of research and conference papers. These have benefited from critical commentary from colleagues, including Professor Martin Mowbray and Dr Desmond McDonnell, at Royal Melbourne Institute of Technology University. We thank our respective families and friends for the kindness, forbearance and support without which books like this would not get written.

The book is dedicated to Dorothy and Bill Watts, both of whom died in 2006.

INTRODUCTION

As book publishers, filmmakers and television producers have long known, crime is an intensely popular and interesting matter. Newspapers would be depleted without crime news like the serial killing of prostitutes in Ipswich (United Kingdom) late in 2006. Television regularly showcases fictional crime series, documentaries and more recently 'reality TV' shows. Novelists since Agatha Christie, Patricia Highsmith and Georges Simenon through to Ruth Rendell, P.D. James, James Lee Burke or Patricia Cornwell have made crime fiction into a literary genre and a best-selling business. Not a year goes by without some special case attracting widespread media and public attention. Cases like the O.J. Simpson murder trial in the United States, Dr Harold Shipman ('Doctor Death') in the United Kingdom, or the Lindy Chamberlain case in Australia, which ultimately saw a dingo found guilty of the murder of her baby, all become stand-out cases. They suggest that 'real-life' crime is as fascinating to large numbers of ordinary people as any television series or crime novel.

Crime is also something around which a number of prejudices and myths circulate. It is widely believed, as if these were matters of fact, that the 'crime rate' is always increasing or that ordinary street crime produces massive economic costs or social pain. These ideas in turn feed a lot of public anxiety about law and order in most modern societies. This anxiety, because it is widespread, is something which ambitious or unscrupulous politicians are quick to seize on as they use 'law and order' issues to attract votes or win elections.

Interest in or anxiety about crime seems also to lead increasing numbers of people to study criminology at university and college and pursue careers in the criminal justice system.

Behind the popular anxieties, the political responses and the media treatment of crime and criminals, much of what the 'average person' in Britain, America or Australia knows about 'crime' and 'criminals' depends a good deal, though not exclusively, on what criminologists do.

Criminology is a social science. Criminologists work closely with other social scientists, including sociologists and psychologists, to research crime and the people who engage in criminal activities. The media routinely draw on this research and use criminologists as experts to comment on crime-related news stories.

This is one of the reasons we have written this book. Today, many universities in the United Kingdom, Europe, the United States of America and Australia have either a criminology department or offer undergraduate and/or postgraduate criminology pro-grammes. It is quite likely that most of the readers of this book will be students in a criminology subject or programme in a university or college. This book is a short introduction to criminology and a guide to thinking intelligently about crime.

A word about this book

We have written this book knowing that there are many large and authoritative criminology textbooks. There are both classics like Vold (1958, 2002) and recent introductory texts like Carrabine et al. (2004) or Walklate (2006). In the United Kingdom there is the massive *Oxford Handbook of Criminology*, now in its third edition, by Maguire, Morgan and Reiner (2002). In the United States there are large and comprehensive textbooks like that by Beirne and Messerschmidt (1995) and Abadinsky and Winfree (1992). Introductory texts, like White and Haines (1996) and Hazlehurst (1996), are available in Australia. Van Swaaningen (1997) reminds us of the very rich and complex work done by European criminologists.

Clearly we think we have something to say. This book has been written with just a few key questions in mind. The first is what is criminology? Secondly, how has criminology come to be what it is today? Finally we ask how do criminologists think about crime? Notwithstanding the apparently simple, even naïve, nature of these questions, they deserve and warrant some careful thought if they are to be properly addressed.

What is criminology?

In regard to the first question 'what is criminology?' we can establish what criminology *is* by asking what it is that criminologists *do*.

One short and very simple answer to this question is that criminologists do research and construct what are called 'theories'. Criminologists research the causes of criminal conduct, measure the incidence and distribution of crime and criminality or carry out victim studies. Or they may evaluate the effectiveness of the various elements of the criminal justice systems like the police, the courts and the prisons. They also do research into public opinion and media reporting about crime, and explore 'public feeling' about the value of capital punishment or the sentences judges and magistrates give to offenders who have committed various kinds of crimes. Criminologists also construct theories about deviance, delinquency and crime of different kinds. Some are based on extensive data collection and analyses. Others draw on large-scale ideas about society, gender, class and human behaviour to explain why some people do criminal things, and why particular groups of people or whole societies have the crime rates they do.

This research and theorizing are found in a large body of criminological literature, comprising many textbooks, even more research monographs, and huge numbers of journal articles. (It is quite a sobering experience to go into a large university library and look at the shelves where all the criminology journals are stored or to carry out a Web-based search of research on, say, homicide or rape.) There is also a constant stream of research reports produced by governments, law-enforcement agencies, community organizations and consultants.

Some criminologists work in specialist research centres. Most countries support at least one prestigious research centre like the Institute of Criminology at Cambridge University or Australia's Criminology Research Centre. Governments and law-enforcement agencies also run their own in-house research units like the British Home Office's Research Development and Statistics Directorate. Most modern criminologists do not just do research, being employed by universities to teach undergraduate students and to supervise postgraduate research. They also belong to national and international professional associations, which are numerous, and they go to any number of annual national and international conferences.

Yet suggesting that criminology is whatever criminologists do is by itself not that illuminating. The fact that criminologists do not always agree about some key questions and issues is far more interesting. Criminologists spend time arguing about how criminology should be done. In this way criminology is just like any other social science discipline, like sociology, economics or political science. Like them, criminology is an intellectual project made up of people who share a number of basic ideas and work practices as well as others who don't always agree with what we can call 'conventional criminology' and who generate controversy.

These dispositions to construct some common agreements *and* to argue about the most basic questions has long been a feature of the history of criminology.

How has criminology come to be what it is today?

Although the word 'criminology' was coined and used first in the late nineteenth century, it took some time for criminology to become the respected academic field of study that it is today. As with social sciences like economics, sociology or anthropology, criminology has a history.

This fact alone indicates why we need to ask how modern criminology has come to be what it is. Whenever we come across a word like 'criminology' (or other names like 'sociology' or 'economics', to say nothing of big ideas like 'rationality', 'justice', 'democracy' or 'truth') we should always follow the lead of the German philosopher Friedrich Nietzsche. Nietzsche was concerned about the relentless urge humans have to produce neat definitions of key ideas. He insisted that each word has its history, and that typically there is controversy about how best to define a given word (1956: 212).

Our ideas and the words we use to talk about them have often been around a long time and are controversial. Understanding the history of a discipline like criminology reveals that people who call themselves 'criminologists' do not necessarily agree with other 'criminologists'. It will also remind us that criminology has not always been the way it is today and that it is unlikely to stay the way it is today over the life-span of readers of this book.

Understanding the history of a discipline like criminology means accepting that it is 'messy'. In this respect criminology is like the other social sciences whose practitioners have always had to deal with many competing views about the 'right way' to do economics or sociology, or . . . Some contemporary criminologists claim, for example, that what they do is a fact-based and 'objective' science. Others reject that approach, arguing that a 'science of crime' based on a model of a natural science like chemistry or geology is impossible. They say that because human conduct is emotional and symbolic, criminologists ought to use more interpretive techniques to 'understand' the motivations and meanings people give to their conduct, including their criminal conduct.

Awareness of the history of criminology helps us to understand why and how different kinds of criminologists do the things that make up criminology today and why some debates about the 'right way' to do criminology continue. It is important that students new to a field like criminology can make some sense of the discipline. Students can best do this by being shown, first, what the different approaches look like and why in particular it is that criminologists do not always agree with each other. It is also important that students do not leave university believing that there is only one way to do criminology. Students graduating from their university or college course to become lawyers, police officers or to work in the criminal justice system ought to be quite clear about why there are differences between criminologists. They also ought to be able to think about the issues and controversies that regularly take place in their community about what 'causes' crime or what governments, the police and lay people should do about it. As the great American philosopher John Dewey (1980: 208) put it, we all have an interest 'in the improvement of the methods and conditions of debate, discussion and persuasion'.

How do criminologists think about crime?

It is important to identify and to think about the ways criminologists think of crime or the people who do criminal things, because thinking is rarely ever just about describing a given situation, requiring that a balance be struck between 'describing' the approaches or traditions of different criminologists and critically 'evaluating' them.

For example, it matters that people studying criminology know what is meant by 'white-collar crime', a 'moral panic' or what Gottfredson and Hirschi (1990) mean when they describe their work as a 'general theory' of crime. This means more than being able to define or describe these ideas. Being well educated or thoughtful means more than being able to recite facts or provide definitions of key concepts. We need to be able to think carefully and critically about the different kinds of research and theories that criminologists produce.

The need to be thoughtful about issues of law and order is suggested by the tendency for 'law and order' to become a political football or the object of populist, media-driven campaigns that can mobilize vigilante-style campaigns to harass recently released prisoners who have a record as sex offenders or who committed a particularly brutal crime. It matters that public debate and policy is informed by good research and careful thinking. The citizens of any democratic society need to be well informed so that they can play their role in helping to produce good policy. For example, in the United States it has long been conventional for politicians, as President George W. Bush did in his Inaugural Address in January 2005, to proclaim their commitment to liberty – and in the case of Bush to criticize 'rogue states' for their abuse of human rights. Yet the United States is among the leading countries in terms of the number of its prisoners subjected to capital punishment: thirty-eight of its states execute people, and it has an unenviable reputation for executing teenagers. In Britain and

Australia there is a popular perception that courts are 'too soft on criminals', a view promoted by elements of the press using inflammatory rhetoric in their reporting of 'law and order' news.

Criminologists clearly have a role to play in promoting more thoughtful public discussion and debate about ideas like 'justice' and what adherence to the rule of law entails. 'Justice' for example is an old and deeply contested idea with its origins in Socrates' provocative inquiry into its nature in Classical Greece. In our own time important philosophers like Alasdair MacIntyre (1988) and John Finnis (2005: 161–92) emphasize the controversial nature of justice. MacIntyre (1988: 9) reminds us of the historical nature of our ideas about rationality and justice when he says:

> So rationality itself, whether theoretical or practical, is a concept with a history: indeed since there are [sic] a diversity of traditions of enquiry with histories, there are, so it will turn out, rationalities rather than rationality, just as it will turn out that there are justices rather than justice.

Some criminologists seem to believe that their commitment to 'scientific methodology' necessarily ensures that they produce 'good research' and that this is all that matters. We are not so sure. By itself methodology, however sophisticated, need not necessarily produce either good research or inform good policy. For research to be good the researcher needs to engage in critical and ethical reflection, and to play an active role in public discussion that can lead to good policy. To do this requires of both criminologists and the larger community of citizens that they engage in what Hannah Arendt (1958: 13) said was the single most difficult thing we can ever do, namely 'to think what we do'.

Our book is aimed at helping to promote thinking what we do.

Structure of the book

We have structured the book around just three questions. The first is what is criminology? Secondly, how has criminology come to be what it is today? Finally, how do criminologists think about crime?

Part I of the book, 'Theoretical traditions and historical perspectives', introduces some of the key issues at stake in criminology; it also outlines some of the distinctive theoretical approaches that have informed the past and the present of the discipline.

In Chapter 1 we start with two basic questions: what is 'crime'? and how do criminologists set about establishing the amount of crime in a given community or society? Here we highlight some of the ways criminologists have defined 'crime' as well as some of the ways they have set about measuring, or 'knowing', the scale of crime in a given society. This discussion helps to indicate that these issues are far from being straightforward or simple.

We then turn to the question: what is criminology? Chapters 2, 3 and 4 provide a brief history of criminology. We do this not because we have an antiquarian interest but because the ways contemporary criminologists do their research or use various kinds of theories is embedded in a history of ideas, assumptions and practices. We need to ask where these ideas have come from, what assumptions criminologists have made and what kinds of practices contemporary criminologists engage in. Though there are dangers in writing any 'history of the present' we have tried to recognize both mainstream kinds of criminology as well as various dissenting views.

There is a conventional idea that the history of a discipline like sociology or criminology is a story of scientific advance and progress. It is tempting for people working in such a discipline to adopt a 'whig' view of their discipline. (The 'whig' view of history assumes that history is a story of endless progress.) Such a view can encourage them to believe that *our* time is the end-point of that history, thus implying that modern criminology is now as good as it gets. Beirne (1993) argues that the history of criminology is not a story of endless progress; neither does it indicate that modern criminology is as good as it gets. Taking an historical and a critical view of criminology is useful because it reminds us of the need to be sceptical about our own time.

We use as a point of departure in Chapter 2 the work of David Garland (1994, 1997), a great modern criminologist, who argues that the history of criminology is less a story of progress than a story about a long-running tension-cum-overlap between two traditions. On the one hand there is what he calls the 'governmental project'. This kind of criminology is preoccupied with practical questions of measuring the amount of crime or devising policies to prevent or control crime. On the other hand there is criminology as a 'science of causes', a pursuit particularly suited to criminologists working in universities. Each of these ideas gives rise to different kinds of criminology, and in ways that persist even today.

Chapter 3 outlines the complex pattern of ideas, vocabularies, research methods and controversies that marks out the development of modern criminology into the middle of the twentieth century. Far from that development being a history of progress, we see a tendency to recycle old ideas and arguments using new words.

Chapter 4 surveys the work of some of the dissenting criminologists, i.e. those who have tried to disturb the practice of more conventionally minded criminologists. Our account outlines the various efforts of 'symbolic interactionists', the 'new criminologists', feminists and 'post-modernists' to urge conventional criminologists to amend their ideas and practices.

This history of criminology reveals that criminologists have always worked with a diversity of philosophical and intellectual assumptions and ideas about quite fundamental questions. These are questions that never go away, like how do we really *know* what we claim to know? Should we try to *understand* or *explain* human conduct? At the start of the twenty-first century, criminology remains what it has long been, a discipline that accommodates many different ideas about 'society', 'history', and the nature of humans and their conduct.

That criminologists entertain many different ideas about these matters partly owes something to the way other social scientists like psychologists, sociologists, political theorists, economists and anthropologists have heavily influenced what criminologists do. The multi-disciplinary nature of criminology in the twentieth and into the twenty-first centuries has meant that many different kinds of sociological, psychological and political ideas and schools of thought have made an impact on criminology. Criminologists have drawn on these theories and models to inform their own approach to describing crime, to explaining why some people commit crime or to recommending ways of preventing or reducing crime. Understanding the different ways of doing criminology and the issues at stake will make for a more informed debate about what criminology and criminologists can offer their communities and governments.

Part II of the book, 'Issues in contemporary criminology', explores some of the ways modern criminologists approach key issues in modern criminology. A short book like this cannot cover all of the issues found in larger criminology texts, like the theory and practice of prisons, sentencing or policing, so these have been omitted. The task of accurately summarizing, for example, how the police and prison systems work in the UK and in the USA, while writing for readers in several countries, was too daunting to even think about.

The case studies or issues we write about enable us to trace out some of the characteristic ways criminologists think about these issues. This means we can assess the strengths and weaknesses of the various theoretical perspectives brought to bear on these problems. In each case we stress the role played by a number of important assumptions in shaping ideas and research into crime.

Chapter 6 discusses how some criminologists explain crime in terms of unemployment and poverty, or what is now referred to as 'social exclusion'. In Chapter 7 we survey attempts by criminologists to explain crime in terms of family dynamics and relationships. We then turn to two contemporary forms of criminal justice policy. Governments in many Western societies are preoccupied with crime control and crime prevention. In Chapter 8 we outline the rationale for the ways governments, acting on the advice of criminologists, set about developing crime-prevention strategies. In Chapter 9 we explore the recent prominence given to the idea that victims of crime ought to play a larger role than they have traditionally done in the sentencing policies and practices of courts. In each case we attempt to identify the sustaining assumptions operating in the development of these criminal justice policies.

In Chapters 10 and 11 two kinds of crime that have played something of a fugitive or marginal role in criminology are examined. We consider why it is that 'white-collar crime', or corporate crime, has played an ambiguous role in mainstream criminology. In the case of 'state crime', too many criminologists, like some other social scientists, notably sociologists, have tended to bypass the issue altogether. In both cases this ambivalence or silence is suggestive of certain intellectual problems that have long dogged mainstream criminology.

Finally in a short Conclusion: 'Towards a reflexive criminology', we ask what prospects there are for some new approaches to the perennial problems addressed by criminologists. This is not the time or place to advance some major new 'theory' of crime. In part this is because we set out to write an introductory book for people encountering criminology for the first time, who (presumably as university students) need a book which lays out the key issues and main lines of research and theory in contemporary criminology. Even so, this does not require that we abstain from the obligation to be thoughtful, or as we say 'reflexive', about some of the important questions criminologists have persistently addressed. This is because criminology is a *practical* discipline.

On being practical and critical

We use the word 'practical' in a way that respects its linguistic and historical origins. Criminology is a 'practical' discipline in that in addressing any issue of practice or human activity it seeks to answer what at bottom is always *the* ethical question, namely: 'What is the right or good thing to do?' Aristotle (1976), writing over 2,300 years ago, insisted that all human action is oriented to some idea of 'the good'. The problem, as Aristotle understood and as Mary Midgley (2001: vii–xiv) reminds us, is that rarely is there agreement about the nature of 'the good'. Criminologists necessarily engage in ethical questions and problems in which the nature of what people believe is good – or bad – is at stake. For example, in an *obvious* sense, when governments pass laws to make certain activities, like abortion, heroin use or stealing cars, illegal, they do so because they believe that these activities are morally wrong. This is because there are people – or victims – who are directly hurt by those activities. Governments also respond to the idea that what are called 'community values' are affronted by these activities.

One problem with trying to define what is morally wrong is that it is rarely possible to get agreement in the complex societies we live in. It is also plain that communities and governments often act without majority support, and even act wrongly or badly. For example, consider the relative moral value of drinking alcohol and the mass murder of hundreds of thousands of people. In 1919 the US federal government introduced a constitutional amendment making alcohol an illegal substance and spent a lot of money, time and effort in enforcing Prohibition. Huge numbers of Americans kept on drinking, their actions helping to consolidate the growth of 'organized crime'. Prohibition was a costly failure. On the other hand the USA has consistently refused to pass legislation making genocide a crime or requiring it to try military officers for grave human rights' abuses. Thinking practically involves being able to think our way through these complexities.

However, taking the more usual sense of the word 'practical', that of 'useful', we are not convinced that criminology is all that 'practical'. We say this even though many criminologists assert that their discipline is 'practical' in that it helps to inform the practices of police, judges, prison officials, probation workers and governments. Many social scientists want, perhaps even need, to believe this about their disciplines. While it sometimes happens that academic research leads to changes in police or judicial practice, there are also very important tensions between academic criminologists and the criminal justice system and its police, judges, prison officials and probation workers. These people work in a range of institutions, some of them, like prisons and police forces, with very long histories. Too often academic criminologists ask questions and pursue issues that are of interest only to other academics or write in ways that can be understood only by other academics. As Pierre Bourdieu (1988) observed, too many of them insist on writing in the 'dead language' of 'academic discourse'. It is not surprising that academic criminologists are often uncomfortably aware that police officers and lawyers believe that criminological theory and research is 'all very well and good, but . . .'. What this usually means is that people in the criminal justice system feel that academic research and theoretical debate has little connection to the work they do.

In saying this we are not suggesting that the people who work in the criminal justice system are always working thoughtfully, effectually or ethically. The routine 'discovery' that some police abuse basic human rights or that some prisons are not nice places highlights how justice can be hidden by the operations of the law. Accordingly complaints that academics are only good for producing *impractical* or *theoretical* research can also be misplaced or, worse, defensive. We like the work of Michel Foucault for this reason. He could not conceal his dismay about criminology:

> Have you read any criminology texts? They are staggering. And I say this out of astonishment, not aggressiveness, because I fail to comprehend how the discourse of criminology has been able to go on at this level. One has the impression that it is of such utility . . . for the working of the system that it does not even need to seek a theoretical justification for itself.
>
> (Foucault 1980: 47–8)

Sometimes people who are critical of the way things get done are often asked to provide an 'alternative'. We need to remember what Foucault (1981: 13) said about criticism. Criticism

> does not have to be the premise of a deduction which concludes: this then is what needs to be done. It should be an instrument for those who fight, those who resist and refuse what is. Its use should be in processes of conflict and confrontation, essays in refusal. It doesn't have to lay down the law for law. It isn't a stage in programming. It is a challenge directed at what is.

No doubt *thinking well* must come before *doing well*. We do not here propose approaches to doing anything new, but do suggest how it is possible to start thinking well.

PART I

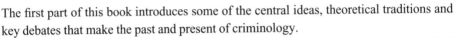

THEORETICAL TRADITIONS AND HISTORICAL PERSPECTIVES

The first part of this book introduces some of the central ideas, theoretical traditions and key debates that make the past and present of criminology.

In Chapter 1 we start with the core idea of crime itself. A few simple questions are asked about the idea of *crime* itself. What does it mean? How have criminologists understood crime? Is crime a straightforward sort of idea? Does the word 'crime' for example name certain human activities in the same way that 'running' and 'jumping' do? Can we count crimes and, if so, how do we count them? Even in this apparently simple exercise we come across some quite complex issues.

These issues suggest that there is more at stake than offering a simple definition or assuming that the 'facts' speak for themselves. As David Garland (1990: 12) observes, this is a problem because 'crime' like so many other kinds of social activities is itself an interpreted matter. Far from being an *objective* matter like the number of wheels on a car, what counts as 'crime' depends on people making all sorts of interpretations and judgements and doing so differently according to time and place.

Attention is then given to one of the key questions that gives grief to some criminologists, namely: How much crime is there in any society at any given moment? Contemporary criminologists like Coleman and Moynihan (1996) talk about the 'dark figure of crime' to refer to the idea that we can determine the actual amount of crime going on in any society. We identify some of the problems associated with attempts to get an *objective* measure of the amount of crime in the USA or in England.

In Chapters 2, 3 and 4 we turn to the history of criminology, focussing on the last decades of the nineteenth century to the twenty-first century. This is not just history for its own sake. As will become clear, contemporary criminologists, like the other social scientists, rely on assumptions, ideas and ways of understanding which have been around for a long time. A history based on a sharp memory reveals that some things change while other things remain constant, an idea which challenges the simplistic idea that the history of criminology is a history of progress.

In Chapter 4 the focus is on some of the important criminologists who have been critical of conventional criminology. There have always been people sceptical about attempts to develop a 'science of crime'. A number of different critical ideas surfaced in the 1960s and 1970s especially which continue to offer important and interesting ways of thinking differently about crime.

1

WHAT IS CRIME?
HOW CRIMINOLOGISTS
THINK ABOUT CRIME

A common-sense approach to criminology suggests that it must have something to do with crime. As Abe Fattah says, the concept of *crime* is as central to criminology as the concept of *society* is to sociology. Fattah (1997: 29) suggests that criminology 'may be loosely defined as the "study of crime" or as the "science of crime" and a definition of crime is therefore essential for our understanding of what criminology is all about'. However, as Fattah goes on to show, 'crime', like so many other key concepts central to the social sciences, e.g. 'poverty' or 'unemployment', is not all that easily defined.

In this respect criminology is just like sociology, economics or psychology. Each of these disciplines can be identified by the vocabularies or 'key words' their practitioners use, as well as by the arguments they advance. We will use the word 'argument' here not so much to suggest that criminologists are always shouting at each other – although this happens sometimes at conferences – but rather as a way of talking about the knowledge-claims we make. The idea of argument which relies on an analytical approach, spelled out by Stephen Toulmin (1961), tries to encapsulate the ongoing process of research and debate which is involved as criminological knowledge is created, criticized and is changed.

One way to begin to come to terms with criminology is to establish how criminologists deal with a key concept like *crime*. We may get a sense of what the discipline is by finding out how criminologists understand this key concept and how they then try to establish how much crime there is in a given society. We also want to spell out a simple but useful analytical framework for thinking about the knowledge-claims made by criminologists and how they use a word like 'theory'.

Let us begin by asking what is *crime*?

What is crime?

Words like 'crime', 'murder', 'suicide' or 'violence' are frequently used by people as if their meanings are self-evident and can be applied easily to some simple *fact* or activity. For many people who are not criminologists, the idea of crime may be so 'obvious' that they do not think twice about it. After all, the newspapers, TV news and Hollywood films make it plain what crime is, so why bother defining it or thinking about it? It is therefore sobering to find a respected criminologist like Fattah (1997: 37) arguing that 'there is no universal or agreed upon definition [of crime] . . . It means different things to different people . . . all attempts to define it are doomed.'

Surely this cannot be right. Don't we have dictionaries that are designed to clear up any confusion? A recurrent idea throughout this book is that concepts like *crime* and *violence* are not as straightforward as many people want to believe. This realization may lead us to reflect on the problems that arise when we use words without thinking.

So let us ask the question 'What is crime?' and start with the *Oxford English Dictionary* (*OED*) definition. The *OED* defines 'crime' both as 'an act punishable by law' or as 'an evil or injurious act'. Already this definition opens up some major issues. This distinction which is an important one needs some thinking about.

The Anglo-American legal tradition has long distinguished between two kinds of act, namely:

- 'acts that are evil in themselves';
- 'acts that are prohibited'.

Is this distinction between 'evil acts' and 'prohibited acts' a sensible one? What does it mean to say that there are some acts that are 'evil in themselves' or that are intrinsically 'evil'?

Crime as a universal evil?

Wilson and Herrnstein (1985), two well-known neo-conservative criminologists, advanced the idea that some activities are intrinsically bad or evil. They say that some human behaviours like homicide, incest, rape, theft and robbery are intrinsically and universally evil. They argue (1985: 22) that crimes like these are 'condemned in all societies, and in all historical periods, by ancient tradition, moral sentiments and formal law'.

Wilson and Herrnstein's claim may sound reasonable until the devil that lies in the detail is disturbed. Mountains of historical and anthropological research contradict Wilson and Herrnstein's claim.

What do we make, for example, of the legal marriages contracted between brothers and sisters in ancient Egypt, an activity usually defined as incest (Boswell 1994: 128)? To be quite blunt about it, all of the activities that are likely to make the readers – and the writers – of this book shudder in horror, like

- cannibalism,
- incest,
- the ritual killing of children for religious or magical purposes, or
- sexual relations between very young people and adults,

have all been normal and admired aspects of some societies, somewhere, at some time.

Even more confounding to the belief that there are universal ideas about what constitutes 'evils' or crimes is the discovery that an activity widely understood to be undeniably 'evil' or unacceptable was not treated as a crime by the relevant criminal law system. How should we understand the widespread sanctioning of European slave traders engaging in the kidnapping of millions of black Africans for sale in the eighteenth-century transatlantic slave trade? What of the wholesale theft of land from indigenous peoples in so-called 'regions of recent settlement' (like Australia, Canada, the USA, South Africa or Brazil)? How should we think about the official sale and distribution of opium in China by the British government into the 1850s? What do we say of the deliberate policy of the British government to starve millions of Indians to death in 1877–78 (Davis 2001)?

This point is well illustrated by the tangled history of attempts to make genocide a crime (Rubinstein 2004). Genocide involves the killing of very large numbers of people for political, religious or ethnic reasons. No one could sensibly deny that genocide is truly evil. The major cases of genocide, beginning with the Armenians in 1916–17 through the killings of Europe's Jews by the Nazi state after 1941 or the US Marine Corps killing of tens of thousands of defenceless indigenous people on Okinawa in 1945 (Cameron 1994), to the killing of millions of people in Indonesia (1965–66), Cambodia (1972–74), East Timor (1976–77) or Rwanda (1994), seem to render the meaning of 'crime' almost redundant. The United Nations Convention on Genocide (1948) has long defined genocide as a 'crime against humanity'. Yet it is governments mostly which organize and carry out the killings. It is governments too that determine and ratify the legal code within the nation state, and it is governments that render the perpetrators of genocide largely immune to prosecution. Governments such as that of the USA – which started a 'War on Terrorism' in September 2001 – have refused to ratify the international anti-genocide convention. Others that have ratified the convention, like Australia, have not passed the requisite legislation to make it a crime in those countries. This allows people alleged to have committed genocide to reside in Australia immune from criminal prosecution.

The same point needs to be made about 'terrorism' especially after the attacks on New York and Washington in September 2001. The US government rightly condemned those attacks on civilians. Yet the US State Department's attempt to exclude state-sponsored terrorism from its definition of terrorism points up the problem, especially when we recall the judgment by the International Court of Justice in The Hague against the American government for its terrorism against civilians in El Salvador in 1987 (Draper 1991). (On that occasion the US government simply refused to accept the court's jurisdiction and refused to pay the hefty fines imposed.)

In short there are problems with claiming that some acts are so evil that they are always universally treated as criminal activities. If the reader believes that Wilson and Herrnstein are right, then he or she should try to nominate one kind of human conduct that has been universally condemned as being too evil to be tolerated. While people may want to believe that 'crime' is whatever is obviously 'evil', the stubborn fact is that 'crime' is not always obvious, objective or simple. Wilkins (1965: 46) made the point that 'at some time or another, some form of society or another has defined almost all forms of behaviour that we now call criminal as desirable for the functioning of that form of society'.

Crime is what the law says it is?

To deal with the problem that there are no universally defined activities that are always criminal because evil, it has been suggested that 'crime' is whatever the criminal law says it is. Michael and Adler (1933: 2) suggest that 'the most precise and least ambiguous definition is that crime which is prohibited by the criminal code'. Yet how useful is the idea that 'crime' refers to those acts 'that are prohibited' by law?

The idea that 'crime' is whatever a given government chooses to define as crime has the merit of being unambiguous, even simple. It certainly reflects a *realistic* approach to the problem. Yet this approach too poses some difficult problems and questions. For example, within countries like the USA or Australia, which happen to have federal systems of state governments each with their own criminal laws and multiple jurisdictions, the same activity may or may not be treated as a crime. This suggests why it was possible that while some American states made anal intercourse – or 'sodomy' – between a husband and wife illegal for much of the twentieth century, it was legal in others. In one American state (Maryland) the legal age at which sexual activity was lawful was set at 9 years, until the late 1950s, while in most other states the age was 16 or 18.

Henry and Milovanovic (1994: 118) draw the conclusion from this circumstance that any idea that 'crime' is whatever governments choose to define as actions punishable by the law forces us to reject the claim that there are *universal* and *objective* forms of criminal conduct. As Sack (1994: 10) points out, there may be a certain degree of 'embarrassment' for criminologists who believe that crime is an objective matter if there can be no account of what 'crime' is outside of whatever 'the law' says it is: criminologists have not succeeded 'in finding another answer to the question than that which is given by the penal code. All attempts that were made by sociologists and criminologists to arrive at a law-free, independent, scientific and authentic definition of crime failed in the past and are doomed to fail in the future.' The idea that 'crime' refers to those acts 'that are prohibited' by law undermines any proposition that there are intrinsic or *objective* qualities that mark certain conduct as criminal conduct.

Nonetheless the claim that 'whatever the law says is criminal is criminal' is significant because it raises important questions about the relations between a society and what gets to be defined by the government of that society as criminal activity. The claim that crime refers to whatever activities are 'proscribed by law' fails to indicate why it is that some behaviours are defined as criminal and made punishable by law, while similar behaviours are not. The question has to be asked: Why is it that some activities are singled out as criminal and made punishable by law, while the same, or similar, activities are not? This question ought to stimulate some interesting research.

Some criminologists have tried to salvage the idea that there is something *objective* about criminal activity by arguing that even if crime is not a universally defined objective problem, it reflects the views of 'society' about 'antisocial' behaviours.

Crime as antisocial behaviour?

Hermann Mannheim (1955: 261) was one of the great figures of British criminology. Fifty years ago he argued that crime was whatever 'society' said it was. Mannheim had no doubt that to confine criminology to the study of crime *as defined by the criminal law* was mistaken:

> [T]he subject matter of Criminology can be limited to the study of criminal behaviour as defined by the Criminal Law just as little as Psychiatry can be

confined to a study of types of mental disease as defined in legal terms . . . it should rather be extended to the study of what Sellin calls 'conduct norms' i.e. norms of behaviour laid down by all the various social groups to which the individual belongs and of which the state . . . is only one.

Mannheim acknowledged that his approach to crime might mean allowing for 'greater vagueness' about the central concept of *crime*. Another view would be that Mannheim's approach completely undermines the possibility of treating *crime* as an objective idea. Writing several decades before Mannheim, Michael and Adler (1933) indicated precisely the problem with claims that 'crime' refers to all 'antisocial' activities. Michael and Adler (1933: 1–2) wrote then that

> Attempts have been made to define crime in moral terms and in social terms. The definition of crime as behaviour which is immoral lacks precision and clarity . . . The definition of crime as antisocial behaviour is hardly more precise or less ambiguous, although it does shift the emphasis from what is thought of as the intrinsic quality of conduct to its social consequences . . .

Given the recent 'rediscovery' of the idea of 'antisocial conduct' in many Western societies, including Britain, by various politicians and parties, it may be useful to also rediscover this critique of the very idea of 'antisocial conduct'.

The problem with taking Mannheim literally is that any conduct that affronted any norm of behaviour laid down by any social group to which a person belonged would become 'antisocial' conduct and thus a 'crime'. Here we see the point of thinking carefully about the assumptions that we make. At least Mannheim spelled out his approach to the concept of crime in a way that lets us think about the consequences of defining crime in a particular way.

Within a single large nation state like Britain or the USA there may be no strong consensus that a given activity is illegal. High levels of disagreement about core values are a persistent feature of modern societies. This is suggested by the regularity with which debates erupt over issues like euthanasia, abortion, illicit drugs, gun-ownership, 'family values' or the right of lesbians and homosexuals to marry.

It is perhaps beginning to be clear why there is nothing inherent in any act or behaviour that renders it a crime. Fattah (1997: 33) points out why any attempt to base a definition of crime on social attitudes is too broad an approach because it extends the idea of crime to actions that, while punishable, do not transgress social rules and are in no sense 'antisocial'. Equally it might be made to apply to activities that are neither condemned by the community at large nor regarded as requiring intervention by the criminal justice system. On the other hand, this approach is too narrow because it excludes activities that are not punishable by law even though they are the same as, or similar to, those acts that are punishable by law.

For example, the fact that one person kills another person does not automatically mean that he or she will even be arrested, let alone tried or punished for murder. Pfohl (1985: 284) notes: 'Some types of killing are characterized as homicide. Others are not. What differs is not the behaviour but the manner in which reactions to that behaviour are socially organized.' Killing is killing, yet what matters is who does the killing, who is killed, where the killing takes place, the nature of the motivation and whose rules about the taking of a life the killing infringes.

More generally we can see that for a long time and across many different societies what we now treat as gross assaults against women, children and slaves were tolerated, even legally sanctioned, while the same assault committed against a male adult would have been dealt with severely. In some countries to this day wives who fail to live up to their husband's expectations can be killed with impunity. Even now in advanced Western societies children continue to be routinely assaulted by their parents in the name of 'discipline' or 'traditional family values', yet this is rarely brought to the attention of the criminal justice system.

For those who like the words to reflect or name some *objective* state of affairs, the concept of crime is going to be a disappointment. If you want the idea of crime to be unequivocal, unmistakable and *objectively* definable, then treating crime as whatever the criminal law or society says it is will not work.

A definition of crime?

These considerations led Fattah (1997: 37) to say that 'there is no universal or agreed upon definition of crime: It means different things to different people' and 'all attempts to define it are doomed'.

There is nothing all that new about this idea. Thoughtful criminologists since Tarde (1886) and Sutherland (1924, 1947) long understood that what counts as 'crime' or is defined as such is relative to time and place.

A thoughtful approach to the idea of crime accepts some of the following propositions. Criminality is not an intrinsic quality of the act and there is nothing about the *reality* of any conduct that makes it a universally *obvious* criminal activity. It is quite clear from the sheer diversity of moral ideas that there do not appear to be any innate human moral reactions that unequivocally and universally underpin social reactions to certain behaviours that lead them to be defined and punished as crimes. Further evidence suggests that within a given society there will be changes in definition and responses to certain activities which may see a hitherto legal activity criminalized or something that has been treated as illegal de-criminalized. The American experience with the 'criminalization' and then the 'de-criminalization' of alcohol consumption in the 1920s and 1930s stands as a paradigm case. In short it seems that ideas about what 'crime' is or what is 'criminal', like so many other ideas, are relative to their social and historical context. (Curiously, if universal ideas about the 'bads' of human existence are hard to define, John Finnis 2005 has made a good case for treating certain things as universal 'goods'.) Finally the thought has to be entertained that ideas about what crime is or what is criminal are shaped by social relations of power and dominance, which means that certain activities may be defined by powerful groups as criminal and can then be written into a system of law, while other harmful, even violent, activities remain lawful.

Yet just because 'crime' is relative to both time and place this does not mean that it cannot be researched, studied or discussed. So long as we do not forget the interpreted and highly conventional basis of any criminal justice system and its definition of crime, it is reasonable to begin with the proposition that 'crime' is whatever a given criminal justice system says it is at a given time.

If what we have said about the problems of defining 'crime' suggests anything, it is that defining human activities is never easy. This conclusion will irritate the many people who like things simple and clear. At any rate we think it best to not offer a misleadingly simple and clear definition of criminology, while stressing that we need to be constantly alert to, and thoughtful about, what we mean by 'crime'.

So how do we start being thoughtful about crime – and all the other things criminologists research and think about? One way is to pay close attention to the way criminologists do their research. We can see what is at stake and what some of the issues are by turning to a key question, that has long helped define criminology's identity, namely: How and what can we know about crime?

How is crime researched and measured?

At the start of the twenty-first century and in many Western societies there is a widespread public perception that crime is on the increase. In the UK since 1997, Tony Blair's New Labour government regularly polled citizens on this issue and it confirms that this is indeed a widespread belief. As Simmons and Dodd (2003: 6) report, over 38 per cent of people surveyed believed that crime had risen 'a lot'. Another 35 per cent believed it had risen 'a little' over the previous two years. The official crime statistics showed that the 'crime rate' had actually fallen by 17 per cent since 1999. This perception seems to be closely related to the newspapers people read: 48 per cent of readers of the populist tabloid newspapers believed crime had risen 'a lot' compared with only 26 per cent of broadsheet, or quality, newspaper readers (Simmons and Dodd 2003: 6).

The perception that crime is always on the rise tempts many politicians to declare 'war on crime' or to 'get tough on crime', especially just before or during an election. The release of any criminological research on the murder rate or the incidence of car thefts is likewise an excuse for a frenzy of media analysis and much canvassing of expert and 'public opinion'.

The 'public' in the USA, the UK or Australia may well believe that the release of statistics on crime rates affords a good basis for forming a view about the incidence of crime. They may well believe this because they assume that crime is either a straightforward or an 'objective' matter. They may then believe that it is easy enough to establish the amount of crime being committed in their community.

Here we can begin to see the value of teasing out the assumptions being relied on and then testing the value of those assumptions. One key assumption here relates to beliefs about the nature of *objective* knowledge.

When people use the word 'objective' they may or may not know that philosophers use this idea to refer to something that can be looked at or known because it is object-like – just like a rock or a chair; that is, *it* is observable or tangible. One persistent assumption made by some criminologists, and by many more citizens, is that crime is just the same as objects like rocks or chairs. Assuming that something is objective is to believe that it exists independently of the scientist or observer who sees it or measures it and who can therefore give us an 'objective' report about its nature.

Conversely we customarily say that because something like a feeling or a dream is hidden in a person and does not have any tangible qualities, it is 'subjective'. This promotes the idea that things like emotions are not tangible or 'objective'.

The 'common-sense' assumption about the objective status of crime assumes that, like the number of chairs in a room, it is possible to establish the number of crimes committed by counting them.

Yet most criminologists know that it is more complicated than that. This is not because there is a dispute about 'reality' and whether crime is as 'real' as or less 'real' than, say, a rock. As Ian Hacking (2000: 16–19) points out, there *is* a difference between an object like a rock – which exists regardless of whether there are human beings around or not – and something like paying rent – which is something we humans have invented or 'constructed'. However, as Hacking insists, the difference is not whether one of these things is more or less 'real' than the other. To test this proposition, Hacking suggests trying not to pay the three months' back-rent you owe! What matters is being able to realise the difference between social categories and natural or physical objects.

Today most criminologists accept and understand that it is not possible to establish an accurate or 'objective' measure of the actual amount of crime – or the crime rate in a given society. As Maguire (1997: 142) points out, this is so partly because of 'the problematic nature of the data, concepts and categories which derive from official and institutional sources'. (See also Coleman and Moynihan 1996.) So why is there this problem?

Part of the problem relates to the social practices involved in collecting crime statistics, while another part has to do with the practical tasks of getting some systematic basis for collecting the statistics. A brief excursion into what this means will make the matter clear.

Do the facts speak for themselves?

Many people and possibly even law-enforcement officials may believe that crime is a 'fact' in the way that the detective in the famous US police drama *Dragnet* of the 1950s suggested when he insisted: 'Ma'am, just give me the facts.'

It is important to make the point that any event that is called a 'crime' and possibly gets to be counted as one is not defined as such until someone decides that the event or activity that happened meets the criteria for being treated as a crime. Far from being an 'objective' fact, the process of converting certain kinds of human conduct into crime statistics involves a complex process of social interpretation and definition.

Say that someone discovers a body which bears all the signs of deadly wounds. Yet is it *obvious* that a crime like murder has been committed? Taylor (1983: 91) makes the case for thinking carefully about this assumption:

> [T]he widespread view of homicide as a highly factual offence . . . [is] thought to
> be evidenced by the existence of a corpse. Homicide is thought amongst experts

to have a very high degree of reportability (in that very few homicides are thought to be unobserved or unpunished). On both counts there is room for scepticism. . . . There are good grounds for questioning the meaning of coroners' reports in cases of non-natural death, and there are increasingly strong grounds for questioning whether the deaths that occur among the terminally-ill, or amongst old people in care, especially in institutional care, are absolutely unaided. Perhaps most routinely of all, there is good evidence to suggest that many more of the deaths occurring in road traffic 'accidents' involving criminal negligence should be appearing in homicide statistics at present.

One famous criminal case in Australia makes this point in striking fashion. In 1998 the Australian press reported extensively on a matter, first brought to the attention of police in the mid-1980s with the discovery of a woman's body in a farmhouse. The dead woman was initially thought to have killed herself and her death was therefore counted as a 'suicide'. This was so in spite of the consideration that the victim had apparently shot herself in the head not once but twice, and with a bolt-action rifle. In the first official inquiry – and acting on police advice and reports – the coroner reluctantly decided to treat this as a 'suicide'. After a decade of investigation, the case was re-opened and a second coroner's inquiry determined that the woman had been killed – and by a serving police officer. (In spite of that official coronial finding, the police officer in question was never tried for the offence.)

The even more famous UK case of Dr Harold Shipman, the Manchester doctor who appears to have murdered in excess of 200 of his elderly patients in the 1980s and 1990s (Walklate 2006: 22–7), makes a similar point. For a long time, and until his trial, all of those deaths had been treated, and therefore counted, as 'natural deaths', enabling Shipman to continue killing. The homicide rate for England had to be adjusted substantially after Shipman was found guilty.

The central point here is that those human actions that become crimes do so only after someone like a police officer or an institution like a coroner's court has defined them that way.

Against the common-sense assumption that 'the facts speak for themselves', human conduct that becomes a crime statistic has been through an elaborate process of selection, negotiation and decision-making. The construction of a 'crime rate' reflects decisions on the part of those people like police and coronial officials who define, classify and record certain behaviours as 'crimes'.

The extent to which conduct is subject to negotiation, even manipulation, before it becomes a criminal statistic was first revealed in a classic piece of research by Aaron Cicourel (1968). His work has been confirmed by subsequent research by Hagedorn (1990), Boyd et al. (1996) and Brownstein (2000). Cicourel examined two police departments in two US cities with substantially the same social, economic and demographic characteristics, except that one city had a significant youth crime rate while the other had a low youth crime rate. Cicourel followed police on to the streets of these two cities to discover that the different crime rates reflected nothing other than quite different policing practices. In one city, an ambitious police force liked to generate high arrest and juvenile process rates. In the other, police preferred to deal with offenders on the spot. This involved the administration of 'street justice' in a back-lane beating if the offenders were black or Chicano teenagers. However, if the offender was a young, white person believed to come from 'a respectable family', then the police officers would go off for a 'serious talk' with the parents. Justice looked different in these two cities. In one, a child who stole a bag of sweets was sentenced to a term in a juvenile detention centre. In the other city, a young, white man involved in a gang rape got away with a 'serious talk' involving his parents and the police sergeant.

Black (1970: 738) likewise showed in his study of policing practices in three US blue-collar, working-class areas, that police preferred to deal with and record serious crimes (felonies) rather than misdemeanours. In his study 72 per cent of felonies were recorded and reported as crimes, but only 53 per cent of the misdemeanours were treated as crimes. Later Black (1980) and Sherman and Glick (1984) pointed to many failures by police to file official crime reports; moreover, in reporting crimes, police made regular and serious errors. More recently Charles Katz followed a special police unit on to the streets as officers gathered intelligence about teenage gangs. He concluded (Katz 2003: 510–11) that the officers disregarded official guidelines in gathering and recording their statistics, and collected it in such *ad hoc* ways that the police administration itself decided the results should not be used: 'Violations of "counting rules" were so flagrantly disregarded that users of police gang data would be unsure as to the nature and reliability of the data' (Katz 2003: 511). Worse, he found evidence that officers were making their research available in the community so that employers and teachers were using it, often to the disadvantage of the young people being labelled – often wrongly – as 'gang members'.

Apart from problems with determining how people or events are to be defined, there are other quite substantial issues involved in the practices of collecting crime statistics.

The problem with official statistics

Criminologists generally talk about 'crime rates', which, like most other social statistics, are usually represented in percentage terms and typically refer to the proportion or number of crimes like homicide or rape per 100,000 of the relevant population.

This talk about the 'crime rate' builds on certain conventions for recording 'social facts' established during the nineteenth century in France by social statisticians like Adolphe Quételet, who began to analyse French criminal data in 1842. This kind of thinking about 'social facts' was given methodological approval by the French sociologist Emile Durkheim (1982) in the 1890s in *The Rules of Sociological Method*.

When it comes to collecting crime statistics it seems that, like the pigs in Orwell's novel *Animal Farm*, not all countries are equal. Some countries, e.g. New Zealand which is both small in population and has a central government, appear to have few problems in getting internal agreement about what constitutes an illegal activity. Other countries, like England and Wales which have published data sets about crimes recorded by the police since 1876, *appear* to have achieved some consensus reflecting the unitary system of government the UK had until the process of devolution got under way in Scotland. England and Wales have since 2002 published an annual report called *Crime in England and Wales* (see the Home Office website: www.homeoffice.gov.uk/rds/index.htm). This is in apparent contrast to countries with federal systems of government like America, Canada, Germany and

Australia. These countries have complex systems, with multiple levels of government (local, state and national) and multiple legal systems. The USA has a particularly complex federal system, with legal powers shared between local government and county level, state level and federal-level legal jurisdictions each able to pass laws about what constitutes an illegal activity. This can mean significant disagreement about what kinds of activities are illegal, to say nothing about different policing and correctional policies.

How does America deal with the problem of gathering information about crime?

The USA

In 1927 the US federal government established a Committee on Uniform Crime Records. In 1930 the Federal Bureau of Investigation (FBI) began to publish its Uniform Crime Reports (UCR), based on police records submitted *voluntarily* by 400 cities in 43 states (Beirne and Messerschmidt 1995: 32–9).

In the twenty-first century the FBI is still releasing its UCRs, relying on police statistics voluntarily submitted now by some 16,000 state, county and city law-enforcement agencies with coverage of 242 million inhabitants in the USA. The UCRs currently focus on crime rates for eight Index Crimes and 21 Non-Index Crimes. The Index Crimes include what the FBI calls 'violent crimes', namely murder, forcible rape, robbery and aggravated assault, as well as other crimes like burglary, larceny–theft, motor-vehicle theft and arson. (There are another 21 Non-Index Crimes, mostly misdemeanours about which the FBI also collects information.) All of this might suggest that the USA now has a very comprehensive collection of information on crime. However, this is somewhat misleading. Index Crimes are those *reported to police*, while Non-Index Crimes measure the *number of arrests made by police*. This simple, perhaps subtle, difference in the way apparently similar information is collected leads to some interesting problems.

The FBI focuses only on Index Crimes. The FBI has for a long time used these rates to give a Crime Index Total and it is this information that the US media and US citizens use to form a view about changes in the rate of crime, and hence the seriousness of the 'crime rate'.

The FBI reports on the number of offences and the crime rate per 100,000 of population, as well as changes in the rate from year to year. The FBI also releases its statistics in a more media-friendly way by indicating, for example, that there is 'a homicide every 22 minutes' or 'a motor-vehicle theft every 20 seconds'. As Beirne and Messerschmidt (1995: 34) observe, these are not 'crime rates'; they are just a neat way of making a point that may or may not alarm 'public opinion'.

If we go back to 1992, the total US population was estimated to be 255,483,870. In 1992 there were 23,760 murders, including homicides and non-negligent cases of manslaughter. The 'crime rate' for homicide is calculated thus:

$$\frac{23,760}{255,483,870} \times 100,000 = 9.3$$

Therefore the homicide rate per 100,000 population in 1992 was 9.3.

For 1999 the FBI reported that there were 15,552 murders, giving a homicide rate of 5.7 per 100,000 of population. In 2000 the volume was 15,586 at a rate of 5.5 per 100,000 (Federal Bureau of Investigation 2001: 15). As the FBI noted, the homicide rate in 2000 was the lowest since 1965, while the number of homicides was well down on the 1992 numbers. In 2002 the volume of murders increased slightly to 15,980, giving the USA a murder rate per 100,000 of 5.6 (ibid.: 19).

As is well known the homicide rate in the USA is much higher than in most Western societies. (By comparison in England and Wales in 2000 there were just 850 homicides, including murder, manslaughter and infanticide.) The USA also stands out in regard to the preferred weapons used. In 65.6 per cent of cases firearms were involved, with handguns in particular used in 51.5 per cent of murders (ibid.: 18). The FBI was also able to gather information on juvenile gang-killings, showing a decline from 858 killings in 1996 to 650 in 2000. As is more typical of homicides everywhere, the bulk of the murder victims knew their assailants (in 44.3 per cent of cases) and in over 30 per cent of cases the assailant was the husband or boyfriend.

The FBI's UCRs make a similar level of detail available in regard to forcible rape, robbery and aggravated assault. On the four crimes that together make up violent crime in 1999–2000, information suggests a significant decline over the 1990s. The total volume and rates of violent crimes in 1991 involved 1,426,044 crimes at a rate of 523.0 per 100,000 population. In 2001 the volume of juvenile gang-related killings rose dramatically to account for 865 killings (Federal Bureau of Investigation 2002: 24). In 2000 the number of offences had declined to 1,424,280, at a rate of 506.1 per 100,000 (Federal Bureau of Investigation 2001: 12). The violent crime statistics for 2000–1 suggests a 33 per cent decline overall in violent crime since 1991.

The FBI's UCRs give a similar degree of detail on crimes like burglary, larceny–theft, motor-vehicle theft and arson. Can we then take it that these official accounts are an accurate account of the number of serious crimes committed in the USA?

There are at least eight basic problems with these apparently objective measures:

- There is a gap between the actual number of crimes committed and those reported to police.
- The voluntary nature of reporting means some of the information is based on estimates only, but it is not clear how much this is the case.
- The FBI's UCR Index does not include certain serious crimes like blackmail or kidnapping which are federal crimes.
- Only the most serious crime in a total crime scene is reported. For example, when a crime incident has occurred involving a combination of burglary, rape and murder, only the murder is reported.
- There is the problem that the Index Crimes measure only crimes legally defined as such. This has some serious consequences for trying to form a comparative view about the tendencies to criminality between, say, the USA and Singapore where the 'crime rate' is very low. Adopting a tough 'law and order' policy in part to stamp out evidence of 'Western decadence', the Singaporean government has made carrying or chewing gum an offence. Similarly some US states make the carrying of ice cream in pockets a crime. These examples demonstrate the impact of social prejudice on what is defined

as a crime, in turn impacting on what citizens of Singapore or the USA 'know' about the level of crime in their society.

- The FBI's Index Crime data set mixes serious crimes like murder, arson and rape with less serious ones like motor-vehicle thefts and larcenies, which could give rise to some misunderstandings on the part of the population when they are reading what is released as the Index Crime Total.
- The Index Crime rates do not let us know about the elaborate social processes involved in converting human conduct into crimes that are recorded as crime statistics. It does not allow for the possibility that some law-enforcement agencies may have an interest in putting the best figures forward to justify their claims to more of the government's budget cake.
- Finally, quite serious crimes involving corporations and governments that may see billions of dollars stolen or many people dead, are left out of the Index Crime rates.

These considerations suggest why we need to approach the US crime rates with a good deal of care. Given the problems that such a federal system faces, how do England and Wales, which have a more or less centralized system of government, fare?

England and Wales

In England and Wales the Home Office's Research Development and Statistics Directorate (RDSD) produces an equivalent national account of crime on an annual basis. Since 2002 this information has been published in an annual report called *Crime in England and Wales* (for example Simmons and Dodd 2003; Walker, Kershaw and Nicholas 2006). This national account of the rate and volume of crime, like the FBI Index Crimes, relies on police reporting and recording procedures and most recently also relies on data gathered by the British Crime Survey (BCS) using interviews with some 47,789 face-to-face interviews with adults, i.e. people aged 16 and over (Walker, Kershaw and Nicholas 2006).

To get some sense of the scale of crime in England and Wales we can note that in 1996, for example, the RDSD claimed that there had been 5,033,800 'notifiable offences'. On the face of it this represented an 800 per cent increase since 1950. (In 1950 there had been 1.1 offences per 100 of population rising to 9.5 offences per 100 of population in 1996.) In the 2002–3 report it was claimed that there was a total of just under 5.9 million crimes recorded by police. This represented a decline in the volume of crime since 2001 of 3 per cent (Simmons and Dodd 2003: 2).

By 2006 and using BCS data (see below for a discussion of what this means), it was claimed that since the peak year (1995) there had been a consistent decline in crime, representing 8.4 million fewer crimes than in 1995. In 2006 the BCS crime rate had fallen by 44 per cent, with domestic crime and burglary falling by 59 per cent and violent crime by 43 per cent between 1995 and 2006. The rate of violent crime has remained stable since 2004. The overall risk of becoming a victim of crime decreased over the same period from a peak of 40 per cent to just under 23 per cent (Walker, Kershaw and Nicholas 2006: 1). It was interesting as ever to note as Walker, Kershaw and Nicholas (ibid.: 3) that people's belief about the crime rate did not match the official data, with an increase of over 30 per cent in the expression of anxiety about increasing crime. How much credence can be put in these kinds of reports?

Some years before, Maguire (1997: 135–88) pointed out the statistical information produced for England and Wales through the 1990s had many of the problems typically associated with official crime statistics because of the techniques and assumptions that are relied on to generate the information. There are problems with establishing the extent of 'crime' in England and Wales similar to those found in the USA.

- As in the USA, there has long been a gap between the 'actual' number of crimes and the crimes actually reported to police. Police, for example, exercise discretion about whether to proceed with investigations of reports made to them by members of the public. It was suggested that around 40 per cent of 'crimes' reported to the police did not end up in the official crime statistics. To deal with this problem the Home Office changed the rules affecting the police approach to recording crimes by introducing the National Crime Recording Standard (NCRS) system in 2001–2. This change had the effect of inflating the number of crimes recorded by police in 2002–3. This was a consequence in part of increasing the kinds of offences that were now to be counted (Simmons and Dodd 2003: 14). The Home Office seems to have sanctioned these changes as one way of adopting a more 'victim-oriented' approach to crime reporting. The NCRS is based on the victim's perception, not the police's, that a crime has been committed (ibid.: 34). The introduction of the NCRS seems to have inflated the 2002–3 statistics by around 10 per cent (ibid.: 35).
- The criminal statistics for England and Wales exclude a significant number of offences detected by policing agencies not under the control of the Home Office. These statistics focus largely, although not entirely, on indictable offences (tried in crown courts) and exclude a large number of summary offences (tried in the magistrates' courts).
- As in the USA only the most serious crime in a total crime scene is reported.
- Further, the information reported in *Crime in England and Wales* mixes up serious crimes like murder with less serious ones. For Maguire (1997: 150) the problem with such crime statistics is that they 'also include large numbers of incidences which it is difficult to claim are any more serious than many of the summary offences and the offences dealt with administratively'. This can create some misunderstandings on the part of anyone casually reading these reports.
- As in the USA, the Home Office statistics exclude some significant kinds of criminal activity, for example, cases of 'white-collar crime' detected by agencies other than the police, like the Inland Revenue, agencies distributing income support; the pursuit of tax evaders by the Customs and Excise departments in respect of failure to pay Value Added Tax (VAT) is similarly omitted.
- The Home Office reports also reflect ongoing changes in legislative definitions of 'criminal' activity along with changes in police practice and special operations carried out by police. For example, police operations against 'football hooligans' or anti-drug campaigns associated with pop concerts can produce apparently dramatic surges in 'crime' and therefore in the statistics.

In effect, far from being an 'objective' or uncomplicated count of crime, official crime statistics like those collected in the USA and England and Wales reflect complex political decisions, as well as policing and legal processes compounded by the assumptions and techniques used by the officials responsible for collecting the statistics. The 2002–3 report points to one of the oddities that attends any official crime-reporting system: reported homicides rose to 1,048 deaths, a rise related to the 'discovery' of some additional 172 murders committed by the Manchester serial killer Dr Harold Shipman. The effect was interesting. As the Home Office reported: 'The total number of homicides was 18 per cent or 157 higher than in 2001/2002. However, the extra Shipman offences exceeded the overall increase and it is likely that the number of homicides actually committed was lower than in the previous year' (Simmons and Dodd 2003: 81). A subsequent judicial inquiry reported early in 2005 that the total number of murders committed by Shipman was now estimated at 250 cases, which may require a further retrospective adjustment to the homicide rate for England and Wales. It can safely be suggested that these kinds of problems are found with local variations in all official crime statistics.

Considerations such as these have driven a variety of exercises by criminologists and policy-makers who believe that an accurate account of the actual crime rate is still possible. This assumption has informed attempts to measure what is referred to as the 'dark figure' of crime, a metaphor that draws on Adolphe Quételet's observation that 'our observations can only refer to a certain number of known and tried offences, out of the unknown sum total of crimes committed' (quoted in Walklate 2006: 30).

The 'dark figure' of crime?

One approach to counting this 'unknown sum total of crimes committed' has been done by carrying out elaborate social surveys that ask citizens if they have ever been victims of crime.

Experimental surveys of this kind were first carried out in the USA in the late 1960s, and in England, Wales and Scotland in the 1980s. Accepting the value of doing this, governments then began to run their own surveys. The US Department of Justice ran its first social surveys in 1972. In Britain the Home Office commenced the British Crime Survey (BCS) in 1982 which surveyed England, Wales and Scotland. Subsequent surveys were done in 1984 and 1988. After 1992 they were done in England and Wales every two years, before annual surveys were begun in 2001–2 following a major review of the British Crime Surveys by Lynn and Elliott (2000).

The BCS is based on a random sample using an elaborate questionnaire. Since 2001–2 this has been given to some 40,000 persons aged 16 and over (Simmons and Dodd 2003). People are asked if any member of their household in the past year has been a victim of one of a number of crimes. If they answer 'yes', then they are asked to fill out a detailed 'Victim Form' for each incident (Walker 1995).

On face value the results from these surveys suggest a considerable under-reporting of crime in comparison to the annual *Crime in England and Wales* reports produced from police records. For example, in 1995 the total of offences recorded by the police in categories covered by the BCS was under 3 million while the BCS reported that nearly 12 million offences had been committed (Maguire 1997: 165). By 2002–3 the mismatch was not as large but it was still considerable. While police records suggested that just under 5.9 million offences had been committed, the BCS suggested a figure of 12.3 million offences (Simmons and Dodd 2003: 9). In 2005–6 the mismatch was still considerable. Allowing for differences in the way the categories are put together, offences reported to police for 2005–6 suggested there had been 5.265 million crimes of violence and property offences, while the BCS data suggested there had been 11 million offences (Hoare and Robb 2006: 2–8).

The BCS has reinforced a 'good news–bad news' story. As commentators have noted, there appears to be 'more crime out there', even if most of it is petty. One of the problems in comparing the two sets of statistics is that the police records and the BCS do not count the same kinds of crimes. It is important to note, given that the results from this survey are used by the media to evaluate Home Office police statistics, that the definitions of crimes used in the BCS research align precisely with police categories only in two-thirds of cases. That is, the BCS research covers only a fraction of the total possible range of crimes. The BCS does not ask about crimes like murder – because there is no one to ask – drug-dealing or certain sexual offences. Equally, when the BCS asked why victims of crime do not report offences to police, as many as 69 per cent of people surveyed replied that they thought the offence was 'too trivial', that police would not be able to help or that they would fix the problem themselves (Simmons and Dodd 2003: 12).

If we are to think carefully about this approach to counting the rate of crime, it seems that the exercise is informed by a number of assumptions. (In Chapter 5 we spell out fully the reasons for identifying the role played by such assumptions.) Among the key assumptions on offer there is the idea that counting 'the dark figure' of crime or the 'sum total of crimes committed' is both desirable and possible. It is also assumed that the 'sum total of crimes committed' is an objective fact about any society and as such it is possible to define and measure the 'crime rate' so as to produce meaningful and comparable information for any society. It is also assumed that the methods of measuring 'the dark figure', such as carrying out a large sample survey, will produce reliable answers to the question. Finally it is assumed that the people who answer such surveys do so reliably and that they accurately represent their experience in terms which make their answers to the survey questions comparable to the statistics collected by police, law courts and coronial inquiries who have applied their tests of significance to determine that a crime has in fact been committed. It is worth saying that all of these assumptions are at least slightly problematic, if not highly debatable.

The official BCS has come under criticism from some criminologists sensitized by feminist concerns about the way masculinist assumptions can render women's experience invisible. Genn (1988) and Painter (1991) point out that the very techniques and assumptions used to define and to measure crime have ignored the actual experience of crime among certain parts of the population, rendering it in effect invisible. Genn (1988: 91) notes that the BCS tends to adopt a 'single crime event' model, which makes good sense when it comes to crimes like burglary or motor-vehicle theft. It is less useful, however, for women trapped in violent relationships, where domestic violence can continue for years and where the woman is victimized frequently. Painter (1991) makes a similar point about relying on a legal definition of crime. This has the effect, for example, of making marital rape legal. Her survey of experiences of rape by women suggested that 14 per cent of women had been raped at some point in their marriage, with over 40 per cent of these women perceiving the act as a rape at the time.

Maguire (1997: 164) argues that the BCS should not be read as offering an account of the sum total of crime. For this reason they should not be seen as providing a basis for validating the police information. Maguire suggests that the BCS simply offers an alternative picture of some of the crimes that are committed.

Conclusion

It is important not to assume that crime statistics, whoever collects them and however they are obtained, are simply and unequivocally an objective measure of crime. This in part is because the criminality of an event is not an intrinsic quality inherent in the act: there is nothing about conduct that makes it an objectively criminal activity. The claim that criminal offences have been committed depends on all sorts of evaluations, interpretations and judgements. In establishing how much crime there is we need to know:

- Who does the counting?
- How do they count it?
- What questions are asked and what assumptions are made in the counting process?

For this reason it is unlikely that we will ever *know* or be able to measure accurately the actual incidence of crime in any society. This claim is clearly at odds with the beliefs held by governments, the media or people working in the criminal justice system, and many citizens in the UK, Australia or the USA who will continue to want to know the *real* extent of crime in their societies. They may well need to accept certain limitations to this aspiration. At the same time there is clearly value in making the effort to do good research on criminal activity.

It should never be forgotten that the human experiences associated with crimes like murder, rape, fraud and deception, burglary and violent assault involve distress, fear, anxiety, terror, pain and loss. Thoughtful and critical approaches on the part of criminologists can help us to deal with the quite real problems that criminal activity creates. The information that we use to measure the crime rate should always take us back to, and not away from, the human experience it is said to represent.

Review questions

Is an objective and/or universal definition of crime possible? If not, why?

Should it matter for criminologists that a simple, single, universal and useful definition of crime is unlikely?

What are the principal reasons that make any accurate account of the numbers of crimes committed difficult to determine?

Further reading

Bottomley, K. and Coleman, C., 1986, *Understanding Crime Rates*, Saxon House, Farnborough.

Brownstein, H., 2000, 'The Social Production of Crime Statistics', *Justice Research & Policy*, Vol. 2, No. 2: 73–89.

Coleman, C. and Moynihan, J., 1996, *Understanding Crime Statistics*, Oxford University Press, Oxford.

Fattah, A., 1997, *Criminology: Past, Present and Future: A Critical Overview*, Macmillan, London.

Maguire, M., 2002, 'Crime Statistics, Patterns and Trends', in Maguire, M., Morgan, R. and Reiner, R. (eds), *The Oxford Handbook of Criminology* (3rd edition), Oxford University Press, Oxford.

Walker, M. (ed.), 1995, *Interpreting Crime Statistics*, Oxford University Press, Oxford.

Wilson, J.Q. and Herrnstein, R.J., 1985, *Crime and Human Nature*, Simon & Schuster, New York.

2

THE ORIGINS
OF MODERN
CRIMINOLOGY

It can seem that the only question about memory worth asking these days is how much you have in your computer. At least this makes the point that a computer without a memory is just a piece of junk. Russell Jacoby (1974) made the same point about people without a memory. Drawing on the work of Sigmund Freud, Jacoby argued that people who cannot remember their past are unable to think or act rationally in the present. Just as the accident victim with amnesia is totally disoriented, so too people without a memory are disoriented and unsure about what to do or where to go. As Harald Weinrich (2004: 136) notes, Freud's point was that the capacity to think well, and so to live well, depends on us having a good memory.

Criminologists produce research, develop theory, teach, give their expert views to the media, and advise governments, the courts and police forces. To do all these things they rely on a vocabulary and a tradition of ideas and concepts assembled into complex criminological arguments. These ideas and this vocabulary have a history which is worth rehearsing.

Many people may well think history is a yawn, and that being interested in the past means you are intellectually 'old fashioned' or some kind of 'fuddy-duddy'. After all, the future is always a far more interesting place. Yet understanding contemporary criminology requires an understanding of how and why it has taken the shape it has. This chapter explores the development of certain ideas in the eighteenth and nineteenth centuries that came to characterize criminology as a social science.

A history of criminology assists us in seeing the partly accidental and evolutionary development of certain ways of thinking about crime, criminal activity and the criminal justice system. We are especially interested in the ways people who identify themselves as criminologists, along with the sociologists, psychologists and anthropologists interested in crime, thought about, inquired into, researched and defined crime, criminal activity and the criminal justice system. Martha Nussbaum (2001), writing a history of ancient Greek philosophy, argues this is just another way of doing philosophy. Writing a history of criminology is likewise best understood as another way of doing criminology. Recalling the history of criminology helps in a fundamental way to answer the question: 'What is modern criminology?'

What kind of history?

If history is important, how do we tell that story or write that history? One way of doing it has been to write what David Garland calls a 'standard textbook history'. This works by telling a story of the 'stages' in the history of criminology, a story which emphasizes the progress made as 'primitive criminology' evolves into 'modern', 'advanced' and 'scientific' criminology. As Garland (1994: 20) puts it:

> The received wisdom of the discipline [can be] simplified into a tale of icons and demons (Beccaria, Lombroso, Burt, Radzinowicz . . .), a few key distinctions (classicism, positivism, radicalism . . .) and an overarching narrative in which ideological error is gradually displaced by the findings of science . . .

This is the kind of history of criminology written by Mannheim (1960), Radzinowicz (1966), or Quinney (1974, 1979). These writers began with a story about how a primitive kind of criminology developed in the eighteenth century. This history suggests that the early attempt to do criminology – mostly by 'amateurs', like philosophers and journalists, who did not understand the 'scientific method' – fortunately evolved into 'modern criminology' characterized by the use of the 'scientific method' to support a rigorous empirical social science (Mason 1996). This is 'whig history' with a vengeance, a history that, as Steve Fuller (2000: 22) says, is 'history written about the past to vindicate the present'.

This is a history that talks of stages such as 'classical criminology' which was created by philosophers and reformers such as Jeremy Bentham in the eighteenth century. This 'stage' gave way to 'positivist criminology', associated with Cesare Lombroso in the 1870s. In turn 'neo-classical criminology', associated with Gabriel Tarde or Cyril Burt, set the stage for a new kind of criminology between the 1890s and the 1920s. These stages in turn made it possible for 'modern criminology' to emerge in the second half of the twentieth century.

Is there anything wrong with writing a history of criminology as a story of progress or of developmental stages? According to Garland (1994: 21): 'The standard textbook history is, of course, broadly accurate – it would be very surprising if it were not. But the broad sweep of its narrative and the resounding simplicity of its generic terms can be profoundly misleading if they are taken as real history, rather than as a kind of heuristic . . .'. (The word 'heuristic' here means any framework for making sense of things.)

Contemporary criminologists like David Garland say that the actual story is not quite so simple. A more accurate history of criminology might point to a far messier, or *contingent*, approach to thinking about and researching crime, the criminal and the law. The 'radically simple' story of stages and progress mistakenly asserts that there was something recognizable as 'criminology' in the eighteenth century – or earlier. Some historians of criminology have claimed that, for as long as there have been 'states', 'theorists' and writing, there have been people who think about these issues who could be called 'criminologists'.

It is more useful to think about contemporary criminology as a set of distinctive intellectual activities and practices that comes to be organized into a recognizable discipline or 'profession' only in the second half of the nineteenth century.

Further, a thoughtful approach to this history also implies that we might stop trying to use a radically simplified chronology of criminology which talks of certain 'progressive' and sequential stages or phases, such as 'classical criminology', 'positivist criminology', 'neo-classical criminology', 'modern criminology' and now 'post-modern criminology'. The idea that the history of criminology is a history of stages ignores the possibility that the way people have done criminology is messier than metaphors of 'progress' or 'stages' allow for. For example, it is clear that most contemporary criminologists do not define themselves as 'post-modern criminologists'. In many respects the work of many contemporary statistically inclined criminologists is not all that different from the pioneering work done by statistical pioneers like Adolphe Quételet in the 1840s or by Cyril Burt in the 1920s. This consideration suggests that there are important continuities between allegedly discrete stages in the way people did criminology.

The simplifying approach at work in the 'whig histories' of criminology also mistakenly asserts that there has been a progressive increase in the 'rational' or 'scientific' treatment of 'reality' as criminology 'matured' or 'progressed'. How for example would those who accept the 'whig' idea of constant progress in criminological knowledge and theory validate such a claim? Do we now actually have better explanations for why people do criminal things than were on offer a century ago?

In a way the kind of history that might better grasp what happened is closer to what Steve Fuller (2000: 24) calls a 'tory history'. This is a history that allows that the figures of the past being written about either got it 'more right' than is now commonly allowed for, or to put this idea more pungently, that what is being done now is simply recycling old ideas using new words to do so.

A revised history of criminology

David Garland (1994) offers another approach to the history of criminology. Garland argues that his 'revisionist' history of criminology reveals two traditions, or what he calls 'projects', operating over the past few centuries, projects which continue to co-exist even now. Garland refers to these respectively as the 'governmental project' and the 'science of causes'. What does Garland mean by this?

As Garland (1994: 18) says: 'By a "governmental project" I mean . . . the long series of empirical inquiries that since the eighteenth century have sought to enhance the efficient and equitable administration of justice by charting the patterns of crime and monitoring the practice of police and prisons.' (The word 'empirical' here refers to the theory that what we know of the world is based on our senses like sight or sound.)

Garland's idea of 'government' is not just about the activities of governments but refers also to institutions like the family, churches and schools as they seek to regulate (or govern) the lives of people by passing laws, making policies or disciplining conduct. This idea of 'government' comes from the work of Michel Foucault (1991), the French philosopher–historian who died in 1984. Families, for example, engage in 'government' by regulating the behaviour of children in activities like cleaning, telling the truth or eating at the table instead of in front of the TV. Governments likewise employ police and health-care workers to control behaviour in the streets or teachers to educate people with approved ideas, values and information.

Garland suggests that across the nineteenth century Western governments increasingly used fact-gathering techniques like censuses and other social statistics to describe the essential features of a range of 'problem populations' like 'the poor', 'the mad' or the 'criminal classes'. Foucault (1991) called this kind of knowledge 'governmentality', making a play on the 'mentality' part of the word. The reference to 'mentality' points to the role of ideas and evidence gathered by experts using techniques like the census. 'Governmentality' includes the variety of *scientific* and statistical surveillance techniques and statistical information used to inform a system of expert administration designed to regulate human behaviour. On this interpretation, gathering crime statistics is just one part of the project of government.

As we argued in Chapter 1 this kind of research work is a central preoccupation of contemporary criminology. It is the kind of criminology produced by in-house police and civil service research units, as well as academic research centres that regularly produce statistics on crime and justice. Much of this work is designed to help governments and police to work out where to put police resources by, for example, identifying areas in cities with high crime rates.

However, Garland says that alongside this activity, criminology also became an academic discipline based in universities, with academics developing an interest in *explaining* why crime occurs. This is what Garland means when he says criminology has also aspired to be a 'science of causes'. According to Garland the 'science of causes' like any science has to make certain assumptions. In this case criminologists who pursue a 'science of causes' promote a 'form of inquiry which aims to develop an etiological, explanatory science based on the premise that criminals can somehow be differentiated from non-criminals' (1994: 18). Garland also refers to this as the Lombrosian project, after the work of the Italian Cesare Lombroso (1911) who published his famous study *Criminal Man* (or *L'Uomo Delinquente*) in 1876. Lombroso was a nineteenth-century 'positivist' who did much to promote criminology as a 'science of causes'. (We will discuss what Lombroso thought and some of the issues with it later in this chapter.)

Garland's main point is that, far from being a history of discrete stages, the history of criminology is better understood as a kind of parallel process in which the 'governmental project' evolved alongside the pursuit of a 'science of causes'. Garland says that the result is 'modern criminology', a tension-filled field of study, teaching and research caught between an 'ambitious science of causes' and a more pragmatic, policy-oriented, administrative project seeking to use science in the service of management and social control. It is tension-filled partly because these two projects operate with different assumptions about the nature of human beings and their conduct, as well as different assumptions about what kinds of knowledge are credible.

Garland's account of modern criminology as a combination of a 'governmental project' evolving alongside a 'science of causes' is a very useful starting point. However, he overstates the point when he suggests that most criminologists today work within either a broadly defined *positivist* tradition or an *empiricist* approach to their research. (The meanings of and debates about these complex and controversial concepts are discussed later.) We will qualify that point by showing that there have always been other criminologists working against those conventions of empiricism and positivism. There are criminologists who have developed an approach to understanding human activity by developing *interpretive* methods. To compound the complexity, another tradition is to be found at work in the history of criminology, best referred to as a *critical*, or *sceptical*, style of criminology. A giant figure in American criminology like Edwin Sutherland (1924 and 1947) was critical early on about the conservative character of conventional criminology. Sutherland (1947) thought this kind of criminology was socially conservative because it focused on the crimes of the poor as opposed to the crimes of the rich and powerful – or what he called 'white-collar crime'. Likewise other early US criminologists associated with the Chicago School of Sociology were heavily influenced by the anti-positivist philosophy of US pragmatists like C. S. Peirce and William James. As we show in Chapter 3 what became an ethnographic approach to criminology, firstly at the University of Chicago, was based on a scepticism about the possibility of ever producing a 'science of crime'. Though sceptical and critical criminologists have never provided anything more than a counterbalance to mainstream criminologists, they have been an important part of the history of modern criminology.

In short we need to modify Garland's account. Contemporary criminology is certainly a tension-filled field of study, teaching and research. There are criminologists who pursue a policy-oriented administrative project seeking to use science in the service of management and social control. There are criminologists like Gottfredson and Hirschi (1990) who relentlessly pursue a 'science of causes'. Finally, as the careers of writers like Stanley Cohen (1997, 2001) and David Garland (1990, 1997, 2001) suggest, a more critical, sceptical style of criminology continues to find a readership.

Nonetheless Garland's idea of a 'governmental project' and a 'science of causes project' at work in criminology provides a good starting point.

Bentham and the governmental project

The first half of the nineteenth century in many countries, including Britain and America, saw the flowering of some of the key institutions that mark out the 'governmental project'. These institutions include the development of the modern penitentiary, the growth of police forces, and the systematic collection of statistical data designed to assist the discovery and regulation of social problems among certain sections of the population. How did this come about?

In countries like France, the UK and the USA the eighteenth century had seen the development of networks of lawyers, journalists, intellectuals and self-declared 'social reformers'. These groups constituted a 'public sphere' based on newspapers, journals and intellectual societies whose members met in coffee-shops, universities and salons run by wealthy and powerful aristocrats. These intellectuals and professionals – or *philosophes* as they were called in France – were committed to a programme of 'enlightened' and critical thought. They promoted the kind of natural science associated with Isaac Newton, the political programme grounded in the liberalism of John Locke, the sceptical empiricism of David Hume and the utilitarian ethics of writers like Jeremy Bentham.

Collectively these writers believed in the promise of a new social and intellectual order based on a broadly defined commitment to *Reason*, or rationality. They advocated the scientific investigation of the social and natural world. They believed profoundly in the capacity of Reason to change human beings and in the power of education and science to make the 'good society'. Indeed all were part of that process which led to what some historians have said is the greatest invention of the eighteenth century, the idea that every human being has a right both to happiness and to freedom.

Their ideas helped to shape a wide-ranging programme of political and intellectual change across Europe and in the American colonies, and played their part in what has been called 'the democratic revolution' that saw Britain lose its American colonies in 1785 and France engage in revolutionary change after 1789.

This was a time when writers and academics were generalists rather than experts in a narrow field. There was no particular special knowledge or response to crime of the kind that marks out the *modern* criminological project, just a preoccupation with the *social problem*.

The 'social problem' referred to the existence of millions of poor, exploited, politically disenfranchised and potentially revolutionary urban, working-class people. The existence of these people, and their perceived potential for trouble, triggered off traditional responses like military repression, political trials and secret police surveillance. It would also sponsor numerous exercises in social scientific research, social policy and democratic reform, especially in the second half of the eighteenth and throughout the nineteenth century. Though no one person can be held responsible for this, one figure stands out.

Jeremy Bentham (1748–1832) was a wealthy gentleman–lawyer, lobbyist and *philosophe* who tirelessly promoted a rational programme of law reform and rational social change designed to increase the sum total of human happiness, or what he called 'utility'. To use Foucault's and Garland's word 'governmentality' we can say that Bentham played a central role in developing a revolution in 'governmentality' that took off in the nineteenth century and was to directly sponsor the development of the twentieth-century idea that governments have an obligation to promote human welfare. Bentham was extremely influential throughout the nineteenth century and continues to be an invisible but significant presence into our own time. Bentham stands as the 'father' of so many distinctively 'common-sense' modern views and practices that we can easily miss his impact.

Bentham is also important because he linked his utilitarianism to his advocacy of the use of scientific evidence as a basis for policy-making, and for a systematic approach to law reform enacted by governments using statutory law.

Bentham was one of the first great modern advocates of treating the law as an agency of social reform. Bentham tirelessly pursued law reform as an instrument for larger social transformation. He was an early advocate of evidence-based law reform. He was an inexhaustible promoter of ideas like privatizing prisons, putting 'the poor' to work, and was ever ready to write constitutions for any country willing to pay him as a consultant. Among his ideas was that precisely designed buildings could be used as schools, prisons or hospitals to regulate the behaviour of almost anyone needing to be educated, imprisoned or cured of disease. He called his design idea a 'Panopticon': the idea that required putting a group of people under surveillance by teachers, doctors or wardens situated in a central point or space in a building, and thereby enabling them to regulate the inmates' behaviour. This idea was to inform the building of prisons like Alcatraz in the nineteenth and twentieth centuries.

His influence, however, runs more deeply than as the promoter of bright ideas. As a rationalist he believed in the power of evidence to persuade people to make necessary social change. Bentham took the proposition from Helvétius, an eighteenth-century *philosophe*, that all valid knowledge is empirical. Bentham believed that all knowledge is based on sensations – like sight or hearing. Grounded in this philosophy of knowledge Bentham sponsored a process of rational social change administered by an expert bureaucracy responsible for an efficient *scientific* system of administration and relying on the systematic gathering of societal facts and statistics. His ideas mattered especially in Britain. Bentham through his social and political networks and his protégés had a tremendous practical and intellectual influence. He was an early advocate for systematic empirical enquiry that ushered in the age of Select Committees and Royal Commissions in Britain. His influence is evident in legislation such as the *Metropolitan Police Act 1828*, the *Poor Law Act 1834* and the *Public Health Act 1848*.

Bentham's promotion of the systematic collection and use of descriptive social statistics to better inform government has led some historians, following Foucault, to suggest that his idea of the 'Panopticon', originally intended as a design principle to construct buildings that could keep the inmates under constant surveillance, should also be seen as a metaphor for governments' collection of social statistics to keep a close watch on social problems or certain groups of problematic people.

Yet Bentham was more than the caricature of Gradgrind, the Benthamite reformer Dickens satirized in his novel *Hard Times* for wanting only 'the facts'. Bentham's passion for change was grounded also in an ethical idea that has proved his greatest legacy: governments, he thought, had an obligation to promote the greatest happiness of the greatest number of their citizens.

Bentham is one of the key figures in modern philosophy and public policy because of his advocacy of the ethical system called 'utilitarianism' ('utility' is another word for happiness or welfare). Bentham was a key advocate of the idea that all humans have a right to happiness. This idea is embedded in the American Declaration of Independence which refers to the pursuit of liberty and happiness. Bentham did not invent the system of ethics called utilitarianism. He drew on the work of writers like Hutcheson and Beccaria (1963), an Italian philosopher of punishment, to develop the principle of utility into the ethical system we now refer to as 'utilitarianism'.

Bentham was a rationalist and a utilitarian. He held that all human action is driven by rational self-interest. Bentham argued that as human beings we naturally and rationally seek to maximize our happiness and minimize or avoid things that give us pain. Utilitarians like Bentham claim that the way we judge something to be good is by asking whether it will make us happy. If the answer is 'yes', then it is 'good'. As individuals we are driven to do only what will maximize our happiness or minimize pain. He drew on this idea to argue that governments ought to promote the greatest happiness of the greatest number of people. At the societal level Bentham argued that any ethical judgement or political process should be judged only against the principle of whether an action or policy will advance 'the greatest happiness of the greatest number'.

Utilitarianism is the belief or value system that has supplied the dominant ethical framework to the cultures of the Anglo-American world. That framework is alive and well in the twenty-first century as evidenced by the thriving state of a neo-classical economics of 'rational selfishness' which informs contemporary neo-liberal policies, as well as Animal Liberation philosophers like Peter Singer. In spite of powerful critiques by philosophers from Kant to Finnis (2005: 112–18), showing precisely why this doctrine is senseless, it retains an extraordinary status in the contemporary Anglo-American world.

This is so probably because of the elective affinity between utilitarianism and any society with an ethic of individualism and a market-based economy: happiness in such societies is readily equated with consuming more goods or having more money. Bentham himself had sponsored the increasingly important belief that it was both possible and desirable to *measure* any increase or decrease in happiness – or utility. Bentham proposed using money as an index of happiness, but votes, public opinion polls or any equivalent metric would do as well. Bentham was one major proponent of the idea that we can quantify our ethical preferences, using what he called the 'felicific calculus'. It has also allowed economists like Becker (1978) to develop an economic theory of crime.

The revolution in government

Bentham stands behind all those attempts to give effect to the 'governmental project' that took off in the nineteenth century. The utilitarian ethic and the practice of a rational, empirically based, efficient legal and administrative system which Bentham promoted was central to the increase in the range and scope of state interventions in Britain from the 1830s on. Given his premiss that it was the duty of government to advance 'the greatest happiness of the greatest number', Bentham helped to unleash the 'Victorian revolution in government' that gathered speed in the 1830s and 1840s.

At the urging of his disciples, utilitarian reformers like Edwin Chadwick, James Mill, Nassau Senior and John Stuart Mill, British governments after 1832 increasingly undertook a range of interventionist, regulatory and information-gathering activities. The 'Victorian revolution in government' involved a reform project designed to make the law more rational and government more efficient by developing an expert-based administrative system which made increasing use of statistics to guide policy-making.

The 'revolution in government' involved a programme of systematic surveillance of social problems, the systematic collection of statistics and the use of inspectors to report on the progress of reform. By the 1850s British governments were relying on an army of inspectors and experts to collect facts about a large number of social problems, including crime, poverty, homelessness, prostitution and 'street children'. The revolution in government also saw Bentham's disciples build and manage the archetypal 'industrial' institutions of the nineteenth century, beginning with workhouses for the poor. Subsequently governments undertook the construction of schools, prisons and hospitals. These institutions treated people as so much raw material to be regulated and re-educated. They relied less on the threat of punishment or pain and more on the efficient management and regulation of the inmates' behaviour.

Garland (1994: 35) explains why this mattered for the development of criminology:

> The various forms of charitable and social work with the poor, the societies for the care of discharged convicts, the management of workhouses, inquiries about the causes and extent of inebriety, investigations into the labour market, the employment and education of children, education, the housing of the poor, the settlements and boys' club movements, could all be identified as the roots of . . . the modern criminological mix.

Why did this happen? There is little doubt that this 'reform' agenda was driven by elite and middle-class business and professional fears that the 'lower classes' would maintain the momentum for democratic change, one that might lead even to socialist revolution (Hobsbawm 1975). Memories of the revolutions in America (1776–84) and France (1789–1814) nourished these fears. The middle-class impulse to reform and regulate was also fed by the unrelenting revelation by reformers, investigators and lobbyists of a plethora of social problems crying out for action. The development of what we call 'social sciences' was implicated in this process.

The statistical movement and a science of causes

Until the mid-nineteenth century, the collection of social statistics had been at best rudimentary and sporadic. The development of statistics flowered in the nineteenth century and was the work of men like Edwin Chadwick and Adolphe Quételet, who possessed of a deep interest in, and passion for, social reform drawing on *scientific* techniques (Stigler 1987: 162–82 and 263–300). In this way the 'governmental project' itself sponsored the development of a 'science of causes' that was to shape the development of modern criminology.

Benthamite reformers who promoted the emergent governmental project relied on an ever-increasing volume of social statistics designed to describe the social, cultural and economic lives of the people by focusing on such things as death rates and suicide rates, as well as crime rates. The architects of the 'revolution in government' required more and more information about more and more of the population, and the development of social statistics played a central role in this process. The need for social facts that led to an explosion in social statistics was well advanced by the 1840s and supported by the growth of groups such as the London and Manchester Societies for Social Statistics. Investigations like Henry Mayhew and his multi-volume studies of London's poor (1861–62) added more colourful kinds of evidence.

It is in this respect then that Garland's distinction between criminology approached as a 'governmental project' and as a 'science of causes' implies a clear-cut set of boundaries between the two than is the case. This becomes apparent as we trace out the development of social statistics and the contribution this made to a 'science of causes'.

The Belgian statistician Adolphe Quételet (1796–1874) made an enormous contribution to the modern 'empirical' social sciences. Quételet's innovations in statistics provided some of the technical basis for the development of criminology as a 'science of causes' based on what can be called a 'broad church' kind of positivism.

Quételet's primary achievement was to develop and apply statistical ideas about averages to many social phenomena, showing how deviations from the average were determined and not a random phenomenon. (He did this by using the curve of normal distribution or a Gaussian distribution.)

Quételet (1842) developed a number of basic ideas about social problems like crime which have persisted into our own time. His data showed that most crimes were committed by younger people aged 15 to 21 and that most serious crimes were performed by males. He claimed to show that many social phenomena were persistent and stable over time, making it possible to talk about an 'average' person by drawing on observations about thousands or tens of thousands of people in each group. He demonstrated that the rates at which various crimes were committed, discovered and punished were likewise regular and varied very little over time. And if crime rates were constant, this suggested to Quételet, that the 'causes' of such phenomena were likewise regular and must be operating according to some 'laws of causality' that could be discovered.

All of this led him to an early version of a sociological model of crime: individuals may commit crimes but they are merely the agent of societal pressures and causes. As Quételet (1842: 6, 108) put it: 'Every social state presupposes, then, a certain number and a certain order of crimes, these merely being the necessary consequences of its organization . . . Society prepares crime, and the guilty are only the instruments by which it is executed.' At some point in the 1840s, Quételet came to see a clear distinction between 'normal distributions' and 'unusual deviations' from this statistical norm.

Like modern criminologists, Quételet found it difficult to resist giving expression to his own class- and gender-bound prejudices, something which sooner or later overwhelms even the most cautious of empirical social scientists. Using techniques for ascertaining a normal distribution, Quételet concluded that while every 'normal' man had a certain tendency to commit crime, this rarely happened. Of more concern was the criminality of the 'statistically' unusual kind manifested by people he thought were degenerates, vagrants, 'gypsies', the 'inferior classes' and people of 'low moral character'. By the late 1840s Quételet, in clear anticipation of Lombroso and Galton, concluded that crime was likely to be a consequence of hereditary and biological defects. In France followers of Quételet, like Guerry, promoted the development of social statistics into recognizably 'modern' forms. In the last decades of the nineteenth century Quételet's work offered the statistical basis for the distinctively 'positivist' idea that the social sciences could and should emulate the physical sciences.

There is no evidence that British social researchers and 'reformers' took much immediate notice of Quételet's work. This was in spite of the fact that by the late 1840s in Britain John Stuart Mill, the dominant philosopher of his age who had been raised by Bentham as a utilitarian and social reformer, was also one of the leading advocates for a statistically based social science and for French 'positivism'. By the 1870s, however, in Britain social researchers like Rawson, Fletcher and Glyde began using the techniques of Quételet.

The word 'positivism' needs some brief consideration here.

Positivism

'Positivism' is a controversial word with a considerable history. Auguste Comte (1798–1857) coined the word 'positivism' (he also coined the word 'sociology'). Like many other key ideas it can be used either as a weapon to insult someone we disapprove of or to help us to talk or think clearly. There is continuing controversy about what the word refers to. This lack of clarity or consensus about its meaning has long been a feature of this word throughout its career. Needless to say there is no single, neat definition of what it means (see Hacking 1983: 42–57).

For contemporary criminologists 'positivism' involves a commitment to a 'common-sense' reliance on scientific method. The practice of this kind of positivism is based on 'operationalizing' a concept so as to render it amenable to measurement, carrying out some data collection and then doing statistical analysis – like regression analysis – on that data. This apparently 'common-sense' approach is often taught in university 'empirical research methods' or 'quantitative research methods' courses and incorrectly assumes or asserts that because it is based on 'common sense' it has nothing to do with theories or philosophy. For those criminologists who are aware of the history of philosophy, 'positivism' will be understood to refer to what a group of mostly Austrian philosophers, who belonged to the Vienna Circle in the 1920s, promoted (Ayer 1959). For other criminologists 'positivism' is what nineteenth-century criminologists like Lombroso stood for. We can see here fruitful grounds for confusion.

An examination of what Auguste Comte meant by 'positivism' helps identify some of the main claims and assumptions still made by many criminologists.

Comte was violently opposed to religious ideas and what he called 'metaphysics'. (In this respect Comte was heavily indebted to the work of eighteenth-century French *philosophes* like Voltaire, Condillac and Montesquieu.) Comte's deep antagonism to religious belief was fed by his faith in empiricism: if something had no material qualities enabling it to be seen, smelled, heard or touched then it did not exist and could not be the proper object of scientific knowledge. 'God' on this account was just a quaint and irrational hangover from the Middle Ages and had no part to play in the development of scientific reason. Comte preferred to put his faith in the achievements of modern sciences like chemistry, physics and medical research. In broad terms Comte thought that the methods of the natural sciences could and should be applied to all forms of knowledge and to what we now refer to as the 'social sciences'. (Unlike twentieth-century positivists, Comte did not believe it either possible or wise to establish definitively that there was a single scientific method: Comte allowed that each science could and should have its own special methods and laws.)

As twentieth-century French scholars like Canguilhem (1990) have shown, Comte and his followers were heavily reliant on biological and medical metaphors and explanations. This biological model fed the development of a new science of society in the 1840s that Comte called 'sociology'. Comte's 'science of society' spoke increasingly of 'social health' and identified 'antisocial' factors using medical metaphors which would come to identify crime as a 'social pathology'. Comte's advocacy of the idea of a science of the societal rested on a number of basic propositions.

1   As an empiricist Comte believed that the only secure knowledge about the world was knowledge based on what was observable. If an idea was not observable or measurable, it could never become the substance of knowledge. (This had serious consequences for many ideas apart from 'God', like 'justice', 'democracy' or 'love'.) Comte relied on one early version of what became known as the verifiability criterion of meaning. This is the philosophical claim that our knowledge of the world ought properly to consist of 'ideas' which are traces of sense data emitted by 'real objects' in the world. In short any word, in order to be meaningful, had to refer to something that was 'real' or observable. Using this criterion, for example, the word 'unicorn' has no meaning and cannot be regarded as playing any part in any scientific claim about the world.

2   Positivism in Comte's hands became a *method of research* based on observation and measurement. Comte argued that any claims wishing to be 'scientific' had to be based on careful observation and precise measurement.

3   Comte further argued that the positivist scientist's goal was explanation: success in explaining anything would be verified when it became the basis of prediction. According to Comte, explaining anything successfully required successful prediction. He did not favour older notions of causality as much as a model of explanation based on the laws of succession. (Laws of succession work by relating events that occur across time, like the claim that 'swallowing cyanide causes death'.) Like Hume and Kant, Comte accepted that *causality* was simply a *metaphysical* idea because causality is not strictly speaking an observable relationship, although in one sense his reliance on the 'laws of succession' was a way of reinstating causality.

4   Finally, Comte adopted *a spectator model of knowledge*. Pierre Manent (1998: 50–85) argues that nineteenth-century social sciences introduced a deterministic logic into its 'science of man' with paradoxical effects. One of these effects was to obscure any real interest in the nature of human conduct. Manent begins by noting that whereas classical political philosophy had adopted the viewpoint of the practical actor – that is a citizen or statesman who participates in the world – sociology early took the 'viewpoint of the spectator'. The viewpoint of the spectator is 'pure and scientific' and accords no real initiative to the agent or agents, but considers their actions or works 'as the necessary effects of necessary causes'. Objectivity on the part of the social scientist implied that the writer–expert was committed not only to eliminating *bias* but also to eliminating the psychological dimensions of experience and even of 'the feeling and willing self' (Bannister 1987: 40).

In short, being a 'positivist' meant for Comte that it was desirable and possible to use what he thought were the methods of the 'natural sciences' – like physics, chemistry or physiology – to do research into social matters like crime. Many of us will doubtless think that this is just common sense.

Yet there are many issues with taking this common sense seriously. Take the idea that scientists just look at the facts and develop theories from those facts. Gerald Holton (1988) has shown how all so-called 'hard sciences' like physics or chemistry rely on 'themata'. (What Holton called 'themata' Gadamer 1994 described as simply rock-solid prejudices without which we cannot think or do science.) 'Themata', or prejudices, are beliefs that we either cannot find facts to support or else refuse to think about, but simply assume to be true. Holton shows, for example, how Newton's famous mathematical account of the laws of the universe in *Principia Mathematica* (1687) relied on a 'thematum' called 'God'.

Notwithstanding these and similar problems with positivism, it matters only that Comte's ideas were enthusiastically, if selectively, taken up in both Britain and America by key figures like John Stuart Mill and Herbert Spencer, each of whom was a key point of transmission of the aggressive and 'irreligious' positivism of Auguste Comte into both Britain and America. Even so, both of these nineteenth-century philosophers were sceptical about the very systemic and rationalist quality of Comte's work, perhaps seeing this as a consequence of Comte's being a Frenchman.

It is important to note that both Mill and Spencer helped to promote and consolidate some of the elements of what 'a proper social science' should look like. In almost every respect their advocacy of a social science was 'positivist', except for one key point. Neither Mill nor Spencer let go of the Benthamite idea that people are individuals pursuing their self-interest and maximizing their happiness by some kind of rational calculation. To this extent they resisted the properly positivist idea that people are driven by factors or causes outside their control.

From the 1840s on, utilitarians like J. S. Mill (1806–73) (himself a pupil of Bentham), arguably the most influential British philosopher of the nineteenth century, constructed a powerful synthesis of liberal individualism, ethical utilitarianism and an empiricist–positivist approach to scientific knowledge. Mill's *System of Logic* (1843) provided a detailed and systematic outline of a *proper* 'positivist' social science. In effect Mill succeeded in codifying the elements of an inductive model of the social sciences. In America, Comte's ideas and vocabulary were spread by Herbert Spencer (1820–1903) on his lecturing tours. Spencer had a major intellectual impact on American academics. His advocacy of a science of 'social physics', or 'sociology', was influential in promoting the development of both sociology and criminology in the USA, as was his commitment to spreading his version of Darwinism which became known as social Darwinism.

Charles Darwin's book *The Origin of Species* (1859) and his subversive assault on the biblical idea that every species of animal and plant was created by God in either one day or seven days (there are two accounts of the creation in Genesis) added further weight to the status of scientific biology in helping to shape the social sciences. Darwin's account of 'racial types', or what he also called 'species', was to have a major impact on the evolution of modern criminology and the idea that criminology should aim to become a 'science of causes'.

Granted the somewhat complex development of European positivism, it is still the case that it was only with the publication in 1876 of Cesare Lombroso's *Criminal Man* that an explicitly positivist criminology was made available to a wide audience. In this book a strong positivist claim was made that factors outside our personal control make some of us criminals. Lombroso's fame rested on his claim that he could *explain* crime through the medium of scientific analysis, because he had discovered that there was a specific type of man – 'criminal man' – whose behaviour was something over which he had little if any control. In effect 'criminal man' was a Darwinian 'throwback'.

Lombroso and the 'science of causes'

Many histories of criminology (Jeffrey 1972) treat the publication of Cesare Lombroso's *Criminal Man* in 1876 as a benchmark event. For these writers, Lombroso's book marks the installation of a determinist 'science of criminality'. In an intellectual context already influenced by Darwin's biology and soon to be shaped by Galton's development of a biologically based sociology, Lombroso's *Criminal Man* (1911) represents one version of a biologically determinist shift towards the *scientific* treatment of the crime problem.

According to Lombroso's account, criminal activity was an example of a 'predictable' and 'habitual' form of conduct which was best understood as something causally determined by 'forces' beyond any person's control. As Cohen notes, the 'positivist revolution' in criminology popularly ascribed to Lombroso's *Criminal Man* (1876) assumed

> . . . not rationality, free will and choice but determinism (biological, psychic or social) . . . the subsequent structure and logic of criminological explanation remained largely within the positivist paradigm. Whether the level of explanation was biological, psychological, sociological or a combination of these ('multi-factorial' as some versions were dignified) the Holy Grail was a general causal theory: why do people commit crime? This quest gave the subject its collective self-definition: 'the scientific study of crime'.
>
> (Cohen 1992: 4)

For Lombroso, individual free will was a myth because 'individual behaviours', including criminal activity, were largely beyond people's control.

From 1876 when Lombroso's book *Criminal Man* appeared, extraordinary interest and acclaim greeted his work. His vivid writing style perhaps explains part of the impact. Lombroso's study of Italian army recruits and prison inmates used both craniometry (measuring skull size) and anthropometry (measuring body shape) in an attempt to identify different *racial types* and subject them to scientific scrutiny and categorization.

In this respect Lombroso's work seemed – and seems – eminently scientific. To this day *real* science is marked by the measurement of things. Lombroso played a part in legitimating the enthusiasm for physical and psychological measurement that has continued down to this day. The mania for measurement would lead to the measurement of schoolchildren beginning with their skull size and routine measurement of their 'intelligence', reading age and mathematical abilities. It was to sponsor the mass testing of soldiers' IQs and the IQs of other groups in the population after 1914. It also encouraged the collection and measurement of the skulls of natives in North America and Australasia, to say nothing of murdered Jews and gypsies in the Institutes of Racial Science that flourished in Nazi Germany after 1939.

Lombroso recalls his 'eureka' moment when opening up the skull of a 'criminal' named Vilella:

> I found on the occipital part . . . a distinct depression which I named median *occipital fossa* because of its situation precisely in the middle of the occiput, *as in inferior animals, especially rodents* . . . at the sight of that skull, I seemed to

see all of a sudden, lighted up as a vast plain under a flaming sky, the problem of
the nature of the criminal, an atavistic being who reproduces in his person the
ferocious instincts of primitive humanity and the inferior animals.

(Ferri-Lombroso in Lombroso 1911: xxiv–xxv; our
emphasis)

Here we see the effect of Lombroso's assumption that it was necessary to treat criminals
as different from the rest of us. He felt confident in this assumption because it seemed to
derive from the dramatic biological revolution unleashed by Darwin's *The Origin of Species*
(1859). Lombroso's talk of 'causes' implies a deterministic view of human conduct in
which our conduct is caused by factors outside our control. Lombroso believed that some
people were 'biologically' disposed to commit crime and that they had no choice. (Some
of us now use the language of genetics to say the same thing.) On Lombroso's account of
a 'science of causes', certain people were inherently 'criminals' and belonged to a 'criminal
class'. They could not help themselves in regard to their 'criminal conduct'.

Lombroso's research was based on the principle that criminals were biological throwbacks to a more primitive version of *homo sapiens*. Lombroso drew on an idea shared by
Darwin, Galton and Freud, that the development of each human from embryo to adult
recapitulates the evolutionary process of the human species. For Lombroso, 'criminal man'
was a poor unfortunate, 'an atavistic being who reproduces in his person the ferocious
instincts of primitive humanity'. His work contributed to what became a veritable tidal
wave of psychological and physical measurements that went on at least into the 1950s.

Lombroso advanced the project of a 'science of causes' in criminology firstly by his
insistence on studying 'the criminal' as a type. He sought to establish a modern science of
the criminal by virtue of his attempt to delineate a definitive anthropological entity: 'the
natural-born criminal'. That is, Lombroso insisted that 'the criminal' was a *type* different
from the rest of us, and was worthy of scientific study. At a stroke Lombroso constituted
the conceptual entity (*the criminal*) that could sustain a discursive and disciplinary
enterprise in terms that were recognizably *modern* and *criminological*, while reassuring his
middle-class readers that they were largely safe from producing or being such throwbacks
themselves.

Lombroso left his readers with the impression that here was a genuine 'criminological
science of causes'. The *criminal* was now being constituted as a conceptual object worthy
of a criminology, defined as a science of causes. And though he should not be given sole
credit for this, by 1890 'criminology' was a word in common use.

Yet in many ways Lombroso's central claim that he had developed a genuine 'criminological science of causes' was the least credible aspect of his work. From the start when
European criminologists met at a series of international conferences beginning in 1883,
French, Italian and German criminologists subjected Lombroso's work to damaging
criticism. (British experts deigned to attend the Geneva Congress of Criminal Anthropology
only from 1896 onwards.) Lombroso's work was frequently and vigorously criticized as
crude nonsense. It is to his credit that Lombroso himself later accepted this criticism, leading
him to radically rethink his position.

This criticism reflects the point that nothing is ever quite simple or straightforward. For
even as Lombroso was propounding his ideas about the causes of criminality, a newer

model of scientific explanation took over in the second half of the nineteenth century. This owed much to the statistical revolution in nineteenth-century astronomy and physics. As Ian Hacking (1990) has shown, more and more scientists stopped talking about *causality* and began talking about the *probability* of something causing something else to happen. Natural scientists came increasingly to accept that many factors could explain why something happened. This idea of multi-causality informed the increasing use by social scientists of statistical techniques like regression and correlation analysis pioneered by Francis Galton and Karl Pearson in the last decades of the nineteenth century. Ultimately this model of causality triumphed in most of the social sciences. In the twentieth century a good deal of academic criminology has been done that involves gathering information and analysing it statistically so as to construct elaborate explanations of crime that point to many factors at work.

Lombroso's work proved to be important in the long run because of the reactions it provoked. Among the many criticisms of Lombroso, Gabriel Tarde's critique stands out. Tarde's intervention proved to be quite influential and his work is often referred to as the 'neo-classical synthesis'. Equally in Britain Lombroso's work stimulated Francis Galton to refine the biological and statistical explanation of social behaviour.

Responses to Lombroso: Tarde and the neo-classical synthesis

Before the end of the nineteenth century, the French criminologist Gabriel Tarde (1843–1904) produced his 'neo-classical synthesis'. This was the result of his criticizing both 'classicism' and Lombroso's 'positivism'.

Tarde (1886) argued that neither Bentham nor Lombroso provided the right kind of basic principles and assumptions that might inform a 'modern philosophy of punishment'. In 1890 Tarde, in *Penal Philosophy*, accused 'classicists' – like Bentham – of overemphasizing the free-will and rationality of the human actor. Equally Tarde accused the 'positivists' of over-emphasizing the machine-like, determined and causal explanations of criminality. In a way he echoes Marx's insight that humans were indeed the makers of their own history, but not of the circumstances in which they found themselves.

Tarde developed a much more sociological idea of crime. That is, Tarde emphasized the distinctively social or collective aspects of human conduct. Tarde argued that 'imitation' was the core social and psychological phenomenon that explained most social phenomena, including crime. As Tarde (1890: 322) put it: 'Imitation is that powerful, generally unconscious, always partly mysterious action by means of which we account for all the phenomena of society.' In terms that later criminologists have found useful, Tarde also argued that another key sociological factor predisposing some people to crime was living in cities. Living in large cities exposed people to what Tarde called an 'agitation of the spirit' that came from being exposed to mass or collective existence which effectively detached people from traditional moral codes. (Here we see one instance of Tarde's ideas anticipating a tradition of sociological criminology promoted by the Chicago School.)

As Tarde was producing his sociological account of crime, in Britain Francis Galton was refining both the statistical basis of the social sciences and providing an influential biological account of human activity.

Responses to Lombroso: Galton and eugenics

Sir Francis Galton (1822–1911) did much to develop a sophisticated and highly credible *programme* of statistically based scientific research that helped to define the modern social sciences evolving between 1880 and 1940. Galton, who was first cousin to the biologist Charles Darwin, was an extremely wealthy, psychologically driven gentleman–scholar (Gould 1989). He gave the world scientific meteorology while he made a major practical contribution to criminal investigations by police with his discovery that fingerprints were unique to each individual. Following Quételet, Galton pioneered the collection of large-scale physical anthropometric measurements in Britain and initiated the first *scientific measurement* of intelligence. He also sponsored the growth of modern empirical psychology and the study of what he called 'individual differences'. To do all this Galton revolutionized statistics with his pioneering work on those key techniques of modern social statistics, regression analysis and the determination of correlation coefficients (Stigler 1987: 290–9). In this last respect Galton quietly re-landscaped the very ground on which social science had stood, moving it away from a simple idea of causal determinism to those very modern ideas of probability and multi-factorial analysis.

Like Bentham, Galton was more than just a man interested in scientific facts: he was also obsessed with the idea that it was possible to use science to improve human well-being. Galton devoted the last decades of his long life to the development of a form of scientific racism. While it is now customary to treat *racism* as reactionary and unscientific, for the first forty years of the twentieth century it was deemed by many to be both scientific and *progressive*. Indeed it is not going too far to say that social sciences like psychology, sociology and criminology were shaped by Galton's ideas about *racial* improvement.

Galton believed devoutly that intelligence and moral commitments to things like hard work and self-improvement were factors that made some people, and even an entire *race*, equipped to succeed in the great Darwinian struggle for survival. And he believed that these kinds of factors were inherited. 'Racial fitness' was the Darwinian notion that people with characteristics such as high intelligence would secure long-term species survival. Conversely 'racial unfitness' referred to all of those characteristics that doomed a race – or a species – to extinction.

Galton was obsessed by the idea that the 'superior races' – naturally the white races – were under threat internationally from the 'coloured races'. Equally he held that the 'racially superior' upper classes – to which he belonged – were under threat from the expansion of 'racially unfit' elements chiefly found essentially among 'the poor' and the working classes. To counter these threats Galton promoted an international movement called *eugenics* (meaning 'well-born'), committed to scientific research, policy-making and education.

In the last decades of the nineteenth century the Darwinian revolution began to feed increasing public anxiety about the mounting evidence of 'racial unfitness'. Everything, from homosexuality and prostitution, alcoholism, poverty, mental deficiency, stupidity, laziness and crime, was treated as a sign of 'racial unfitness'. All were understood to be natural in their manifestations and to be biologically transmissible. (Versions of this idea have returned since the 1990s to inform aspects of the social sciences including criminology, to say nothing of the way the popular understanding of the human genome project has been constituted.)

Eugenicists argued that only by adopting what they called 'racial hygienic' measures would the 'racially fit' survive. Racial hygiene meant encouraging the 'racially fit' to breed, while discouraging the 'unfit' by sex education, or preventing them from reproducing by contraception (called 'racial hygiene'), or, when all else failed, using compulsory sterilization.

Galton's preoccupation with collecting and analysing the results of his preoccupation with the size of people's skulls or their body shape and later their intelligence were to have fateful consequences. To make sense of his measurements, Galton sponsored the development of regression analysis. Subsequently Galton's disciples, especially William Cattell (at Columbia University) and Karl Pearson and George Yule (at London University), elaborated and refined most of the basic statistical techniques (including regression analysis and chi-square) to make them the indisputable methodological core of modern empirical social sciences.

From the start the highly sophisticated statistical techniques developed by Galton were oriented to practical policy outcomes. These statistical innovations were all part of a project to identify those in the community who were *unfit* as a prelude to state intervention.

It is important to note that there were, especially after 1920, two kinds of eugenicists (Kevles 1985). 'Negative eugenicists' took a strong biologically determinist line and were inclined to emphasize coercive policies like compulsory sterilization. In terms of practical policy measures, the *negative eugenic* project designed to identify and prevent unfit people from breeding achieved only partial success. Numerous states in North America, and several European countries, including Nazi Germany, passed compulsory sterilization legislation. (Virginia compulsorily sterilized its last victim, an Afro-American woman, in 1969.) It is also the case that under its medical killing programme, the Third Reich killed around 200,000 psychiatric patients and children with intellectual and physical disabilities.

The more numerous *positive eugenicists* saw biological, social and cultural factors as all playing a part in a much wider range of policy interventions aimed at enhancing the welfare and health of the whole population (Burleigh 1994). This refusal to explain everything in terms of biology also provided a research programme in which researchers could argue about the relative weight of biological *and* social factors in causing crime or poverty or whatever. Among the numerous practical interventions sponsored by eugenicists were:

- systematic IQ tests, and the study and normalizing of children's educational development, including age-based norms for reading, writing, etc.;
- professional training of teachers, social workers and prison workers;
- state provision of maternal and child welfare programmes;
- epidemiological studies of disease patterns as well as mass inoculation campaigns;
- mental hygiene movements to medicalize the treatment both of mental illness and physical and intellectual disability;
- medical testing of children;
- the study, diagnosis and treatment of juvenile delinquency;
- birth control and sex education clinics usually called 'racial hygiene' centres;
- sexually transmitted disease clinics;
- national nutritional research and campaigns to improve diets;

- campaigns to abolish slums and provide quality welfare housing;
- promotion of physical education, kindergartens, free playgrounds, national parks, urban planning and other preventive projects.

Eugenicist thinking provided the dominant progressive social scientific paradigm up to 1940. Most significant, progressive and rationalist intellectuals and academics in the Anglo-American and European world espoused variations of eugenicist ideas. Those who directly or indirectly supported such ideas included economists (Keynes and Pareto), psychologists (Freud, Pearson, Stanley Hall, Burt, Spearman and Thorndike) and many first-rank educators, doctors and physiologists, social workers, urban planners and leading policy-makers.

Moreover, it helped establish a technical–statistical basis for social and epidemiological research, able to compute and analyse large data sets. In 1929 a British Parliamentary Joint Committee on Mental Deficiency estimated that there were at least 350,000 'mental defectives' in the UK. The committee claimed that this represented a doubling of 'defectives' since 1908; three-quarters of these came from families 'persistently below the average in income and social character'. The defectives included 'insane persons, epileptics, paupers, criminals (especially recidivists), unemployables, habitual slum dwellers, prostitutes, inebriates and other social inefficients' (quoted in Kevles 1985: 112). Even so, confronted with this 'evidence' the British government on this occasion did not pursue the favoured eugenicist policy of compulsory sterilization of the defectives. The reliance on large-scale statistical analysis has achieved an unquestioned and canonical status within the empirical social sciences of sociology, psychology and criminology into our own time.

By the start of the twentieth century some of the characteristics of criminology as a distinctive modern social science were either emerging or in place. Out of the eugenic impulse to know more and do more about social problems came an increasingly scientific and highly technical interest in the causes of crime. Garland (1994: 39–40) says this involved

> an avowedly scientific approach to crime, concerned to develop a 'positive', factual knowledge of individual offenders, based upon observation, measurement and inductive reasoning [where scientific explanation amounted to causal explanation] . . . identifying in particular the characteristics which appeared to mark the criminal off from normal law-abiding citizens . . .

The practical interest in managing crime and criminals, or what Garland (1994) has called the 'governmental project', was helping to identify the kinds of questions with which criminology in the twentieth century would be preoccupied. Equally by the start of the twentieth century, and courtesy of the pioneering work of Galton, the methodological and technical basis for a science of causes had been laid down. This would enable later mainstream criminologists to pursue the elusive search for the explanatory factors that produced both *crime* as well as explain the conduct of *the criminal*.

Like most of their American colleagues, British criminologists, for example Charles Goring, rejected the narrow mono-causal version of 'positivist' research represented by Lombroso. One of the chief consequences of Galton and Pearson's style of statistical analysis was that it emphasized the idea of probability rather than strictly mono-causal explanations and insisted on identifying the many factors, or 'variables', involved in a given social problem like crime.

Those of Galton's followers interested in crime initially called themselves criminal anthropologists. Havelock Ellis, an early British eugenicist, produced *The Criminal* (1914), a landmark in criminal anthropology based essentially on the works of writers like Marro, Von Baer, Nacke, Laurent and Perrier. Like so many other eugenicists, Ellis distanced himself from Lombroso-style explanations. He concluded:

> The criminal . . . in some of his most characteristic manifestations, is a congenitally weak-minded person whose abnormality, while by no means leaving the mental aptitudes absolutely unimpaired, chiefly affects the feelings and volition so influencing conduct and rendering him an anti-social element in society.
>
> (1914: xv)

This approach was evident in other early modern British criminological research like Charles Goring's *The English Convict* (1913). Goring did his empirical data analysis at Karl Pearson's Biometric Laboratory at London University, the nerve centre of the British eugenics movement and sophisticated statistical analysis. Heavily reliant on a mass of social statistics, Goring refuted Lombroso's biological 'throwback' thesis, and the idea that there was a distinct 'criminal type'. Far from assuming that there was a distinct 'criminal type', Goring argued that criminality was an extreme version of characteristics all normal people share. He argued that the specification of causes must be central to any objective science of crime but that this must be based on very large data sets carefully interrogated with techniques like regression analysis. As a eugenicist, Goring found that genetic factors were operating in the development of criminal behavioural traits in certain persons. He believed, for instance, that 'low intelligence' and 'poor physique' correlated highly with criminal conduct. He argued that crime would flourish as long as 'we allow criminals to propagate' and that government must 'regulate the reproduction of those constitutional qualities – feeble mindedness, epilepsy, inebriety, deficient social instincts, insanity – which are conducive to the committing of crime' (Goring 1913: 14).

Conclusion

An historical account of the rise of modern criminology points to a number of factors. Fear of social disorder posed by large numbers of poor, urban, working-class people led reformers influenced by Bentham to document and to try to regulate problems like poverty and crime. This 'governmental project' led to persistent exercises in gathering social statistics in the interests of social order. In 1876 Lombroso's famous biological account *Criminal Man* showcased a more ambitious if controversial attempt to develop a 'science of causes'. More influential in the long run and less rigidly determinist was Francis Galton's sponsorship of a statistically informed model of the social sciences. Galton's use of statistical techniques like regression analysis was ultimately to sustain a more successful though no less 'positivist' account of human behaviour than Lombroso's.

Review questions

What are the main characteristics of the 'governmental project' and a 'science of causes' in criminology?

What are the key elements of a broadly defined positivist style of criminology, and what is your assessment of them?

How do arguments couched in terms of probability differ from those expressed in terms of simple causality?

What was Tarde's critique of older criminological arguments?

Further reading

Beirne, P., 1993, *Inventing Criminology: Essays on the Rise of 'Homo Criminalis'*, SUNY Press, Albany, New York.

Gottfredson, M. and Hirschi, T., 1990, *A General Theory of Crime*, Stanford University Press, Stanford, CA.

Gould, S.J., 1989, *The Mismeasure of Man*, Penguin, Harmondsworth.

Stigler, S., 1987, *The History of Statistics*, Belknap Press at Harvard, Cambridge, MA.

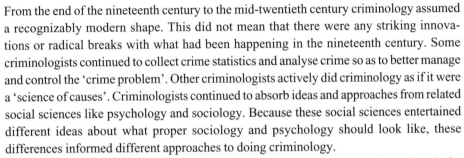

THE CONSOLIDATION OF MODERN CRIMINOLOGY

From the end of the nineteenth century to the mid-twentieth century criminology assumed a recognizably modern shape. This did not mean that there were any striking innovations or radical breaks with what had been happening in the nineteenth century. Some criminologists continued to collect crime statistics and analyse crime so as to better manage and control the 'crime problem'. Other criminologists actively did criminology as if it were a 'science of causes'. Criminologists continued to absorb ideas and approaches from related social sciences like psychology and sociology. Because these social sciences entertained different ideas about what proper sociology and psychology should look like, these differences informed different approaches to doing criminology.

The practical approach to criminological research and theory shaped criminology in the UK until the mid-twentieth century, reflecting the role played by the criminal justice system as the primary employer of British criminologists. Conversely, US criminology took on a slightly different character reflecting the way criminologists sought employment in universities, where their activities began to take on a certain kind of theoretical and academic character as well as many of the features of a profession. This movement into US universities facilitated cross-fertilization between modern criminology and other social sciences like psychology and sociology.

These paths of development are well illustrated by tracing out first the work in Britain of Cyril Burt and his advocacy of a statistically based *scientific criminology* (Burt was primarily a psychologist with a practical interest in juvenile delinquency). From his position at London University Burt dominated British psychology from the late 1920s until the 1970s and heavily influenced the development of British criminology.

We then turn to the American experience, looking to the success of the ecological model of crime developed by sociologists at the University of Chicago. The movement of criminology into America's universities also made it possible for dissent to be voiced. As early as the 1920s, some sceptical criminologists began developing a kind of *critical criminology*. From the margins, as it were, key figures like Edwin Sutherland challenged the preoccupation of mainstream criminologists with certain kinds of crimes, most notably those perpetrated by working-class and racially marginal people. Sutherland insisted on addressing the crimes committed by professional and corporate elites. Now elevated to the Pantheon of classical criminologists, Sutherland's contribution is more honoured in the breach.

In spite of Sutherland's best efforts, mainstream criminologists maintained their traditional interest in a narrow spectrum of crime. They responded eagerly when the

Harvard sociologist Robert K. Merton published a magisterial sociological theory of crime and deviance. At the time it seemed that Merton had established the theoretical foundations for a criminology able to engage in empirical research while using a vocabulary informed by the grand sociological model developed by Talcott Parsons. In this way, by the middle of the twentieth century criminology began to take on a settled character.

This chapter charts that development. It also outlines some of the key assumptions that underpin the consolidation of criminology as a social science. Let us start with the contribution of Cyril Burt.

Scientific criminology: Cyril Burt in Britain

If contemporary criminologists agree about anything it is that no single explanation of what 'causes' crime is possible. It is agreed that many factors come together to make criminal activity possible. This idea rests in part on the statistical techniques developed by the work of Galton and Pearson. Though he is not responsible for this idea, Sir Cyril Burt (1883–1971), himself much influenced by Galton and Pearson, did much to make this idea credible. After all it was Burt's research in the 1920s that pointed to at least 170 explanatory variables operating that *explained* a young person's slide into delinquency (1965: 600).

It is ironic that Burt has been revealed as one of the great scientific frauds of the twentieth century. Burt's international reputation rested on his claim that intelligence was inherited and that intelligence correlated highly with class and race. Burt claimed to have found and measured the IQs of identical twins separated at birth to demonstrate that heredity and not upbringing shaped intelligence. However, Burt had done no such thing. It was discovered after his death that he had invented much of the data and even the assistants he claimed had helped him (Kamin 1974).

Notwithstanding this, Cyril Burt was one of the most influential psychologists of the twentieth century, and his work significantly influenced the development of British criminology. Burt's career is typical of the way criminological research in Britain was initially conducted in the prison service or by psychologists, probation officers and those working with offenders. Unlike the USA where the university system played an early and key role in shaping criminology, the criminal justice system was the primary site of British research until the mid-twentieth century. Many of the key criminologists were practising psychiatrists, psychologists, probation officers and administrators. Until the 1960s in comparison with the USA, British criminology had a relatively slender foothold in universities. The *practical* interests of pioneering British criminologists like Cyril Burt did not mean that their work was unsophisticated. Key figures like Burt and Mannheim, who both had university positions, exercised a powerful influence. British criminology had a more persistently *practical* tone, even though its practitioners relied, like their US counterparts, on a blend of theoretical propositions, a mix of research methodologies and some fundamental social prejudices.

Burt's career began as a psychologist working for London County Council (LCC). After his groundbreaking work on juvenile delinquency done at the LCC, Burt became the doyen of British psychology as Professor of Psychology at London University from the late 1920s until the early 1960s.

In 1925 Cyril Burt wrote *The Young Delinquent* (1965). This was an exemplary exercise in the new style of statistically inclined scientific criminology not least because of his emphasis on the many interwoven factors that he claimed produced criminal conduct. Burt rejected mono-causal explanations typical of older-style positivist social science. Burt favoured multi-factorial analysis and explanations couched in terms of probabilities. In his work for the LCC Burt had assessed thousands of schoolchildren between 1916 and 1925, before analysing the mass of data to reveal the magnitude and correlation between feeble-mindedness and delinquency.

Burt was also a committed eugenicist. By the 1920s eugenics had swept across the *modern*, advanced and scientifically trained professions. There were few sociologists, psychologists or criminologists between 1920 and 1940 in Britain, Europe or the USA who were not more or less committed eugenicists. Cyril Burt was no exception.

At first glance Burt's book *The Young Delinquent* sits curiously with his status as a eugenicist. As a eugenicist he took the pessimistic view that it was not possible to attack factors grounded in heredity because 'nothing can root out an inborn tendency' (1965: 604). However, as a *scientific psychologist* he emphasized the role of the *mental* over the genetic, saying: 'A crime . . . is only a symptom. It is a mental symptom with a mental origin. And there is now a definite body of ascertained knowledge, tracing mental symptoms to their causes, just as medical knowledge tracks down the sources of bodily disorders' (1965: 4).

Burt (1965: 14) rejected the idea of an inherently *delinquent type* of young person. He argued that 'the line of demarcation between the delinquent and the normal child is an arbitrary one. At bottom it is a social rather than a psychological distinction': 'no deep gulf exists to separate the sinner from the saint . . . It is all a problem of degree, of a brighter or darker grey. This graded continuity, the normal melting into the abnormal by almost imperceptible shades is entirely in accord with what we now know of most other forms of mental deviation . . .'. To arrive at his view of delinquency, Burt applied a battery of IQ tests, psychoanalytic interpretive techniques and physical measurements of heads and chests to a cohort of 197 schoolchildren. Burt pointed to huge numbers of variables that 'explained' the slide into delinquency (1965: 600). Those of most importance included defective discipline, poor family relationships and certain personality styles, while poverty and 'low intelligence', he argued, was of less importance.

With uncommon and perhaps suspicious precision Burt reckoned that environmental factors accounted for 29.9 per cent of a delinquent, while heredity accounted for 26.5 per cent. Therefore, he concluded (1965: 599–600): 'Crime is assignable to no single universal source, nor yet to two or three . . . It is almost everywhere the outcome of a concurrence of subversive factors: it needs many coats of pitch to paint a thing thoroughly black.'

As Garland (1994: 53) says: 'The influence of Burt's work, and especially its eclectic, multi-factorial search for the correlates of individual delinquency, was to become something of a hallmark of British criminology in the mid-twentieth century.' Burt's legacy sustained generations of researchers devoted to the study of the delinquent. Leading British criminologists like D. J. West (1967, 1972, 1982) and David Farrington (1978, 1994, 1997), for instance, have continued to offer explanations of juvenile crime and 'antisocial behaviour' in a similar way to Burt in terms of the specification of an array of 'causal factors', as well as the factors pointed to as 'causal'.

Unlike their British colleagues, US criminologists were established in universities and developed links with other key social science disciplines – like sociology – even before the nineteenth century had ended. This institutional factor was to ensure that US criminology flourished as an academic and professional entity.

American criminology: the Chicago School

One of the factors that influenced the evolution of US criminology was the way the expansion of US universities in the second half of the nineteenth century provided an institutional base for the development of criminology as a profession. Burton Bledstein (1976: 88) says this 'culture of professionalism' evolved because members of these professions took major social issues and made them topics suitable for research *in the university*. As Bledstein (1976: 327) argues, US

> universities quietly took divisive issues such as race, capitalism, labour relations and deviant behaviour out of the public domain and isolated these problems within the sphere of professionals – men who learned to know better than to air publicly their differences. The university not only segregated ideas from the public; intellectual segregation occurred within the development of each new department in the university.

This professional culture meant that only experts accredited as such could pass comment on or join scholarly debates. This meant that outsiders were ruthlessly excluded by such practices as peer review of research work and the use of an increasingly technical vocabulary. Schools and departments came to be identified as places where only certain specialized theoretical or philosophical debates could occur.

The development of the Chicago School of Sociology (with its strong emphasis on research into crime) was one result of these American traits.

At the turn of the century the University of Chicago and its School of Sociology hosted the first discernible scholarly *tradition* in criminology in North America. This School, established in 1892, just two years after the university was opened (Bannister 1987), supported the justly famous project of urban sociology represented by such notable figures as Park (1915), Thomas (1923) and Thrasher (1927).

Much of the early theoretical and research work of the school touched directly on crime. Between 1915 and the 1940s, it produced a distinctive body of theoretical and empirical research on a range of social problems, including crime. Its work helped to consolidate the impression that in the USA sociology and criminology were properly scientific disciplines. Several things distinguish the approach of the Chicago School including its ecological account of crime and its emphasis on careful measurement and description.

The Chicago School's theoretical approach to crime was very much shaped by the city itself. Chicago had expanded after 1865 to become a huge urban and industrial metropolis, characterized by working-class radicalism, poverty, the arrival of waves of immigrants and, of course, crime. By the 1920s Chicago would be synonymous with the *organized crime* associated with figures like Al Capone. Chicago was a kind of natural urban laboratory replete with various social problems ideally suited to the research interests of Albion Small, the first Professor of Sociology at Chicago, and his colleagues, for example Robert Park.

The Chicago School is best known for its development of an ecological explanation of human conduct. The ecological idea suggests that distinctive patterns of human conduct are shaped by the organization or design of space in which that conduct occurs. Park and his colleagues argued that the social and spatial characteristics of life in a city provided a space, or an ecology, in which particular activities like crime became possible. The Chicago School argued that just as any natural habitat shapes the opportunities for food-gathering or reproduction for species living there, so too a city environment shapes human behaviour. It pointed to the way the design of streets and the location of businesses shaped human behaviour, allowing for certain kinds of activities and not others, or rewarding some people and punishing others.

This was not a new idea. Nineteenth-century middle-class reformers had long argued that city slums *caused* poverty and unemployment. The Chicago School developed a refined version of this idea showing how the different geographical 'zones' in a great metropolitan city were characterized by different densities of population, the diverse character of neighbourhoods and communities and the natural life-cycle of city growth, characterized by concentric rings of development. These features helped to give each city distinctive socio-economic patterns of life. This ecological idea has not lost its grip. There are many contemporary advocates of the ecological approach who argue that it is possible and desirable to design spaces so as to prevent crime. This might mean installing video cameras in shopping centres, removing certain corridors or designing walkways that discourage purse-snatching.

Though they are best known for developing an ecological theory of crime, members of the Chicago School, like their British colleagues, also promoted the idea that no single factor explains criminality. William Healy (1915: 22) made the case that a search for a single theory of crime was all very well and good, but that

> no general theories of crime, sociological, psychological or biological, however well founded, are of much service when the concrete issue, namely the particular offence and the individual delinquent, is before those who have practically to deal with it . . . [and that while] collected statistics and groups of facts concerning criminality are offered from time to time . . . [they lead] for the most part only to controversy.

Its members rejected the Lombrosian pursuit of a mono-causal account of crime in terms of inherited criminal traits. In rejecting that account of the biological basis of criminality, members of the Chicago School argued that most people doing criminal things were *normal* people living and acting in an abnormal urban environment, particularly in inner urban zones characterized by poverty and various kinds of deprivations.

Much of this work was broadly *positivist* in the way Beirne and Messerschmidt define this approach:

> [S]everal variants of positivism have dominated the thinking of most criminologists regarding crime and crime policies . . . Thus criminal behavior tends to be viewed

rather like the behavior of billiard balls (they move predictably according to certain laws of motion): the subject of criminology – the criminal – behaves according to certain sociological, historical, psychological or economic laws . . .

(1995: 359)

Key members of the School like R. W. Park, E.W. Burgess, W. I. Thomas, Frederick Thrasher, Clifford Shaw and Henry McKay used various 'objective' measures of delinquency and crime rates and tried to show how these 'correlated' with, for example, urban densities. Thrasher's (1927: 45) study of juvenile gangs suggested that 'science proposes to discover what is typical rather than unique and does so, in the first instance, by making classifications. Interest therefore centers not so much on the individual gang itself as in the characteristics that distinguish it from other types of collective behavior.' Thrasher (1927: 57) provided a formal account of 'the gang':

> The gang is an interstitial group originally formed spontaneously, and then integrated through conflict. It is characterized by the following types of behavior: meeting face-to-face, milling, movement through space as a unit, conflict and planning. The result of this collective behavior is the development of tradition, unreflective internal structure, esprit de corps, solidarity, morale group awareness and attachment to a local territory .

(It can also be observed that this definition defines many masculine organizations, including armies, football clubs and corporations.)

In 1942 Shaw and McKay produced their *Juvenile Delinquency in Urban Areas* which sums up the Chicago School's approach. In it they correlated changing urban patterns with changing (but always 'objective') rates of crime and delinquency. These were meticulously mapped so as to show the clustering of high delinquency areas that were also the areas of inner-city decay. Shaw and McKay concluded that there was a clustering of the symptoms of urban pathology like poverty, crime, sickness and school truancy found in the deteriorating inner-city areas where 'stable families' and 'conventional moral values' were in short supply among the adults and young people. Meanwhile, out in the affluent suburbs, all was well. While inner-city gangs were disposed to 'deviant' values, middle-class families were the bulwarks of conventional or 'all-American' values – a theme replicated later in a more interesting way by Robert Merton. It may be that Shaw could not help but give voice to the values he formed when growing up in rural Indiana.

Certainly such sweeping generalizations required that Shaw and McKay forget a good deal of what had recently happened in America. They were writing barely a decade after the end of Prohibition. This experiment at making alcohol-use illegal ended finally because the mass of Americans were not prepared to do without alcohol and were prepared to break the law and buy it from bootlegging gangsters. These generalizations suggest too that middle-class prejudices were easily dressed up as scientific findings and so rendered an unimpeachable basis for various legislative or policy exercises in 'crime control'.

Shaw and McKay could not countenance the possibility that the rates of delinquency and crime were anything but *objective* measures of 'social disorganization'. They asserted that it was always the moral values of 'the criminal' and 'delinquent communities' that were the problem, rather than governmental neglect or the promotion by elite groups of their own interests against those of others in the community.

Yet the USA is a large and diverse place, as are its universities. Even in the 1920s not everyone in Chicago was convinced about some of the directions criminology was taking.

Towards a sceptical criminology: Edwin Sutherland

Apart from the ecological framework and the attempt to measure core features of the urban ecology, some members of the Chicago School became well known for their insistence on practising a home-grown style of anthropological research.

Some of those in the Chicago School were followers of the social psychologist G. H. Mead and his idea of the 'socially constructed' or 'synthetic self'. As a result some Chicago sociologists came to exhibit greater sensitivity to the expressive, symbolic and constructed character of human conduct. In part this shift towards a more cultural and interpretive approach reflected a disenchantment with the positivist preoccupation with scientific method. The insistence on the interpreted or meaningful nature of human action transcended the limitations of positivism and helped facilitate the development of an interpretivist tradition in US sociology and criminology (Bannister 1987: 55–9). In effect, they developed an urban anthropology that involved researchers going into the streets and bars to do participant observation. The American pragmatic tradition of Peirce, James and Dewey provided a striking critique of positivism and did it in ways that were picked up on in the subsequent development of the 'symbolic interactionist' tradition – discussed in more detail in Chapter 4.

Another more eclectic kind of scepticism was represented by Edwin Sutherland (1883–1950). Sutherland, born into a Nebraskan academic family, was a 'socialist' whose idea of sociology has much in common with an American tradition of critical sociology represented by Thorsten Veblen and, later, by C. Wright Mills.

Sutherland studied sociology at the University of Chicago, where he researched the unemployment problem and then taught courses there between 1913 and 1921. Described by his mentor Hayes as 'cautious yet progressive', Sutherland argued for the practical relevance of sociology and criminology. In 1921 Sutherland began work on one of the finest American criminology textbooks, published simply as *Criminology* (1924, 1947). Though dated in some ways, the book can still be read with profit. In it Sutherland identified criminology as 'a primarily sociological enterprise' (1924: 11). His position was exemplified in his deft and apposite observations drawn from the work of sociologists from the Chicago School like W. I. Thomas and Florian Znaniecki and the pragmatists like John Dewey and William James.

His scepticism was on view when he argued (ibid.: 24–6) that it was 'quite unsafe to generalize about criminals'. Similarly he (ibid.: 20) observed that any attempt to equate crime simply with law-breaking was a 'purely formal and quite inadequate' approach. In contesting the broad-church version of positivist criminology, Sutherland chided his colleagues for treating words like 'crime' and 'crime rates' as if they referred in some simple way to an objective reality (ibid.: 30–40). Sutherland argued that it was necessary to examine the ways policing practices produce crime statistics. Indeed, for Sutherland, the construction of such statistics was itself a good topic for research (ibid.: 54).

His progressive instincts were revealed in his rejection of the Durkheimian idea that 'normal crime' rates enhanced 'social solidarity'. Sutherland maintained that crime reduction could be achieved better through anti-slum or anti-poverty campaigns (ibid.: 68–70). In these ways Sutherland pushed hard against the conventional and 'right thinking' boundaries of mainstream criminology.

Sutherland is best known for two major claims. The first is his suggestion that crime is learnt by imitation through association with others for whom such behaviour is a normal way of life. This is his theory of 'differential association'. His other, far more interesting, claim is that criminologists have been preoccupied with the crimes committed by working-class people while the more serious and costly crimes committed by corporate entities and governments are ignored. Sutherland's 1947 theory of 'differential association' is a more developed version of Gabriel Tarde's 'neo-classical', or sociological, theory of imitation.

Sutherland rejected the idea that the disposition to engage in crime can be explained in terms of genetic inheritance. Equally he rejected the possibility of explaining crime in terms of general human needs and values – like striving for status, the love of money, happiness or the avoidance of frustration. He argued, rightly, that these motivations explain non-criminal behaviour just as well as they do criminal behaviour. The crux of Sutherland's theory is that people learn the techniques and motivations for doing crime depending on whether they are exposed to 'favorable or unfavorable definitions of law violation'. Translated this means only that where a group of people habitually engage in, for example, illegal car use, graffiti or shoplifting, those who associate with this group are likely to fall into bad ways.

Beirne and Messerschmidt (1995: 424) argue that Sutherland's theory should still be seen as 'one of the most fertile causal accounts of crime'. This assessment may be something of an overstatement. It makes sense of some of the minor and repetitive kinds of crime in which inner-city working-class young men engage, like football hooliganism or juvenile shoplifting. Yet there are several major problems with Sutherland's argument.

Firstly, there is the problematic assumption that crime is best understood as a *behaviour*, that is a repetitive, regular and predictable pattern of conduct. This account is closely attuned to the emergent behaviourism found in US psychology departments in the 1920s and 1930s associated with J. B. Watson and, later, B. F. Skinner. Sutherland's model of human conduct is extremely mechanistic, even crudely behaviourist, surprisingly so, given his awareness of Mead's and James's work. For instance, the idea that people, by dint of exposure to a certain culture, inevitably absorb values favourable to law violation is a version of the 'person-as-cultural-dope' model. Secondly, Sutherland's claim is so vague as to defy any attempt to evaluate it. What, for instance, does 'association with criminal patterns' mean? Finally, while it might work well for crimes like shoplifting or for drug- and alcohol-related offences, Sutherland's theory fails to account for crimes like murder or spectacular mass murders, spontaneous homicide, kidnapping and most 'white-collar crime'.

If Sutherland's 'differential association' theory is a good example of what can happen when criminologists don't think as clearly as they might, his work on 'white-collar crime' is a refreshing antidote to that problem.

Sutherland argued that most of what comes to be called 'crime' by elite and powerful groups of law-makers, administrators, judges and police, is the conduct of working-class, minority racial and poor people. As Sutherland (1949: 3) explained: 'criminal statistics show unequivocally that crime, *as popularly understood and officially measured*, has a high incidence in the lower socio-economic class, and a low incidence in the upper socio-economic class' (our stress). From this *empirical* fact it has often been concluded by many criminologists that poverty, unemployment or being working class *causes* crime, a story with enormous and recurrent appeal to an academic community and its audiences. (We will return to his work on white-collar crime in Chapter 10.)

If Chicago proved to be the home both to the Chicago School and to the lucid scepticism of Sutherland, US criminology would also be shaped by sociology coming out of Harvard University. In the 1940s, Harvard was home to Talcott Parsons and Robert K. Merton. It was Merton who authored another kind of sociologically based criminology.

Robert K. Merton and the synthesis of sociology and criminology

The possibilities of applying a 'sociological imagination' to criminology were grasped by Robert K. Merton, whose much praised theory of 'anomic deviance' was to influence the way mainstream criminology developed in the middle decades of the twentieth century. Merton gave criminologists an authoritative language and a set of theoretical frameworks complementary to already established traditions of US social scientific research. To see what it was that Merton said and why he said it, we need to take a small side-step.

Merton was a colleague of the influential Harvard sociologist Talcott Parsons (1902–79) and much of Merton's work was a working out of Parsons's ideas. Parsons was one of the great systems-building sociologists.

Parsons's kind of sociology had its origins in the work of Auguste Comte (1798–1857). Other core elements of this evolving tradition of sociology were outlined by Herbert Spencer (1820–1903) and Emile Durkheim (1858–1917). Parsons had studied in Germany in the mid-1920s, where he read Max Weber. In the late 1920s Parsons began working at Harvard in the Economics Department. In 1930 he then shifted to the new Sociology Department under Pitrim Sorokin where he started developing a grand new sociological synthesis. Influenced by the economics of Alfred Marshall and his own studies in biology, Parsons was also familiar with Emile Durkheim's sociology. Parsons creatively reinterpreted and integrated the work of Weber, Durkheim, Marshall and Pareto, producing his model of a generalized 'theory of social action' (Camic 1991).

Parsons (1971) provides one of the most elaborate and abstracted kinds of social theory ever written. Parsons drew on Durkheim's theory of social order and on Max Weber's account of social interaction as rational action. It was this 'structural functionalist' synthesis with which many sociologists after 1940 would identify (Gouldner 1971).

Like the word 'positivist' it is easy to overstate the level of consensus around 'structural functionalism'. Anthony Giddens (1984), a strong critic of Parsons's style of sociology, for example, describes 'structural functionalism' as the 'orthodox consensus' or thread running through much sociology over the course of the twentieth century. (For a different view see Alexander 1987.) The claim that there is a single sociology called 'structural functionalism' overstates the extent to which 'structural functionalism' excluded other kinds of sociology. Secondly it exaggerates the level of agreement among the writers said to belong to this tradition. The key writers in the structural functionalist tradition often disagreed over fundamental questions of theory and method. Durkheim told a gloomy story about the tensions of the modernizing process, while Parsons offers a more cheerful account of how 'modernity' reflected the progressive realization of allegedly universal functional values necessary for human survival. (See Mestrovic 1997 for a critique of this view that ironically he finds at work in both Parsons *and* Giddens.)

However, despite the differences and tensions there is sufficient agreement about the core ideas of 'structural functionalism'. Those who draw on structural functionalist theory have made five important claims. Some of these ideas continue to circulate in both academic work and in popular culture, and it is therefore useful to see them spelled out as a prelude to thinking about them.

Structural functionalist sociology relies heavily on biological metaphors and analogies with the human body to talk about both 'structure' and 'function'. This kind of sociology relies on biological metaphors that treat 'society' and its 'members' as if it were speaking of the human body. (It is quite significant that Comte, Spencer and Parsons all studied biology and drew on its vocabulary to create biological metaphors for use by sociologists.) Biologists routinely talk about the *structures* of a body (organs such as the lungs, kidneys, eyes and brain, etc.), as well as processes (like digestion, the auto-immune system and reproduction) that perform special *functions.* That is, this combination of *structures* and *functions* is needed to keep the body healthy and well. Each part is connected to another part of the social body so that mutual dependence ensures the survival of the whole.

According to this story, 'society' has a similar organic quality. Society has structures and its parts often called *social institutions* – like the family or school – are deemed to fulfil *functions* vital to the survival and well-being of 'society'. If any part of society becomes pathological, then the whole is at risk. And just like the body's immune system, 'society' will react to pathology (or disorder) by trying to fix itself.

According to most structural functionalists, all societies naturally incline to social order. Society is represented as a kind of external *thing* that *causes* people to act in particular ways. Many people still talk about how 'society' *requires* us to marry or to work hard. Any normal healthy society will force its members to think, and act in accordance with its requirements for order and stability. Using organic metaphors, structural functionalist sociologists argue that like the body's organs, what they called *structures*, like class, gender or ethnicity, and *institutions*, like the family, schools, churches and government, work in the same way to maintain health or social order. The way things already are is the basis of social order and is as necessary for the survival and health of a society as, e.g., the kidneys or liver is to the health of the body.

Social order is also *moral* order. Social order is guaranteed when everyone accepts the moral values of society and when all members of the community accept their roles. Social order depends on there being a moral consensus that is actively inculcated through a variety of educational processes. This is accomplished through a process which American sociologists called *socialization.* This means that there is a general agreement in the society about social values and ways of seeing the world. According to this theory, society establishes standards of behaviours, ideas and values which are *functional* to that society.

A broadly 'positivist' model of scientific method supplies an appropriate methodology for social sciences like sociology and criminology. Durkheim (1982) took it for granted that his type of sociology required the use of proper *scientific* rules and methods to establish the laws of social action and human behaviour. He argued that the processes and 'structures' of any society are objective – or external – realities. As a sociologist Durkheim claimed that there were rules for good sociological method. In particular he maintained that sociologists needed to study *social facts* and not facts about individuals. (He was worried that facts about persons would encourage psychological explanations into sociology and thereby subvert it.)

As we saw in Chapter 1 'social facts' refer to stable patterns of activity on the part of large numbers of people that can be expressed statistically. This gives rise to calculation of things like the death rate, the birth rate, or the crime rate. Typically they come in the form of statements like: 'The crime rate for males aged 24–30 is 35 per 100,000 of population.' Durkheim liked 'social facts' because he thought they pointed to the underlying stability of social structures that tend to change, if at all, very slowly. He did not treat going to church or school, or committing a crime or suicide, as an individual activity involving personal choice or decision. Rather Durkheim claimed that society caused some people to go to school, form families or to act deviantly or criminally.

In this tradition sociology, when it is done well, produces structural explanations. This tradition has long rejected the idea that we can explain anything useful about social life by referring to personal beliefs, or motivations, and individual action because these features are said to characterize 'psychological' explanations. The properly sociological explanation is 'structural'. Durkheim claimed that structural features of society, like a breakdown in moral values (which he called 'anomie'), religious practice, or a sudden increase in wealth or a rise in unemployment, *cause* the crime or suicide rates to rise or fall, and it is the study of social facts and their structural causes that sociologists need to focus on (Durkheim 1951).

Merton, who accepted most of this model, used it to produce one of the most admired accounts of criminality and delinquency in the twentieth century, calling it the 'anomic theory of deviancy'.

In 1938 Merton wrote a short article entitled 'Social Structure and Anomie' which developed and extended Durkheim's account of deviance. In doing so he influenced significantly the development of Anglo-American criminology in the middle decades of the twentieth century. Like his mentor Parsons, Merton (1969a) was committed to the assumption that the key social problems of his time, whether they were 'crime', 'deviance' or economic inequality, arose from the structural and institutional aspects of social life rather than from the choice, needs or desires of individual people.

Like Durkheim, Merton rejected psychological, or individualist, accounts as well as biological explanations of why people do deviant or criminal things. Merton, like Durkheim, wanted to establish the social structural conditions that *caused* deviance. He (1969b: 255) set out to establish in terms that were unmistakably 'sociological' and 'structural' that 'some social structures exert a definite pressure upon certain persons in the society to engage in nonconforming rather than conforming conduct'.

Merton argued that 'society' sought to offer a good quality of life for its citizens. This, he argued, could be achieved by establishing certain social goals which were legitimate for all of its members because these are the things worth striving for. Any society also generates legitimate, regular and institutionalized ways for its members to achieve these goals. Merton claimed that all societies link their aspirations to particular sets of moral beliefs and thereby create institutions that try to realize those social goals. According to Merton, 'social order' is the result of people being satisfied because they have conformed to social expectations.

However, what happens when there is a gap between the social goals and the social institutions? Merton suggests that this can occur because the social goals may all be successfully socialized into people but the institutional means may not be available for everyone to achieve these goals or, worst of all, there is no social consensus about goals. This lack of a society-wide consensus about social goals Merton, following Durkheim, calls 'anomie'. The definition of anomie is that it is a society that can no longer produce binding moral values or rules.

Merton argued there was an inclination for some groups and individuals to become 'anomic' when they focus on achieving socially accepted goals, but are not concerned about the means by which they realize those desires. Merton said that 'anomie' can develop in some groups if they want the material goods (like money, nice cars, houses or status) at any cost, even if it means cheating, stealing or murdering to obtain the valued outcomes. For example, a student may want to pass an exam, but rejects the *right* way of passing exams by attending classes, reading and studying. Rather, he gets what he wants by illegitimate means, like cheating or breaking into the school's computer system to get the examination papers.

It is important to remember that Merton was writing at a time when many Americans were affected directly by the mass unemployment and the social and political dislocation of the 1930s. Merton understood that America was a society where there was a huge gap between social expectations and the means to achieve them. The dominant opinion-makers, speaking on behalf of 'American society', held out the promise that everyone could have an affluent life-style. The so-called 'American Dream', as it was articulated in the 1930s by Hollywood, Al Capone or the churches, proposed that hard work gave rise to material success. Herbert Hoover, who was elected President in 1928, had promised a 'chicken in every pot'. However, Merton understood that the means to achieve this were not equally available to all Americans, because the country was profoundly divided by class and racial divisions, and inequalities of power and resources. (Like most male sociologists of his generation, Merton ignored gender inequalities.) In consequence Merton said that America was a poorly integrated society producing massive social contradictions.

Merton argued that there were at least five typical ways in which these tensions and strains manifested themselves in the USA. Individuals handled these strains and tensions in diverse ways, ranging from full conformity to outright rebellion. In effect this is a five-point scale in which four of the points are deviant.

Merton argued that most Americans lived their lives in the light of these goals and behaved in a conformist way. They conformed to the 'American Dream' as a set of legitimate goals and they accepted and believed in the normal means to achieve this by working hard, saving money and leading sober, family-centred lives. As a structural functionalist he necessarily believed that 'were this not so, the stability and continuity of

Table 3.1 Merton's model of social adaptation

Modes of adaptation	Cultural goals	Institutionalized means
1 Conformity	+	+
2 Innovation	+	−
3 Ritualism	−	+
4 Retreatism	−	−
5 Rebellion	±	±

Source: Merton 1969a: 263.

society could not be maintained' (1969a: 264). Whether Merton was right about this is an entirely different matter since he had no empirical evidence then or later to validate his claim. Even more interesting is the question of how any researcher would ever go about validating this claim.

Apart from the vast crowd of conformists, Merton argued that some Americans chose to use 'illegitimate', that is, deviant and criminal, means to achieve the legitimate goals associated with the 'American Dream'. Public gangsters like Al Capone exemplified the rich, powerful, hardworking, successful, patriotic American who pursued the success goals of American society but who also just happened to break the law in order to achieve the American Dream.

Equally some Americans adopted the strategy of appearing to believe in the 'American Dream' without actually doing so. In this way the actual behaviours and strategies adopted were likely to miss out on achieving the 'Dream' because they either took no risks or else aimed too high. According to Merton (1969a: 275), 'ritualism' was the 'adaptation' most favoured by lower-middle-class Americans. Again a sceptical reader might well ask how would Merton ever validate this claim.

For other Americans, none of these options worked. For some, retreat from the 'Dream' was a strategic choice. 'Retreatism' is the territory of the stereotypical deviant who abandons the 'American Dream' and any of the normal institutional places where it might be lived out. This is a form of private protest without any significance except that social control measures need to be directed against this 'reserve army of misfits'. Here, in this category, are all traditional deviants and criminals who populate the nightmares of white, urban, middle-class academics, like the psychotics, the outcasts, the vagrants, the no-hopers, the criminals, drunkards and drug addicts.

Finally there was the truly sinister possibility that some Americans might reject the whole idea of the 'American Dream'. Rebellion becomes the politicized or at least the highly public form that deviance can take when a significant number of persons reject the 'American way'. In Merton's time the Communist Party of America clearly met this criterion, while the creators of the TV cartoon series *South Park* might do so now.

Merton's has become a much praised, often cited statement of a classical sociological position. Yet Merton's work is a curious, even contradictory, mix of social criticism and conservative sociology. Merton is a social critic when he recognizes that America was – and is – a society profoundly fractured by poverty, class, racial and regional differences, with a highly unequal distribution of cultural, political and economic power. (Diamond

1998, well before George W. Bush stole the American presidency in 2000, wittily describes contemporary America as a 'kleptocracy'.) Having allowed that this is the way things are, Merton then superimposes on this insight the recurring and deeply conservative sociological idea, found in Comte, Durkheim and Parsons, that 'society' is always well-ordered and rests securely on a widespread moral consensus which only a few deviants ignore or flout.

It was this latter aspect of Merton's work that rendered it attractive and interesting to criminologists. Merton (1969a, 1969b) provided a core part of what by the 1950s and 1960s had become the dominant theoretical framework to the way criminology should be done. Merton did not invent a new approach in criminology so much as add a layer of sociological legitimacy to the long-standing and conventional treatment of crime and criminals already established as normative in US criminology. Criminals were represented, in Merton's terms, as the stereotypical deviants, who had abandoned the American Dream and any of the 'normal' institutional places where it might be experienced. He sanctioned a preoccupation with petty street crime. Equally Merton reinforced the well-established positivist prejudices of most criminologists that prescribed the foundational value of large-scale data collection and analysis for 'good scientific criminology'.

The criminological consensus

By the middle of the twentieth century criminology, especially in the USA, seemed to be taking on a settled and self-assured identity. Courtesy of Merton, transatlantic criminology secured its intellectual foundations on a bedrock of a broadly defined positivist methodology. In spite of mainstream criminology's self-portrait as an *eclectic* discipline, there was a solid mainstream of shared assumptions and practices from the 1950s to the 1970s.

While acknowledging the difficulty of reducing quite complex ideas to simple formulations, it is possible to say that Anglo-American criminologists between the 1950s and 1970s were largely wedded to a 'broad-church' kind of positivism. To a considerable extent this continues to be true of many practising criminologists at the start of the twenty-first century.

Allowing for the usual caveats about such a generalization, there were at least five core elements at the methodological heart of this 'broad-church' model of positivism.

1   There is the idea that good research relies on scientific method. Those who subscribe to a 'broad-church model' of positivism claim that there is a distinctive set of methods used by the successful natural sciences like physics and chemistry. These are characterized by the use of various tests of replicability or statistical analysis that can establish whether the research is credible or reliable. Emulating the methods of the natural sciences can establish the facts and produce good explanations that are predictive and that can also produce law-like statements even if these have to be expressed as probabilities.

2   The only proper objects of scientific knowledge are *observables*. Subscribers to a 'broad-church model' of positivism hold that good science should only work with what can be seen and measured. In the social sciences, *observables* include social facts

such as the crime rate or the suicide rate; social facts like crime rates are important basic points of reference. 'Social facts' are believed to represent repeated or institutional activities, like going to school, going to church or committing crime. Thus the crime rate as we saw in Chapter 1 is a classic social fact. These can be studied as objective facts, which, like all facts, are said to be independent of the observer, and which can then be treated in a neutral and scientific way. As such, non-observables like emotions or psychological states of mind cannot really become observables. One way of partially relaxing this criterion is to allow for *operationalization*. Operationalization is a process where if you can define a non-observable so that it becomes measurable, then it can become the object of *proper* scientific knowledge. One example of how research has been done on a non-observable phenomenon like 'love' occurred when the researcher defined 'love' as the level of correlation between the measured time two people 'in love' spent gazing into each other's eyes and their responses to a questionnaire.

3   Subscribers to a 'broad-church model' of positivism assume that human behaviour is predictable because it is causally determined, thereby allowing it to be scientifically studied. Human behaviour is predictable because it is causally determined by forces and factors (or variables). That is because human behaviour is (i) observable and measurable, and (ii) humans are sufficiently predictable to allow for the identification of regularities. Emile Durkheim, who did so much to prescribe the rules for doing scientific sociology at the end of the nineteenth century, allowed that individuals can do things on their own volition. Yet this capacity of people to act is always represented as 'fortuitous', 'capricious' or 'contingent'. This means that such activities verge on being irrational and certainly not able to be fitted into a truly intelligible framework making it part of truly *scientific* knowledge.

4   Modern social scientists are skilled technicians and experts. This is because they are 'spectators' (Manent 1998).

5   Finally, the 'spectator view of knowledge' leads directly to the idea that the social sciences should be value-free. This is what the American sociologist Eubank (1937: 179) meant when he said: 'Sociology sets up no moral judgment and sets up no ethical standards for human conduct.' The claim is a simple one: as an *objective* science, its exponents – sociologists, criminologists, economists or psychologists – should observe a strict neutrality in questions of ethics and public morality, and neither make nor rely on ethical principles or claims. This idea has become a common-sense view. However, what it means and whether value-freedom is either possible, desirable or useful are quite different matters.

Of course most criminologists in the mid-twentieth century, like those who continue to work within a broadly defined positivist framework, do not always explicitly spell out or acknowledge these kinds of philosophical claims. It is more normal for these kinds of ideas to sit around in the background of their research activities. Typically the researcher relies on or uses these assumptions to provide a foundation for a particular set of research practices. While this is not the place to critically evaluate these assumptions or beliefs, it is possible to say that each of these ideas is contestable and that they have been exposed to devastating criticism over the last century or so.

In Anglo-American criminology into our own time, the positivist model provided a powerful and widely admired account of how to do good criminological research. This meant gathering bus-loads of criminal statistics and filtering them through the by-now canonical research method model (laid out half a century ago by the likes of Goode and Hatt 1952, Hyman 1955, Moser 1958 or Blalock 1960).

In turn this kind of methodology has sustained a particular set of propositions about 'crime' and 'the criminal'. It has meant in particular that 'crime' and 'the criminal' were – and are – understood as obvious and objective *social facts* embodying the repetitive and institutionalized character of the social world. 'Crime' and 'the criminal', like all facts, were independent of the observer, which meant they could then be treated in a value-neutral and scientific way. Good criminological research would sooner or later reveal the patterns of causality which any science of causes needed to 'discover' if it were ever to be taken seriously. This consensus view of criminology certainly did not involve any *theoretical*, i.e. speculative, let alone critical, dispositions.

This kind of criminology was epitomized in 1969 in Britain with the first of the reports by D. J. West (1969) (the *First Report of the Cambridge Study in Delinquent Development*). Based on an 8-year study of 400 boys, the West study was typically hailed by Radzinowicz as an 'instant classic' to be placed alongside such other great research as the work of Robins, the Gluecks and the McCords. West's report came to the entirely predictable conclusion that the 'social level' of the boy's family was the most important single factor in discriminating 'poorly behaved boys' from the rest. Equally predictably, in hailing this work as a classic, Radzinowicz insisted, as Burt and the Chicago School had done before, that there was no single causal theory of crime. This sense of themselves as empiricists and *practical men* sponsored a degree of eclecticism. This did not, however, entail that there was much basic disagreement about the fundamental view held of the nature of 'social order', 'social facts' or the interests of 'society'.

In terms of the kinds of substantive claims advanced by Anglo-American criminologists about crime and criminality in these middle decades of the twentieth century, there are five that matter. We are not saying that all criminologists actively held to, or could articulate, each of these assumptions as assumptions. We are suggesting only that these assumptions provide the bedrock on which most empiricist–positivist criminology rested and to some considerable extent continues to do so. These claims need to be identified clearly as a prelude to assessing the extent to which there has been any consistent effort to think outside these conventional ideas.

What should we think about such conventional ideas as the following? There is a single, unitary and coherent social and moral consensus against which *deviance* and crime can be defined, or bench-marked. This idea in turn supports the idea that social deviations or criminal behaviours are in fact breaches of a dominant, single, unitary and coherent moral code.

Deviance and criminal conduct are sufficiently stable, making them amenable either to study or to conceptualize sociologically or criminologically. The qualities defining certain patterns of conduct as *deviant* or *criminal* are inherent in those forms of conduct or behaviour itself and not in the relation between the behaviour, the society or the perceiver or detector of the conduct alleged to be deviant or criminal. That is, *crime* and *deviance* are somehow observable, fixed and determinate markers of the conduct itself.

The relations–distinctions between *crime*, *deviance* and *difference* are in fact conceptually coherent or even real distinctions. Crime is 'clearly criminal', while minor differences are clearly deviant. All that distinguished these elements in Durkheim's (1951) original magisterial account were the degrees of serious deviation from 'societal norms'.

The positivist search for a 'general theory of deviance' or a 'general theory of crime' is a sensible and credible exercise, justified by the unity of these behaviours, and by the censures they attract across the otherwise variable range of cultures, situations and contexts.

The credibility and appeal of all these ideas to sociologists and criminologists – and to the broader intellectually and professionally trained members of Anglo-American societies in the middle of the twentieth century – cannot be overstated. In the 1950s and the 1960s it provided a credible master narrative which issued in a secure sense that the key problems facing modern society had all been identified and, with them, the methods for answering them had all been discerned.

What Gouldner (1971) called 'American sociology' enjoyed great secular authority as the very model of proper social science. In a liberal democratic society engaged in the struggle to defend the Free World from international communism, the social sciences (like psychology, economics, sociology and criminology) played many important roles: they identified and measured political sentiment; they monitored the level of social integration, the state of social values or the satisfaction of consumer needs; they could offer expert advice on the social problems of the day. Collectively the social sciences combined the appearance of intellectual diversity and debate appropriate to a liberal–pluralist society with a steady source of intellectual support for the legitimacy of the basic interests and assumptions of the social order.

Conclusion

At the heart of conventional criminology in the mid-twentieth century was the foundational idea that the 'crime rate' and 'the criminal' were both *obvious* and *objective* 'social facts' reflecting the repetitive and institutionalized character of an ordered, coherent society built around agreed-on moral values. 'Crime' and 'the criminal' like all real *facts* were independent of the observer, which were available to be treated in a scientific, value-neutral and methodical way. It was confidently expected that any criminologist who paid due respect to these methods of scientific research would sooner or later discover the patterns of causality which any science of causes needed to 'discover' if it were ever to be taken seriously. All this seemed so obvious and commonsensical a matter as to require little if any justification.

Yet that orthodoxy came under attack in the 1960s and 1970s. It is to this period, when many problems with conventional criminology were discovered, that we now turn.

Review questions

What are some of the links between the eugenics of the 1920s and 1930s and modern-day social science?

How do multi-factorial explanations differ from more traditional causal explanations?

What is 'anomie'?

What are some of the different ways Burt and Merton would explain delinquency?

Further reading

Burt, C., 1965, *The Young Delinquent* (3rd edition), University of London, London.
Gouldner, A., 1971, *The Coming Crisis of Western Sociology*, Avon, New York.
Merton, R.K., 1969a, 'Social Structure and Anomie', in Cressey, D. and Ward, M. (eds), *Delinquency, Crime and Social Process*, Harper & Row, New York.

DISSENTING CRIMINOLOGY

Into the 1960s many criminologists were convinced that their discipline was a credible and successful social science working with a widely accepted set of theoretical models producing high-quality research. Yet the 1960s and 1970s proved to be decades when conventional criminology was exposed to substantial, even damaging, criticism. That criticism continues unabated into the early twenty-first century as various kinds of critics snap at the heels of mainstream criminology.

As we indicated in Chapter 3 there had always been sceptics or critics like Edwin Sutherland, which is why thinking about the history of criminology in terms of stages can be misleading: ideas and people don't always fit easily into such 'boxes'. What does mark out the 1960s and 1970s is the scale and seriousness with which various 'radicals' and sceptics in both the UK and the USA questioned the dominant consensus in criminology.

Some worried about the problems involved in doing criminology as an objective 'science of causes' which ignored both the complexity and the interpreted character of human activity. These critics, writers like David Matza (1960), Howard Becker (1963) and Aaron Cicourel (1968), drew on the 'symbolic interactionist' tradition in US sociology in developing their critique of the orthodoxy. These critics vehemently rejected the conventional assumption that crime was an objective fact enabling the collection of masses of *empirical* data as a basis for explanatory theory. Moving beyond criticism, they proposed some new ways of doing criminology.

Others, more politically engaged and influenced by Marxist ideas, argued that social interests, political ideas or ethical principles would and should intervene in ostensibly *objective* criminological theory or research. The development of 'neo-Marxism' and a New Left movement in the 1960s in the UK was especially important in sponsoring, albeit briefly, a radical criminology in the 1970s. Three young, radical criminologists, Ian Taylor, Paul Walton and Jock Young (1973), proclaimed the need for a 'new criminology'. They argued that conventional criminology, which they called 'correctionalist criminology', was politically and socially conservative. Dissent of a different kind came from the women's movement as feminists pointed to the problems of invisible gender biases at work in social sciences like criminology.

If the force and fury of those decades of dissent has faded somewhat at the start of the twenty-first century, those who practise conventional kinds of social sciences continue to be subjected to critical and sceptical scrutiny. We conclude this chapter with a brief survey of some of the contemporary responses to conventional criminology produced by 'post-modernist', 'deconstructionist' or 'post-structuralist' critics.

We begin with those writers who rejected the idea that crime was an objective reality, insisting instead that, like all other kinds of human activity, crime was socially constructed in a process of symbolic interaction. In effect, crime was all a matter of interpretation.

The symbolic interactionist critique of conventional criminology

Colin Sumner (1994: 215) provides a crisp assessment of the basis of the first major challenge mounted to conventional criminology in the 1960s when he argued that

> every student of criminology soon discovers . . . that it really is so odd that lay people usually see labelled criminals and deviants as biologically defective, when occupations actually exist with public codes of conduct, handbooks, rules, 'sciences', textbooks, diplomas, degrees, and charters for the specific purpose of systematically identifying and treating people as criminals and deviants. A lot of work goes into the professional and bureaucratic production of social deviants. It must – because it is not at all obvious who they are.

One of the key figures in this critical challenge was Howard Becker. An American sociologist, Becker (1963) challenged the dominant and conventional idea that both crime and deviance were *objective* and therefore amenable to a *naturalist* scientific treatment. His challenge to traditional ways of thinking about 'the criminal' and crime was made clear when he argued that what is called 'crime' is the consequence of efforts by some people to define a situation as a 'crime' or certain kinds of behaviour as 'criminal' (Sumner 1994: 203). This meant that the two concepts central to criminology, namely *the criminal* and *crime*, were best understood as the consequences of social practices involving interpretation.

This response to conventional criminology we will refer to as the 'symbolic interactionist' challenge. In broad terms 'symbolic interactionism' is a tradition with its base essentially in US sociology, although it relied on strands of thinking coming out of continental Europe. What we refer to as 'symbolic interactionism' actually includes diverse groups of sociologists and criminologists pursuing various lines of thought.

One group, who actually called themselves 'symbolic interactionists', was led by Herbert Blumer (1969). Their emphasis was on the symbolic nature of social interaction and the idea that social reality is *constructed* by people. Another strand came from Germany and Austria courtesy of 'phenomenologists' like Alfred Schutz (1972) who introduced into America the ideas of his own teacher, Edmund Husserl. Schutz influenced the work of Peter Berger, best known for his work (with Thomas Luckmann) (Berger and Luckmann 1969) called *The Social Construction of Reality*. These 'phenomenologists' were interested in how people experienced their social relationships and made sense of their experiences. Harold Garfinkel (1967) developed a parallel 'school' called 'ethnomethodology'. Others like Howard Becker (1963) and Erving Goffman (1959, 1968a, 1968b) called themselves 'labelling theorists'.

While there are some important differences of emphasis between these groups, for simplicity's sake we will treat them collectively as 'symbolic interactionists'. Writers like these and others provided an important critique of the dominant style of criminology in the 1960s and 1970s. Why did they say what they said? Should we take their arguments seriously?

The 'symbolic interactionists' challenged two of the main assumptions or propositions of conventional criminologists. They were critical of the claim that criminal behaviour was *caused* by a mix of innate, genetic or psychological variables like ineffective child-rearing, family pathology or social disorganization. This criticism rested on their scepticism that crime was an *objective* fact. That is to say that 'symbolic interactionists' were especially critical of the central claim of conventional criminology that

> crime and deviancy were a non-rational, determinate product of under-socialisation, and thus devoid of any human choice, creativity of meaning . . . an account based on efforts to isolate the presumed factors propelling a pathological few to break the rules of an assumed social consensus . . .
>
> (Muncie 1998: 222)

Symbolic interactionists argued instead that crime was the work of people acting, choosing and making sense of the world as best they could. This meant that crime was something people *chose* to do rather than being *forced* to do it. Even more provocatively symbolic interactionists said that crime, far from being some inherent quality of conduct, was better understood as the consequence of some people – working as social control and policing agents – labelling or defining the conduct of other people as 'criminal'. For symbolic interactionists, 'social reality' is not some objective reality in which whatever is meant by 'society' can be understood as a natural *fact* or thing. Rather social reality is understood as something people actively construct in a rich web of social interactions and social institutions like families, schools or workplaces. These interactions are sustained and constructed symbolically, especially via the most crucial of all fields of symbolic activity found in human language. In this sense, say the symbolic interactionists, the symbolic nature of social reality is both primary and overwhelming. Writers like Clifford Geertz (1974) insist that all human action accord is always symbolic action. Human reality is an interpreted reality. This means that social action is constituted out of symbolic material like ideas, rules, words and values. Language and non-linguistic communication like gestures and body posture supply the essential basis of interaction between people. For symbolic interactionists, social reality is whatever people define as real and make real by virtue of their symbolically charged interactions.

Symbolic interactionists insist that social reality is not an objective or external fact because they make an important distinction between the meanings of 'objective' and 'subjective'. They acknowledge that objective knowledge is certainly possible of *objects* if objects are defined as entities lacking consciousness; *subjects*, however, are typically living, sentient creatures like human beings who possess a lot of capacities objects lack, chief of which are the capacities to think, speak, act, feel and orient action to valued ends. All of these capacities point to the quality of 'subjectivity' – which is what 'subjective' means. Implicit in this distinction was a question long addressed by philosophers: Is the knowledge that we think is possible of objects – like chairs or stones – either worthwhile or possible when applied to 'knowing' subjects?

This entails that the things that a criminologist researches, like a 'criminal' or 'delinquent', are not like the objects studied by a natural scientist, like a 'tree' or a 'rock'. It means a 'criminal' act is not an objective phenomenon. Rather it is made real only because of the meanings we have given it and the definitions applied to it.

For symbolic interactionists all social encounters require constant interpretation. This continual reading of signs helps people work out what is happening. For example, if someone walks into your kitchen with a knife in his or her hand, is this an offer to help cook dinner, an invitation to share a bad-taste joke, a threat implying the possibility of serious injury, or an experiment in establishing how social interactions work?

It is not surprising that symbolic interactionists think differently from positivists about knowledge and truth. Symbolic interactionists tend to dismiss the preoccupation with how we can know anything with certainty, a preoccupation often expressed as a question: How can we know the *truth* reliably?

'Symbolic interactionists' argue that if people define a situation as real, then that definition is real in its consequences. Unlike the structural functionalists, the symbolic interactionists do not treat the world as something simply to contemplate scientifically or philosophically. Rather they treat the world as the place where people – including themselves – have to live by making sense of their world and acting on a daily basis on the basis of those beliefs. Sense-making and acting are practical activities and give rise to practical issues.

In this respect the US symbolic interactionists drew on the native tradition of pragmatism. From the 1880s a group of philosophers led by C. S. Peirce (1839–1914), William James (1842–1910) and John Dewey (1859–1952), and working out of Harvard, the University of Chicago and Columbia University, developed a philosophical perspective which came to be called 'pragmatism'. (Pragmatism is still alive and well in the USA and is currently represented by 'neo-pragmatists' like Richard Rorty (1979, 1999) and Ian Hacking (2000).) The US pragmatists have long stressed the role of social practices and experience as the grounding of knowledge-claims. Pragmatists suggest that only people who can afford to sit around in a library and contemplate the world from afar are likely to see questions like 'What is the truth?' worthy of serious enquiry. As Richard Rorty (1999: 7) puts it, we should ask 'not is it true, but rather what is it good for?'

As Chapter 3 suggested, the ideas of pragmatists like James and Dewey and Dewey's colleague G. H. Mead (1863–1931) sustained the development of an urban ethnography tradition in both sociology and criminology based at the University of Chicago. By the 1950s and 1960s this had evolved into a significant alternative to conventional *scientistic* criminology.

For symbolic interactionists all knowledge is active and interpretive. Accordingly good criminological knowledge requires that researchers be active in developing their knowledge, typically through techniques like detailed ethnographic description or participant observation. Symbolic interactionists claim that all competent social actors possess the normal array of social and interpretive skills with which they can interpret and act in their world – more or less – successfully. Their research agenda involved identifying the various truth practices of people, practices that they say produce whatever a given group calls 'knowledge' or 'beliefs'.

Participant observation is one of the preferred ways symbolic interactionists obtain information about people's experience. This means leaving the safety of the library or researcher's office and going out on to the street, hanging out in courtrooms or following police as they do their work. Their preference is to do research on interactions between small numbers of people (like prisoners and prison officers or police and young people) and how each actor interprets the other in their ongoing interactions.

Symbolic interactionists say observations gained from within social settings like an office or a street corner offer more insight and understanding of the values, knowledge and belief systems of people's lives as well as what they actually do. Symbolic interactionists do not use controlled experiments or large-scale samples/questionnaires to develop their knowledge. They favour interpretive and descriptive material about people's life-worlds, focusing on the meanings people give to certain things.

One important consequence of this view of reality is the rejection by writers like Garfinkel (1967), Goffman (1968a, 1968b) and Schutz (1972) of many of the usual categories of sociologists like 'class', 'social order' or 'deviance'. (For a brilliant summary of this approach see Athens 1997: 117–25.) Garfinkel claimed that these categories are either meaningless or have no greater validity than the categories of other non-sociologists, and that sociologists would be better advised to study the ways ordinary people know, organize and act in their world using their language categories. For this reason symbolic interactionists are usually critical of the kinds of structural explanations favoured by conventional criminology. This means they do not generally try to advance *causal* explanatory theories which are reliant on sociologists' concepts as structural functionalists do, but prefer to focus on the interpretive schemes that ordinary people use. For this reason they are generally not interested in developing macro-social explanations. Needless to say this provokes a lot of huffing and puffing on the part of some sociologists, criminologists and social theorists who rightly see this as an assault on their claims to know more and better than ordinary people, though they struggle to defend the claim they have privileged access to reality.

Symbolic interactionists and criminology

The development of a well-defined symbolic interactionist movement within sociology in the 1960s had a significant impact on criminology through the work of writers like Erving Goffman and Howard Becker. One effect was to move attention away from offenders and towards police and court officials. Goffman and Becker challenged orthodox positivist criminology, which assumes that deviance and crime are objectively real transgressions of the social order requiring the development of specialist–expert knowledge (by way of diagnosis, classification and measurement), and professional corrective interventions (therapy, treatment, etc.). They developed the idea that social-control agents create and regulate people through their definitions of what is deviant or criminal. That is, they *create* deviance by defining and thereby constituting it. Becker (1963: 9) summed up this view of deviance in a classic formulation of 'labelling theory':

> [S]*ocial groups create deviance by making the rules whose infraction constitutes deviance*, and by applying those rules to particular people and labeling them as

outsiders. From this point of view, deviance is not a quality of the act the person commits, but rather a consequence of the application by others of rules and sanctions to an 'offender' (Becker's stress).

In effect Becker argued that there are neither clear nor objective distinctions between the 'criminal' and the 'non-criminal': ordinary people broke social rules all the time without being labelled either deviant or criminal. The converse was also possible, namely that a person could be treated as a deviant or a criminal without having broken moral or legal rules. One reason why this is possible is because criminal conduct is not necessarily morally deviant, while morally deviant behaviour is not always criminal.

Some critics have complained that this is an argument for ethical relativism, where any and all moral values become equal. This is not a well-founded response. Goffman, for example, worked from a clear-cut and defensible moral and critical framework which not everyone would find easy or comforting. In his study of 'total institutions' like prisons, hospitals, monasteries or armies, Goffman (1968a) inserted the memory of the Nazi death camps like Auschwitz into the consciousness of sociologists. Goffman claimed that the death camps and the concentration camps worked like contemporary hospitals, prisons, schools, orphanages or homes for the elderly in stripping individuals of their 'dignity, liberty and identity' by rituals and 'rites of passage'. These rites of passage included putting people into uniforms, making them wash or have their hair cut or giving them new names, new roles or just numbers to identify them. Goffman's most powerful insight, but one which he did not do much to extend or develop, was to recognize the terrible power that lay within many institutions, ostensibly set up for 'welfare' or 'social protective' purposes, to do terrible harm to the people who became inmates or clients.

Apart from this quite powerful ethical insight what value was there in the interactionist approach?

The interactionist critique persuaded some criminologists to become more interested in the ways powerful groups set about defining conduct as criminal. Piliavin and Briar (in Rubington and Weinberg 1968) produced a much admired account of interactions between black juveniles and police showing that black youths stood a far higher chance of being stopped and/or arrested for criminal activities; police argued for this on the grounds that research statistics vindicated their belief that blacks were far more likely to offend. Piliavin and Briar concluded that this became a self-fulfilling prophecy. As we saw in Chapter 1 Cicourel (1968) produced a very influential study of the way police used their discretion when dealing with young people in ways which were reflected in apparently *objective* crime rate statistics. Sudnow (in Rubington and Weinberg 1968) produced another influential account of the social processes at work in the criminal justice system. Sudnow started with the discovery that in the USA plea-bargaining often saw the serious offence of burglary reduced to a petty theft plea by a defendant. Sudnow found that police, lawyers and judges used a stereotype of 'normal crime' in place of a formally legal definition drawn from the statutes so as to arrive at a faster legal process in a system already overwhelmed by too much complexity. This was a new kind of criminology which began to point to new kinds of political and ethical issues.

It was work like this that played a role in provoking a more explicitly political treatment in the UK on the part of academics who gathered at the National Deviancy Conference

(NDC). So let us turn to British criminology and the development there of a different kind of *alternative* criminology represented best by the work of the 'new criminologists'.

Radical criminology in the UK

The growth of a radical criminology was very much part of the ferment in ideas and political action that characterized British UK life in the 1960s and 1970s. In the late 1960s, some of the newer UK universities hosted a revival of Marxist political and social theory and constituted what is often called the 'New Left' – a loose collection of radical students, unionists and professionals interested in radical and democratic reform while opposed to Soviet-style Marxism. Its growth reflected larger social and political processes. The university systems in many countries were enjoying unprecedented growth fed by the admission of large numbers of students. US military involvement in Vietnam after 1965–66 encouraged a broad movement of dissent and radicalism around the world, some of it centred on university campuses. As Stan Cohen (1992: 79) recalls: 'By the end of the sixties, all the walls insulating crime and deviance from academic sociology, and from left or radical political thought, were beginning to crack.'

The NDC brought together radical sociologists and criminologists like Jock Young (1971), Stanley Cohen (1973, 1974), Ian Taylor and Laurie Taylor (1973), Geoffrey Pearson (1975) and Paul Rock (1973). The NDC was also attended by writers like Stuart Hall (1974), pursuing a separate but related initiative at the Centre for Contemporary Cultural Studies (CCCS) at the University of Birmingham.

The CCCS began a long-term inquiry into British 'youth cultures', and writers associated with it, like Stuart Hall, Mike Brake and David Hebdige, claimed that 'transgressive behaviours' exhibited by young people (in youth 'subcultures') were symbolic expressions of working-class resistance to middle-class hegemony. From this neo-Marxist perspective youth cultures were expressions of two different logics. On the one hand young people could be seen as collectively resisting the power of dominant classes (or what members of the CCCS called 'class hegemony'). Alternatively a youth culture could be seen as the result of co-option by powerful elites selling them popular music, clothing or advertising offering them fake forms of opposition and rebellion.

Colin Sumner (1994: 262) claims that the NDC was 'a dynamic hotchpotch of inter-actionists, anarchists, phenomenologists and Marxists. Nevertheless right from the beginning it was clear what it was against.' Paul Young (Walton and Young 1998: 18) would later characterize the NDC as a rich mix combining the anti-positivist and critical elements of labelling theory with an interest in theorizing total social structures. All of this was 'transposed into a society that was more aware of relationships of class and transfixed at that time with the emergence of ebullient and dynamic youth cultures'. Sumner (1994: 262) says that what the NDC did especially well was focus on the 'more collective features of the conflicts between a deviant group or subculture and the establishment forces aligned in disapproval against it'.

Stan Cohen's (1973) work on 'moral panics', a concept with which his name has ever since been synonymous, is rightly regarded as one of the more permanent and admired achievements of writers associated with the NDC. His work on 'moral panics' also provides a good starting point to identify some links between the symbolic interactionists and what became the 'new criminology'.

Stan Cohen on 'moral panics'

Working with some of the same assumptions relied on by US 'labelling theorists', Stan Cohen (1973) investigated the social processes at work in the media response to gatherings of young people on Bank Holidays at seaside resorts like Brighton. Cohen was particularly interested in the media's representation of groups of young people as 'folk devils' in ways that shaped public opinion and policy responses by governments.

Cohen developed the notion of 'moral panic', a term used by Jock Young, to describe this process of labelling. A 'moral panic' was a condition, episode, person or group of persons defined by the mass media as a threat to 'social values'. Cohen formalized this account by describing the media's labelling processes in terms of a set of typical stages: 'The moral barricades are manned by editors and right thinking people; socially accredited experts pronounce their diagnoses and solutions; ways of coping are evolved or more often resorted to; the condition then disappears, submerges or deteriorates' (Cohen 1973: 7).

Cohen drew on Howard Becker's work in his account of the 'moral entrepreneur' as a key player in moral panics who is recognized by his or her attempt to persuade others to adhere to a particular symbolic moral universe. Cohen argued that moral entrepreneurs are people with specific ways of *seeing* who use their power to make their versions of morality dominant. This, he argues, involves stigmatizing those identified as deviants. (In the USA, Goffman's 1968b study of stigma pointed to the role of feelings like shame when a person believes he or she has offputting features – like a dripping nose or being gay – as well as the way people use the marks of stigma to control others.)

Cohen focused on the strategies used by the mass media. His work suggested that it did not really matter what the young people referred to collectively as 'Rockers' or 'Mods' actually did. What mattered was how the media represented them to a mass audience. Cohen said that the media did this by distinguishing sharply between those who define what is right and those identified as deviant.

To manage or normalize 'deviants', moral entrepreneurs like journalists and their editors initiate and help sustain moral crusades aimed at transforming public attitudes to specific issues or sections of the population like young people, single mothers, families on welfare or 'the unemployed', etc.

Normalization of 'deviants/criminals' is achieved by bringing about changes to certain professional practices and to legislation. Moral crusades create 'moral panics'. Typically 'moral panics' involve the moral entrepreneurs telling tales of mischief or evil, or pointing to flagrant violations of an alleged basic cultural value. Whether these violations are 'real' or 'imagined' hardly matters, says Cohen. The ways the stories are told do three things: they excite widespread moral outrage; they authorize punitive and other action; and they mobilize interventions by agencies like police or social workers against the alleged perpetrators.

The success of moral entrepreneurs depends on their ability to mobilize a wider community response. This, says Cohen, relies partly on the seriousness of the perceived threat of 'the problem' as much as it does on their ability to create public awareness of the issues. The force of the resistance they encounter and their capability to offer persuasive solutions also matter.

As Cohen pointed out, the media plays a major role in the process of creating a moral panic. People with greater access to the media and those with cultural credibility have a greater chance of influencing the extent of the moral panic. Those with immediate access to the media obviously include the journalists, but also all 'right-thinking people' like church leaders, judges, experts and professionals.

Cohen's provocative account of moral panics was picked up and developed by Stuart Hall (1974) when he analysed the relationship between deviance, politics and the media. Sumner (1994: 269) says Hall argued for the 'first time in the sociology of deviance, that the process of rendering a social group deviant was a question of open political struggle. It was not a simple, given fact that a group was deviant, but a matter of hegemonic contestation.'

Hall explicitly rejected the idea that there was any real social or moral consensus, as Parsons's style of sociological criminology asserted. Rather Hall insisted that any moral consensus was an activity or practice that deployed ideology and was therefore always open to challenge and debate. By 'ideology' Hall meant to refer to a 'map of a problematic social reality' (1974: 279). Any consensus reflected the political achievement of elite politics, mobilizing the state and its agents, the media and 'public opinion'.

Far from being a simple, static function, maintaining a moral consensus was a process of constant contest. This idea seemed to catch something of the lively cultural politics of the 1970s. Indeed, the very drive to install consensus politics had the effect of creating a political, deviant 'counter-culture'. Hall, unlike some others at the time, did not go on to claim that people or groups identified as deviant were self-consciously political or politically aware actors.

It was in this context of political and intellectual ferment that in 1973 Ian Taylor, Paul Walton and Jock Young published *The New Criminology*.

The 'new criminology'

Taylor, Walton and Young, key members of Britain's 'New Left' who had gathered at NDCs since the late 1960s, were clearly out to shock the establishment. Walton and Young (1998: 2) later characterized the state of criminology in Britain before their intervention as 'fat cat criminology': 'Before the National Deviancy Conference, and the works that followed, British criminology was big science, with Home Office funding and dominated by one fat cat university, Cambridge.' Needless to say the 'new criminologists' did not teach at Cambridge, nor at Oxford.

As Muncie (1998: 221) suggests, the 'new criminology' was

> a fierce attack on traditional positivist and correctionalist criminology, arguing that this tradition acted as little more than an academic justification for the existing discriminatory practices in the penal and criminal justice systems . . . [It] sought to illustrate how crime was politically and economically constructed through the

capacity and ability of state institutions within the political economy of advanced capitalism, to define and confer criminality on others.

In some 250 pages Taylor, Walton and Young (1973) surveyed and commented critically on the entire history of criminology. They argued that the political processes involved in 'discovering' or defining deviance or crime ought to be the starting point of any critical criminology. In calling for a 'politicization of criminology' they argued that criminologists ought to declare what values they stood for, because 'a criminology which is not normatively committed to the abolition of inequalities of wealth and power, and in particular of inequalities in property and life-chances, is inevitably bound to fall into correctionalism' (ibid.: 279).

The 'new criminologists' claimed that there were two crucial weaknesses characterizing all previous criminology. Firstly there was its isolation from 'sociology'. (This is an odd claim, given the way Parsons's style of sociology had been assimilated into mainstream criminology.) Secondly there was its relatively ambivalent relationship to the other social sciences. Taylor, Walton and Young demanded what they called a more robust *social theoretical* framework for criminology, a social framework that was free from all the psychological and biological assumptions they claimed were embedded in conventional criminology.

The 'new criminologists' unambiguously opposed *orthodox* criminology. Like the symbolic interactionists, Taylor, Walton and Young (ibid.: 150–4) rejected the key positivist and/or conventional criminological assumption that crime was a real, objective phenomenon best identified as an individual pathology that was *caused* by a mix of biological, psychological or sociological pathologies and constituted an offence against an objective normative consensus. In place of that assumption they suggested that crime was a rational and a meaningful social activity, often created out of the contradictions of a class society.

Not content with their assault on conventional criminology they also turned their sights on *orthodox sociology*. By this they meant both the scientistic, abstracted empiricism that relied on lots of numbers and multiple statistical correlations as well as the very sophisticated version of high social theory offered by sociologists like Parsons and Merton (ibid.: 9–14).

As if that was not enough the 'new criminologists' rejected *orthodox Marxism*. By this they meant 'old-style' Marxism which offered a determinist, even reductionist, explanation of conduct in terms of *economic* interest. The 'new criminologists' rejected the simplistic Marxist idea that all crime was the work of the 'dangerous classes', a 'lumpen-proletarian' class riddled with false consciousness, 'demoralized, even defeated by its poverty' (ibid.: 209–36).

The ambitions of the iconoclasts were as elevated as the mix of elements they drew on because their position, as this summary suggests, was a complex one. The 'new criminology' they argued for was nothing less than a formal, fully developed, social theory of deviance. They argued that such a theory would involve

a political economy of criminal action, and of the reaction it excites, [thereby identifying] the formal elements of a theory that would be adequate to move

criminology out of its own imprisonment in artificially segregated specifics. We
have attempted to bring the parts together again in order to form the whole.

(ibid.: 279)

They claimed to have constructed just such a fully realized social theory of deviance. If so,
it was done in only a very few pages (ibid.: 270–8). They outlined the *scope* and the
substance of a fully 'social theory of the deviant act'. They said that any adequate theory
of the deviant act must be able to specify the underlying causes of that act. This, they said,
would identify the wider structural considerations such as the overall context of inequalities
of power, wealth and authority, constituting in short a *political economy of crime*. Such a
theory must also be able to specify its immediate origins, and this amounts to a *social
psychology of crime*. As well as doing this, such a theory must also be able to focus on the
actual deviant act by asking how the behaviour relates to the causes. Finally, such a theory
must be able to specify the immediate origin of the social reaction.

So did they deliver what they had promised? And how well has the 'new criminology'
stood the test of time?

Problems with the new criminology

Looking back at his contribution to the 'new criminology' a few years ago, Jock Young (in
Walton and Young 1998: 24) ended with a complacent flourish: 'There we have it, and there
is very little in it that one would find fault with today.'

As far as it went, Taylor, Walton and Young's 1973 book was a well-targeted critique
of the orthodoxy. Yet it was also a book with very serious weaknesses. Critics like Colin
Sumner (1994: 281) have pointed out how

> at the level of form the book was unkempt. Arguments were overdrawn, critiques
> were ill-developed and often unfair and key positions were fudged. In terms of
> substance, we were urged to abandon all prior conceptions of deviance, yet for
> what? In truth a pittance; a parody of the complexity of crime and deviance.

By far the most developed part of their work drew extensively on the 'symbolic
interactionist' tradition. Oddly the neo-Marxist component was not so fully developed
or explicated. For example, having apparently rejected a conventional economically
determinist Marxism they simply – and silently – reinstated it (1973: 209–10). They did
this, for example, when they argued that a 'fully developed' Marxist criminology would
explain how 'particular historical periods, characterized by particular sets of social
relationships and means of production, give rise to attempts by the economically and
socially powerful to order society in particular ways' (ibid.: 220). These neo-Marxist
elements in their work were more fully developed in 1975, in a follow-up book called
Critical Criminology.

As for the substantive claim to have outlined a 'new criminology', their proposal
amounted to a few pages of abstracted and often incoherent theorizing about crime. If their
critique of all previously existing criminology was wide-ranging, detailed and trenchant,

they were able to suggest only in a sketchy way what such a 'new criminology' might actually look like. This was always going to pose a credibility problem.

One basic objection that came from various kinds of criminologists was that the 'new criminology' had gone too far and had relativized reality and 'real crime' out of existence. Two kind of 'relativism' are at stake here. Epistemological relativism says there are no objective or universal truth-claims as all human knowledge is historical and incomplete because dependent on cultural beliefs and assumptions. Ethical relativism is the idea that there are no universal or objective ethical values because any ethical claims are relative to time and place. Some of their critics suggested that it was this attempt to 'relativize' the ideas of deviance and crime that effectively destroyed the basis of any inquiry into those ideas. As Sumner (1994: 262) suggests: 'The NDC was to stretch the meaning and viability of the radical meaning of deviancy to its absolute limit – so far in fact that it collapsed under the strain.' (As we will see the 'new criminologists' accepted the force of this criticism and beat a hasty retreat.)

Left-realist critiques

This criticism was advanced by some of the UK's leading radical criminologists like Geoffrey Pearson who called themselves 'left-realists'. As the term implies this is a kind of criminology that uses categories like 'class,' 'power' and 'oppression' to challenge the politics of conventional criminology while insisting that crime remains an *objective*, or real, problem.

As a 'left-realist' Geoffrey Pearson (1975: 120) claimed that the 'new criminology', based on a 'radical sociology of deviance', had created an intractable problem. Pearson observed first that the 'new criminology' proposed that 'deviance' and 'crime' were not *things* possessing the usual *objective* thing – like qualities previously attributed to them by mainstream criminology. That is, radical deviance theory had demonstrated that it was no longer feasible or desirable to treat the core concepts of *crime* and *deviance* as if these were the names of physical objects as are 'bucket' and 'rock'. Rather these words referred to quite complex forms of human conduct and to no less complex reactions which involved interpretations and judgements. This implied that for people to say that a crime has occurred involves interpretations of actions like punching or shooting as well as attempts to assess psychological states of mind like motivation or intention.

Secondly, Pearson accepted that the radical sociology of deviance had demonstrated that detecting 'deviants' or 'criminals' was part of a continuing social practice involving contest and resistance. Words like 'crime' and 'deviance' were part of an unending political and moral contest, involving struggle and contest between powerful people on the one hand and on the other people who lacked access to significant economic, political or cultural resources.

After pointing to the quite subversive implications of the 'new criminology', Pearson said they had gone too far: he maintained that the radical theory of deviance was an 'escapist' response to a 'real' problem. Pearson insisted that radical deviance theorists refused to address 'the hard moral questions' about issues of crime in which moral judgements could not be evaded. For him, some behaviours were unacceptable and he found the 'romanticizing' of deviance unhelpful. Pearson was not persuaded by the proposition that all activities and behaviours are inherently morally neutral until someone comes along to judge them. Indeed so apparently persuasive was this criticism that Jock Young had within two years repudiated his own contribution to the 'new criminology' and like Pearson now claimed to be a 'left-realist'.

Pearson is surely right to suggest that not all conduct is morally equivalent or acceptable. This is a proposition with which many writers who work within the symbolic interactionist framework, like Goffman (1968b), would agree.

Yet it is not clear that the 'new criminologists' were in fact arguing that 'anything goes'. This is certainly not an implication of the empirically well-grounded argument that powerful people or organizations including governments or media organizations have the capacity to define some problems as worthy of attention while rendering invisible other problems that may be far more serious or harmful.

Our problem with Pearson is that he has both conflated and confused two quite separate points. Firstly it is an empirical matter to determine whether or not there are any universally valid or objective moral laws or norms, or indeed whether there is within a given society a society-wide ethical consensus. (One problem rarely confronted by those who claim that there are universal and/or objective moral ideas is what is to be the evidence for such a consensus: is it what people *say* or what they *do*?) We have already argued that the idea that there are universal ethical norms has not yet been made empirically.

Secondly there is the question of whether there is a hierarchy of values such that some activities are clearly ethically far worse or more injurious than others are. It is pretty clear that all human activity is ethically informed. From Aristotle (1976) to Charles Taylor (1977: 15–44) philosophers have made a strong case that all human activity and interaction is inherently ethical, because it is oriented to some idea of the good, however that idea of the good is defined or defended. For Taylor, people are 'self interpreting animals' for whom ethical deliberation is a central part of the human experience.

The essential problem is that even within the same community we do not agree about what is the right or the good thing to do. Ever since philosophical debates began in classical Athens – itself a relatively small and homogenous community – we have known that we live in a world of competing ideas about justice and 'the good'. The great liberal theorist Isaiah Berlin said that our fate is to live in a world where there is an irreducible diversity of ethical values. Factually the idea that there are universal moral rules, laws or criteria which can be invariantly applied to a given practice to produce invariant evaluations does not stand up to scrutiny in the face of the intractable fact of diverse practices and evaluations. This problem is not resolved by Pearson's assertion that some actions are *inherently* or *objectively* good or bad.

Again it is clear that few of us would disagree that *in principle* there is a hierarchy of values. The difficulty again is in getting agreement about what the hierarchy should look like. Pearson is not entitled to conflate these two quite separate issues. There is a clear distinction to be made between arguing that there are no universally valid or objective moral laws or norms and the argument that some activities are clearly ethically far worse or more injurious than are others. It is entirely reasonable to hold to both propositions, since advancing the first proposition does not mean that you cannot make the second case.

Further, if Pearson wishes to make a *realist* case for objective, universal, moral norms, then he needs to engage with that problem properly. Apart from stamping his feet and saying that 'there are' objective crimes and 'universally practised moral laws' because he says so, Pearson has no sensible suggestions for dealing with the fundamental problem, namely the absence of any universally acknowledged or practised *objective* moral laws.

Notwithstanding this, Pearson's case was deemed sufficiently persuasive by one of the 'new criminologists'. Just two years after they had unveiled the 'new criminology' one of its authors declared himself to be a freshly minted 'left-realist'. Jock Young (in Taylor, Walton and Young 1975: 13–14) announced that 'sceptical deviancy theory' offered 'no coherent alternatives' to 'correctionalism' other than 'an abstracted and individualistic idealism'. In his (1975) contribution ('Working-Class Criminology') Jock Young said that the symbolic interactionist critique was exhausted as a political or a theoretical position, possessing only the virtues of being a 'moral gesture'. In effect the new criminologists rejected the *constructivist* emphasis of the symbolic interactionists. Young, and to some extent Taylor and Walton, opted to return to the structuralism and the *objectivism* which underpinned their kind of neo-Marxist social theory.

In his self-critique Young now claimed that the earlier position was overly preoccupied with the 'expressive' side of deviance. He considered that they had over-emphasized the significance that deviants gave to their conduct. In this self-critique Young said that they had ignored the role of the state while they had over-stressed the 'free will' of 'the individual'.

In short Young (1975: 17–18) claimed that they had inserted an 'idealist' position into what should have remained a more 'materialist' or a properly Marxist kind of theory.

> The deviant himself is seen to embody expressively an authenticity which allows him to cut through the taken-for-granted world of conventional culture . . . he was accorded an unreal ability to transcend the exigencies of everyday life. [It was a] crude attempt to utilize Marx's notion of alienation with a view to seeing in deviant behaviour the activity of men struggling against institutions of constraint and what later we were to term 'normalized repression'.

(Indeed, though this is a larger point, the new criminologists seem to have got quite confused as they struggled to deal with the criticism they were facing. While proclaiming the *objectivity* of crime, the category of *deviance* itself was simply dropped from their theoretical vocabulary! Hirst's contribution to their 1975 book explicitly disavowed the possibility that a Marxist theory of deviance was even possible!)

Young simultaneously announced his retreat from the new criminology while outlining the basis of 'left realism'. Young railed against those of his colleagues who had embraced 'labelling theory', claiming that the new criminology of the NDC was a 'crass inversion' of utilitarianism that merely 'idolized the deviant'. He claimed (1975: 68) that he and his colleagues had 'developed a criminology that does not deal with property crime and a criminology whose subjects live in a world not of work, but of leisure'. Accordingly the 'new criminology' was a 'Romantic', or 'idealist', position.

In effect Young tried to reinstate the idea that crime was both objectively 'real' and was open to causal explanations. He claimed that there really was a consensus on crimes against the person and property. Young (ibid.: 82) claimed that there was an objective 'consensus about crime operating throughout society', a consensus that 'corresponds to the uniformity of the mode of production dominating the social order'. This involved Young stitching a Marxist structuralism and a Parsonsian functionalism together. Crime, in short, was 'objectively real' especially when 'it' was done against working-class victims. Some behaviours really were psychopathic and irrational. At the heart of Young's recantation was the simple idea that there *really* is a *reality* about crime that justifies an objectivist framework.

Young also insisted that a causal theory, just like that long advocated by positivists, was possible and desirable. He claimed that it really was the case that certain 'ecological areas' were 'socially disorganized' in ways that *caused* deviant behaviour. Once again crime was understood to be *caused* by economic deprivation and/or by anomie. Given this socially objective consensus, 'left-realists' claimed that the working class was right to support 'law and order campaigns' because deviance and crime were *real* problems, just as conventional criminologists had been saying for a long time.

The idea that crime is a natural, obstinate and ever-threatening fact of life, perpetrated by an objectively discoverable body of people ('criminals'), has proved remarkably resistant to critical thought. It has been long central both to popular ideas about crime as well as to mainstream criminologists. The reaction of conventional criminologists to all the 'to-ing and fro-ing' of the new criminologists was therefore not all that surprising.

Mainstream responses

The response from most orthodox or mainstream criminologists to the new criminology was to ignore it. As the work of contemporary criminologists we survey in the rest of this book suggests, the symbolic interactionists and the new criminologists might as well have saved their breath. Those who bothered to notice the new criminology had responses similar to Pearson's. Writers like James Q. Wilson (1975) were critical of the new criminology for what its exponents said amounted to the relativizing and trivializing of quite serious problems by sponsoring a form of 'radical' or 'sociological chic'. (This was a term popularized by the New York novelist Tom Wolfe who wrote about wealthy New York celebrities hosting smart parties attended by gangsters and Black Power revolutionaries in the 1970s.)

For mainstream criminologists like Wilson (1975) and Wilson and Herrnstein (1985) the work of the new criminologists was simply anathema. Like Pearson they stamped their feet, asserting as positivists had long done that knowing the *truth* about the world requires simply achieving a correspondence between the *facts* and our knowledge. The point and purpose of scientific method was to discover the facts, do careful measurements, and test and refine theory. That the new criminologists appeared briefly to flirt with the unthinkable merely proved from the perspective of the mainstream the lack of credibility of their position.

Yet the need for careful thinking about previously unexamined assumptions was made evident by a new group of critics, and this criticism has proved a lot harder to ignore.

Feminist critiques

In spite of their ambitions to be comprehensive, the new criminologists had missed the obvious, as had so much of conventional criminology. As feminists began to point out in the 1970s and 1980s, it was decidedly odd for a discipline like criminology, claiming to offer a comprehensive social theory of deviance, to somehow have ignored the existence and the role of women.

Feminism is one of the major social movements of our time. (Alaine Touraine 1986 offers a classic account of the role and character of social movements as a source of social transformation in the twentieth century.) The social activists, academics and professionals who shaped the women's movement of the 1970s and 1980s asked one basic and useful question: Where have women, who make up half of the population, gone?

'Second-wave' feminism began in the 1960s with the work of people like Betty Friedan (1963), Germaine Greer (1967) and Kate Millett (1971), whose insights and arguments were subsequently expanded into a substantial body of feminist research and political action. ('First-wave' feminists like the suffragettes had led the struggle at the start of the twentieth century to get women the vote and have their basic civic rights recognized.) Feminist theorists argued trenchantly that too often the theory and research done by male philosophers, historians or social scientists had forgotten that women were a central part of social and historical experience. Feminist criminologists from Carol Smart (1975, 1997) to Susan Walklate (2004) used the intellectual and political assumptions of feminism to show how, even among radical criminologists like Taylor, Walton and Young (1973), women were rendered invisible by a mainstream criminology better called 'malestream' criminology (Carrabine et al. 2004: 85).

Referring simply to feminism is unhelpful if we fail to recognize the diversity of liberal, Marxist or socialist, radical and, most recently, post-feminist (or post-modernist) feminisms. In what follows, though we cannot observe or be sensitive to these distinctions, we can indicate the kind of critique they offered of 'malestream' criminology.

When feminists talk about social reality they focus on issues of gender relations, the sexual division of labour and gender-based inequality. For many early feminists males were the dominant gender and they constituted a patriarchal society. Feminists pointed to the historical evidence that men *as a group* have traditionally owned most of the wealth just as they have dominated state institutions like government, the courts and the state bureaucracy, as well as intellectual and creative institutions like universities and art galleries, to say nothing of business corporations. Moreover, the relative lack of women in academic research and theory had less to do with the way women had been inactive or invisible and more to do with the way they were ignored and largely written out of history. In criminology, feminists like Smart argued that women both as victims and criminals had been completely ignored (Smart 1975, 1997). This is not to say that the problem can be fixed by simply taking established criminological theories and adding the word 'woman' or 'girl' here and there.

Most feminists have rejected the idea that biology determines their destiny and instead say that sex and gender are the product of social and cultural ideas informed by the power of men in patriarchal society. Feminists also say that you cannot understand human action unless you relate it to a person's position in the pattern of gender relations found in a given society. In a patriarchal society most women are exploited, oppressed and dominated. For radical and separatist feminists, marriage, family life and heterosexuality are effectively mechanisms for the domination of all women.

Feminists insist that social order is maintained by various forms of gendered violence. This includes both the threat of as well as actual violence. The threat of rape or domestic violence, for example, is said to be one way of keeping women in their place; the fear of poverty if women reject their *normal* domestic obligations is another. For many feminists, patriarchy can be effectively challenged only when enough women become aware of their own oppression and when they appreciate what causes them to be oppressed.

Most feminists take a critical approach to 'malestream' knowledge. Their role as researchers is to provide critical analysis of the status of women while supporting emancipatory practices that enhance women's lives.

As might be expected feminists have raised interesting questions about the nature of knowledge. For most feminists the social sciences have been part of an apparatus of culture and knowledge that supports the continued oppression of women. Feminist research uses a variety of methods to inform, criticize, politicize and enlighten. Some feminists argue that all forms of rational knowledge reliant on 'scientific method' are positivist *and* reflect male-centred values and practices designed to reinforce male power, and as such must be rejected. Others argue that it does not matter what methods are used so long as their application to research reflects as accurately as possible the experiences of those women being studied. Other writers, like Cain (1990), Stanley and Wise (1983) and Hammersley, Ramazanoglu and Gelsthorpe (1992), call for the development of new feminist research methods that allow for the development of knowledge and realities that were previously overlooked.

Modern feminists tend to agree that sexism is codified in both the body of knowledge known as 'criminology' as well as in the penal and justice systems.

Feminist criminologists argue that 'criminality' itself is primarily a masculine idea. Representations of the 'criminal' or 'delinquent' have traditionally been based on the figure of the male. Categories like 'youth' or 'adolescent' have long been masculine, defined in effect, but always implicitly, as ideal–typical male subjects (Carrington 1989, 1993). In the case of young offenders, feminist criminologists analysing the category of 'adolescence' observed how it was defined in terms of 'scientific' notions of storm and stress, conflict and dichotomy. The language of adolescence has been constructed using implicitly masculine concepts. Barbara Hudson made the point forcefully that adolescence was defined as a stage that the young person (that is male) was expected to 'grow out of', so that adolescent maladjustments could be 'tolerated': 'but femininity is what a girl is supposed to be acquiring, so that any signs that she is rejecting rather than embracing the culturally-defined femininity are treated . . . as necessitating active intervention and urgent re-socialisation' (Hudson in McRobbie and Nava 1984: 44; see also Cain 1989a). The penalty many women and girls have paid as they entered the criminal justice system was not necessarily because of their criminal behaviour, but resulted rather from their failure to act in appropriately feminine ways.

The result, as feminist researchers have shown, is that certain activities performed by men are defined as 'normal' but the same activity on the part of a woman becomes abnormal or immoral. Feminists point out that for too long domestic violence has not been recognized as a major criminal problem. 'Victimless crimes' like prostitution by women fall into this category. Prostitution in many countries is criminalized; their activities are unlawful, rendering prostitutes (most of whom are women) subject to penalties while those who pay for the sex (usually men) typically escape prosecution. For others, for example McRobbie (1991), the same could be said about perspectives like sub-cultural theory. Neo-Marxists, for example, viewed 'deviance' and 'youth culture' as symbolic expressions of male working-class resistance to bourgeois culture, while McRobbie (1991) observed how such interpretations ignored the experience of young women.

Secondly feminists argue that women are either invisible or are significantly misrepresented within criminological theory and research (Smart 1975; Heidensohn 1986; Cain 1989b; Carrington 1989, 1993; Walklate 2004). In other words, the part played by women and girls as victims and perpetrators in stories of delinquency and criminality are rarely considered (Gelsthorpe 1989). Although it was acknowledged that girls and women were capable of criminal and delinquent acts, female criminality was usually bench-marked against male experiences of criminality, rather than the other way around. The primary concern was safeguarding the sexual virtue or chastity of women, especially young women, and ensuring that they went on to fulfil their designated sex role as compliant wives and nurturant mothers. Conversely the involvement of women in what was and is generally seen as masculine activities was and is usually perceived as bad. Sex before marriage – especially with more than one partner – riding motorcycles, wearing black leathers, being confident, ambitious, competitive (especially against boys), swearing, getting about the town, using public space, brawling, spitting or being assertive were behaviours that were and are considered to be 'unfeminine'.

For feminist criminologists like Kerry Carrington (1993), what gets women and girls into real trouble is their refusal to accept their *legitimate* sexuality, their refusal to be integrated into a culture of femininity. Girls who enter the masculinist public spaces of the street, of visible youth culture, demonstrate their defiance of a 'culture of femininity'. Drawing on a case study from her book *Offending Girls* (1993: 102–4), Carrington noted how

> Cheryl was punished by the courts for not participating in that culture . . . She routinely invaded the male space of the street and the local youth subculture, spending her time 'walking the streets', 'chucking laps', that is racing up and down in cars . . . She did not confine her activities to the bedroom . . . Cheryl was being punished by the courts for her invasion into the male territory of the street-based youth culture. It could be suggested that the juvenile justice system operates on a double standard of morality, punishing girls and not boys for their participation in the spectacle of youth culture.

Feminists argued that infringements committed by women were either not seen as *different* or not as seriously criminal as offences committed by men. Historically the primary offences committed by women, and especially young women, have been 'status offences' such as being 'in moral danger', being 'incorrigible' and being 'out of parental control' or being 'wayward', rather than the criminal offences committed by men such as robbery, assault and vandalism. For feminist criminologists, the prevalence of double standards is also reflected in the treatment of male offenders. Male offenders are deemed to be *criminal*, while females who found themselves in the criminal justice system were as likely to be defined as sick, emotionally unstable or suffering from psychological and psychiatric disorders.

To date, the impact made by feminist criminologists has been substantial and, unlike other critical and dissenting traditions, they have been hard to ignore. This is as it should be. After all feminists had simply made the point that somehow a large number of researchers committed to a realist perspective had failed to observe, let alone address, the existence of that half of the population who were women. That point was irrefutable. However, the difficult questions this raised about conventional criminologists' claims to objectivity and to knowledge based on empiricist principles were again avoided.

It is perhaps too soon to say whether the same fate awaits the most recent kind of dissident criminology. Since the 1980s a distinctive body of critical, sceptical theory has made its mark both in the universities and in the larger intellectual and creative culture of the West found in creative media like literature, film and architecture. We will refer to this pattern of ideas as 'post-modernism'. We turn to this version of dissenting criminology and to the work of Michel Foucault.

Post-modernist dissent

There are many perspectives and approaches that we refer to here as 'post-modernism' (see Harvey 1990; Bauman 1991; Giddens 1990; Turner 1990; Anderson 1995). Sometimes other terms like 'deconstructionism', 'post-structuralism', 'discourse theory', 'cultural studies' or the 'new historicism' are used. It is important to note that Michel Foucault, the writer whose work has had some impact on criminology and who we treat here, refused to regard his work as either 'post-structuralist' or 'post-modernist'.

What we are calling 'post-modernism' is a complex, contradictory and difficult set of ideas to summarize simply and quickly. In some ways it is easier to say what post-modernists reject than what they stand for. David Harvey (1990) suggests that post-modernists reject what he calls the 'Enlightenment project'. What was the 'Enlightenment project'?

Harvey (ibid.: 27) says that the men who made the Enlightenment believed that

> there was only one possible answer to any question. From this it followed that the world could be controlled and rationally if we could only picture and represent it rightly. But this presumed that there existed a single correct mode of representation which, if we could uncover it (and this was what the scientific and mathematical endeavors were all about), would provide the means to Enlightenment ends.

This Enlightenment project and the scientific rationalism of the twentieth century that grew out of it were not just about a philosophy of science but a belief in social progress. Harvey says the Enlightenment project promoted a belief in '[l]inear progress, absolute truths and rational planning of ideal social orders'. In one sense the kind of history of criminology we have sketched out here suggests that mainstream criminology is part of that 'Enlightenment project'.

Rather than get bogged down in definitional squabbles, we address the work of Michel Foucault who offers a useful introduction to the ideas that matter.

Michel Foucault (1926–84) was one of the most famous and important intellectual figures among the star-studded cast of French intellectuals of the 1960s through to his death from AIDS in Paris in 1984. Foucault spent much of his time writing a distinctive blend of philosophy and history. In a series of books that were quickly translated into English he argued that what constituted 'madness', 'deviance' or 'crime' changed greatly according to the particular period of time and specific cultural context.

In the early 1970s Foucault became involved in a French prisoners' action group. A subsequent visit to Attica Prison in New York State rocked him and led to his research on what he called the 'genealogy' of the prison, published in 1977 as *Discipline and Punish*, a book which forced criminologists to take notice of him. This work persuaded some criminologists to take seriously his kind of scepticism about conventional social sciences.

Foucault offers us a critical framework for thinking about all knowledge-claims. He insists that all knowledge-claims are expressed in 'discourses'. The idea of discourse refers to a structured set of propositions produced about the world. A 'discourse' claims that reality is a certain way because a number of people have agreed about what is real, or have identified certain problems as deserving of further attention. (The idea of discourse is close in a lot of ways to the older idea of 'paradigm' made famous by T. S. Kuhn 1970 who used the idea to revise the history of physics.)

The power of discourses lies in their ability to determine what can be said, what is credible and what is counted as *truth*, or *reality*. Foucault argued that all knowledge of reality is mediated by discourses (reliant on particular kinds of language uses and various techniques for knowing things), so we can never claim to know reality as it *really* is. (To 'see' his point, try to think about the world without using particular language categories and the discourses of which they are part.) He suggested that there is no way of escaping the power of any one discourse, except by moving into another. Apart from particular discourses, there is no single master discourse which gives us absolute or direct access to reality, nor for *obvious* reasons can we appeal to reality to resolve disputes between different discourses. There is no non-discursive way of saying that reality is really 'this way' because we never have direct access to any part of reality except by means of particular discourses.

The idea of discourse is useful because there is an important distinction to be made between the things that we can know about directly, because we experience them ourselves, and those we cannot, because we do not have the experiences that make that kind of knowledge possible.

There are many things and processes that we can experience on a first-hand basis. We experience our coffee as hot or agree that the chair we are sitting on is black. Yet there are also many things that we want to know about that we are unable to know so directly or experientially. In disciplines like criminology or sociology we want to know about the number of people who have performed *criminal acts*, or how many *crimes* were committed in a specific year, or how many people were unemployed or went through divorces. It is not always clear how we can find out about these things.

This means that researchers have to use what Bohme (1975) calls 'constructive schemes' that will help them to know about such things. This means that for problems like *crime*, *unemployment* or *poverty* the researcher first needs to 'conceptualize' – or define – what a category like *crime* is so that the concept can then be applied to those parts of reality he has selected by naming them. Then comes the use of particular research techniques that can gather in *data* or *facts*. Discourses are important here because both the conceptualizing of the things researchers want to find out about as well as the research techniques used are constructed out of the prevailing discourses. Foucault insisted that there is no distinction in the social world between what people refer to as 'real' (or 'material') and the 'symbolic' when trying to elucidate the basis of language and meaning. It implies too that the relationship between discursive categories (*language*) and social action and practices (*social reality*) like criminological research are so interlinked that they should be seen as mutually determining or shaping each other.

Foucault held that discourses constrain what people can do, say or think. Discourses say what is to be defined as *real* and what is not, and what can be thought about and what cannot.

To this idea, derived in part from sceptical philosophers like Nietzsche and Wittgenstein (1953), Foucault added the insight that power and knowledge are linked together. Foucault insisted that language is not a neutral medium that conveys information in non-partisan ways through ideas that are formed independently of personal history, politics, prejudices or cultural inclinations. He argued that discourses involve the political use of language. As William Connolly (1983) argues, discourses are institutionalized and structured meanings that constitute our ways of thinking and acting in particular politically charged directions. Connolly argued that some discourses are more important than others, because some groups of people have more power or authority than others to establish what it is possible and not possible to think, know, speak and write about. This idea of discourse points to the way the practices of professional doctors, teachers, counsellors, youth workers, social scientists and other professionals who work inside organizations are shaped by ideas designed to administer other people's health, schooling or well-being. It is also highly relevant to the way disciplines like criminology work.

Foucault's ideas about discourses were designed to administer a 'therapeutic shock' to the simple confidence we might feel when we think that we have got an *objective* or *scientific* grip on things. Foucault was deeply sceptical about the *rationality* said to characterize Western intellectual history. We see here how Foucault challenges the Enlightenment idea about the rationality of one scientific way of knowing the world.

The social sciences (or the 'human sciences') were of particular interest to Foucault. He claimed that if we understand how language is organized into 'discourses' then we will also gain insights into the way power works. For Foucault the main achievement of the modern social sciences (like criminology, sociology, psychology, psychiatry, economics or medicine) was to define, categorize and regulate people by using criteria like *rational* to define the irrational and *normal* to define the abnormal. In effect, for Foucault the social sciences are part of an apparatus of control and regulation.

Foucault often talked about the effects of power in discourses. He suggested that people who claim they have the truth are actually using a variety of techniques to force other people to accept those claims. The power of social scientists and professionals rests in part on their ability to impose their particular ideas on others, which rely not on superior intellectual capacity, but on political techniques like ridiculing people with alternate views, or excluding them from committees, research grants or university jobs, etc. Finally, Foucault's concept of discourse rejects the idea that any language and its vocabulary is simply a passive reflection of reality. Here he attacked some philosophical ideas long assumed to be true by most criminologists.

As with the work of the symbolic interactionists and the new criminologists the impact of this perspective on conventional criminology is best described as marginal. Reputable criminologists like David Garland (1990, 1994, 1997) have drawn on the work of Foucault to reconstruct the history of criminology. Fattah (1997) also offers a critique of 'modernist' criminology combining a 'post-modernist' scepticism allied to a humanist ethic. Other criminologists, like De Haan (1990), Henry and Milovanovic (1991), Hunt (1991) and Carrington (1993, 1997), have explored the implications of post-modernism for renovating modern criminology. Post-modernist ideas have also made themselves felt in related areas like socio-legal studies, feminist theory and the sociology of deviance.

Conclusion

Most contemporary criminologists continue to promote a conventional kind of criminology that looks often remarkably like the orthodoxy of the 1960s. Most practitioners of criminology continue to parade their credentials as *practical researchers* and *experts* who rely on their common sense about what the key problems in criminology are or what good 'scientific method' looks like. This means, to all intents and purposes, a degree of reliance on a variety of *empiricist* or *positivist* assumptions. It means, too, a comfortable sense that the traditions of criminological research and theory can continue to be worked over within a smoothly unfolding disciplinary history. As with so many other areas of intellectual activity or human conduct, when a small group of critics challenged orthodox criminology, most conventional criminologists simply kept on doing what they had been doing. They did so while paying lip-service to the idea that it was a 'good thing' to have some debate or criticism on the margins of the discipline. This is why a judgement by Colin Sumner, while it is accurate enough, doesn't seem to make all that much difference. As he puts it: 'The time has passed for behavioural concepts of social deviance, degeneracy, inadequacy or even criminality. No-one seriously concerned with social science can take them as valid scientific concepts' (Sumner 1994: 311).

It is safe to say that the great majority of criminologists remain committed to doing 'bread-and-butter criminology' and carry on doing conventional criminology as if the various dissenting traditions had never been. Conventional criminology keeps sailing on, undisturbed by radical critics and post-modern sceptics. This may mean one of two things. It may mean the critics and sceptics are profoundly wrong and so should go unheeded. Or it may mean, as we suspect, that the persistence of old habits of mind in mainstream criminology is testimony to the profound capacity of many of us to believe what we want to believe.

None of this is to deny the value of the efforts made in the past by sceptics or critics and in the present by criminologists influenced by 'post-modernist' ideas who continue to challenge the orthodoxy. The real significance of the various dissenting traditions explored in this chapter is that each opened up a window of opportunity for criminology to begin to be a more thoughtful enterprise. That opportunity will continue to beckon.

Review questions

What are the key assumptions about the nature of social reality that the symbolic interactionists relied on in developing an alternative kind of criminology?

What are the strengths and weaknesses of the symbolic interactionist critique of orthodox criminology?

What are the strengths and weaknesses of the new criminologists' critique of mainstream criminology? Were their critics right when suggesting that there are clear cases of human behaviour that are objectively or inherently wrong or criminal?

Do feminists have a point in their claims about the invisibility of women in mainstream criminology?

If Foucault's idea of discourse is taken seriously what are some of its implications for contemporary criminology?

Further reading

Anderson, W.T. (ed.), 1995, *The Truth About the Truth: De-Confusing and Re-Constructing the Postmodern World*, G.P. Putnam, New York.

Becker, H., 1964, *The Other Side: Perspectives on Deviance*, Free Press, New York.

Foucault, M., 1980, *Power/Knowledge: Selected Interviews and Other Writings, 1972–1977*, Pantheon, New York.

Sumner, C., 1994, *The Sociology of Deviance: An Obituary*, Open University, Buckingham.

Swaaningen, R. van, 1997, *Critical Criminology*, Sage, London.

Taylor, I., Walton, P. and Young, J., 1973, *The New Criminology: For a Social Theory of Deviance*, Routledge & Kegan Paul, London.

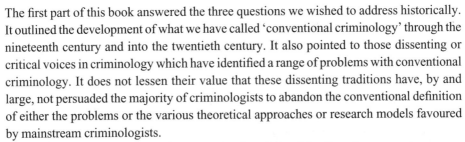

PART II

ISSUES IN CONTEMPORARY CRIMINOLOGY

The first part of this book answered the three questions we wished to address historically. It outlined the development of what we have called 'conventional criminology' through the nineteenth century and into the twentieth century. It also pointed to those dissenting or critical voices in criminology which have identified a range of problems with conventional criminology. It does not lessen their value that these dissenting traditions have, by and large, not persuaded the majority of criminologists to abandon the conventional definition of either the problems or the various theoretical approaches or research models favoured by mainstream criminologists.

In the rest of the book we give extra depth and detail by focusing on contemporary criminology and how criminologists think about crime. We do this both *thematically* and *analytically*.

We begin (Chapter 5) by arguing that we need to look analytically and critically at criminology by treating it as a body of knowledge or arguments. We do not assume that all readers of this book are already equipped to approach the issues analytically and critically, and we offer them guidance on how this is to be done. We show how it is possible to develop analytical and critical capacities by reading actively. By reading actively we can develop deeper insights into what is being said as well as form a view about its credibility. This means we can assess the strengths and weaknesses of the various theoretical perspectives brought to bear on these problems. In the chapters that follow we stress the role played by a number of key assumptions in shaping criminological ideas and research on a range of key issues and problems.

We do not pretend that this is an exhaustive treatment of all the research or all the issues which modern criminology addresses. As has already been suggested this book does not try to cover all the standard themes in criminology, like policing practices or prison systems or specific kinds of crime like homicide or property crime. The issues that we address can, however, make some claim to being important, as well as offering some insight into how contemporary criminology works. They also serve to reveal something of the underlying assumptions and arguments that characterize mainstream modern criminology in a time of constant change.

We have selected six themes or issues. In Chapters 6 and 7 we discuss some of the ways criminologists try to explain crime. Chapter 6 outlines the ways criminologists explain relatively minor yet persistent kinds of crimes like theft and burglary in terms of unemployment and poverty – what is more often now called 'social exclusion'. This is a long-standing preoccupation in criminology. In Chapter 7 we consider another traditional approach to explaining crime. Criminologists have long argued that the conditions of family life, ranging from family size to 'dysfunctional' family relationships or 'broken' families, play a key role in producing criminals or criminal behaviour.

Chapters 8 and 9 look at two kinds of policy ideas that have proved popular in attempting to prevent crime. In Chapter 8 we explore the current interest in crime prevention in many Western societies. We outline some of the reasons that might explain the interest governments, acting on the advice of criminologists, have displayed in developing crime-prevention strategies. In Chapter 9 we explore the relatively recent prominence given to the role of victims of crime in shaping such things as sentencing policies and practices on the part of courts. In each case we identify some of the sustaining assumptions that operate in the development of these criminal justice policies. As we indicate, there are important political as well as theoretical issues at stake here.

Then, in Chapters 10 and 11 we look at two kinds of crimes which play an ambivalent role in criminology. We suggest that 'white-collar', or corporate, crime has long had an uncertain status in mainstream criminology. In Chapter 11 we address the problem of 'state crime'. It is a problem because criminologists, like some other social scientists, notably sociologists, have tended to bypass the subject altogether. In both cases we think that this ambivalence or silence is suggestive of certain intellectual problems which have long dogged mainstream criminology.

Finally in a short conclusion ('Towards a reflexive criminology') we highlight some of the perennial problems that dog conventional criminology and discuss the possibility that a more thoughtful kind of criminology might evolve.

A SHORT GUIDE TO READING AND THINKING ABOUT CRIMINOLOGY

What all criminologists do is to undertake research that enables them to make claims that certain states of affairs obtain. This research is typically published in various books, research articles or reports. It is designed to persuade any reader that what he or she reads can be believed. People who are encountering criminology for the first time need to be able to read and think effectively about what they are reading. They need to pay attention to the techniques of persuasion being used. How is this to be done? We offer here a very simple but robust approach to reading actively by directing attention to some of the key elements found in criminological arguments.

When we use the word 'argument' here we could just as well have used the word 'knowledge'. This is because the 'knowledge' found in books, reports and research articles in social sciences like criminology or sociology is typically presented in the form of 'arguments'. In saying this we acknowledge the later work of Ludwig Wittgenstein (1953) and of one of his protégés, Stephen Toulmin (1961), who provided an incisive account of the way people develop the 'stuff' that makes up knowledge.

For Toulmin (1961), an 'argument' is a structure – or perhaps 'grammar' is the better word – of elements that make up 'knowledge'. An argument relies on a number of elements designed to convey a belief or claim about the ways things are, and to do so in a way that persuades other persons that these propositions are credible, or can be believed. In this regard what we offer here is an introduction to the rhetoric of criminology.

People frequently misuse the idea of *rhetoric* as if it involves some kind of trickery or else think it can be used as a term of abuse, such as when people say: 'Oh, that's all rhetoric.' Properly understood, 'rhetoric' refers to the ways writers set out to persuade people of what they have to say and the use they make of things like mathematics, statistics, logic, images and, of course, language.

We suggest that people new to a discipline like criminology can get a good grasp of what is going on by paying attention to certain key elements in the reading they do. In what follows we begin with a simple analytic framework for thinking carefully and critically about the *arguments* of criminologists. An analytical approach identifies the key parts of any such argument.

Thinking carefully about criminology can be assisted by asking how well each of these elements work together. Thinking about criminology involves paying attention to the structure of any argument as well as the way each writer uses language. We pay particular attention to the role of metaphors in thinking. As writers like Lakoff and Johnson (2003) have shown, metaphors are fundamental to the way we think about the world. We briefly outline some of the ways metaphors work.

On arguments

Let us begin with an example of a short criminological argument. It is adapted from a recent Australian current affairs TV show whose host was interviewing a crime expert. The dialogue went something like this:

> *Interviewer*: So should Australians be concerned about crime?
> *Expert*: No, I don't think so. The rate of serious crime is trending downwards.
> *Interviewer*: Oh really?
> *Expert*: Yes, the work I have done on NSW police reports shows that the NSW homicide rate for the last year was down by 5 per cent on homicide figures over the past three years, reported sexual assault offences had tumbled by 13 per cent over the same period and armed robbery was seriously down. The only increase was in car theft, which had increased slightly, by 3 per cent.
> *Interviewer*: So recent press headlines about a crime wave in Sydney shouldn't be taken too seriously?
> *Expert*: That's right.

Though it may seem like an oversimplification, here in embryo are all the elements of any kind of argument mounted in criminology. There are only four central elements in any argument that matter.

First, there is the *question* (or *questions*): *Should Australians be worried about crime?* Questions provide the motivation for thinking about the world or for researching some issue. They also guide us towards the answers and the evidence we might look for. Second, there is the main *claim* (or *claims*) which answers that question: *Australians don't need to worry about the crime rate because it is declining.* Third, in everything from discussions in pubs to the most sophisticated research papers or books, it is expected that we offer either reasons or evidence for the claims we make. In a social science like criminology it is certainly expected that the writer presents some relevant *evidence* or *reasons* to sustain or support the main claim/s. *Here the evidence presented is in the form of crime rate statistics like homicide rates over a number of years.* Finally and most crucially we will find that there are certain *assumptions* being made which underpin each of these elements. Assumptions are just that: they are things presumed often without being spelt out. Here there are a number of assumptions, including the following:

- it is possible to establish why there is public anxiety about crime;
- public fear of crime is linked to movements in the crime rate;
- crime rate statistics reflect the actual offences committed;
- any reduction in crime rate statistics ought to lead to a lessening of public anxiety; and
- fear is a rational response to evidence.

As we argue below, assumptions are the single most important part of any argument – and the trickiest to deal with because mostly they are invisible.

All of the elements of this very simple argument, namely question/s, claim/s, evidence and assumptions, provide the analytical structure of the far more complex arguments criminologists develop in research articles and whole books. What criminologists do when they do criminology is ask certain *questions* and make particular *claims*, using certain kinds of *evidence*, while relying on certain *assumptions* to do all of these things.

Because we rely on this analytical framework in Chapters 6 to 11, we need to say a little more about the elements that constitute an argument. We also make some suggestions about how we can use this analytical framework to think about the arguments that make up criminological knowledge. To make the value of this framework very clear we suggest that active reading begins by using a framework like this with every piece of work that readers encounter.

Questions

Leaving aside arguments in pubs (or bars) and over dinner tables, academic research is always driven by explicit questions which are called 'research questions'. (Even everyday arguments rely on implicit questions. Many a discussion about a political election begins with a question like, 'Who will win?')

In reading the work of academic writers it is vital that the reader both identifies and understands the question a writer is addressing, because this may in part indicate why different writers are disagreeing – different questions elicit different answers. The reader also needs to be in a position to assess whether the question has been answered or how well it has been answered. Understanding the question is central to assessing the value and credibility of an author's argument.

In most academic writing, the research question is spelt out in the introduction to the article or book. Such questions tend to combine mixtures of words like 'what', 'why', 'how' and 'where', while some more sophisticated pieces of research and writing may ask 'how can we compare . . .?'

It is important to pay attention to the questions being asked, because different disciplines ask different questions. Most criminologists tend to ask certain kinds of questions, before they then get into debates about how best to answer those questions.

Among the key questions criminologists ask are:

- What is crime?
- How do we explain crime?
- How do we know crime and how do we measure it?
- Who commits crimes and who are the victims?
- What can we do to deal with crime, what can we do to deal with those who do it and with those who suffer from it?

In thinking carefully and critically we can observe that not all questions are equal. There are *good* questions and *bad* questions. An example of a bad question is: 'Why is the moon made of green cheese?' Asking this question involves a logical fallacy called 'begging the question'. This fallacy involves relying on a wrong assumption when framing the question. This is not wise. (A better question would be, 'What is the moon made of?') Even so it is not possible to avoid making assumptions when framing the question.

As lawyers in a courtroom understand, no question is ever innocent. All questions rely on prior assumptions. That is, asking a question presupposes certain prior knowledge or beliefs. Every question relies on a raft of assumptions including fundamentals like

- the question is answerable;
- the writer's own theoretical premises are sound (we will say more about this when we talk about assumptions).

Claims

In most scholarly writings authors make it clear, usually in the introduction and in the conclusion to their work, what their main claim, or their answer to the question, is. This is also referred to as the writer's 'thesis'. The idea of 'claim' here refers to the main idea or point that the writer wants the reader to accept. In any large-scale and complex piece of writing or research the main claim can be a very large and complicated structure of ideas and propositions.

In being thoughtful about an argument we need to evaluate the claims being made. For example, we should ask how well an author has answered his or her research question. We also make other judgements like how much it addresses an urgent or pressing practical or ethical issue, or how much it illuminates a previously not-clearly-understood part of the human or natural world, or the extent to which it stands previous ideas on their heads.

Like questions, claims depend on an array of unstated assumptions. For instance, in any piece of research based on evidence collected in an experimental laboratory setting, the credibility of the claim depends on the assumption that the results of the research can be reliably extrapolated into other social settings. Thus, there are many examples of research carried out in psychology laboratories on the effects of televised film and cartoon violence on young children's disposition to emulate the violence they saw. How good is the assumption that the evidence collected in a laboratory is applicable to what happens in a family's living-room?

Evidence

All of the modern social sciences appeal to evidence. Like their colleagues in the other social science disciplines, criminologists collect, discover or use certain kinds of evidence to support their arguments. For this reason disciplines like economics, sociology, psychology and criminology are treated as *empirical* enterprises. (By contrast other disciplines like mathematics or some kinds of philosophy work by using forms of deductive or axiomatic reasoning.) Leaving aside temporarily some important conceptual issues about what is meant by 'empirical', it is plain that the credibility and value of the social sciences rests on the belief that they tell us things that are *real* or are discoverable *in reality* because of the evidence they have assembled.

If social sciences' arguments are to have any credibility it will depend on the author of the argument appealing to something she or he regards as evidence. In social sciences like criminology, the failure to supply evidence is rightly seen as a fatal weakness. Equally a lot of critical attention is paid to the relevance and quantity of the evidence as well as to the ways it was collected. As we will see, different kinds of criminologists collect different kinds of evidence. For some *crime statistics* are vitally important, while for others it may be evidence collected as participant observers or in psychology laboratories.

For some criminologists it is also important that the evidence can be gathered in the same way time and time again, the idea being that reliablility is guaranteed by repeating the process of gathering information. Without completely discounting the importance of good and relevant evidence, sometimes this concern results in the author overlooking the point about the nature and validity of the assumptions being relied on at each step of the argument.

There are a number of important things to note about what counts as evidence.

Firstly, different social science disciplines look for or accept different things as evidence. For example:

- In literary studies, scholars generally pay a great deal of attention to the words and language used in novels, plays or poetry when they make claims about 'what Shakespeare really meant when he said . . .'.
- Some psychologists rely on information gleaned from carefully designed and managed experiments run in specialized laboratories or from the use of 'instruments' like Aggression or Impulsivity Scales.
- In some areas of sociology a great deal of emphasis is placed on large-scale surveys which use questionnaires administered to large numbers of people which are then processed statistically using various tests of significance.

Since criminology relies on a number of disciplines, this means that criminologists draw on a range of diverse evidence.

However, just to complicate things, within any given discipline there are usually alternative ideas (and practices) to the mainstream view about what good evidence looks like or how it is obtained. For example, some sociologists believe ethnographic or participant observation research is far better than large-scale sample surveys.

Thirdly, there is a more general point. We live in a world which offers a vast, even overwhelming, amount of potential information. Somehow we need to select the evidence which is most relevant.

In regard to each of these three points, assumptions play a major role, by shaping the questions we ask, by making claims and by helping us work out what kinds of evidence we can discover, invent or use.

Assumptions

What we are calling assumptions are the most crucial part of any argument. An assumption is what you have to presuppose to be the case in order to proceed to ask a question or to select certain kinds of evidence. They help to define our questions, shape our claims and select our evidence. They are what we referred to in Chapter 2 as 'themata' (Holton 1988) or 'prejudices' (Gadamer 1994), and they are what are needed to do any kind of science or any kind of thinking. They make up the basic 'constructive schemes' (Bohme 1975) or patterned ways of thinking which Foucault (1980) called 'discourses'.

The problem with assumptions, however, is that they are just that, assumptions. A defining feature of any assumption is that they are rarely, if ever, spelt out. Therefore establishing what assumptions are operating in a given piece of scholarship is not always easy. Assumptions are often found in the white spaces between the words and by what is not said as much as by what is said. They are quite elusive and have to be inferred or 'thought out' rather than identified by reading them.

How do we identify the assumptions that are working in any particular argument? One way is to look at the sequence of elements within a given piece of research or writing and to ask what the author had to assume when she or he asked the question, or selected or 'discovered' the evidence. We can generally identify the assumptions being made by asking some simple questions. What kind of question is being asked and/or what kind of answer is being looked for? For example, is the question descriptive, predictive, taxonomic, analytical, interpretive, explanatory or evaluative? What assumptions have to be made by the author in determining the kinds of relevant evidence that need to be to used or discovered? In turn, what assumptions does the author need to make about the central aspects and concepts representing the reality which she wishes to write about or to discover in order to first select the kinds of stuff that will work as evidence? What kinds of assumptions will need to be relied on to warrant the linkage of the evidence to the basic claims being made?

Asking these questions will, by and large, help in the identification of the core assumptions that, as it were, hold an argument together. Once this has been done it becomes possible to think about the assumptions being made and so assess the general value or credibility of the argument. If an argument is relying on credible assumptions, it is likely to be a better argument than one that does not.

Apart from working out from the grammar of the argument what the assumptions are, it often helps to identify the vocabulary being used. This is because we tend to package up our beliefs about the world. Some key words mark out particular kinds of belief systems and so provide clues to the fundamental assumptions being made. Christians, for example, use words like 'grace' and 'sin'. Feminists emphasize the role of 'patriarchy' and 'sex role socialization', while economic liberals talk about 'the market' and 'market forces'. Even the doing of research relies on belief systems. For example, researchers reliant on empiricist and/or positivist assumptions will talk about 'co-variance', 'variables', 'representative samples' or the 'operationalization' of concepts, while social constructionists will talk about 'symbolic systems' or 'discursive practices'. Over time practised readers become adept at detecting these linguistic markers associated with particular belief systems.

What we mean, then, by 'assumptions' is a polyglot assembly of beliefs sometimes grouped into what are referred to variously as 'theories', 'paradigms', 'ideologies' and 'belief systems'.

Though we do not have the time to argue out the case here, we assume that no one, and certainly not criminologists, ever comes to think or do research by just looking at *the facts*. People generally rely on their assumptions to live and work – and to do research – and do not usually like having to examine what are often fundamental and cherished beliefs. These beliefs form part of their basic identity. In this way criminologists, like the rest of us, come with already formed theories and beliefs with which they will do the kind of criminology they do. This possibly explains why controversies between different kinds of criminology can never be adjudicated by appeals to evidence, just as we cannot expect a debate about abortion between a conservative Catholic and a secular liberal to be resolved by appeals to evidence. Someone who is a Marxist for example will rely on different beliefs or assumptions from someone who is a Christian or a feminist.

Broadly speaking, there are three kinds of beliefs that inform the arguments we construct.

1   Most of us have beliefs about the fundamental nature of reality that can then become assumptions inside a particular argument. These 'ontological' beliefs may include the Christian idea that all aspects of reality are God-made and therefore reality is both orderly and spiritual. Alternatively people may hold to an existentialist belief that no one made the universe, which just happened in a single 'Big Bang'.

2   We hold beliefs about the nature of good and evil and whether humans can or should live good lives and how they should do this. These are political and ethical theories which address questions about how to achieve justice or the good life.

3   Finally we also hold to 'epistemological' or 'methodological' beliefs to do with how we know anything about the world. Some of us will appeal to faith, others will appeal to reason or rationality, while others prefer to stick to the facts. In the social sciences these beliefs provide some of the basic issues about which endless controversy swirls. This is where the idea of theory comes into play.

'Theory' in criminology

Though some will grumble about it, most criminologists accept that modern criminology is a very diverse discipline. People often use the word 'theory' to describe this diversity. But what does this word mean? In part it means precisely what we have been talking about in terms of 'assumptions'. The authors of most modern criminology textbooks observe, for example, that criminology is made up of numerous and competing theories, like:

■   control theory (Hirschi 1969);
■   differential association theory (Sutherland and Cressey 1978);
■   labelling and symbolic interactionist theory (Becker 1963); and
■   functionalist and neo-Marxist subculture theories (Cohen 1974; White 1989).

They will also point to the impact of 'social theories' like structural functionalism, Marxism, feminism or labelling theory on criminology or point to the role played by psychological theories like psychoanalysis or neo-behaviourism. One of the great books of the 1990s, by David Garland (1990), is an attempt to systematically compare the work of different theorists from Durkheim to Foucault to develop what he calls a 'social theory of punishment'. As Garland (1990: 286) argues, 'each of the different traditions of social theory provides a specific set of tools in the form of a specially adapted conceptual vocabulary designed to explicate a particular aspect or dimension of social life . . . each of these interpretative vocabularies has its use in understanding punishment'. Yet, it is interesting that nowhere does Garland, like so many writers, spell out what he means by the idea of theory!

While academics esteem 'theory' quite highly, they also use the concept in ways that are not always clear or simple. So what does 'theory' mean? There is no simple answer because 'theory' has at least five quite different meanings. We need to be able to identify and respect the differences in the ways 'theory' is used.

In the first sense of the word, 'theory' refers to a statement advancing an explanation or prediction. When academics do this they typically draw on what are said to be the practices and assumptions of natural sciences like physics. In a natural science like physics, 'theory' refers to quite tightly defined generalizations (or 'laws') having explanatory and/or predictive capacity. This approach is often seen as a key feature of what is defined as the 'positivist' approach to constructing a *proper* social science. This is broadly the sense writers like Gottfredson and Hirschi (1990) are relying on when they use the word 'theory'. Theory here refers to a pattern of knowledge-claims said to be *inductive* and based on the collection of a lot of data, or facts. According to an influential account by Carl Hempel (1965), this produces a 'covering law' statement which takes the form: 'When facts A and B occur, then by virtue of covering law X, the consequence C must follow.' This whole statement becomes a *theory*, said to be capable both of explaining and predicting the events of the world.

In the second sense of the word, 'theory' is defined as any statement that interprets some aspect of social reality or human behaviour. This idea of 'theory' belongs to a different tradition from the idea of theory as a scientific law found in the natural sciences. People who belong to this interpretive tradition say that explanations and predictions may work quite well with chemicals or rocks, but do not work too well with human beings because of the capacity of humans to act according to their desires and feelings, or their moral, religious or political beliefs. Karl Popper (1974) even suggested that the very fact that people know that a scientific prediction has been made about them may lead them to change their behaviours and so thwart anyone trying to predict what they will do. This second sense of 'theory' implies that we need to understand people's feelings, beliefs and desires, and that we will best do this by interpreting other people's behaviour and actions by *understanding* their feelings, beliefs and knowledge.

In this tradition writers like Max Weber and Peter Winch have stressed the value of asking people to give accounts of their motives, reasons or beliefs in performing some act. Winch (1958) argues that to describe the motives or reasons of people is to grasp their meaning and this permits us to *theorize*, or understand, why people do what they do. (Weber thought this made a *causal* account of human action possible: Winch did not agree.) This points to some large disagreements between people working inside this tradition. This way of thinking about 'theory' belongs to a tradition of 'interpretative' social science.

Behind the positivist and the interpretive approaches to 'theory' lurk some really large assumptions and debates about the nature of human knowledge and even the nature of reality itself. These assumptions and debates in turn inform arguments about how best to do social science or criminology.

The history of criminology can in part be written as a history of how these two perspectives about how best to do social science help to shape the way criminologists do criminology. Much of our later discussion will draw attention to these differences. Yet there are another three ways in which people use the word 'theory'.

A third way in which 'theory' is used refers to what are called meta-narratives and interpretive traditions which offer large-scale understandings and explanations of human behaviour or social development. Examples include traditions like 'Marxism', 'liberalism', 'socialism', 'psychoanalysis' or 'feminism'. These narratives offer to make sense of events – and possibly even to transform social reality. Some feminists might, for example, explain why women's wages are on average less than those paid to men 'because employers tend to be men living in a patriarchal society'. Here 'theory' refers to an interpretive scheme relying on concepts like *class* or *gender* which are then used to name actors and explain actions on the basis of some large assumption, such as that (patriarchal) 'structure' determines 'action'. The point of this kind of theory is to produce a whole way of seeing the world, which is why they are sometimes referred to as 'worldviews'. It often seems that these large interpretive schemes are resistant to criticism or to *facts* brought in from other frameworks. One important question here is whether it is possible to have facts that do not belong to some larger interpretive or theoretical framework.

In a fourth sense, 'theory' can refer to what look like guides to action or practice in the way a recipe informs the practice of baking a cake. There are numerous books that outline how to be effectual parents, managers or social workers, and which are used to inform workshops used to train parents and professionals of various kinds. In this sense 'theory' is understood as a reflection or representation of some practice which is now re-presented as a set of components and ways of ordering the components so as to guide or produce good practice. In this sense, what we are doing in this chapter is offering a *theory* of reading.

Finally 'theory' can also be used pejoratively to mean idle, silly or impractical speculation. This is the sense in which one person may say dismissively to another: 'You are just a theorist.' Here 'theory' refers to ideas which in the eyes of the critic engage a variety of invalid arguments, irrational beliefs or prejudices, and it is mostly used by people who see themselves as better qualified by their experience or practice than the theorist. This meaning of 'theory' raises some legitimate questions about the kinds of ideas that academics generate and their value to practitioners.

In short, 'theory' refers to different kinds of intellectual activities. To summarize: 'theory' can refer to:

- any statement claiming predictive or explanatory value;
- any interpretive statement in which the theorist is interested in issues of meaning (Turner 1990: 7–8);
- traditions of ideas (or what are called 'meta-narratives'), like Marxism, feminism, psychoanalysis, or liberalism, which offer large-scale understandings and explanations of human behaviour or social and historical development;
- recipes for action or practice, in much the same way that a recipe helps us to bake a cake;
- an individual, in a dismissive way, as 'just a theorist' or as impractical.

Why this matters

We need to be able to identify and respect these differences. We need, in particular, to be able to identify and be thoughtful about the way these different approaches to theory-making inform the assumptions that particular writers, and the larger traditions to which they belong, are using or relying on.

Paying attention to the role of our theoretical frameworks and of our assumptions is central to the ability to be thoughtful about the claims made by criminologists – or anyone else. We go so far as to suggest that the essential issue about most arguments is not the quality of the evidence *per se* or what methods were used to get the evidence so much as the assumptions being relied on. We may be well advised to focus on testing the value of the assumptions being relied on rather than engage in a forensic testing of the evidence *per se*.

That is, we can normally grant that the *facts* or evidence adduced in favour of a claim are as they are – *true* or accurate accounts of a state of affairs, or else are the result of normally diligent methods of getting some evidence together. This, however, does not necessarily make the argument all that credible.

Assumptions and the theories they help to make up are important because they help select the information or things to be used as evidence, and then they are used to help make links between specific kinds of evidence and the claim. Like everyone else criminologists rely on assumptions to frame their questions and select their evidence.

It is vital that we are able to identify the assumptions being made or relied on, for several reasons. Thinking critically about the assumptions will encourage and produce a better and more robust identification of all of the problems – or the strengths – of a given 'argument' advanced in a research project or article.

Because assumptions are rarely spelled out, discerning the assumptions being made has the effect of encouraging a greater than usual level of attention to the formal elements and design of the argument. Having identified the assumptions, it then becomes possible to assess the value and robustness of the design and especially of the assumptions. That is, we can ask how credible or reliable are the assumptions being used to select out or to call up or constitute the data/evidence in the first place. Establishing the credibility of the assumptions used to warrant the advancing of the evidence can assist us in testing the extent to which the evidence actually supports the proposition.

We will demonstrate the value of this approach to reading criminology in the following chapters by applying this analytical framework to some of the ways that criminologists do criminology.

There is one other very basic observation to make about what criminologists do. All of the thinking they do relies on the devices that make up any human language. One of the fundamental devices, some have said that it is *the* fundamental device, of language is metaphor. Because we 'swim' as it were in a 'sea of language', and this is definitely a metaphor, we may not notice the effect this has on the way we think.

On thinking and metaphors

Since Perelman and Olbrecchts-Tyteca's 1969 breakthrough text, there has been a revival of interest in the rhetoric of both the social sciences and the natural sciences. By 'rhetoric' we mean both the techniques people use to make their claim to know something credible as well as the study of those techniques. The study of rhetoric involves understanding how we try to be persuasive (McCloskey 1998: 185–6). We engage in rhetoric any time we set out to persuade others of something we believe to be true. Rhetoric addresses the problem of knowledge. I may know that I have just seen a UFO or that '$E = mc^2$', but how do I persuade you?

As McCloskey (1998) has argued, we rely on a number of rhetorical techniques to secure all of our knowledge-claims. Those techniques include appealing to evidence, or *facts*, using various forms of logic and tests of validity, the construction and use of narratives, and the use of metaphors. The skilful use of each of these four elements constitutes a 'framework of authority' which all writers use when endeavouring to convince an audience. To accept the value of focusing on the techniques of persuasion that a study of rhetoric entails, among other things, refusing to accept that there is only one 'royal road' to credible knowledge. This means refusing to accept positivist claims that statistical tests, for example, exclusively provide the only secure grounds for true knowledge. It means also rejecting those interpretivist claims that secure knowledge is gained only by mastery of hermeneutical and symbolic techniques.

Why we need to be interested in rhetoric is crisply summed up by Nelson, Megill and McCloskey (1991: 3) when they write: 'Scholarship uses argument, and argument uses rhetoric. The rhetoric is not mere ornament or manipulation or trickery. It is rhetoric in the ancient sense of persuasive discourse.' As they (ibid.: ix) argue:

> Rhetoric of inquiry turns away from modernism and foundationalism in the philosophy of science. It rejects the notion that there can be a single autonomous set of rules for inquiry – rules standing apart from actual practices. It appreciates the importance of rhetoric – the quality of speaking and writing, the interplay of media and messages, the judgement of evidence and arguments . . . It seeks merely to increase self-reflection in every inquiry.

One of the central elements in this turn to rhetoric has been a recognition of the central role played by metaphors both as a normal part of language use and, therefore, of all thinking.

As George Lakoff and Mark Johnson have demonstrated, we literally could not think or act without metaphors. Human thought processes are largely metaphorical. As they (2003: 3) note:

> Metaphor is pervasive in everyday life, not just in language but in thought and action. Our ordinary conceptual system in terms of which we both think and act is fundamentally metaphorical in nature . . . Our concepts structure what we perceive, how we get around in the world and how we relate to other people.

As one illustration of this, they point to the way we think about *arguments as war* in terms of a whole series of ordinary phrases:

1   Your claims are *indefensible.*
2   He *attacked every weak point* in my argument.
3   His criticisms were *right on target.*
4   I *demolished* his argument.
5   I've never *won* an argument with him.
6   You disagree? Okay, *shoot*!
7   He *shot down* all my arguments.

They (ibid.: 4) go on to say:

> We can actually win or lose arguments. We see the person we are arguing with as an opponent. We attack his positions and defend our own. We gain and lose ground . . . Many of the things we do in arguing are partially structured by the concept of war.

To fail to acknowledge the way we think metaphorically is to fail to understand a great deal.

As the metaphor of *argument as war* indicates, the essence of a metaphor is understanding and experiencing one kind of thing in terms of another. It involves a translation of meaning from one place or thing to another. (Think of the change if we dropped the metaphor of argument as war and thought of *argument as a dance*.) Metaphor involves a process of transferring or carrying over meaning by making an association between two apparently unrelated areas or objects that the metaphor now somehow connects.

Metaphors abound in social sciences like criminology. They are at work when criminologists talk about the causal link between delinquency and the 'broken family' (Wells and Rankin 1986, 1991). The metaphor ('broken') turns something literal, namely a group of people comprising a marriage or a family, into something figurative, namely 'a mechanism' like a dishwasher that is 'broken'. It may well also imply that there are expert 'technicians' who can go in and fix the 'broken family'. There is a metaphor at work, too, when criminologists talk about an 'alienated stratum of young people'. There are two metaphors at work here, namely the idea of 'alienated' – as in estranged or alien – and 'stratum', a geological idea suggesting a hard and durable layer of rock underground or hidden from sight. This metaphor applies a meaning that converts the highly visible, colourful and energetic *presence* that characterizes most young people into a separate, distinct and problematic layer of hardened young people who are strangers to the rest of us.

Metaphor is critical to our understanding of the outside world and the objects of criminological research like 'criminals', 'broken families' and 'delinquents'.

Metaphors play a huge variety of intellectual, emotional, creative and illustrative functions. They allow us to understand and imagine things in ways a *literal* description does not. For example, criminologists might refer to an 'epidemic of crime'. Using a medical metaphor like 'epidemic' constructs and shapes people's understanding in terms of something that is 'infectious' or highly 'contagious'. For example, it implies that healthy normal people could 'catch it' if they associated with or came too close to certain other groups of people. Understood as an 'epidemic', delinquency or crime is clearly dangerous, a threat to 'community health' and in urgent need of treatment if the infection isn't to become widespread. As in medical contexts, the use of the term in relation to societal issues also implies that there are 'experts' who can 'treat' the problem with appropriate technical solutions. As Nikolaus Rose (1990: 123) has observed, talking in this way has a lot to do with the way certain acts 'come to symbolise a range of social anxieties, the decline of morality and social discipline, and the need to take steps in order to prevent a downward spiral into disorder.' There are, moreover, different kinds of metaphors or, to put this differently, there are different uses to which metaphors can be put.

Metaphors operate at the most basic conceptual level. They make thought itself possible by constituting an order of things. Constitutive metaphors help set up basic conceptual systems that we then use to define, explain and know the world. Metaphors used constitutively involve very big and very basic concepts such as *society*, *God the Father* and *culture*. For example, from the perspective of functionalist sociology, *deviance* or *delinquency* is explained by reference to a particular constitutive metaphor of *society* as organic, a 'living system'. The use of figurative terms borrowed from nineteenth-century natural sciences characterized social relations in terms of something called 'society' as an organic assemblage somewhat like a biological or botanical system such that to speak of a person as a 'member' of a society drew explicitly on biological/physiological ideas. (Recall here that arms and legs are biologically speaking 'members'.) The biological metaphor of 'society' has framed the way some sociologists have thought and in this way it has helped establish the basic discursive practices of sociology and criminology. These two social sciences have made heavy use of ideas like *structure*, *function* and *social pathology*. From this basic metaphor other subsidiary metaphors emerge referring to notions of *social order*. It means that analogies can be made between the proper functions of parts of the body deemed necessary for a healthy life and the proper roles of people and institutions for social well-being – hence socialisation theory. Those individuals who do not *internalize* their appropriate social role are identified as maladjusted and as such they jeopardize social order (Klamer and Leonard 1994: 20–50). This is a very powerful and seductive metaphorical system because it makes what it is difficult to understand, like the conduct of particular people, intelligible, and once we have that metaphor in place it is extremely difficult to change it.

Metaphors are often used in teaching or for describing and clarifying strange or unfamiliar phenomena. In this way metaphors work pedagogically to solve the basic problem of how we can move from what we know to what we don't know. Pedagogic metaphors *build a bridge* between what people already know and what they don't know. Talking about 'feral adolescents', a 'lost generation' or 'casualties of change' is to use pedagogical metaphors. 'Feral' suggests a wild, unsocialized and dangerous being. It conjures up an image of dishevelled, long-haired, young people living in make-shift tepees deep in some rainforest who are committed to radical ecological politics. A metaphor like 'lost generation' has been used to talk about youth unemployment. It delivers a powerful message about young people as both victims and threats. A comparable metaphor is youth as 'casualties of change'. This metaphor is used to suggest that young people bear the brunt of major socio-economic change. They are simultaneously victims who deserve our understanding, sympathy and support; and they are threats as lost or as casualties. As such they are 'not integrated into society' and run the risk of becoming disaffected and so can pose a threat to 'social order'.

The heuristic use of metaphors offers another powerful illustration of their role. Used heuristically they evoke comparisons and point up resemblances between things, and help show us how we can think and talk about an observed phenomenon in terms that are already familiar to us. As Klamer and Leonard (1994: 112) observe, our heuristic use of metaphors proceeds 'by taking a fertile metaphor and relentlessly articulating the nature of its subsidiary domains, probing the properties of that terrain, and testing the connections . . .'. Ideas like 'lifecycle', 'culture' and 'subculture' are good examples of the fertility of heuristic metaphors in fields like youth studies and criminology.

An heuristic metaphor helps begin an inquiry. Classic examples of such metaphors in criminological research and deviance theory include 'life-cycle' or 'life-stage' models. The 'life-cycle' metaphor, for example, allows us to not only explain, but to extend our inquiry, to develop models, to describe in greater detail what is happening. (Such models, it might be added, also operate as useful pedagogical metaphors.) Classical notions of adolescence as a 'precarious', troubled and troublesome phase (Stanley-Hall 1904; Coleman 1961) in the transition of the 'life-cycle stages' from childhood to adulthood invite us to treat those to whom that category is to be applied as passing through a distinct and unique stage. Life-cycle metaphors borrow from the natural and biological sciences, enabling us to treat adolescence as a temporary status with specific cognitive, emotional and intellectual features. They include the very idea of adolescence as a 'transitionary' and typically troubled phase of 'storm and stress'. The heuristic power of such metaphors enables us to organize our thinking about particular aspects of young people and our relationships with them.

The very term 'subculture' can be used heuristically because it establishes a relationship between the collective activities of particular young people and the wider 'mainstream' culture. As 'subcultures', they are described by some as 'resistant' to the 'dominant hegemonic culture', as Hall and Jefferson (1976) did. Members of the Birmingham CCCS in the 1970s and 1980s operated with a neo-Marxist understanding of subculture that positioned working-class young people in symbolic struggles against social order and assumed a clash between class and generation.

An heuristic metaphor can be expanded by relentlessly articulating the nature of its subsidiary domains. Adolescence as a period of 'storm and stress' constructs 'the adolescent' as turbulent, unpredictable, hurricane-like, susceptible to fits of rage and full of anxiety, angst, trepidation and apprehension. Such a metaphor suggests a danger and threat. It invites us to imagine 'the adolescent' as in need of careful monitoring and governance as they tread the uncertain and rickety 'path' to responsible adulthood.

Deviating from the path of adjustment has been central to deviance theory, and depending on how far they deviate from the norm there is the risk of becoming 'dysfunctional', delinquent or even criminal. In such instances we tend to hear warnings of 'anomie' (i.e. to be without anchor), alienation and 'youth on the margins' as opposed to being in the 'mainstream'.

There is real value in paying careful attention to the use of metaphor in criminological theory and research. A central feature of this research has been the use of metaphor to perform a variety of illustrative, framing and cognitive functions, helping us to understand *crime*, *deviance* and *criminals*. Each of the traditions that we have identified at work in criminology relies on and uses different kinds of metaphors in ways that matter deeply. When structural functionalists use words like 'structure' or 'social forces' they are using metaphors, because these words are not literally descriptive. Likewise when symbolic interactionists use terms like 'social actor', 'moral panic' or 'social script' they are relying on metaphors. Understanding the cognitive role and function of metaphors and showing how specific metaphors constitute the objects of research and theory becomes a very important source of deep insight.

Some may argue that displaying an interest in metaphor is pointless and *unscientific* because such an interest belongs more to domains like literature and poetry and has little if anything to offer in the way of practical, real or scientific insights. To such criticism we can make a simple response. Criminological research and theory as we know it would not be possible without the use of metaphor. All researchers use particular metaphors in their daily work. Metaphor silently but powerfully informs the thinking of researchers and theorists, usually without there being any awareness of the metaphors being used, their capabilities or their traps.

Conclusion

In this chapter we have presented a simple approach to reading and thinking about the work of criminologists. We have done so because we think that such central activities as reading and thinking need to be done with some kind of method in mind. We have offered a basic but robust approach to reading actively by directing attention to some of the key elements found in any academic writing. By reading actively and looking for these elements readers can develop a sharper insight into what is being said as well as forming a view about its credibility. We then briefly outlined the key role played by metaphors in shaping the way criminologists think about the world.

In the following chapters we begin to apply this analytical framework to some of the themes conventional criminology addresses, a process which serves to introduce the discipline of criminology.

Review questions

What are the key elements of arguments?

What role do assumptions play in criminological arguments and research?

What are some of the key ways in which the idea of *theory* is used?

Why does metaphor matter?

Further reading

Lakoff, G. and Johnson, M., 2003, *Metaphors We Live By* (2nd edition), University of Chicago Press, Chicago, IL.

Nelson, J., Megill, A. and McCloskey, D. (eds), 1991, *The Rhetoric of the Human Sciences*, University of Wisconsin Press, Madison, WI.

Perelman, C. and Olbrecchts-Tyteca, M., 1969, *The New Rhetoric*, D. Reidel, Dordrecht.

EXPLAINING CRIME: UNEMPLOYMENT AND CRIME

The decades since the mid-1970s have seen sweeping social, economic and political changes in most Western societies. Whole industries and occupations have disappeared as a mixture of 'free-market' reforms, new global production and distribution strategies, and information technologies like the Internet have transformed the workplace and the home. In countries like the UK, the USA, Canada, Australia and much of Europe, these changes have been accompanied by entrenched long-term unemployment, wage cuts, increasingly insecure employment and underemployment, and mounting evidence of socio-economic inequality. Many writers (Robertson 1992; Castells 1998; Giddens 1999) have found it convenient to use the idea of *globalization* to describe or explain these changes.

It is perhaps not surprising, against such a backdrop, that some criminologists and sociologists have pointed to these kinds of changes and used them to explain contemporary crime. In the 1980s US writers like William Julius Wilson (1987) began to talk about an 'underclass' of permanently unemployed, poor and largely black and immigrant communities. The emergence of an 'underclass', said Wilson, explained the persistence of property crimes and crimes of violence. In the 1990s British policy-makers began to talk about persistent 'social exclusion' characterized by long-term unemployment, poverty and crime. In 1999 Tony Blair's New Labour government established a 'Social Exclusion Unit' to carry out research and develop policies designed, among other things, to address the crime problem. (This unit has subsequently been renamed the Social *Inclusion* Unit – no doubt on the advice of PR consultants.)

Yet this current interest in linking poverty, unemployment and crime is hardly surprising: the history of criminology is replete with attempts to link these three aspects of modern societies.

In this chapter we explore the idea that unemployment (in particular) and poverty (in general) are linked to crime. Our question is: Is there a causal link between unemployment and poverty on the one hand and crime on the other?

Far from being unique to our time, this idea is part of a longer history of what Ian Taylor (1997) has called a 'political economy of crime'. For well over two centuries social scientists and criminologists have argued that poverty and unemployment 'breed' crime (Box and Hale 1982: 21). Yet the fact that an idea has been around for a long time does not automatically make it a good or credible idea.

If we are to answer our question there are several other questions that require careful and thoughtful treatment because they will help to expose the assumptions people rely on when arguing that there is a causal link between unemployment and crime.

- What do we know about unemployment?
- How good is the evidence about the spread and duration of unemployment?
- What do we know about crime and how do we know it?
- Are we entitled to draw a direct causal link between these two phenomena? That there may be a statistical correlation is one matter. What this correlation – or coincidence – means, and whether it is significant, is another.
- In the case of the alleged causal connection between unemployment and crime, what kinds of assumptions do we need to rely on about the character of human conduct?
- How much is human activity *caused* by external factors? Or is human conduct better understood in quite different ways?

These questions provide an analytic framework for our discussion.

An old 'new' idea

The idea that unemployment in particular and poverty in general are causally linked to crime is far from being new. The Industrial Revolution of the eighteenth and nineteenth centuries was a period like our own, full of dramatic and radical change. By the 1820s in Britain, the first society to go through the full rigours of industrialization, the link between poverty and crime was simply assumed to be a fact. The passage of the New Poor Law legislation in 1834, which treated the poor and the unemployed as 'dangerous', 'antisocial' and deviant, testified to the popularity of this idea. The Act of 1834 sponsored the establishment of prison-like institutions called 'Poor Houses', to which people wanting welfare support had to surrender themselves.

Across the Channel in the same decades pioneering social scientists like Quételet and Guerry began collecting and analysing French crime statistics. In his influential *Treatise on Man*, Quételet's 1842 pioneering work on social statistics, which he called tellingly his 'social physics', he claimed to have revealed the laws shaping all human conduct. Quételet (1842: 1–3) pointed to a 'constancy of crime' under the economic conditions of large-scale industrialization and impoverishment. He claimed that the consistency with which crimes were committed from year to year in the same numbers and by the same kinds of people – mostly men aged between 21 and 25 – was evidence that free will and choice were less important than the laws of human conduct.

Back in Britain Russell in the 1840s was pointing to a link between British business-cycle downturns, or what we now call 'recessions' or 'depressions', and the number of prisoners appearing in courts. For the rest of the nineteenth century a link between poverty, unemployment and crime achieved common-sense status.

That idea was reinforced when a major social and economic crisis erupted in the 1930s, sparked by falling prices and rising unemployment. In the course of what became known as the Great Depression many social scientists (Shaw and McKay 1942) discerned a clear link between unemployment, poverty and crime. Robert Merton (1969a), when developing his structural strain theory of deviance, pointed to the role played by paid work in opening up legitimate social and economic opportunities. Rusche and Kirschheimer (1939: 45) argued that 'the prisons help to control the labour supply by jettisoning inmates when labour is scarce and filling up when labour is abundant'.

It is not therefore surprising perhaps that in the 1970s and 1980s, as many Western societies experienced levels of unemployment not seen since the 1930s, people would again begin to draw a link between unemployment and crime. Criminologists have not been timid about making that link. Increasing rates of unemployment in the 1970s in the leading economies of the West, motivated criminologists to carry out research on the unemployment–crime link. Greenberg (1977) and Jankovic (1977) in Canada suggested that there was a causal connection. Other Anglo-American researchers (Block and Heineke 1975; Brenner and Harvey 1978; Fox 1978; Cohen, Felson and Land 1980) drew the same conclusion. Brenner (1977: 4) insisted, in terms suggesting both excessive precision and unwarranted confidence, that a 1.4 per cent increase in the 'unemployment rate' in the USA in 1970 was 'directly responsible for some 51,730 total deaths including 1,740 additional homicides, 1,450 additional suicides and 5,520 additional state mental hospitalizations'.

On through the 1980s and 1990s criminologists, policy-makers and the media in the UK and the USA routinely claimed that unemployment was a key cause of crime and juvenile delinquency (Ericson, Baranek and Chan 1991). White (1989: 26) argued that in a time of high unemployment:

> [A]t the economic level, it can be suggested that more and more young men will turn to crime to make ends meet.

There is an extensive international literature on this link. (For a small sample of this literature over the past quarter century see Cohen, Felson and Land 1980; Chiricos 1987; Hale and Sabbagh 1991: 400–17; Weatherburn 1992; Bagguley and Mann 1992; Britt 1994: 99–108; Wilson 1996; Crutchfield and Pitchford 1997; Mathers and Schofield 1998; Shihadeh and Ousey 1998; Ainsworth-Darnell and Roscigno 2001; Bellair et al. 2003.) Typical of this explanatory framework is British research by Farrington et al. (1986: 99–108) who examined the careers of over 400 young men in London and concluded that 'crime rates were higher during periods of unemployment than during periods of employment'. Chiricos (1987: 187–211) likewise concluded from his meta-analysis of some sixty-five research studies that unemployment rates were 'positively' linked to crime rates. Distinguishing between the different types of crime, like property crimes and violent crime, and between periods in which the crime was committed, Chiricos argued for a strong relationship between property crime and unemployment rates. Likewise Dickinson (1994) claimed he could demonstrate a clear link between rising unemployment in the UK and an increased incidence of burglary for young males under 25. Other criminologists have suggested that if unemployment did not automatically switch young people on to criminality, it did impel those already showing 'delinquent tendencies' to move into criminal activity (Farrington et al. 1986: 99–108; Bagguley and Mann 1992).

The claim that there is a positive link between crime and unemployment was extended into the contention that many 'Western' countries were witnessing the emergence of an 'underclass' (Wilson 1987, 1996; cf. Bessant 1995).

The 'underclass' is a metaphor used to define a section of the population who live in what has been called 'a culture of poverty', allegedly characterized by welfare dependence, the experience of long-term and possibly even inter-generational unemployment. Most recently, especially in the UK and Australia, social scientists and policy-makers have adopted the concept of 'social exclusion' in preference to talking about an 'underclass'. The concept or metaphor of *social exclusion* has a geographical connotation and typically refers to the spatial concentration of large numbers of welfare-dependent people experiencing long-term and sometimes inter-generational unemployment.

This notion of an *underclass* is in fact an old idea dressed up as a new metaphor. In the nineteenth century it was referred to as 'the perishing classes', 'the black people', 'the masses', the 'lumpen proletariat' or simply as 'the poor'. As Payne and Payne (1994) note, metaphors like 'underclass' or 'the socially excluded' have helped to make discussion possible between 'left-leaning' and 'right-wing' criminologists. Macnicol (1987: 295) recognized quite early that the 'ideological thrust of this rediscovery [of the underclass] was a curious combination of reformist social engineering . . . and a conservative "social pathology" perspective which emphasize[s] cultural deprivation'.

In both the UK and the USA neo-conservatives like Murray (1990, 1994) waged a 'war' on both 'crime' and the 'welfare state' in the 1990s, suggesting that the 'welfare state' predisposed members of 'the underclass' to crime. This idea informed proposals to reform the welfare state so as to encourage a more positive orientation to work. By the late 1990s the assault on welfare programmes marketed as 'workfare' or 'welfare to work' initiatives and ostensibly designed to create a more 'flexible' labour market was widely believed to have worked because the USA appeared to have relatively low levels of unemployment. This assessment depended on the fact that the USA had an unemployment rate below the average (or mean) for the thirty countries that belong to the Organization for Economic Co-operation and Development (OECD). Since the OECD includes most of the big developed countries, including most European economies, this looked to be a strong point. Much of the talk about the lower than OECD average rates of unemployment in the USA has, however, avoided taking into account the effect of the staggering rates of imprisonment in America. By 2000 over 2 million Americans were in prison, a rate of imprisonment that, among other things, actually reduced the unemployment rate by about 1.5 per cent. To put this another way, if its prisons had been emptied, the US unemployment rate would be the same as the OECD average for 1999–2000. By the middle of the first decade of the twenty-first century official unemployment rates in most OECD countries were at their lowest levels in twenty-five years, reflecting in most countries a return to high-growth economies and in the USA the economic stimulus consequent on military intervention in Iraq since 2003.

From the neo-conservative perspective social-security benefits not only created increased crime rates and disincentives to work but also had undesirable social effects, like high rates of illegitimacy. This last effect is said to reflect the *fact* that benefits payable to single mothers function as an alternative to waged work. In some instances claims have been made that the complete abolition of all welfare and related benefits will not only produce a more moral society, but will break the 'cycles of dependency', poverty and crime (Novak 1994: 37). In the UK 'welfare reform' introduced by the Blair government and in America by Presidents Clinton and George W. Bush have gone some way to implementing these ideas.

On the left, though for different reasons, social democrats and social liberals have made an equivalent argument about the crime–unemployment link (Freeman and Soete 1994). As Taylor (1997: 473) argued, claims about a close, essentially determinate relationship between crime imprisonment and economic distress lies at the core of nearly all the socially reformist, Keynesian and even Marxist theoretical and analytical writing on crime that emerged in North America and Europe from the mid-twentieth century through to the late 1970s.

Part of the liberal–left argument (Cunneen 1990, 1994; White 1994, 1995) was that increasing crime rates would only be reversed if new employment programmes were established and existing ones extended, if state support for the jobless was increased, and if there was greater social equity and justice.

Given this apparent consensus between 'Left' and 'Right', it is highly likely today that many people in the UK, the USA or Australia would accept, as a matter of common sense, that unemployment *causes* crime.

Yet other criminologists have not been so sure about this link.

Sceptics

North American research gently undermined the claim that unemployed young people were especially at risk of becoming criminal. In the USA, Duster (1987: 51) argued that 'unemployment surely does not cause crime in any simple linear fashion, and certainly not in any direct one-to-one relationship. In [the USA] the easy demonstration is the Great Depression.' Heidensohn (1989: 184) argued that comparisons of trends in crime and unemployment rates at best produced ambivalent results, concluding that 'not everyone accepts that there is a positive and causal link'.

In England too some queried claims that unemployment and financial hardship encouraged people to commit crimes in order to alleviate that material hardship. In one meta-study of some fifty other criminologists' research designed to test the 'economic recession causes the crime rate to rise' argument, Box (1987) concluded that while income inequality was strongly related to many crimes – with the exception of homicide – the relationship between overall unemployment and crime was 'inconsistent'.

In Australia, Christine Alder (1986: 212) argued that 'there is not a simple, direct, inevitable relationship between unemployment and crime'. Other criminologists like Devery (1991) agreed that, even though the correlation between those who are materially deprived and criminality might seem 'obvious', there was actually no evidence to demonstrate that it was their disadvantaged position that causes them to commit crime. Weatherburn (1992) also argued for some caution, claiming that much of the research did not show a consistent disposition on the part of crime rates to closely shadow changes in unemployment rates.

Research like this has led some criminologists to argue for a more nuanced treatment of the issue. As Stern (1982) had pointed out, the assumption that unemployment causes crime (and related social pathologies) might have got the link the wrong way around. Stern (1982) suggested that mental illness or distress might 'cause' unemployment, leading on to criminal conduct. Even more subversively, he noted, drawing on Wiers's 1945 study of links between economic growth and delinquency rates in Wayne County (Detroit), that perhaps periods of economic prosperity rather than recession were more likely to increase the crime rate. In the UK, Field (1991) has suggested, in like vein, a strong relationship between economic boom conditions leading to an increased propensity to violent crime.

As long ago as the early 1980s Box and Hale (1982: 22) had tried to move the debate to new ground when they suggested that a better explanation of the link between crime and unemployment was called for. They argued that increases in unemployment generate an 'ideologically motivated response to the perceived threat of crime posed by the swelling population of economically marginalized persons'. Rather than looking to a direct causal link between mounting unemployment and crime, this kind of explanation looks more to a link between changes in economic downturns and shifts in the beliefs of people in the general community. Allen and Steffensmeier (1989) suggested the value of looking beyond simple links between crime and unemployment by focusing on more complex combinations of factors like under-employment, low wages, low hours of work and low wages to better explain the patterns of crime. They noted that while in aggregate full employment seemed to relate to low arrest rates for their sample groups of young men (13–17 and 18–24), factors like poorly paid and part-time work were more likely to explain high arrest rates but only for the older-age-group men.

In short, if there are many criminologists wanting to make a clear and confident link between unemployment and crime there are others who are quite sceptical about such a link. How then should we think about this issue?

Analysing the argument

In order to assess the argument that unemployment causes crime we need to analytically untangle a number of issues. There are three issues that matter and we address them in sequence. All of them go to basic and usually unexamined assumptions with which criminologists who want either to establish or to reject a link between crime and unemployment start. Firstly there are assumptions made regarding what we know about unemployment and the 'unemployment rate'. Then there are assumptions made concerning what we know about the 'crime rate'. Since we have already addressed this issue in Chapter 1 we will not repeat ourselves too much. Finally there are assumptions made about the nature of human conduct and causality that are relied on in making arguments about a crime–unemployment link.

So let us start with the first assumption. Given that part of the debate about the links between crime and unemployment depends on attempts to correlate the crime rate and the unemployment rate, we need to ask what is the 'unemployment rate' and how is it counted?

Counting unemployment

For people who rely on a thirty-second TV news item in which the newsreader says something like, 'Today Britain (or the United States or . . .) registered the highest – or lowest – unemployment rate in X years', it sounds all very simple. It may seem simple until you start to think about it: how do you count 'the unemployed'? It is perfectly reasonable to ask how many *chairs* are in a room and to then set about counting the chairs. However, unemployment is not susceptible to that kind of counting exercise. The 'unemployment rate' is not the product of some simple process of counting because the data used to establish that rate does not come from an actual *count* of the numbers of unemployed or jobless people.

Against the naive view that human conduct is just *out there* waiting to be observed or counted, social scientists have to develop what Bohme (1975) calls 'constructive schemes'. Gary Wickham (1992: 139) argues that the modes of *knowing* discrete elements of a population depend much more on political and administrative practices than they do on whatever is meant by 'reality'. Wickham argues that the ways we *know* or *count* particular types of people, like 'the unemployed', 'the mentally ill' or 'the criminal', do not simply 'reflect' *reality*, but rather express the interests and needs of governments and the technical methods of experts. What does this mean?

To establish something like the unemployment rate the experts or statisticians develop a constructive scheme that requires that they do two things.

1   They begin with a category, in this case 'unemployment'. The experts have to work out how it is to be defined (or 'operationalized') as well as devising a technique to do the 'counting'.
2   The experts can then use that definition to count those people (and only those people) who meet the criteria provided for in the definition of the category. In this way a kind of group of persons is constituted by the category.

Some people start to get annoyed about this and say, 'But this is all nonsense. Why make something that is simple so complicated? Doesn't unemployment simply refer to all those people who do not have paid jobs?' That may sound like common sense. But defining unemployment in that common-sense way would mean that we would find that there was a huge population of 'the unemployed'. We would have to include babies and infants, children at school, young people in universities and secondary or junior colleges. We would also have to include people in prisons and hospitals, people who don't want to work in regular jobs, to say nothing about all those women raising children in the home and other people doing domestic and caring work, and all the elderly.

Then there is the problem that ever since it was coined, probably by Alfred Marshall, the great British economist in the 1880s, 'unemployment' has referred to the involuntary experience of being jobless. That is, unemployment is something that is done to you: you cannot choose to be unemployed.

It is for such reasons that a category like 'unemployment' *invents* a reality to which the category can then be applied. All that this means is that before we can begin counting we need to carefully define what is meant by unemployment. Note that we are not saying here that unemployment is not real. On the contrary, the experience of unemployment is quite real to people who are jobless, just as its social or economic repercussions are very real and can be quite devastating, for the unemployed person and his or her family and friends. However, the way unemployment is counted depends on all sorts of prior questions and assumptions that are put together into a constructive scheme by those people whose job is to establish the unemployment rate.

In short, measuring unemployment and determining the unemployment rate depends heavily on

- the criteria used to determine who is to count as unemployed; and
- answers to the practical question of how you actually *discover* who is to count as unemployed.

Short of going out into the streets and asking everyone who walks by if they are unemployed, or knocking on every door or every house and apartment in the country, how do you count the unemployed?

For the last century or so most Western governments have in fact periodically knocked on the doors of all houses, apartments or dwellings in major statistical exercises called 'censuses'. But these are immensely expensive, complex, high-energy exercises and cannot be done more than once every 5–10 years. In the meantime governments and businesses need more statistical data collected on a more regular basis. So let us start with the basic issue: How do we *count* the 'unemployed'?

Since the 1950s as part of an international movement among developed nations to produce roughly comparable social data, governments have adopted International Labour Organization (ILO) guidelines and constructive schemes to carry out the measurement of unemployment. (The ILO, like the World Health Organization, is part of the United Nations' framework.) The ILO's definitions of 'employment' and 'unemployment' are used to establish the unemployment rate – partly to make possible international comparisons with other countries.

The ILO definition of 'unemployment' and the 'unemployment rate' says that to be unemployed you must first be in the 'labour force'. If you are not in the labour force you cannot by definition be unemployed! (If you are not working and you are not looking for work you will be defined as a 'discouraged worker', but you are not definitionally 'unemployed'.)

To be in the labour force you have to be aged between 16 and 65 years and to have worked for income for one or more hours per week in the survey period or else have been actively looking for work in the survey period. To be 'counted' as in the labour force, a respondent to the questionnaire needs to be able to satisfy these criteria. Defining and counting the labour force gives us a Labour Force Participation Rate which is the percentage of the total 16–65-year-old population who are in the labour force.

The *unemployment rate* is the percentage of people aged 16–65 years who are in the labour force and who have not worked for one or more hours of paid work in the survey period but who have actively looked for paid work in that period.

A person in the sample and who is answering a questionnaire can officially be defined as unemployed only if he or she:

- is over 15 years of age;
- has 'actively' looked for work in the prior four weeks;
- is able to start work in the survey week; and
- has not worked for more than one hour during the survey week.

On the second point of how practically a government discovers who is unemployed using these criteria, the ILO relies on a representative sample survey. In Australia the Bureau of Statistics uses a representative sample of 30,000 households. The sample is carefully designed so as to be representative of the whole population. The sample group is also regularly changed as the Bureau replaces a proportion of its sample with new people every few months. The results of this exercise can then be periodically compared with results obtained from the national census, which uses the same criteria and questions as are used in the smaller survey process.

Needless to say, while this looks like a sensible solution to the two problems of defining and then 'counting' the unemployed, it faces many problems.

Problems with the definitions and measures

Firstly we need to keep in mind that when a government announces the 'unemployment rate' that *is not an actual count of the people who are unemployed*. Rather than a count of the actual numbers of jobless people, it is a statistical aggregate based on the sampling of a small number of households. It is important to also recall that the data that are collected use certain definitions of who is to be counted as 'unemployed'.

Secondly the international definition of who counts as unemployed excludes many people. For example there are people who are jobless but who have given up 'actively' looking for work and so are not counted as unemployed. They are placed in a separate category, the 'discouraged worker' category. The definition of the 'labour force' does not include those who continue their full-time education. Those who stayed on at school or who have gone back to school or university because they cannot find work are not counted as unemployed. Likewise, as we have already seen, in the USA prisoners are not counted as part of the unemployed population.

Another problem with the definition of unemployment is that it excludes people who are '*under*-employed', i.e. those wanting full-time waged work, but who have not been able to get it. This category includes people who have worked over one hour per week and therefore do not count officially as being unemployed. There are many people who want waged work, but who have not been able to get it. Despite this they are not officially counted as unemployed because they may have worked in the survey period, or they are under, or over, the appropriate age, and/or they have not 'actively' sought work, or finally because they are in some form of full-time training or education.

The issues involved in working out the proportions of young people who are unemployed as a prelude to establishing a 'youth unemployment rate' have become quite notorious. The levels of youth unemployment, generally in the order of 18–30 per cent internationally, have accompanied the near-complete disintegration of the full-time youth labour market in most Western economies. (This shift has been accompanied by an immense increase in school retention rates and by a big increase in the numbers of young people combining schooling and paid work.) Intuitively it seems reasonable to assume that many young people stay in the education system because they cannot get full-time employment. However, although they are full-time students, many also work 15–26 hours a week at the pizza parlour or somewhere similar to help support themselves. The question is this: Are they in or out of the labour market? When is a full-time student *only* a full-time student and not a member of the labour force?

In short, any unemployment rate data have to be treated with considerable caution because the data are based on a selective sample (albeit a large one) and because they use criteria that exclude large numbers of those people who are out of work at any one time.

There are also significant gender effects embedded in the assumptions that go into the various research and administrative categories, some of which bear heavily on the presumed links between unemployment and crime.

Finally it is not surprising to find that there are few consistent, historical, long-term data sets that would enable us to say very much about links between unemployment and crime on a historical–comparative basis across the twentieth century either within a single country like the USA or between countries. Until countries began using the ILO framework in the 1950s, all sorts of different data were collected at different points using fundamentally different conceptual approaches as well as administrative techniques for collecting the data. Using the assumptions made by empiricist social scientists, we are simply not entitled to make too many claims about long-term historical trends relating to unemployment and crime for the twentieth century.

Contrary to common-sense assumptions, data sets like the 'unemployment rate' purporting to represent the incidence of joblessness are not a simple picture registering the actual numbers of unemployed persons. What this means is that criminologists who want to demonstrate a link between unemployment and crime confront some basic problems when they try to use the unemployment rate as if it were simply an accurate, or objective, reflection of something like the real extent of joblessness.

There are equivalent issues that are no less intractable when it comes to establishing the 'crime rate'.

Counting the 'crime rate'

At least there is now an international agreement about the constructive schemes used in collecting unemployment data. For crime data there is no such international agreement. It is hard enough often getting the various levels of government within one country to agree. As Wundersitz (1993) points out, for countries with federal systems of government, like the USA, Canada and Australia, this means that the systems of policing, sentencing and imprisonment produce quite different counts of crimes. This in turn creates major problems if we want to compare the crime rates for different countries.

We also need to repeat the point that collecting the data that go into the 'crime rate' is not like a photograph of reality but involves as we have shown apropos the 'unemployment rate' the use of 'constructive schemes'. This means that the collection of crime data reflect certain conceptual approaches and depends heavily on the data-gathering techniques used. Some criminologists have well understood the problem which the use of constructive schemes sets up for anyone wanting to believe that the crime rate is an *objective* picture of reality.

Edwin Sutherland was one such criminologist. Knowing this he argued strongly against the thesis that criminal behavior was *caused* by unemployment or by the poverty associated with unemployment. Sutherland said this for three reasons.

First, the unemployment–poverty crime link

> presents a generally skewed picture of crime given that it omits almost entirely the behaviour of 'white-collar criminals' . . . criminologists have tended to restrict

their attentions largely to cases processed through the criminal courts. Given the vast majority of defendants passing through the system come from the lower socio-economic classes this would suggest a narrow view of the 'crime problem'.

(1994: 24–5)

The problem of white-collar crime is important for people who want to draw some link between being unemployed and/or poor and criminality. This is precisely because white-collar crime involves people who are employed, frequently in senior positions inside companies and governments, and/or who have an upper-class background or enjoy high incomes (Alaheto 2003: 335). As Sutherland (1994: 25) put it:

[T]he generalization that criminality is closely associated with poverty obviously does not apply to white-collar criminals. With a small number of exceptions, they are not in poverty, were not reared in slums or badly deteriorated families. Even if poverty is extended to include the economic stresses that afflict business in a period of depression, it is not correlated with 'white-collar criminality'. Despite the relative wealth of those in the corporate world crimes in the field of investment and management have escalated rapidly over the past few decades. This neatly inverts the traditional correlations made by criminologists between poverty, unemployment and crime.

Sutherland also points out that many of those who commit 'white-collar crimes' are never convicted and their crimes never recorded. ('Out of court' settlements result in further 'non-convictions'.) Unlike the 'crimes' of people from working-class backgrounds, the unlawful acts of white-collar criminals are 'often less visible' and relatively 'immune because of the class bias of the courts and the power of their class to influence the administration of the law' (ibid.: 23).

To this we should add the relatively recent discovery that significant numbers of adults placed in positions of responsibility over children and teenagers, have been systematically engaging in sexual abuse and rape, physical violence and emotional abuse against those young people (Burkett and Bruni 1995). Most Western societies have been rocked in the past two decades by the revelations of abuse by priests, welfare workers, teachers and volunteers. They have been even more alarmed by the evidence of systematic cover-ups by governments, church leaders and bureaucrats. In 2003 in Australia the Governor-General (a former Anglican Archbishop) was forced to resign following evidence of his complicity in one such cover-up. To date criminologists have failed to incorporate this pattern of persistent conduct into their theory of crime.

Thirdly, there is the larger problem that Sutherland pinpointed when he (1994: 25) noted: 'Criminological theory has not adequately explained lower class criminality. Thus, the emphasis on socio-pathic and psycho-pathic factors have not been related to cases involving "white-collar" or corporate crime.' Whether criminologists have explained lower-class crime adequately or not is arguable. Sutherland is surely right, however, to suggest that by failing to include white-collar crime in the normal or mainstream criminological conceptual framework there is no capacity to test the adequacy of any of the usual theories advanced to explain *normal* crime committed by 'lower-class' or 'poor people'. Sutherland highlighted the point that there are major issues about the kinds of conduct that get to be defined as 'criminal' and who gets to be identified as likely to engage in criminal activity. He has suggested why it is that many forms of criminal activities fail to be regarded as criminal or being subjected to policing has major implications for any attempt to draw a simple causal link between unemployment–poverty and crime.

Apart from these substantive problems there are also problems associated with the data-gathering techniques used. As we showed in Chapter 1, there are many serious problems with *measuring* the extent or 'rate' of crime that are similar to the problems of measuring unemployment. These problems are the source of many complaints from both academics and government officials about the lack of credible crime statistics. Any statement regarding the 'crime rate' is problematic given that we don't really know what the true state of criminality is.

As we showed in Chapter 1, collecting crime data depends primarily on the activities of police. Criminologists have raised many questions about how infractions of the law get to be officially recorded and classified as statistical data. One key factor is police discretion. There are many factors that influence reports of an offence to law-enforcement agencies. These include the insistence of the complainant that the police officer pursue the matter; the complainant's deference to and demonstrated respect for the authority of the police officer; the officer's perception of the social status and resources of the complainant to successfully support the complaint, and so forth. Such factors influence the likelihood of reporting, and the selection and representation of the alleged offence that defines the substance of the report. In short, social and normative judgements and decisions to pursue or not to pursue a given offender lie behind each and every crime statistic.

It is widely known and accepted that young people, especially young men, make up a disproportionate number of those who are targeted for special police attention, which leads to them being defined and treated as criminal offenders. It is also well established that *special* populations, like young indigenous people, gay and lesbian people, and coloured and ethnic minority young people, attract disproportionate police attention. Whether this attention is deserved is certainly open to question. There are many issues about the precise nature of offences committed by young people. As Gordon Tait (1994: 73) argues, 'most of the "offences" relate to fairly minor thefts or property offences, particularly shop lifting. They [young people] also generally get filtered out of the legal system, with only about 10–20 per cent of young "offenders" being convicted.'

Christine Griffin (1993: 3) has likewise been concerned about the treatment of young people:

> The mainstream perspective is positivist, empiricist and conservative, presenting itself as an apolitical and mainstream perspective. It is characterized by the tendency to investigate young people as both the source and the victims of a series of 'social problems', adopting the victim blaming thesis in the search for the causes(s) of specific phenomena.

Increases or decreases in official rates of crime do not indicate whether the figures are the product of an increase in offences or a consequence of specific policing policy and practice. Increased juvenile crime rates may have nothing to do with any actual increase in the number of unlawful activities on the part of young people. They may reflect only changes in the law or increased police attention being given to certain groups due to media or public concern about their perceived threat to social order. O'Grady (1992) investigated one apparent very large increase in juvenile crime rates in Melbourne and an hysterical 'moral panic' initiated by the media. He found that the apparent 'juvenile crime wave' reflected a government decision to take minor offences and convert them into criminal misdemeanours. The offences included failure to wear an approved bike helmet, travelling on public transport without a valid ticket, failure to provide an address, misbehaviour like placing feet on public transit vehicles' seats and smoking cigarettes in non-smoking areas.

Because official crime rate statistics are the outcome of social practices, they cannot be regarded as *objective* or impartial measures of the 'crime problem'. Our first point is only that mainstream criminologists have failed to adopt a sufficiently wide-ranging and inclusive idea of what crime is and who commits it. A preoccupation with reporting or counting the crimes of certain groups of people, groups who are more readily noticeable or who are unable to protect themselves by avoiding detection or prosecution, has sanctioned a biased view of the crime problem and generated a lot of idle chatter about the crime rate. This means, secondly, that the connection between unemployment–poverty and crime may not be as clear-cut as many people seem to believe. At the least, people who are alarmed by media reports about increases in the crime rate should be warned that the 'crime rate' and the 'unemployment rate' are not simple reflections of any actual or objective pattern of human conduct.

Mainstream criminologists who are statistically inclined will doubtless continue to insist that the statistical analysis they do and the discovery of correlations between unemployment and crime rate data point to a causal link between these two phenomena. They do so because of the assumptions about causality entertained by many criminologists who argue for some kind of 'causal' link between crime and unemployment.

The idea of determinism

Ultimately the value of social sciences like criminology rests on the credibility of the insights they often give into human conduct. This gives rise to fundamental questions that have exercised many people over the past few centuries. We refer to the problem of human conduct itself and the debate between those who insist humans exercise free will and those who insist that all human conduct is causally determined.

This problem may be framed as a series of questions. Are we humans constrained by factors that stimulate us or force us to behave in entirely predictable ways? Alternatively do we exhibit a wider variety of choice and decision-making than determinist accounts typically allow for? We are not here debating some quite basic constraints like our biological dependence on water or food or such constraints as our bodily shape preventing us from flying unaided through the air. Rather, how much choice do humans have about what we do, with and to each other?

This debate is informed by certain key words like 'explanation' and 'understanding'. Is it the case as people who accept a broad-church kind of positivism that human conduct can be *explained* in terms of external or *structural* factors typically rendered by sociologists and criminologists as social forces and factors? Alternatively, symbolic interactionists and social constructivists have argued, it is more the case that human conduct can better be *understood* in terms of the motives, feelings and needs of people.

These are fundamental questions. They are attended by a series of subordinate questions of method. For example, are we able to measure or otherwise statistically calculate the role of factors that are said to exercise causally determinative effects? Alternatively, are we to give more weight to the reasons which people themselves give us? Or should we give more weight to the reasons offered by experts or observers, reasons that are assumed, irrespective of what the people whose conduct we are examining say, to possess more explanatory power?

These are all important questions to which many complex answers are possible and have, indeed, been offered. Since this is an introduction to criminology and not a philosophy book, we will not undertake a long-winded account of the various arguments. What is at stake is suggested by arguments like those advanced by Gottfredson and Hirschi (1990) in their *General Theory of Crime*.

Gottfredson and Hirschi (ibid.: 90) adopt the courageous tactic of opting for a single explanation: they argue that lack of self-control is the cause of all crime. They claim that people who are impulsive, insensitive, physically expressive, risk-takers with low frustration tolerances will tend to engage in criminal acts. Their identikit of the 'criminal offender' emphasizes low capacity for self-control. This results in failures in activities that require planning, delayed gratification, verbal and cognitive abilities required in schools and higher education. Those who lack self-control have trouble making friends, 'flock together' with other people who lack self-control and are deviant, and ultimately prefer 'to gravitate to the street' (ibid.: 157–8). That these are the characteristics conventionally associated with young, working-class males suggests something of the social prejudices at work in this account.

Gottfredson and Hirschi seem to have written their book in complete ignorance of Edwin Sutherland's powerful reminder of how mainstream criminology simply blanks out white-collar and elite crime, a point reiterated by Simon (1999).

A determinism is also operating when Gottfredson and Hirschi insist that lower-class or working-class families are the original source of delinquent and criminal problems in later life. Crime, it seems, is only ever the result of ineffectual child-rearing practices, involving a failure to discipline bad behaviour. Their insistence on the issue of lack of self-control (ibid.: 96) leads them, perhaps recklessly, to dismiss the role played by factors which other criminologists have often reached for, like 'socialisation, culture or positive learning of any sort'. This leads them (ibid.: 165) to insist that the 'most significant employment–crime fact is the tendency for people who commit crime to have unstable job profiles – that is to have difficulty finding jobs and keeping them'. What should we think about such an explanation that proposes a *structural* and causally determinist explanation of criminal conduct?

One American criminologist, Jack Katz, rejects this kind of structural determinism quite brutally. Katz (1988: 3) points out, firstly, that many of those people who fall into the supposed causal categories, like those who are unemployed or poor, do not commit the crimes that the research predicts they will. Secondly, many of those who do commit crimes do not fit the designated causal categories. For example, many white-collar criminals are employed, earn big incomes and live in affluent, high-status areas. Likewise most paedophiles and people who sexually abuse children and young people persistently are professional, middle-class teachers, priests, welfare workers and businessmen. Finally, many who do match the predictive indicators of criminality, and who do eventually commit the crimes it has been predicted they will commit, go for long periods without engaging in those criminal activities. Any one of these problems should give reason for alarm. Taken together, they constitute a devastating critique of explanatory theories of crime like that offered by Gottfredson and Hirschi.

Jack Katz (1988) has provided a major critique of much of the literature arguing for causal links between the unemployment and crime rates. The mainstream positivist tradition has long insisted that we can *explain* social phenomena by looking for the external factors or social structures that constrain humans to act in predictable ways. Katz suggests that a theory or an approach to explaining human conduct that looks for a direct causal relationship between factors such as poverty–unemployment and crime is unduly simplistic.

Katz calls the 'poverty causes crime' argument a 'sentimental theory of crime causation'. He suggests that the focus on causal relationships between structures of economic inequality and human conduct – like criminal activity – assumes that human conduct can be explained as a result of external factors coercing or constraining us to act in a particular way. This approach leaves little if any room for the possibility that there are feelings, desires or motivations impelling people to commit criminal offences.

Katz belongs to a long-standing, albeit minority, tradition of sociologists and criminologists who, like Lonnie Athens (1997), insist that we are better advised to try to *understand* human conduct as something people largely *choose* to do. This has been a minority tradition because among the key constitutive ideas at work in mainstream sociology has been a deep suspicion of 'psychologistic' approaches to social life. This probably reflects a desire by sociologists to erect a clear boundary between themselves and competing disciplines like psychology.

Zygmunt Bauman (1978: 12) has put the case for treating the motives, feelings and desires of people seriously when he argued that 'men and women do what they do on purpose':

> Social phenomena, since they are ultimately acts of men and women, demand to be understood in a different way than by mere explaining. Understanding must then contain an element missing from the explaining of natural phenomena: the retrieval of purpose, of intention, of the unique configuration of thoughts and feelings which preceded a social phenomenon, its only manifestation, imperfect and incomplete, in the observable consequences of action.

As Katz (1988: 2–3) suggests, causal explanations based on large data sets generally fail to consider the expressive, ethical and purposive quality of people's conduct. Katz is right, along with criminologists like Cohen (1992: 46–53) and Athens (1997), to insist on taking into account the complex overlapping of distinctly human motivations for a whole range of behaviours like pride, a sense of injustice, patriotism, righteous anger and revenge.

At the heart of this approach is the proposition that, far from being *objects* on whom external factors work causally, human beings are *subjects* impelled by ideas, feelings and desires, both of their own and of other people with whom they interact. It is these ideas, feelings and desires that impel them to act. These intentions, as Charles Taylor (1977) has argued, are often expressed and articulated in publicly available ways, using the linguistic and other expressive and symbolic technologies that we all use to make sense of the world and to interact with each other. This is not to say that we do what we do for reasons or because of feelings that are always clear or readily available to us; for not all of us can always give accounts of why we do what we do. Given the role played by feelings, fantasies and desires in most if not all human conduct, including scientific and intellectual work, we should not overstate the case that human conduct is always rational or the conduct of rational agents.

And as the sometime 'new criminologist' Ian Taylor (1997) reminds us, good socio-logical theory is attentive to the symbolic and cultural dimensions of social life. Our states of mind, our feelings and the motives that impel us to act may have little if any direct relationship to factors such as material deprivation or employment status. This is not to doubt that some criminal conduct is driven directly by such motivations as greed or the desire to obtain money by illegal means or to hurt someone or even to kill them.

For Katz and, before him, Max Weber, human conduct is social because it involves complex interactions between people. It is also mostly meaningful action for which actors are able to give more or less reasoned accounts of why they did what they did. These accounts are offered in terms of motives, feelings and desires, allowing that these are states of mind formed in interaction with others. Research by Bessant and Watts (1993) and Bessant (1996) on young people who regularly engaged in fighting and stealing from shops found that of those young people interviewed some came from conventionally defined working-class families while others came from high-income and high-status families. They found that the dominant account offered by these young people pointed to their rarely experienced opportunities to feel strong, effective, competent and adventurous. That is, fighting and shoplifting gave them opportunities to define and meet challenges to their bravery, their honour or their skill. They did not do these things because they were poor or without waged work.

Accounts that emphasize the causally determined nature of human conduct, whether by recourse to arguments about culture, socialization, institutional sanction or economic deprivation, are underpinned by a determinist view of human action. Without lurching into the equal and opposite silliness of saying that all human conduct is perfectly and freely willed, it is clear that human action is action for which each person is normally responsible and accountable. ('Normally' here allows that some people may be acting with diminished responsibility because they are mad or brain-damaged, affected by drugs or simply mistaken.) This does not mean that the motivations are always ethically legitimate or rational. Neither does it deny that there are sometimes severe constraints on what we can do, arising out of people's perceptions of the kinds of resources or power available to them, or out of the kinds of power relations in which we invariably find ourselves.

Conclusion

The current credibility of claims that jobless people are likely to be involved in something like a 'criminal economy' draws on long-standing ways of thinking about working-class and/or low-income people.

We have argued that there is no *obvious* basis to be found in whatever criminologists mean by reality for claiming a straightforward or direct *causal* link between increases in the unemployment rate and the crime rate. The popularity of the belief that it is only 'poor', young and unemployed people who steal and do unlawful things is simplistic. It misrepresents individuals and groups already disproportionately subject to coercive practices and the unremitting gaze of professionals, police and the state. It is ironic that 'radical' criminologists who are concerned about the evil consequences of capitalism, like unemployment or poverty, may well be lending support to a contemporary political culture in which old ideas about *the individual*, rational economic activity and the free-market economy have been recently revived. The preoccupation with crimes committed by the *poor* ignores the kinds of crimes committed by white-collar, professional and elite groups. The complacent recycling of old prejudices is no victory for clear thinking or criminal justice policies that are both effective and socially just.

Any unquestioning acceptance of official statistics as if they are a simple, passive or objective reflection of something like the real incidence of offences in a community will result in a failure to acknowledge the social practices and processes that lead to the construction of the statistical data. When this happens talk about 'crime rates' will become more modest and thoughtful.

Review questions

How important are the techniques and assumptions involved in counting the unemployed for assessing arguments that assert a causal link between unemployment and crime?

How credible are causal and determinist arguments, especially those based on secondary social statistics, in helping us to understand why people do what they do?

Is Jack Katz right to call economic explanations of crime that are preoccupied with poverty and unemployment a 'sentimental theory' of ' crime?

Further reading

Bagguley, P. and Mann, K., 1992, 'Idle Thieving Bastards? Scholarly Representations of the Underclass', *Work, Employment and Society*, Vol. 6, No 1: 112–26.

Griffin, C., 1993, *Representations of Youth*, Polity Press, Cambridge.

Katz, J., 1988, *Seductions of Crime: Moral and Sensual Attractions of Doing Evil*, Basic Books, New York.

Muncie, J., 1998, 'Reassessing Competing Paradigms in Criminological Theory', in Walton, P. and Young, J. (eds), *The New Criminology Revisited*, Macmillan, London.

Payne, J. and Payne, C., 1994, 'Recession, Restructuring and the Fate of the Unemployed: Evidence of the Underclass Debate', *Sociology*, Vol. 28, No. 1, February: 1–20.

EXPLAINING CRIME: CRIME AND THE FAMILY

Along with poverty and unemployment, *the family* has also been identified by modern criminologists as a major source of crime and delinquency. Given the scale of the social, economic and cultural changes that have taken place since the 1970s in the UK, the USA and Australia, it is not surprising that the temptation to find *the family* responsible for the crime problems of our time has proved so irresistible.

On the one hand there have been many significant changes in family life and family formation in most Western societies since the 1970s. These changes include a move away from marriage, a decline in the numbers of children being born (the fertility rate), an increase in the divorce rate and the emergence of new kinds of family formation – there are now many more single-parent families, more 'blended' families (i.e. new families put together after divorce and remarriage), and even gay and lesbian marriages often involving children. These changes have been accompanied by a great deal of public discussion about their meaning. There are many metaphors available to characterize these changes, including 'family breakdown', the 'death of the family' and the decline of 'traditional family values'.

Criminologists have not been slow to pick up on these themes. At the heart of one of the most influential 'theories of crime', that of Gottfredson and Hirschi (1990), as we saw in Chapter 6, is a story about certain kinds of families that fail to raise their children to be law-abiding or morally conventional. As Cook (1997) and Walklate (1998) observe, the increase in the number of single-parent households, lack of parental discipline and of parenting skills, 'dysfunctional' family relationships and even 'large families' have all been blamed for increases in the crime rate over the past three decades.

As is the case with arguments about how unemployment and poverty cause crime, there is a long history to this, ostensibly contemporary, preoccupation with families. There is a long tradition in criminology that seeks to explain crime by linking it to 'bad families'. Given the political and policy implications of this alleged link we need to ask how credible are the explanations seeking to establish it. As we argued in Chapter 6 there is more than a suspicion that there are social prejudices at work in the way conventional criminologists understand crime and they produce a narrow-minded kind of criminology. These prejudices emphasize the relationship of poverty and working-class life to crime while blanking out white-collar crime. It is important in reading research by criminologists on this issue to ask about the assumptions they make so as to identify the constructive schemes they are using.

This chapter looks at empirical research on the link between families and crime. We begin by considering some of the studies of families and crime carried out in the first half of the twentieth century. We then turn to the 'human development' model (Farrington 1994, 1997). Using our analytical model for thinking about arguments, we look at the kinds of claims made and the evidence used, before turning to the assumptions relied on by those who assert a causal link between bad families and crime. We need to ask what does it mean when some criminologists claim that certain families are 'antisocial', 'pathological' and/or 'dysfunctional', making them 'criminogenic' – or 'crime-causing' – families? What role do various assumptions about families and their responsibility for the primary socialization of their children play in these explanations? To what extent can empirical or statistical measures permit links to be made between these patterns of family life and the kinds of conduct represented as *crime* and delinquency? Implicit in this treatment and in these questions is a scepticism about the extent to which modern criminology can actually be credited with having progressed in its theoretical or conceptual understanding of what explains crime.

An old–new idea: families and crime

It is not surprising that theories of child development and studies of the family became increasingly important in the UK and the USA from the 1920s on. An early indication of what was to come is found in Cyril Burt's 1925 study of juvenile delinquents (1965). Burt gave early support to a model of *normal* child development in the 1920s and 1930s. As we indicated in Chapter 3, Burt promoted a multi-factor theory of delinquency, blending elements of psychoanalytic theories with eugenicist ideas about biological and psychological deviations from the norm.

The work of Burt presaged a much wider cultural shift, in Western societies, characterized by the increasing authority and appeal of psychological arguments and therapies. Phillip Rieff (1978) has written a deeply ironic history of the evolution of persistent and widespread psycho-therapeutic ideas. He focuses on the impact of ideas loosely associated with Sigmund Freud and the various schools of psychoanalysis on the cultures of both the UK and the USA, especially after the world war of 1914–1918. Nikolaus Rose (2000: 116–60) points too to the persistent intersection of an interest in liberal ideas about *the self* and the startling growth in the credence given to psycho-therapeutic ideas during the twentieth century. In this context the use of psychological theories by criminologists is part of a broader shift in social and intellectual practices.

Among the key ideas this broader intellectual shift set loose, courtesy of Sigmund Freud's psychoanalytic theory, was the core idea that certain experiences in infancy and childhood have life-long consequences. As Jacoby (1974) reminds us, Freud's deeply unsettling account of the conflict between infantile sexuality and the demands of social existence was quickly reworked by former disciples of his, such as Adler and Klein. These neo-Freudians wanted to reduce the shock value of some of his core ideas, for example, that all children are sexually alive from birth. Donald Winnicott (1964, 1968, 1971) and John Bowlby (1940, 1953a, 1953b, 1965), two British child psychologists who worked in an eclectically psychoanalytic way, shaped the theory and practice of professionals working in child-care and welfare and of some criminologists in regard to those children who displayed *maladjusted* and/or *antisocial* behaviours. Both men became advocates of a psychological approach to the diagnosis and treatment of delinquency.

Bowlby and Winnicott advanced one central idea: *maternal deprivation*, an idea which has had a long career. Both claimed that the absence of a mother and of the nurturing love and warmth mothers offer in the early years of childhood was likely to produce all kinds of problematic attitudes and behaviours in adult life.

What was at stake was suggested in a speech Winnicott gave to English magistrates in 1964. Winnicott outlined his hope that courts would use 'psychological methods' to 'investigate' particular cases of 'antisocial behaviour'. He argued that the origins of delinquency could be found in the 'disruptions' to parent–child relations during the formative years of a child's life. Winnicott claimed that delinquency was a consequence of the instability brought about by an absence of controls in the 'normal stages' of 'emotional growth'. Delinquency was, in effect, a search for maternal love. In a later work, Winnicott (1984: 116) put it:

> When a child steals outside his own home, he is still looking for his mother . . .
> he is seeking with more sense of frustration, and increasingly needing to find at
> the same time the parental authority that can and will put a limit to the actual effect
> of his impulsive behaviour, and to the acting out of the ideas that come to him when
> he is in a state of excitement.

As a result of these disruptions the 'antisocial child' begins to look beyond the family milieu in order to obtain the sense of 'emotional security' denied by his or her immediate family.

Using the same approach, John Bowlby also argued repeatedly over a long career that the absence of 'maternal love', particularly in the child's first five years, was central to any explanation of delinquency or of adult criminality. Indeed he argued that the 'prolonged separation' of the child from his/her mother (or mother substitute) during the first five years 'stands foremost among the causes of delinquent character development' (1953a: 41). Bowlby supported this claim with a study of forty-four working-class, adolescent 'thieves'. (It is worthy of note that Bowlby did not study a group of adolescent children of 'upper-class' parents who relied on child care provided by nannies and boarding schools.) In this study he drew on the considerable authority of the classic 'experimental research design' when he compared the emotional make-up of this group with a control group matched in terms of social background, age and sex (Bowlby 1965). He claimed that the former group included many more of those described as 'affectionless characters'. According to Bowlby, many of them had experienced prolonged periods of separation from their mothers (or foster-mothers) in their infancy, in part because of the war-time evacuation of British children after 1939. Bowlby claimed that the clear consequence of the maternal deprivation they experienced was a propensity to engage in later life in 'antisocial' forms of behaviour.

Winnicott's and Bowlby's claim that the origins of delinquency were best explained by the quality of specific emotional relationships between children and their parents had a lasting influence on generations of counsellors, probation officers, psychologists and social workers in the UK and the USA (Rose 1990: 160–6; Rose 2000).

Yet there were critics of this approach who were alarmed by the simplicity of the explanations. After all, it explained possibly complex patterns of human conduct by reducing it back to a single determining factor. Michael Rutter (1972) criticized the 'maternal deprivation' thesis on the grounds that Bowlby (like Winnicott) was offering only a single-cause explanation for quite complex activities. Rutter also noted that the 'maternal deprivation' argument rested on a number of unwarranted assumptions about the nature of family life. One obvious and problematic assumption concerned the central role played by the mother during the 'bonding' process. The other parent, the father, seemed to have disappeared completely from view. According to Rutter (ibid.: 123):

> While loss is probably an important factor in one of the syndromes associated with 'maternal deprivation', a review of the evidence suggests that in most cases the damage comes from 'lack' or 'distortion' of care rather than any form of 'loss'.

Rutter (ibid.: 126–7) suggested that

> it is not maternal bonding that needs to be studied but rather the nature of the relationship itself . . . It should be appreciated that the chief bond need not be with a biological parent, it need not be with the chief caretaker and it need not be with a female.

Although Bowlby offered a more complex explanation of motherhood and bonding than is often allowed by his critics, a somewhat simplistic rendition of the deprivation thesis was nonetheless absorbed by generations of child-care 'experts' who believed that mothers were the indispensable emotional factor in 'successful' child development (ibid.: 127). The influence of Bowlby's and Winnicott's ideas was in evidence when Sheldon and Eleanor Glueck (1950) published one of the first major US studies to focus on family relationships and delinquency.

The Gluecks were prominent Harvard criminologists who carried out a longitudinal study of a group of more than 500 officially defined 'delinquent boys' matched with 'non-delinquent' boys from Boston. The conventional idea that girls were incapable of delinquency, or if they were delinquent then their kind of delinquency did not matter, points to certain 'malestream' assumptions at work. The Gluecks assembled a vast range of social, psychological and biological data that could identify and *predict* which boys would end up 'delinquent'. They claimed that the results of their research demonstrated a link between family life and juvenile delinquency.

The Gluecks (1950: 261) argued that delinquent behaviour could be predicted by a number of key factors, including the extent to which a boy was disciplined by the father and the nature of the mother's supervision of the boy. They also drew attention to the extent of affection of the father and mother for the boy and to the general 'cohesiveness of the family'. The idea that the internal workings of families were primarily responsible for the creation of delinquent behaviour, was central to the Gluecks' explanatory theory of delinquency and crime.

These claims were highly influential, perhaps because they tapped into popular anxiety on the part of some parents or else simply reaffirmed long-standing social prejudices about lower-class families. Yet there have been critics. In a detailed analysis of the Gluecks' research, Laub and Sampson (1988: 360) identified a number of shortcomings in their study, the most serious of which were the general lack of systematic attention to the influence of 'external', or socio-economic, factors on delinquency and the failure to acknowledge the processes by which 'offenders' were 'officially' defined as such. Laub and Simpson said the Gluecks' work was 'superficial' insofar as it ignored the complex ways in which 'external' factors impacted on young people and their families. Despite such reservations, however, Laub and Sampson (ibid.: 375) supported the Gluecks' central contention that 'family process variables' (like parental supervision, attachment and discipline) were important factors in explaining delinquency.

Others have made trenchant criticisms of the work of Winnicott, Bowlby and the Gluecks. Feminist writers argued pointedly that their arguments ignore the socially constructed nature of 'motherhood' and the ways in which women are positioned in terms of their reproductive roles and functions. Utting, Bright and Henricson (1993: 20) argued that any account of parent–child relationships should focus not on the presence of a particular carer but rather on the 'quality of care' experienced by the child. This is an important observation in a context where increasing numbers of women are pursuing 'dual careers' as both employees and mothers, and where there is an increasing reliance by many families on paid child-care. Naffine (1997) argues that the notion of 'mother–child bonding' relies on some highly questionable assumptions about the *natural* role of women in the process of child-rearing and ignores the way men's and women's roles and relationships were being constructed and reconstructed over the course of the twentieth century. This criticism also implies that there is a conservative politics at work, given the way some criminologists and sociologists are reasserting the value of women's traditional roles.

Researching the 'criminogenic family'

Since the pioneering work of Bowlby, Winnicott and the Gluecks there has been a proliferation of research focusing on the links between families and crime. Criminologists' efforts to identify the role of the domestic rumblings of family life in the creation of crime and delinquency have never been less than exhaustive. These claims in the research literature often bear a striking similarity to more popular ideas about the 'failing' or 'dysfunctional' family which are to be found in media commentary on crime and delinquency (Cook 1997). In what follows we begin by briefly outlining the kinds of claims linking variously the 'broken family', 'big families' and 'failing families' to crime.

The 'broken family' seems to have attracted the most persistent attention among empirical researchers. Researchers use the metaphor of 'broken home' or 'broken family' to refer to the absence of one or both parents because of divorce, separation or bereavement. Why such a family should be more 'broken' than one with both parents present is not exactly clear.

A great deal of research has attempted to correlate the 'broken family' with the onset of delinquency. Wells and Rankin (1986: 87) note that between 1980 and 1985 at least sixty-five major studies were conducted in the USA alone on the relationship between 'broken families' and crime. Such interest is partly attributable to the popular belief that the 'broken home' *per se* leads to 'antisocial' behaviours among the young (Young 1997). Into the twenty-first century criminologists continue to 'discover' that 'broken families' like single-parent families produce significant numbers of delinquent and criminal young people (Chung et al. 2002; Dembo and Schmeidler 2003a, 2003b).

Other criminologists have looked to the problems of family size. This is generally understood as the problem of 'large families', usually defined in terms of the number of children in a household (Regoli and Hewitt 1991: 181–206). Leflore (1988: 640) typically observes that large families generate a lot of problems and internal tensions, markedly affecting the ability of parents to adequately care for their children. Another US study, by Tygart (1991: 535), argued that in larger families parents found it more difficult to supervise their children adequately. In the best known of contemporary longitudinal British studies (Farrington 1978, 1994: 14–15) the research data are used to argue that large families correlated with delinquency.

However, it is the link between the *quality* of family relationships and crime that has increasingly come to occupy many criminologists. Contemporary criminologists have increasingly tried to show that delinquent or offending behaviours result from failings in parent–child relations. In the late 1970s, Patricia Morgan (1978: 94) reviewed many of the US and UK studies of families and crime. She concluded that the origins of criminal behaviour among the young were to be found in 'quarrelling, discordant homes with violent or insane parents' or in 'disharmonious families' where there was 'tension' or a 'lack of warmth'. James Q. Wilson and Richard Herrnstein (1985: 366) likewise elaborated an account of the role played by 'deep-seated temperamental problems' exhibited by 'pathological parents' who 'lack the desire to change their children's offending behavior'. Loeber and Stouthamer-Loeber (1986: 13) also found that 'poor parental supervision or monitoring, erratic or harsh parental discipline, parental disharmony, parental rejection of the child and low parental involvement with the child (as well as anti-social parents and large family size) were all important predictors'.

All too often this means that criminologists start to talk about 'parental failure'. 'Parental failure' is said to be evident in poor emotional relationships between parents and their children or in the inability of parents to exercise effective child-rearing or good 'parenting skills'. This kind of criminology clearly believes it is possible and desirable to identify certain families in terms of their 'dysfunctional' and/or 'criminogenic' features.

David Farrington is arguably the best known and certainly among the most published of UK advocates for a 'human development' approach to the study of 'criminal careers'. For this reason it is worth paying some detailed attention to his promotion of long-term or longitudinal studies to establish the impact of families on delinquency and crime.

Farrington began work with D. J. West, a leading figure at the Cambridge Institute of Criminology, on a 'prospective longitudinal survey' of over 400 'traditional' working-class British boys in 1961. His research team found that one in five of the boys committed an offence (mainly theft, burglary, or unlawfully taking and driving away an automobile). This research team spared no effort in trying to identify every conceivable relational factor that might be correlated with delinquency.

Reseachers interviewed the boys at regular intervals from the ages of 8 and 32 years. They also surveyed the boys' parents with regard to factors such as income, family size, employment, child-rearing practices and 'degree of supervision'. They also interviewed the boys' teachers to establish general patterns of school behaviour among the children while the boys' peers were invited to 'rate' factors such as degree of 'daring', 'dishonesty', 'popularity' and 'troublesomeness'. Farrington's team 'tested' the boys at various stages of the life-cycle for intelligence, 'impulsivity' and educational attainment; and they 'assessed' the impact of the boys' living conditions, their employment, relationships with parents, leisure activities and other pursuits such as 'drinking, fighting and offending behaviour' (Farrington 1994: 9).

On the basis of this research Farrington reached a number of conclusions about the relationship between parenting and delinquency. He and his colleagues argued that the quality of parental supervision and discipline was vital in preventing the onset of 'anti-social behaviour'. Farrington (ibid.: 12–15) suggested that 'cool, rejecting parents tend to have delinquent children ... [as do] parents who let their children roam the streets unsupervised from an early age [while] ... warm, loving parents tend not to have delinquent children'. This is highly significant because

> offending is part of a larger syndrome of anti-social behaviour that arises in childhood and tends to persist into adulthood. There seems to be continuity over time since the anti-social child tends to become the anti-social teenager and then the anti-social adult, just as the anti-social adult tends to produce an anti-social child.
>
> (Farrington 1997: 362)

In effect 'antisocial conduct' can be the first stage in a criminal career. By 'criminal career' Farrington means that we can specify that those people who commit criminal offences have had a career marked by 'onset', when they begin to commit offences, 'duration', or the period of time over which they commit the offences, and 'desistance', when they stopped offending.

Farrington's definition of antisocial conduct is interesting. In an early attempt to say what they meant by antisocial conduct, West and Farrington (1977) had defined 'antisocial' by such things as 'unstable job record, heavy gambling, heavy smoking, drug use, drunk driving, sexual promiscuity, spending time hanging around the street, anti-social group activity, violence and anti-establishment attitudes' (1997: 364).

By the 1990s Farrington (1997: 363) was defining 'antisocial' conduct in terms of being 'troublesome and dishonest' in primary school, and being a 'bully' and engaging in aggressive and frequent lying at 12–14 years of age. By 18 it included heavy drinking, heavy smoking, using prohibited drugs, heavy gambling and engaging in early, unprotected and promiscuous sex.

In spite of an abundance of data, Farrington (1994: 14–15) drew only the most cautious and tentative conclusions: 'it is difficult to establish which (factor) causes what, or how all these different factors interact to produce delinquency'. (As we have argued already, this recognition of the enormous numbers of variables that go into *explaining* or *predicting* delinquency or criminality has been a hallmark of empirical research by criminologists since before 1914.) As Utting, Bright and Henricson (1993: 11) point out: 'It is important to recognize that statistically significant "predictors" ... rarely, if ever, approach the realms of certainty.' They add that 'attempts to target and stigmatize young children as "potential offenders" using statistical predictors are likely to mis-identify a proportion of children who will not turn to crime, while missing many others who are equally at risk' (ibid.: 18).

Despite his reservations, Farrington was still able to outline a number of factors that 'contributed' in one way or another to the onset of delinquency. Of these Farrington claimed that 'family factors' were important in accounting for delinquent behaviour and that, in particular, 'erratic and inconsistent discipline' was a major cause of delinquency (1994: 10). Moreover, 'the presence of adverse family background (poor parental supervision, cruel, passive or neglecting attitude of the mother, parental conflict) doubled the risk of a later juvenile conviction . . . We can show that family factors predict delinquency independently of other factors . . .'.

Other studies in the USA, New Zealand and Australia have replicated Farrington's longitudinal and multivariate analysis (see Utting et al. 1993 and Utting 1994 for an overview of these studies). Such longitudinal studies are invariably characterized by the use of vast sample sizes followed over very long periods of time. Inevitably, this has resulted in the accumulation of a large body of 'data' which, subject to the usual qualifications, is used to *predict* the onset of delinquent behaviours. However, the sheer magnitude of the studies, as well as the array of factors under scrutiny, always seem to make it difficult for the researchers to state with absolute certainty which factors are likely to predict delinquency. As D. J. West (1982: 38) had pointed out:

> No survey . . . can hope to provide a complete map of cause and effect. The most one can expect to do is to identify within an infinitely complex system of interacting influences some items that make a significant contribution to delinquency.

Equally curiously, however, and in spite of all the qualifications that these 'empirical' researchers routinely advance about the ability of their research to adequately *predict* delinquency, they insist that 'family dynamics' are vital in explaining delinquency. Graham and Bowling, in a UK study of 2,528 young people aged between 14 and 25, found a close connection between offending and 'poor quality' family relationships. They note: 'Both males and females who were less attached to their families were more likely to offend than those who were relatively content at home' (1996: xii). This study identified 'low-parental supervision' and truancy as key factors in offending behaviour among the majority of young people in the sample. At least Graham and Bowling moved beyond laying responsibility for this at the feet of mothers in concluding (ibid.: xii) that 'low levels of parental supervision' were closely dependent on the quality of parent–child relationships, particularly between boys and their fathers.

These then are the kinds of claims made by contemporary criminologists looking for causal links between certain features of family life and the evolution of delinquent and criminal activity. That these arguments coincide with a good deal of populist and simplistic commentary on display in TV shows like *The Oprah Winfrey Show* or *The Jerry Springer Show* does not necessarily mean they should not be taken seriously. Equally, the fact that this kind of research mimics the views of fundamentalist Christian propaganda and neo-conservative think-tanks that promote 'right thinking' views about the proper role of women, permissive approaches to sexuality and divorce, or the sinfulness of gays and lesbians may likewise just be a coincidence. Some careful and critical thought may indicate why there are some very real problems with drawing too quick-and-easy a link between certain kinds of family life and crime.

Some critical thinking

As we have seen there are three ideas about how 'bad families' cause crime: bad families may be 'broken families', they may be 'large families' or they have poor quality emotional dynamics.

Let us start with the idea that 'broken families' produce delinquency and criminal activity. In discussing the problem of 'broken families' we need to keep in mind the fact that most modern societies like the UK, the USA or Australia have had very high rates of divorce and separation since the 1960s and 1970s. This means that divorce, parental separation, single-parent families and what is referred to as 'blended families' have now become, if not actually dominant forms of family experience, certainly very normal and widespread.

'Broken families' and large families

When the empirical research is reviewed and the arguments analysed carefully it does not support a robust connection between 'broken families' and delinquency. In one large US study, psychologist John Rankin found that 'broken homes' correlated significantly only with three types of self-reported juvenile misconduct, namely running away from home, truanting and fighting (this study relied on two national samples totalling 2,242 children). Even in these cases, however, it was difficult to state with any certainty whether such outcomes were directly related to the family structure. Rankin (1983: 47–8) concluded that 'the relationship between broken homes and running away and truancy does not seem particularly strong'.

In another 'meta-analysis' of some sixty-five US studies of 'broken homes' and delinquency, Wells and Rankin (1986) concluded that 'broken homes' produced slightly higher levels of delinquency among children when compared to the results of 'intact' family households. Wells and Rankin (ibid.: 87) found that the correlation between 'broken homes' and delinquency was 'stronger for minor forms of juvenile misconduct or what are called "status offences", and weakest for "serious forms of criminal behaviour"'. They argued that the type of 'break-up' in households also tended to affect levels of delinquency. Wells and Rankin (ibid.: 89) concluded that 'delinquency is slightly stronger for families broken by divorce and separation than by the death of a parent'. This conclusion has been supported in other general reviews of the literature on this issue, suggesting that the relationship between 'broken families' and delinquency is weak, or not at all strong (Jeffs and Smith 1990: 35; Regoli and Hewitt 1991: 206; Lovry 1994: 6).

One of the key problems in the literature claiming to find a causal link between 'broken families' and crime is a failure to specify the particular factors characterizing families – broken or otherwise – that are supposed to lead to crime. It is simply not clear what it is about the 'broken family' – in comparison with the so-called 'intact family' – that causes delinquency or criminality. As Wells and Rankin (1986: 8) note:

> Despite the sizeable body of empirical research extending back to the turn of the century, the broken home question remains unsettled and ambiguous. A major

shortcoming in the literature is the virtual absence of any systematic conceptual specification and corresponding empirical measurement of the broken home as a sociological variable. Although it seems straightforward on its face, more careful analysis reveals it to be a summary gloss for a multiplex combination of family structural and interactional conditions.

Is it the well-established empirical finding that *single-parent families* are over-represented in those families who are income poor? Much of the research on the 'broken family' relies on the assumption that the problems characterizing 'broken families' originate within the family. Yet the ability of parents in any kind of family to maintain their own relationship or to love, care for and supervise their children is affected by many factors other than their inherent parenting 'skills'. Holman (1995) points to the role of inadequate incomes, unemployment, the withdrawal of community, health and education services, and the experience of racial tensions and community conflict. As Utting, Bright and Henricson (1993: 22) argue, how parents and their children deal with these kinds of experiences is far from being a simple matter.

Or is it being assumed that the absence of one of the parents has a negative effect on the family's psychological or social dynamics, effects that are somehow missing in 'intact families'? Is it simply an article of faith that any 'intact family' is necessarily better than a broken one that is on display here? That idea seemed to be on display in 1998, when Peter Saunders, a former Professor of Sociology at Sussex and commentator for the CIS, a neo-conservative think-tank in Sydney (2000–2006), shocked an Australian conference by claiming that any 'intact family', even one where the father engaged in persistent domestic violence, was better for the children than a 'broken family'.

In short, rather than providing a robust basis for explaining why some people commit offences, the research focus on family structures, especially those associated with 'broken families', has failed to specify what the factors are, both within and outside the family household, that lead to delinquency or criminal conduct. By focusing on 'the family' as the pivotal site of crime creation, criminologists have tended to fall into the popular trap of regarding some families as more 'normal', 'acceptable' and 'complete' than others. The metaphors, and they are only that, of 'broken' and 'intact' signify a way of thinking and valuing certain models of the family that reflect cultural assumptions or prejudices found among those who do this research.

These observations can also be made of the claim that *large families* are criminogenic. As with the broken-family model, the link between the number of children in a household and delinquency is, at best, weak. For example, though Farrington (1994: 14–15) argued for a correlation between family size and delinquency, he also allowed that this was secondary to the nature and quality of family relations, particularly between children and parents. Similarly Leflore (1988) in a US study found only a tenuous relationship between family size and delinquency, concluding that 'the home environment may be more important than family structure variables for some youths'. As Rutter and Giller (1983: 109) argue, the claim that there is a close connection between family size and offending is largely 'unfounded'; and as Utting (1994: 18–19) put it, family size may be considered at best one of a range of influences that may, or may not, have a bearing on the emergence of delinquency.

That by and large working-class, coloured and immigrant families, and low-status families in the UK, the USA and Australia, have tended throughout the twentieth century to have more children than white, middle-class or elite couples has of course nothing to do with the fixation on family size in the criminology literature. This last observation gives rise to the question of how certain social prejudices may have entered into the 'constructive schemes' of modern criminologists looking for a causal link between the quality of parent–child relations in some families and crime.

The human development model

There are some very powerful elements in the constructive schemes at work in conventional criminology. There is the very simple idea common to most criminologists that 'antisocial behaviour' or 'crime' is a readily identifiable, even measurable and objective, phenomenon. Then there is the idea of a quasi-organic process of human development in which like the interplay of wind, soil and a garden stake shaping the growth of a small sapling into a tree, so everything done to a child before it is five, fixes its future in ways that cannot be undone. Finally there is the simple idea that human conduct can be readily explained by 'causal factors' like the quality and quantity of maternal love and that a life-long chain of causality is at work.

This constructive scheme has exercised a high degree of influence in the 'human development' model in criminology.

Let us begin with the way the 'human development model' is promoted and the assumptions that this model rests on. This model is on display, along with an assumption that is on this occasion fully outlined, when David Farrington (1997: 361) writes that

> criminal behaviour does not generally appear without warning: it is commonly preceded by childhood anti-social behaviour (such as bullying, lying, truanting and cruelty to animals) and followed by adult anti-social behaviour (such as spouse assault, child abuse, and neglect, excessive drinking and sexual promiscuity). The word 'anti-social' of course involves a value judgment, but it seems likely that there would be a general agreement among most members of Western democracies that these kinds of acts interfered with the smooth running of Western society.

There are several early warning signs about this claim. Firstly, it is simply quite unclear what meaning the idea of 'antisocial behaviour' might ever have, except perhaps to designate forms of conduct the researcher dislikes – and which on this occasion, he allows, 'involves a value judgment'. Look at the things said by Farrington (1994) to constitute 'antisocial' behaviours. They include being 'troublesome and dishonest' being 'aggressive and frequent liars', being a 'bully' and engaging in 'heavy drinking', 'heavy smoking', 'using prohibited drugs', 'heavy gambling' and early, unprotected and promiscuous sex. (It is salutary to remember that West and Farrington (1977) had earlier included having an 'anti-establishment attitude' in their definition of 'antisocial', as well as redundantly making 'antisocial group behaviour' a marker of 'antisocial behaviour'.)

It is hard to know how seriously this definition of what constitutes 'antisocial' conduct should be taken. Recall firstly that Farrington has asserted that his idea of 'antisocial' conduct is shared by 'most members of Western democracies'. Numerous health and social surveys in the UK, Australia and the USA, however, suggest that many, if not most, young people at 18 have engaged in 'heavy drinking', have 'used prohibited drugs', and have engaged in frequent, often unprotected, sexual activities. A substantial minority of young people are also engaged in 'heavy gambling' and 'heavy smoking'. The proposition that these activities signify 'antisocial behaviour' is highly problematic in societies where these attributes and activities are also widely practised and used as hallmarks of sophisticated behaviour by many adults. One empirical basis for saying this is the evidence of the widespread use of cannabis and amphetamines, illicit drugs in Victoria (*The Age*, 30 January 2005). Police began compulsory drug and alcohol testing of drivers in December 2004. Two-and-a-half times more drivers tested 'positive' to drug use than they did for alcohol use.

Further, does Farrington really want us to believe that the behaviours he refers to as 'antisocial' – either singly or in aggregate – are actually capable of 'interfering with the smooth running of Western society'? The proposition that heavy drinking, smoking and gambling are antisocial activities might come as something of a surprise to the liquor, tobacco and gambling industries. Those industries constitute a substantial proportion of many modern countries' economies as measured by Gross Domestic Product. They also provide employment for millions of workers, supply major sponsorships for sporting and cultural events, and generate through the tax systems very large revenues for governments.

The very ubiquity of behaviours such as bullying, cheating and lying (and we could add other behaviours to Farrington's list which social scientists have identified – such as nose-picking and farting in public) might suggest that they have hardly impacted on 'the smooth running of Western society'. Indeed, among certain elites, sexual promiscuity and/or lying on the scale associated with various well-known but nameless US Presidents, UK Prime Ministers, cabinet ministers or corporate bosses suggests that far from being 'antisocial' these behaviours are widely practised, highly praised and valued behaviours. (This is not to say that sections of the tabloid media will not from time to time selectively 'out' sexually active members of the political or corporate elite.) The idea that there is some kind of *causal* connection in place between 'antisocial' forms of human conduct, the selection of which plainly reflects only Farrington's value set, and criminal conduct is so questionable as to be laughable.

If we turn to the core idea of the human development model there are further major problems. Central to this model is a proposition that on the face of it might seem commonsensical: as Graham and Bowling argue, the risk of children becoming delinquent is powerfully determined by the quality of parenting. Graham and Bowling (1996: xii) argue that 'low levels of parental supervision', levels closely dependent on the quality of parent–child relationships, particularly between children and fathers, is the crucial factor leading to delinquency. To make their case on this point more convincing, however, they would need to show that most modern Western families who are not producing delinquent children are actually practising 'pro-social' family life characterized by rich, expressive and close relationships between parents, including fathers, and their children.

However, it is striking that we do not actually know much about 'normal' families because criminologists do not research them. Every one of the hundreds of research articles we consulted in writing this chapter is research done on families with delinquent or offending children. The vast bulk of these families are low-income and/or working-class and/or ethnic-minority families. Further, Graham and Bowling seem to have overlooked the persistent sexual division of labour in most Western societies. This means that women continue to take on a major domestic role in terms of child-care and domestic labour. This feature of modern family life, easily confirmed by numerous modern family work-time studies, suggests that fathers have long been 'absent presences' in the great majority of presumably 'normal' twentieth-century families.

There are problems, too, with the way the human development literature develops the 'parental deficiency model'. Writers like Campbell (1987) and Farrington (1994: 11), for example, all argue that parental inability to exercise 'consistent and firm discipline', maintain 'effective communications' and practise 'conflict resolution' are key factors in 'criminogenesis', or the manufacture of criminality. These writers argue that deficiencies in these *skills* produce families that are discordant, argumentative and lacking in parental support and supervision

There are some complex issues here. Firstly, the sample base of Farrington's 1994 study was working-class families. Like every other criminologist who has done research on this question, he has not researched other kinds of families, like the families of elite or middle-class professionals to establish the extent to which the so-called 'pro-social parenting skills' are actually practised in them.

The fact that Farrington and his colleagues have chosen to focus on low-status, working-class families is a key problem. Are any of the observable differences between the poor, ethnic-minority and working-class families and elite families to be properly understood as deficiencies or simply as differences, and whose judgement about this is to prevail? The preoccupation with researching low-status, working-class, coloured and immigrant families is a traditional bias among conventional criminologists. Why are the alcoholism, sexual promiscuity, emotional abuse or drug-taking of elite families or middle-class families not researched to the same extent as these activities on the part of the lower classes? Is it not possible that too many class and ethnic biases have been allowed to silently inform this research? Have not all manner of assumptions and prejudices about the obvious deficiencies of 'the poor' and working-class families, many of them especially in the UK and the USA, found among minority or immigrant communities, shaped the kinds of research done and the conclusions drawn?

This failure to establish a properly comparative basis for saying what kinds of practices make up 'modern family life' in culturally diverse, radically unequal and multi-ethnic societies like the UK, the USA or Australia is a serious weakness in this research. (Though it is no more than suggestive, Kracauer's 2003 account of Mormon families in Utah still pursuing 'traditional family values', including polygamous marriage, suggests that parts of this culture are rife with domestic violence, rape, incest and psychological abuse and a murderous preoccupation with gun-ownership.)

More generally we can say that the quality of the emotional life and parenting styles in Western families is both very diverse and grounded in a huge variety of historical, cultural, ethnic, occupational, class, religious and psychological traditions and practices. Ought not US criminologists to take into account that theirs is a society with both indigenous peoples and immigrant populations, including significant populations of Afro-American peoples, Catholic Irish, Catholic Italians, Catholic Mexicans, European Jews, Buddhist Vietnamese and Muslim Arabic peoples?

In an area notoriously subject to fads, fashions and advice-mongering by well-meaning experts, this might suggest that it is unwise to reduce ideas about effective parenting to a single set of expert-derived criteria for what is to count as 'effective parenting skills'. (Over the twentieth century expert advice from Dr Spock through to Dr Phil has variously suggested beating children, making them pray a lot, administering cold showers and cod liver oil, family conferencing, complete permissiveness, cognitive therapy and exposure to dispute-resolution processes as desirable parenting practices.)

In making this observation we are not saying that anything goes. It is undeniable that a small number of parents engage in unacceptable behaviour by any standard, including the murder of their children. It is a sad fact that the most likely killer of a child under 12 years of age in Britain and Australia is the child's mother. Equally there is evidence to suggest that some families across a wide spectrum of ethnic and class backgrounds engage in brutal, emotional, sexual or physical abuse of their children.

The core question remains: what is to count as a parenting deficiency and what are to be understood simply as differences in child-rearing practice or as differences in managing family relationships?

The research methods that sustain human development research have the effect of blanking out the social world in which the research is being done, a world which – minimally – includes both the world of the researcher and the world of the research population. Positivist researchers like to reduce their analyses to single or 'cluster' explanations of complex social practices.

Such researchers are presumed or required to adopt a position of scientific detachment involving *value neutrality*, allowing him or her to faithfully administer technical research methods to the specified area of study. A study like Wiesner and Capaldi's (2003) is the very model of a modern longitudinal research project using 'multinomial logistic regressions' and providing 'descriptive' tables outlining Bayesian Information Criterion (BIC), Log Liklihood and Posterior Probability of Correct Models. Wiesner and Capaldi (2003: 245) can then with all seriousness say such things as:

> The average posterior class membership probabilities for the six class solution, with class assignment based on maximum posterior probabilities. Conventionally, values close to one on diagonal elements indicate good classification quality. Although the average posterior class membership probabilities and a further inspection of the individual posterior class memberships' probabilities indicated that classification errors were small for the majority of the study participants, classification quality was somewhat lower (though still acceptable) for the chronic LL [low level] offenders and the decreasing HL [high level] offender classes.

C. Wright Mills (1963) famously had to translate the high-grade theoretical gibberish produced by Talcott Parsons (1950) when he had achieved his most magisterial 'Grand Theorist' voice. A similar exercise is clearly indicated for empiricists like Wiesner and Capaldi. After all, they simply wanted to tell us that if you look at six groups of 'at risk' males aged between 9 and 24, they do not appear to have any clear distinguishing social factors, like their family structure or parenting practices, to explain the various kinds of offences they committed. Or as Wiesner and Capaldi (2003: 254) put it, 'the analyses revealed relatively few factors that discriminated among differing offender trajectories in the multivariate analyses'.

In locating the onset of delinquency in the 'family dynamics' of poor or working-class families, this kind of research both abstracts and objectifies whatever is meant by 'delinquent' conduct from its wider social and economic contexts. Yet parenting practices cannot be easily divorced from their specific cultural, ethnic, class, religious or social circumstances. Without an appreciation of such matters, many so-called 'empirical' studies actually practise a kind of moral nihilism which obliterates any recognition of or sensitivity to moral frameworks that may be quite different from those of the researcher. Moral nihilism is a consequence of simultaneously following 'the rules' for securing 'scientific value neutrality' while surreptitiously reinserting the researcher's own ethnic, class or religious and moral frameworks into the research findings. The favoured categories at work in human develop-ment research, like 'adequate parental supervision', 'impulsivity', 'sluggishness' or simply being 'at risk', reveal more about the strange bestiary of ethno-centric, gendered and class-centric prejudices of the researchers than anything meaningful about the world to which they are applied. By refusing to explicitly outline, let alone defend, the researchers' own moral and social evaluations about what constitutes 'antisocial' behaviour or 'effective parenting practices' or 'close emotional relationships', much of this research simply produces vacuous and unreflective empirical findings masquerading as objective outcomes. Such research is actually blind to the diversity of the social contexts in which the parenting practices or family relationships of specific communities are socially and historically located.

Researchers like Farrington simultaneously ignore their own cultural norms and preferences while using them to identify deficiencies in the lives of low-income, working-class, Muslim, Afro-American or indigenous families. These families are invariably described in terms of their deficits. It is *they* who lack economic resources and have 'reduced' access to significant political or cultural resources.

Pretending that there are timeless or objective criteria for establishing what constitutes 'effective parenting practices' or 'close emotional relationships' is simply unintelligent, even stupid. Assuming that parenting practices or emotionally expressive behaviours found only among small numbers of professionally educated, white, middle-class people make for better families is likewise unhelpful.

As Stan Cohen (1974, 1984, 1992) has repeatedly pointed out in relation to UK criminology, the very *selection* of factors for study in a lot of research mitigates against any simple notion of *objectivity*. Human development studies have been informed by a rhetoric which discursively emphasized the role of *objective* 'scientific investigation', the 'opera-tionalization' of research categories like 'antisocial behaviours', the collection of 'data', and the use of sophisticated statistical processes to establish the *causes* of crime and delinquency. Such an approach rests on assumptions both about the objective role of the investigator in the research process and about the subject(s) under study.

As Hil, MacMahon and Buckley (1996) have argued, questions about the meaning of 'the family', the relationship between the family and the state, and the nature of policing are all strenuously avoided or regarded quite simply as irrelevant. Further, the contested and problematic nature of 'crime' itself, the core category in criminology, is rarely if ever acknowledged. In a similar way, the label of 'offender' or 'delinquent' is applied un-questioningly to thousands of young people in an attempt to identify the particular range of factors that differentiate them from the 'law-abiding majority'. This attempt to separate out 'offenders' from the 'rest of us' and to record their social attributes is itself symptomatic of a distinctively modern way of thinking about the causes of criminal deviance (Abbott and Wallace 1992; Young 1997).

Just as we need to recognize the complex nature of family relationships, so it is important to avoid labelling families as simply 'good' or 'bad' – a simplifying polarity implicit in many empirical studies of families and crime. Rather, as Frost and Stein (1989: 5) insist, 'we need an analysis which helps us understand the positive and negative aspects of the family experience for children and young people'. By presenting a one-dimensional view of 'the family', human development research tends to buttress oppositional categories that pit one representation of 'the family' against another. Accordingly, families are thought of as 'normal–abnormal', 'functional–dysfunctional', 'broken–intact', and so forth. This rendering of oppositional categories is further underpinned by the assumption that it is possible to demonstrate a quantifiable difference between law-abiding and 'criminogenic' families. This reflects a wider disciplinary idea that treats certain families, communities and neighborhoods as threats to the social order. Particular households are thus homogenized as 'problem families' and regarded as in need of intervention and regulation (Cook 1997). The process of identifying the particular characteristics of such families through research studies provides the justification for incursions by the state into the lives of working-class families (Parton 1991: 10; see Hunt 1991). The families routinely subject to the most heavy and sustained research and policing are those from the poorest and most disadvantaged sections of the working class (Donzelot 1979; Carrington 1993; Hudson 1993: 3).

As Mike Donaldson (1991: 2) points out, an adequate understanding of 'working-class' families would draw on 'the whole lives of its members, changing and changed by each other as they stand in structural opposition to capital, its forces and agencies'. Donaldson (ibid.: 73) is also right to insist that the daily life of the family-household is acted out in a multiplicity of ways according to the essential divisions of age and gender. The 'struggle to create order and meaning out of precariousness and scarcity, to provide a measure of security in a very uncertain world . . .', involves managing various household 'clocks' (ibid.: 73). Too much criminology research fails to think about 'working-class families' in this way. It would also be useful to know more about the diverse ways in which all kinds of families, up and down the hierarchy of socio-economic opportunity and power, construct their daily lives and interactions. The organization of 'family time' and relationships between members is, however, severely disrupted by problems associated with unemployment and inadequate income. At such times, families strive to manage increasingly fraught and fragile relationships (Altatt and Yeandle 1992: 144). For those on the margins of economic life – the long-term unemployed, the isolated and disaffected – the family household becomes less a source of respite and support and more a place in which the pressures of the outside world are acted out.

Finally, it is especially striking that the empirical research on working-class families has the effect of actually silencing or muffling the voices of the subjects. Elaine Scarry (1985) has pointed out that certain forms of state violence have the effect of silencing the victims of that violence. It is not stretching the meaning of 'violence' too far to see a similar effect being produced by conventional social science research. Hil and McMahon, in a commentary on juvenile justice research, noted that the resulting literature is remarkable for its lack of attention to the views and experiences of those actually caught up in the criminal justice system. We continue to know little about the lived experience of those involved in processes of criminal justice or about the ways in which these experiences relate to everyday life in communities and neighborhoods.

(1995: 4; see also Hil and McMahon 2004)

As if to compound this silence, much of the existing research takes the meaning of 'the family' for granted. In most cases, no effort is made to offer even the most rudimentary defence of the tacit belief that only a middle-class, 'intact', 'nuclear family' with a traditional sexual division of labour where father works and mother is the carer is able to secure freedom from the onset of delinquency. The possibility of alternative family forms and the influence of gender, class and ethnicity on family relationships are rarely explored in detail. The sole-parent household is regarded as deviant to the culturally loaded norm of the 'complete' or 'intact' nuclear family. This narrow view of 'the family' is made worse by the tendency to ignore the diverse and competing interests in family households. Rarely does one get the sense that families are complex, interactive institutions in which power and interest play a significant role in determining relationships in them.

Yet such matters are crucial in enabling us to understand the ways in which family relationships are constructed and acted out in daily life (Funder 1995: 4). As Mike Donaldson (1991: 2) reminds us, the 'terrible intimacy' of family life is reflected in the complex relationships that exist in this ever-changing and culturally diverse social institution. Thus:

> It is necessary to see families not as unified entities that can only be represented by the concept of a 'household head', usually male. [Rather they should be seen] as flexible and interactive groupings comprised of men and women, children, young people and older people, whose collective and separate interests need to be protected and supported.

(National Council for the International
Year of the Family 1994: 9)

Conclusion

As Pat O'Malley (1996) has argued, the resurgence of individualistic explanations of crime in the 1980s and 1990s has helped to re-generate an interest in 'the family' as the source of crime. Garland (1996), too, notes how a discourse of 'responsibilization', where crime is attributed to 'individual failure' on the part of the offender and his or her family, renews a traditional criminological interest in family life. Equally the spectre of an 'underclass' whose populations are supposedly prone to outbreaks of lawlessness has led many researchers to stress the prevalence of dysfunctional families among low-income people and the unemployed (Wilson 1996).

While the sheer volume of studies in this area is testimony to the importance assigned to 'the family' by criminologists, the conclusions are extremely biased in terms of the preoccupation with researching poor, working-class and minority families. The families of white, elite, high-income, powerful, wealthy people, strangely enough, never get to be researched for evidence of 'antisocial behaviours', the quality of emotional life or the resident moral attitudes of family members. Equally strangely, criminologists continue to make the quite unwarranted assumption that only poor, working-class and ethnic-minority families get to be 'broken', display sub-standard care of their children and exhibit deficiencies of morality or pro-social conduct.

Criminologists and penologists have – perhaps unwittingly – contributed in large measure to the *new* emphasis on moral individualism. They have done this insofar as they have asserted the importance of individualized notions of justice – mainly by reference to the ideological conduit of 'responsibility' – and completed studies on offender motivation and situational crime prevention (Brake and Hale 1993). These 'conservative criminologies' signal a *new* era in criminology devoted to the actuarial exploration of the 'crime problem' (Garland 1997). The family is rarely far from the gaze of such criminologists.

In short, criminological discourse in this area is important not for the success or otherwise in identifying particular causal variables within the family household, but because it reflects the partial and highly selective way in which the discipline has, over the course of the twentieth century, focused on 'working-class' and 'poor' families to *explain* crime.

Review questions

Is it useful or desirable to talk about 'the family' as if the term refers to a single, coherent, social institution that generates uniform parenting practices or child–parent relationships?

Are there any moral or social biases at work in the development of the 'parental failure' type of explanations of delinquency and criminality?

In what ways does the feminist critique call into doubt empiricist accounts of family-based explanations of crime?

Further reading

Farrington, D., 1987, 'Implications of Biological Findings for Criminological Research', in Mednick, S., Moffit, T. and Stack, A. (eds), *The Causes of Crime: New Biological Approaches*, Cambridge University Press, Cambridge.

Heidensohn, F., 1986, *Women and Crime*, Macmillan, London.

Henry, S. and Milovanovic, D., 1994, 'The Constitution of Constitutive Criminology: A Post-Modern Approach to Criminological Theory', in Nelken, D. (ed.), *The Futures of Criminology*, Sage, London.

Hunt, A., 1999, *Governing Morals: A Social History of Moral Regulation*, Cambridge University Press, Cambridge.

CRIMINOLOGY AND THE LURE OF CRIME PREVENTION

Law and order issues have become a staple of public debate and electoral politics in most Western societies. It sometimes seems that electoral campaigns have become political auctions in which the competing parties and candidates seek to outbid each other in terms of who is toughest on law and order. In the UK Tony Blair's New Labour won the 1997 election in part because of its tough law and order policy (Bottomley et al. 1998). It subsequently issued several White Papers, including its *Justice for All* White Paper (Home Office 2002), and introduced fourteen Bills addressing the 'crime problem'. In the USA the elevation of George W. Bush to the White House in 2000 rested on his reputation as someone who had been tough on crime when he was the Governor of Texas, signified in part by his willingness to not exercise clemency on behalf of inmates of Death Row. As David Garland (1996: 460) observes, contemporary politicians are nowadays moved easily to 'make punitive pronouncements' so as 'to express popular feelings of rage and frustration in the wake of particularly disturbing crimes'. These tabloid reactions rely on what he calls 'a criminology of the alien other which represents criminals as dangerous members of distinct racial and social groups which bear little resemblance to "us"' (1996: 461).

It is perhaps not surprising that crime prevention has become a central element in public discussion in the media and public policy debates at the start of the twenty-first century or that crime prevention has become a major theme in contemporary criminology, reflecting a drift towards the 'commercialisation of criminology' (Israel 2000). Many criminologists regard crime prevention as the central reason for doing criminology.

In this chapter we explore two aspects of crime prevention. One is the way criminological arguments inform policy. Our intention here is not to provide a detailed analysis of the technical merits or demerits of specific crime-prevention initiatives. This has already been done well by writers like Graham and Bowling (1996), Hazlehurst (1996), Gilling (1997), Sparks (2000) and Newburn (2003). Rather we examine the way criminologists have approached the idea of crime prevention as a policy practice. Why has crime prevention become so popular among policy-makers over the past two decades? It matters that we are able to think about the value of criminological arguments when they start to have policy or political consequences. We examine some of the assumptions built into the constructive schemes and arguments advanced by criminologists advocating crime prevention.

We look also at the politics of contemporary crime-prevention discourses. Sitting alongside a traditional politics whose exponents run a 'get tough on crime and criminals' line, backed up by the power of the state, we also see at work a neo-liberal politics which adapts a discourse of 'risk' and the 'risk society' (Beck 1992) based on mobilizing individuals and communities to take more responsibility for crime prevention. Here we see relatively novel ideas about crime prevention as a policy practice found in societies with political cultures dependent on an individualist vocabulary associated with neo-liberalism.

We examine a tense exchange between Adam Sutton, a leading proponent of the criminological *relevance* of crime prevention, and his critics in the late 1990s (Sutton 1996; O'Malley 1997). This offers an ideal case study of some of the issues at stake in current debates about crime prevention. The nature of this exchange and the various claims made about what 'crime prevention' *means* reveal some of the central issues at stake in contemporary ideas about crime prevention.

The meaning of crime prevention

Traversing the landscape of crime prevention can seem rather like hacking through the dense undergrowth of an Amazonian rainforest. This is not simply because the history of crime control seems to be so murky. It also has much to do with the proliferation of competing definitions, typologies and political meanings associated with the idea of crime prevention which has the kind of lushness associated with tropical plant growth. Moreover, there is not always much light at the bottom of it all.

There is a plethora of ideas about crime prevention. Crime prevention has been informed by ideas of correction, deterrence, rehabilitation or reintegration, ideas which are not always commensurable. As Gilling (1997: 1–8) reminds us, it has also been seen as 'pro-active' or 'reactive', and best administered variously in relation to offenders and victims, neighbourhoods or entire 'problem populations'. Some criminologists, for example Van Dijlk and De Waard (quoted in Sutton and O'Malley 1997: 2), have defined crime prevention in a way that downplays the role of the criminal justice system as 'the total of all private initiatives and state policies, other than the enforcement of the criminal law, aimed at the reduction of damage caused by acts defined as criminal by the state'. Others, like Pease (1997: 965), note that 'the police lead in primary prevention' through activities 'seeking to reduce crime opportunities without reference to criminals or potential criminals'. Garland also argues (1990: 18) that legal punishment is best thought of 'as a legally approved method designed to facilitate the task of crime control'. Crime prevention has also been defined in terms of a range of approaches. Some emphasize 'primary crime prevention' which focuses on victims rather than on the motivations of offenders. Then there is 'situational crime prevention' which seeks to change people before they engage in crime. Others look for 'tertiary crime prevention' strategies which seek to put an end to the criminal career, sometimes permanently, as advocates of capital punishment no doubt intend. For others, crime prevention is about some general philosophical or moral position, or, quite simply, in the Benthamite tradition, as something that both promotes the well-being of a community and is eminently desired by the majority of the population.

There is enough here already to suggest why aiming at any simple or essential definition of 'crime prevention' is problematic.

A common-sense approach would suggest that, however it is defined or intended, crime prevention extends throughout all of the formal and informal networks of the criminal justice system. The contemporary emphasis on crime prevention points also to an increasingly intricate relationship between the criminal justice system, elements of corporate finance, like the insurance industry, as well as the security industries, and citizens mobilized into projects like The Neighbourhood Watch. It certainly also includes community safety programmes and a wide array of 'risk management' policies. Crime prevention is now being constituted as a normal responsibility, not solely of governments, but of all *active* and *responsible* citizens. This has been accentuated since the 11 September 2001 attacks in the USA when, as part of the so-called 'war on terror', governments in the UK, the USA and Australia have called on their citizens to be alert and to report 'suspicious people' to the authorities.

Criminology and crime prevention

Historically, criminology and crime prevention have gone hand-in-hand. Whenever people have thought about crime, so remedies have been proposed designed to prevent its occurrence. But this is where any symmetry ends. As we have argued in earlier chapters, from the earliest expressions of criminology to the most recent criminological research and theory, there is great diversity in theories of crime as well as in the strategies proposed to curtail 'criminal' behaviours. The contemporary state of criminology reveals a highly complex ensemble of ideas and perspectives, for reasons that are indicated by a potted history of criminological thought about crime prevention.

From its onset criminology conceived of the theory and practice of punishment as having a part to play in crime prevention. In the late eighteenth century the Italian legal philosopher Beccaria objected to the, then-normal, public spectacle of punishments like hanging, flogging, burning or beheading. His approach to crime prevention was informed by his preference for a proportional system of administrative justice in which offenders could expect a sentence *appropriate* to the crime. As a proto-utilitarian, Beccaria like later utilitarians, including Bentham, believed that the purpose of punishment was to act as a general deterrent to crime rather than to engage in or even to celebrate punishment for punishment's sake.

In early-nineteenth-century Britain and America, Bentham and his disciples took this logic further by insisting that the proper objective of criminal justice should be the reform and rehabilitation of the criminal. They argued that rather than simply punishing criminals, rehabilitation was what was needed to facilitate improved 'habits and thoughts' among errant individuals. The shift from physical discipline and punishment to 'mind control' and moral regulation was part of a broader set of strategies aimed at controlling and even reforming the 'dangerous classes'. These strategies have become a central motif in what writers like Garland (1997, 2001) call the 'regimes of liberal governance' into our time.

Garland's reference to 'regimes of liberal governance' derives from the work of Foucault. Foucault (1991) called this the 'modern' idea of government. This is another way of talking about the way *society* is made up of *individuals* each of whom is presumed to be a rational, happiness-maximizing, somewhat egoistic person who enters freely into relations with others, especially in the economic processes of the market (Taylor 1997). It presupposed, as Schneewind (1998) points out, an 'autonomous individual' who voluntarily practised rational self-control in the interests of *society*. Societies like Britain and America in the eighteenth and nineteenth centuries drew heavily on the ethics of utilitarianism, liberal political theory, and classical and neo-classical economics to produce cultures of practice in which these ideas can be seen at work. (Needless to say, because nothing is ever simple, older *communitarian* ideas grounded in Christian religious and moral ideas also helped shape the actual cultures of these societies. Communitarianism promotes the idea that the interests and traditional values of the community take priority over the needs or interests of the individual. The individualism of Christianity helped make a bridge between the newer kinds of individualism and more traditional conceptions of moral life.)

Garland's 2001 account of 'liberal government' is typified by the Benthamite project to make individuals responsible for regulating themselves in morally or socially appropriate ways. This philosophy informed attempts to instil proper moral and religious values among prisoners in Pentonville in England and Port Arthur in Australia. These exercises in moral rehabilitation ran parallel to similar practices evolving in the great institutions of the nineteenth century like the industrial schools, factories and the workhouses. These gave expression to Bentham's Panopticon principle, which holds that if people feel as if they are under constant surveillance they will self-regulate. All these institutions were conceived as places where an effort to regulate the behaviours of the poor and working-class populations of the new industrial cities might best be made. A key change, however, and one sponsored by Bentham and his protégés, was to move away from detailed regulation by teachers, wardens, prison chaplains and other supervisors and towards installing, as it were, autonomous systems of self-regulation into each *member* of society.

The rise of 'liberal government' did not mean that older communitarian ideas about the virtue of retributive justice of the 'eye for an eye' kind faded away. As is so often the case, the highly intellectual ideas of people like Beccaria and Bentham variously shunned or ignored the widespread moral–emotional appeal of vengeance, treating it as irrational and unworthy. Most of us have a well-developed capacity for seeking retribution, or vengeance, something that those who have opposed capital punishment have not always understood. These ideas supported tough policing and penal policies in the nineteenth century, as they do into the twenty-first century. Nevertheless, the two ideas simply co-existed. Things got even more complicated in the second half of the nineteenth century.

As we saw in Chapter 3, the shift to a project of moral training and of rehabilitating those who had committed criminal offences enjoyed considerable support in the first half of the nineteenth century. The second half of that century saw the flowering of a positivist framework of socio-biological explanations of crime. From the 1860s on, the success of the Darwinian biological 'revolution' encouraged a determinist model of social science. Foucault called this a 'bio-politics'. As we have shown, this took the statistical work of writers like Quételet, who were convinced that human conduct was governed by immutable laws, and began to move towards what we now call a genetic model of explanation. In Italy the idea that criminality had a biological basis informed Lombroso's account of 'criminal man' as an atavistic or evolutionary throwback. In England Galton's science of eugenics was the chief expression of this 'bio-politics'. Galton and his protégés like Pearson ushered in the intensive practice of empirical observation and bio-statistical measurement designed to distinguish the characteristics of racial types in the anthropometric project that Lombroso and Galton promoted. The physical measurement of body and skull shapes that anthropometrists practised quickly gave way after 1900 to an even more elaborate measurement of *intelligence* and subsequently of a vast array of social, emotional and cognitive processes. This disposition to measure and to construct standards for the *normal* development of reading, writing or other cognitive and social skills continues unabated at the start of the twenty-first century, suggesting, if nothing else, the scientific authority and appeal that 'numbers' continue to exercise, perhaps as a device to dispel anxiety in the face of uncertainty.

Criminologists' research seemed to suggest that various educative and medical interventions – like compulsory sterilization of the 'unfit' – would aid the quest for 'racial' or 'social' hygiene. Crime prevention in this sense was to be increasingly characterized by an attempt to clean out the criminal element from the social body, a leading motif in what became a complex of practices that made up the 'racial hygiene' movements. The 'criminal', as a lesser being, was to be eliminated either by the negative eugenicist programme, making systematic use of medical technologies like contraception and sterilization, and/or by the positive eugenicist programme through initiatives of state-sponsored public health, education, psycho-therapeutic interventions and moral restraint.

This eugenic impulse continued to play an important role in shaping approaches to crime prevention until the 1930s. It was supplemented in Britain by the work of psychologists like Burt, Bowlby and Winnicott, in the middle of the twentieth century, who initiated a shift towards 'human developmental' concerns that turned especially on mother–child relationships (Rose 1990). The rise of child-guidance clinics and the growth of various therapeutic intervention strategies in Britain reflected attempts to manage crime by promoting improved family relationships. In America, in the 1930s and 1940s, a major preoccupation with crime prevention emerged through early therapeutic interventions with 'pre-delinquent boys'. One modern expression of this idea is the promotion of parent effectiveness training (PET).

This focus on the individual–family link was partially displaced in the post-war period by the rise of other sociological explanations of crime creation. For instance, the Chicago Area Project in the 1940s was an attempt to address the urban problems identified by the Chicago School of Sociology. Clinical intervention was thus to some extent replaced by a liberal version of community development which involved the recruitment of outreach youth workers and the provision of recreation activities, family support and so forth – an approach evident in many current approaches to crime prevention. Such measures were designed to provide an outlet for the criminogenic urban poor, thereby lessening their propensity to engage in antisocial behaviours.

Following broadly in this tradition, the later works of US sociologists like Merton (1969a), Matza (1960) and various labelling and sub-cultural theorists argued that socio-economic conditions have a major role to play in the creation of crime. The more sceptically inclined argued that involvement in the criminal justice system merely made matters worse for the offender and society as a whole. (Edwin Schur's 1974 proposal for 'radical non-intervention' was the logical outcome of this radical–sceptical train of thought: Schur proposed that with regard to problems like delinquency or some kinds of mental illness the best thing to do was nothing.) Other writers, among them Oscar Newman (1972) – through his notion of 'defensible space' – and US journalist Janet Jacobs (1962), argued that crime was an outgrowth of a fragmented urban environment in which high-density municipal housing had eroded the quality of life for its beleaguered residents. Although charged with 'architectural determinism' and 'social abstractionism', their ideas led to the emergence of 'environmental criminology' with its focus on the opportunities for and constraints on crime, spatio-temporal organization and the deleterious effects of behavioural 'contamination' (Gilling 1997). According to this body of thought, crime prevention was most likely to occur through systematic programmes of urban renewal and improved (and safety conscious) environmental design.

While these theoretical developments were taking place, criminologists continued to hack their way through the metaphorical Amazonian jungle in search of the specific dispositional or causal factors leading to crime and delinquency. Influential figures in the UK like Mannheim remained unconvinced by much of the research, arguing that too much criminological work on juvenile delinquency consisted of 'half-baked truths and slogans, of unwarranted generalizations derived from a small body of observations and inadequate samples' (1955: 13). The favoured explanations (typically inner-urban deprived environments, 'dysfunctional family life' and 'antisocial' personal attributes) continued to be researched, but without any startling results. As Gilling (1997: 46) observed:

> [W]hile criminology continued its elusive search for dispositional factors that separated the criminal from the law abiding, others had to live with the consequences of its spectacular failure to make inroads into steadily rising rates of crime . . . Rising crime and its repercussions . . . became a problem for others besides criminologists and the agencies of the criminal justice system.

This 'spectacular failure', and the apparent conclusion that 'nothing works', provided a context which made possible the emergence of contemporary crime-prevention ideas.

Contemporary crime prevention

What we have in the UK, the USA and Australia in the twenty-first century is an uneasy juxtaposition of neo-liberal and 'rational choice' theory framed by talk of risk sitting cheek by jowl with neo-conservative calls for a 'get tough on crime and criminals' approach that calls for more police, tougher sentences – and in the USA the reintroduction of capital punishment. This is what Carrabine et al. (2004: 103–7) call 'contradictory criminologies'.

Crime prevention is now part of the vocabulary of modern political discourse, even though in practice it remains mostly subordinated to more punitive or 'get tough' approaches to criminal justice. Most political parties in Western states now advocate some form of crime prevention as a means of dealing with the crime problem. The sub-text of such approaches is that crime prevention conveys a more thoughtful, sensitive and *constructive* approach to crime control, while retributive punishment is counter-productive and serves only to satisfy a collective thirst for some kind of vengeance. The fact that talk of prevention is prevalent in political circles, with continual references to the need to 'get tough on crime and its causes', is itself evidence of the credibility given to such issues in current public discourse.

It is conventional to use a single term such as 'neo-liberalism' or the 'New Right' to refer to the character of the political culture in countries like the UK, the USA or Australia. This misstates the complexity of the situation. In terms of economic policy, the older social liberalism associated with the idea of a 'mixed economy' in which government and the market co-operated combined with a 'Keynesian welfare state' has given way to a neo-liberal policy discourse which focuses on smaller government and more room for the market (Mishra 1984). Since the 1990s this in turn has sponsored talk and policies promoting the value of 'globalizing the economy' through free-trade agreements and by deregulating the market.

This has occurred at the same time as various kinds of neo-conservatives have promoted a restoration of traditional values and institutions like the family grounded in certain kinds of Catholic and evangelical Protestant religious beliefs. Aune (2001: 6–9) points to four strands of 'conservative' thought in the USA:

- traditional conservativism represented by the Rockford Institute and the League of the South;
- libertarianism represented by journals like *Public Choice*;
- 'fusionists' associated with the *National Review* and former President Ronald Reagan; and
- neo-conservativism, exemplified by James Q. Wilson, journals like *Commentary* and Rupert Murdoch's *The Weekly Standard*.

Weaving in and around these networks are the increasingly powerful and well-funded fundamentalist Christian churches.

The result is a contradictory political culture and policy framework. Free marketeers and neo-liberals have never favoured the kinds of regulation of individual sexuality or lifestyle vigorously promoted by the Christian Right. Notwithstanding the contradictions and tensions inherent in this coalition, the political cultures of the UK, the USA and Australia have been reshaped by the advocacy of economic liberal values and neo-conservative values.

The Reagan presidency sponsored a major shift in US public policy. In the UK the Thatcher government effected a similar fusion of traditional conservative and neo-liberal economics. The evolving policy framework saw merit in freeing market forces from the dead hand of excessive government intervention and excessive union power. In the 1980s, and without detecting any obvious contradiction, the Thatcher government and the Reagan presidency simultaneously sponsored the rediscovery of 'traditional values'. Espousal of these 'traditional values', addressing themes like sexual morality, family life and respect for authority and law and order, entailed more, not less, government intervention. It also sponsored the development by labourist and progressive parties of an ensemble of conservative and 'middle-ground' ideologies (like Tony Blair's New Labour and Bill Clinton's 'Third Way'). The Australian Labour Party governments of Hawke and Keating (1983–96) took what might be called a 'social democratic' road to 'Third Wayism', promoting neo-liberal economic and social policies, while retaining the allegiance of their working-class constituency with a social wage policy (Bessant et al. 2006).

One result has been a renewed emphasis on notions of *individual* and *community* responsibility. Individuals, families and communities are being urged to take greater responsibility in the search for solutions to social and economic problems. Simultaneously neo-conservatives have moved to reinstate 'traditional values' and individual responsibility as part of a critique of the conventional sociological approach which explained social conduct in terms of 'social structures' widely seen by neo-conservatives as a 'cop-out' from taking individual responsibility. This point was memorably made when Prime Minister Margaret Thatcher observed that 'society does not exist' (Abbott and Wallace 1992).

John Braithwaite (2000) argues that this has involved a major restructuring of relations between the state and its citizenry by means of what Miller and Rose (1990) called 'governing at distance'. As Rose (2000: 323–4), using the 'steering, not rowing' metaphor made famous by Osborne and Gaebler (1993), argues, this has meant that modern governments become the '[p]artner, animator and facilitator for a variety of independent agents and powers and [that it] should exercise only limited powers of its own, steering and regulating, rather than rowing and providing'.

Contemporary academics have hardly been immune to these intellectual and policy shifts. In the social sciences there have been moves to revivify neo-classical economics, while rational choice theory has resurfaced in disciplines like sociology. In criminology this has meant a move to explain offending behaviour using 'neo-classical' ideas of voluntary, purposive and rational–calculative individual human action. Rational choice theorists argued that people engaged in crime as a conscious and 'mundane' activity to maximize economic or other benefits. Crime could not be explained simply by reference to 'social conditions' or other external 'forces'. As Gary Becker (1968, 1978), one of the leading Chicago free-market economists, showed, it was possible to concoct an economic theory of crime. This encouraged other rational choice theorists, such as Cohen and Simpson (1997) and Shover (1998), who have argued that corporate criminals are rational, calculating and instrumental individuals who carefully considered the risks and sanctions when assessing each opportunity to commit a criminal act. Accordingly crime was a 'moral aberration' for which the offender alone was responsible. Similarly Erlich (1975) argued that capital punishment should be treated as the 'shadow price' for murder. He used an econometric model, 'crunched some numbers' and showed that 'seven lives would be saved by each execution'. As Hudson (1993) noted, this view fitted neatly with the prevailing drift towards what has become known as the 'justice model', in which individual responsibility was regarded as the hallmark of rational calculative action.

All that was left for the 'expert' criminologist was to offer recommendations to identify those elements defined as the 'situational' and 'dispositional' antecedents of offending. It was suggested that 'situational crime prevention', with its focus on 'opportunity reduction', reflected a 'criminology of the real world'. Those promoting this view presumably believed that criminologists were finally addressing the 'hard facts of life'. This was clearly better than peddling obscure and irrelevant 'left-wing ideologies' or 'sociological excuses' for what was properly a personal moral deficiency or a failure to accurately conduct a rational assessment of the costs and benefits of an action (Gilling 1997: 65).

The obvious flaws in situational approaches to crime prevention included allowing a limitless capacity for 'freedom of choice' while overemphasizing the economic motives of action at the expense of the denial of 'expressive' crime, like 'crimes of passion'. (Rational actor theorists have responded that while nothing may deter a deranged killer the threat of execution might well deter most potential murderers.) Situational approaches to crime prevention have continued to remain integral to contemporary crime-control practices in a number of Western policy communities.

Situational crime prevention has significant elective affinities with neo-liberal and neo-conservative politics because it understands crime as something individuals *choose* to do. As Israel (2000) suggests, it may also have something to do with changes to the terms on which university-based criminological research is now being funded, so that research designs are both more competitive and more sensitive to their commercial implications.

Through the 1990s crime prevention took another 'new turn'. Experts began to talk about 'community safety', an idea grounded in a hotchpotch of neo-conservative and neo-liberal and left-realist discourses. It has ushered in various approaches to crime management based on notions of 'community development', 'partnership', 'community policing' and 'private policing'. These approaches have involved everything from anti-crime groups, vigilante groups patrolling streets and subways, Neighbourhood Watch-type programmes, citizens' associations and, in the case of the UK, a proposal to use the unemployed as an ancillary police force.

Each approach has its own 'theory' of crime causation, appealing variously to environmental and situational influences, individual moral failure, family breakdown, urban decay, unemployment, the rise of an 'underclass' and increasing poverty – or, as it is now called, 'social exclusion'. However, the shift towards 'community safety' has involved a move away from the narrow emphasis of rational choice theorists on opportunity reduction and has resulted in a model of crime prevention grounded in the apparently spontaneous actions of 'active citizens' in alliance with the official law and order agencies. As Gilling (1997: 180) points out, this focus on the community

> is a very strange change to have occurred, because the restructuring of the state continues, and the situational approach still posseses a much stronger elective affinity with the strong state required as a corollary for determining the logic of privatization and managerialism. In what was once coined The Great Moving Right Show, community safety perversely appears to be moving in the opposite direction.

This is a possibly overly benign view given the history of earlier exercises in political cultures under the sway of communitarian belief systems. Robert Gellately (2002) recalls that one of the first efforts to mobilize citizens to engage in crime prevention was the exercise undertaken by the German Gestapo in the 1930s. The Gestapo created neighbourhood networks of informants to make up for the numerical deficiencies of Gestapo agents, a system that the secret police (or *Stasi*) of the communist regime in East Germany took over, holus-bolus, after 1945. The sinister overtones of that exercise has, if anything, been heightened since the terrorist attacks in New York and Washington on 11 September 2001, and the Underground bomb attacks in London in 2005, by the move to establish agencies with responsibility for homeland security in the USA and by governments mobilizing support for citizens to inform authorities about 'suspicious persons'.

Crime prevention has of course moved well beyond such relatively simple 'communitarianism' over recent years. One of the most significant developments that has complemented 'community safety' has been the ascendancy of the notion of 'risk'. Its absorption into the policy and practice of crime control in Western states marks the return to pre-eminence of individualistic explanations of crime causation.

Crime and risk

Over recent years, criminology, along with other social sciences, has embraced the vocabulary of risk with a view to identifying predisposing 'risk factors' and proposing initiatives to prevent further offending (Bessant, Hil and Watts 2005).

Typical of the discourse of risk-based crime-prevention initiatives is the proposal for one 'crime prevention strategy' in Australia. Like countless other parallel approaches in Western countries, the Queensland Labour government has adopted what might be called a 'blunderbuss' approach to crime prevention, outlined in a succession of policy documents (Queensland Criminal Justice Commission 1992; Task Force on Crime Prevention 1999). The Task Force on Crime Prevention proposed a highly 'mixed' approach to crime prevention, including a criminal justice model involving control by law-enforcement agencies and the criminal justice system. To this it added support for a 'situational approach' including 'design, organization and management' of the environment for 'opportunity reduction purposes', as well as community-based approaches like initiatives to 'target "at risk" groups and communities'. Finally it added on developmental approaches designed to prevent 'the development of risk behaviors through early intervention and adolescent interventions' (ibid.: 9).

In a summary table of breathtaking scope the *Getting Tough on Crime* policy identifies both *risk factors* and *protective factors* under such headings as 'childhood factors', 'family factors', 'school factors' and 'community and cultural factors'. Much of this depends on a mountain of recent 'empirical' research on the theme of 'pro-social' and 'antisocial' behaviours and the 'risk factors' that are associated with them, as exemplified in the work done in Sweden by Stattin, Romelsjö and Stenbacka (1997: 198–223).

Although promoted as if this policy framework rests on solid empirical and scientific evidence, the use of indices of 'risk' and 'protection' points to a level of fantasy and plain silliness that is deeply worrying. Any reader can ask her- or himself if the characteristics identified by Stattin, Romelsjo and Stenbacka (ibid.: 199–200) as indicators of 'antisocial' behaviour are anything more than a bundle of prejudices about the world of the 'typical' young, male, juvenile delinquent. The research cited identifies a range of 'predisposing causes' in its list of family factors, including 'poor parental supervision and discipline', 'substance abuse', 'family conflict and disharmony', 'father absence', 'long-term parental unemployment', 'rejection of child' and 'abuse neglect'. Equally it identifies the protective factors which will prevent these risks eventuating, including 'supportive caring parents', 'family harmony', 'responsibility for choices of required helpfulness'(!), 'strong family norms and morality' and 'parental attachment to the labour market'. This research seems to presuppose that 'pro-social' qualities essential to 'family functioning' are widely distributed in any modern Western society, such as the ability to relate closely to others, 'caring', social extroversion, role-taking ability, co-operativeness, social responsiveness, reflective rather than impulsive conduct, impulse control, emotional stability, self-efficacy and a sense of fairness (Stattin, Romelsjo and Stenbacka ibid.: 199–200). It is surely a matter worthy of more research to establish the extent to which such 'pro-social' qualities are found among contemporary business leaders or politicians to say nothing of academics in the UK, the USA or Australia. Far from treating this sort of stuff as 'scientific' or helpful in developing viable crime-prevention strategies, we see here evidence more of moralistic prejudices devoid of real insight into the world of 'normal' virtues and the real conduct of ordinary people. Great modern ethical philosophers like Tzetvan Todorov (1996) and Mary Midgley (2001) remind us of the real ethical complexity of people's lives.

The manifest failure to clarify the meaning of what looks like a large number of moralizing judgements is matched by an unwillingness to think about the connection between 'criminalization' and broadly conceived 'policing' strategies. Indeed, nowhere in the *Getting Tough on Crime* policy documents is there any reference to the role of policing in constructing the 'crime problem'. This 'problem' is largely taken for granted, as is so often the case in conventional criminology. Nowhere is there any critical or reflective analysis of the official crime rate statistics, let alone of their essentially problematic nature. This is significant given that Queensland is one of the Australian states with a larger than average indigenous population and one which also boasts of disproportionately high arrest and imprisonment rates for its Aboriginal population. The question of whether a massive 'all-of-government' initiative involving millions of dollars and the employment of large numbers of professional and ancillary personnel is necessary needs to be asked, given the way that the 'crime problem' in Queensland is routinely overstated. No doubts are raised about whether the calibration of the risk posed by crime is accurate, which is surprising given, as Utting (1994) reminds us, the notorious unreliability of predictive instruments. Finally, despite the acknowledgement of 'social factors', the document asserts that no costings or funds are to be provided for the many proposed initiatives. One is left with the distinct feeling that programmes requiring the investment of millions of dollars (such as job-creation schemes, strategies to alleviate growing family poverty, etc.) will go unfunded while the domiciliary interventions and 'early intervention' approaches will prove more attractive to governments. In short, while the document makes the grandest of all crime-prevention gestures, its outcomes are likely to be as piecemeal, short-lived and patchy as countless other such approaches (Cohen 1984).

Australian criminologists have been centrally involved in the construction of the Queensland strategy and are active more generally in the crime-prevention industry. Everywhere, criminologists, psychologists and child development experts are busily setting about the provision of the technical instruments and empirical data required for the assembly of crime-prevention initiatives.

The enterprise conjures up all of the authority with which modern social scientists seek to render themselves credible and authoritative. The empirical studies typically involve large samples. The Swedish study by Stattin, Romelsjo and Stenbacka (1997) which the Queensland government relies on draws on a sample of 7,500 young people. The Australian study by O'Connor (1992), also relied on by the Queensland government, used a cohort of 1,125 young people. (Equally research adopting a more intensive psychometric methodology tends to work with smaller samples; see Caspi et al. 1995.) This research appears to be endlessly busy. There is endless referencing to all of the other studies. There is a persistent and intensive obsession with measurement associated with 'instruments', and metrics of 'impulsivity', 'sluggishness', 'aggressivity', and all of the other 'signs' of 'anti-social behaviour' and their correlations with criminal offending (Anderson et al. 1997). We see in almost all of this research an endless recycling of research methods concerned with measurement and taxonomies that recycle the preoccupations of earlier social scientists at the end of the nineteenth century and for much of the twentieth century (see Chapter 3).

In the early twenty-first century there is a large international industry devoted to the prevention of crime. This is exemplified by the so-called Best Practice Bureau of the International Centre for the Prevention of Crime (ICPC). Supported financially by the governments of the Netherlands, the UK and Canada, the ICPC prides itself on documenting what prevents crime, how crime prevention works and the support available for prevention. Its list of 100 'best-practice' approaches covers a wide range of interventions under the following headings:

- What Prevents Crime = Designing the Physical Environment and Social Control, Supporting Young Persons and Families, Enhancing Responsibility, Breaking the Cycle of Crime.
- How to Prevent Crime = City Action Plus, Partnerships by Police, Business and Other Entities.
- Support for Crime Prevention = National Leadership and Funding Programmes.

What do we find if we examine one of these approaches more closely? In one programme ('The Skill Development Program for Poor Children' in Ottawa, Canada), 'disadvantaged children' were offered a range of free 'non-school skill development' programmes, including sports activities and 'co-operative games'. In many of these crime-prevention programmes the initiatives are supposed to support young people and families. There are references to 'skills programmes for poor children', 'pre-school programmes for "at risk" children' and programmes for 'parenting skills' to 'prevent anti-social behavior in disadvantaged children'. The coercive nature of the programme is reflected in the following statement: 'Children were *aggressively recruited into the program and special efforts were made to reach non-participating children*' (ICPC 1997: 16; our emphasis). The Ottawa programme makes extraordinary claims about its supposed effectiveness in reducing 'antisocial' behaviours, as well as its overall cost-effective 'lessons'. Yet quite why specific programmes should be put in place simply to cure 'antisocial' behaviours is neither indicated nor argued for. Quite which 'skills' were developed through judo, ballet and scouting is not mentioned. It could, of course, be possible, as was the case with the French 'Bonmaison' programme and various wilderness programmes, that 'delinquency', however defined, was reduced – if only temporarily – because the children and young people concerned were kept occupied and under strict supervision.

Indeed, as Cohen (1984) had observed of earlier crime-prevention programmes, rarely are sports activities or other 'quality of life' initiatives either necessary or desirable in themselves. It often takes a 'crime problem' to ensure that these facilities are put in place.

This applies to a range of crime-prevention initiatives that target 'at risk', 'disadvantaged' or 'poor' children, young people and their families.

This of course is not to dismiss those programmes and initiatives that may in fact provide interesting activities for young people or that actually help to protect neighbourhoods and communities from predatory crime. Indeed, it would be dangerous and shortsighted to entirely write off crime-prevention strategies as just another covert attempt to impose greater state regulation on certain problem populations. Criminologists can demonstrate some positive results from crime prevention. Few would argue with the positive benefits of reducing crimes of violence and burglary on public housing estates. One recent study (Bessant et al. 2003) of inner-urban housing estates in Melbourne documented the very serious effects on tenants of the failure to adequately police those estates. One of the effects of unregulated illicit drug-dealing in these public housing estates was a very high level of violent assault and theft that deterred some homeless families from applying to live on them. Likewise there are strong arguments for programmes that effectively deter telephone-booth vandalism, credit-card fraud, motor-vehicle theft, domestic violence or violence against gays and lesbians (Grabosky and James 1995). As Cohen has argued (1984), it is entirely defensible to promote those things that produce safer streets and usable public amenities, and which promote justice at the local level and enhance the quality of life in neighbourhoods and communities.

However, too much contemporary crime reduction and risk management continues to be informed by a largely conservative discourse that serves to displace or even block alternative approaches that centre on fundamental issues like human rights or social justice. As Hughes (1998: 156) puts it, the 'continuing emphasis on *crime* prevention . . . acts to systematically exclude other readings of the relationship between social problems and social order'.

Criminologists of both the political Left and Right have also been active in promoting criminology as a discipline that is wedded to *practical outcomes*, often to the exclusion of what alternative and more equitable models of crime prevention might look like for our time.

Criminology, 'relevance' and crime prevention

The current enthusiasm for crime prevention is both a major promise and a central problem for criminology. From an administrative, or *practical*, perspective, any legitimacy and value that criminology has is dependent on its capacity to influence good policy. For criminologists with a more theoretical orientation, the relationship between their own research and policy questions may be more problematic or might simply go unrecognized. While criminologists have oscillated, often wildly, between these positions, the dominant tendency has been to engage in the imperatives of the *practical*–preventative project. Central to debates in this area is the question of 'relevance'. Quite simply, should criminology be linked to a problem-fixing policy agenda? The question is, of course, never put in such stark terms, even though the tension apparent between theory and practice has often dogged the discipline.

The key problem we immediately run into is, as Pat O'Malley (1996: 67–8) suggests, this: *whose* agenda, policy or theory are we talking about? What in this context does 'relevance' mean? What role should criminologists play, if any, in relation to the crime problem?

There is little point indulging in well-worn debates like 'Whose side are we on?', especially at a time when the kinds of traditional distinctions made between 'Left' and 'Right' have ceased to make much sense (Giddens 1999; Unger 2005). Equally it is still important to critically reflect on the positions adopted by criminologists in respect of crime prevention.

A good place to start with such an exercise in critical thinking is to report on a lively and symptomatic exchange that took place between three criminologists in 1996. The debate was between Adam Sutton (1996) putting the case for a 'relevant' criminology wedded to policy concerns, and Stan Cohen (1996) and Janet Chan (1996) who took a somewhat more sceptical position.

Adam Sutton (1996: 61) self-identifies as a 'practical criminologist' uncompromising in his belief that criminologists should be concerned primarily with linking their work to practice:

> For criminology . . . the major promise is of renewed relevance . . . of shrugging off 'nothing works' pessimism and helping to shape and give direction to programs rather than offering only critical perspectives.

As Sutton (ibid.: 61) sees it:

> Clearly for criminology the promise is of relevance: crime prevention provides major opportunities to translate the discipline's liberal and critical issues into enlightened policy.

Sutton (ibid.: 61) believes it is vital that criminologists be relevant:

> Crime prevention is too complex and too contested ever to be dismissed simply as a set of techniques for social control. Years ago, as an administrative criminologist, I was drawn to it because it seemed to be the only way to ensure continued relevance of the discipline which can and should inform policy. Even now, despite the difficulties and costs to myself and others associated with [it] . . . I see no viable alternative.

Even so Sutton is sceptical about the shift on the part of managers of state enterprises and government departments towards imperatives oriented to 'key performance indicators', 'outcomes', 'cost effectiveness', 'evaluation' and quality assurance. Notwithstanding this concern, Sutton believes that criminologists should get on with the practical business of 'programme development, implementation and review' (Sutton and O'Malley 1997: 2). This approach, says Sutton, should be administered in the areas of 'organizational' as well as 'individual' offending if 'responsible, law abiding behaviour' is to result. At the same time, criminologists should not lose sight of the social conditions which make such responsibility a reasonable expectation (ibid.: 9).

Sutton is particularly scathing about the role played by theorists and sceptics, and their 'critical discourse' in respect of crime prevention. Critical or dissenting criminologists, he says, merely eclipse crime-prevention approaches or, worse, open the door to '"nothing works" cynicism' (Sutton 1996: 62). Among the theorists he condemns are those who question the focus on street crime, the symptomatic and narrow concerns of situational prevention and those who see the eradication of crime through social justice (ibid.: 63). Sutton's response to critical perspectives is indicative of his irritation with any kind of substantive critical and theoretical analysis – even though he recites the ritual call for 'a broader context of *well-grounded* social theory and advocacy' (ibid.: 63; our emphasis).

Sutton's certainty about the authority and relevance of criminology has numerous royal precedents – like King Canute's instructions to the sea or Queen Victoria's incredulity when told that there were lesbians. His position reflects a dogmatism grounded in the belief that a properly constituted criminology, that is, one that is scientific, objective and empiricist, will also be judged practical *because* relevant.

Neither Chan nor Cohen is inclined to agree. Chan (1996: 27) suggests that

> The danger is in trying to prove our relevance and assert our expert status; we allow the narrow and practical aspects of crime prevention to dictate our field of inquiry.

She adds (ibid.: 27) that the drive to relevance may be dictated by other, 'external', imperatives:

> In a climate of fiscal constraints in universities and research institutions, the attraction of funding from client-focused, program-specific contract research is difficult to resist. And crime prevention is undoubtedly a gold mine for crime trend analysis, community studies and evaluative research.

More importantly, however, Chan points to the certain intractable problems inherent to many crime-prevention models and practices. On this basis she suggests (ibid.: 28) that 'crime prevention' is far more interesting than it seems at first to be:

> It is indeed difficult to keep a narrow focus on the practical issues of crime prevention . . . the mind is drawn towards the more theoretically challenging questions . . . such as the history and manifestations of the crime prevention concept, its relationship with other recent trends such as privatization and decentralization and community partnership in crime control, its impact on various models of private and public policing, etc.

Chan adds (ibid.: 28) that 'perhaps it is our own imagination, not the lure of crime prevention, that limits where we take the subject of crime prevention'. Indeed, by insisting that criminology be linked directly to policy and practice, without regard to the social or political context in which such matters are discussed, Sutton not only fails to see Chan's point but also confines criminology to a narrow and subordinate role. Thus 'relevance' in this sense becomes an intellectual straitjacket worn by those who appear to have abandoned any attempt to reflect on the current enthusiasm for crime prevention.

Stan Cohen (1996: 10) likewise takes on the issue of relevance by insisting that

> the single-minded pursuit of criminalization as the index of achievement for progressive social movements seems to be misconceived. The lure of criminalization is more problematic than the lure of relevance.

By this Cohen means that the 'crime-busting' approach integral to Sutton's brand of crime prevention simply reflects too many of the narrow concerns of conventional criminology as a social science discipline. Cohen maintains that the language of 'success' or 'failure' associated with crime-prevention programmes imposes a narrow, technical approach that shifts attention away from the 'big questions' about the nature of modern societies and core issues like what, if any, principles of social justice might inform public policy-making (Cohen 1985).

As if to contest Sutton's avowedly 'moral' stance on prevention, Cohen (1996: 12) insists that progressive criminology requires

> an informed ideology that makes very explicit our own criteria for claiming either success or failure – and that explains how such criteria differ from those used by others or produced by flipping pennies.

These criteria are defined by the ways we think about the nature of the 'crime problem'. For some progressive or neo-Marxist criminologists, like Rob White (1997: 182), crime prevention can be a worthwhile project. However, for White, it can be worthwhile only if it is informed by recognition of what he means by 'structural' factors like 'class', 'wealth' and 'poverty' which he argues are involved in producing crime. Perhaps, as Cohen suggests, these *apparent* theoretical or political differences are papered over by the continued use of a lexicon of crime prevention, often to the exclusion of the more genuinely transformative logic of progressive social movements or radical theory.

The narrowness of the conventional criminological preoccupation with crime prevention is further illustrated by its apparent failure to locate itself in its actual social and political contexts. Indeed, by submitting themselves to a 'practical' agenda, indicated by a logic of 'relevance', criminologists may actually contribute to many of the dangerous or regressive trends evident in contemporary society.

How might this be so?

There are two interconnected ways this might happen, and each is linked both to the contemporary processes of socio-economic change referred to as 'globalization' and to the hybrid neo-conservative–neo-liberal project of governance producing new kinds of government activity and policy-making.

Firstly, if certain theorists of 'globalization' (Martin and Schuman 1997, Chomsky 1996) are right in their assessment, then 'globalization' is likely to sponsor new kinds of criminal activity as well as embed socio-economic inequality in Western societies. Castells (1998) has identified some of the elements of a new 'global criminal economy' which include arms- and weapons-trafficking, money-laundering, the smuggling of illegal immigrants, the development of a global trade in women and children sold to the sex industry and a new market for body parts from both live donors and executed criminals. In each case the flow of trade is from 'the desperate poor to the needy rich' (Scheper-Hughes and Wacqant 2002).

The processes of economic change that have seen large-scale de-industrialization in many parts of the USA, the UK and Australia have also been accompanied by increasingly successful political campaigns run around cutting 'the tax burden'. This policy exercise in turn has run parallel to a determination to either cut expenditures on welfare or to discipline welfare recipients in new welfare-to-work programmes so as to end 'welfare dependence'. As Hogg and Brown (1998: 215) note in their illuminating analysis of contemporary crime prevention, the devolution of 'crime prevention' activity back to the 'community' is powerfully aligned with 'the small-state' rhetoric of many contemporary Western governments.

The consequence, especially if governments are actually pursuing cuts to public welfare, health care and education, is that such policies will promote increasing social and economic pain for people who lack the capacity to take advantage of new kinds of globalizing industries like information technologies and financial services. These policies may actually contribute to an increasingly spatially *segregated* social order. Market forces, already well and truly in place, will compel low-income earners to live in neighbourhoods with cheap housing. Equally those with sufficient wealth and property will use that wealth to buy expensive technological security to protect themselves from *outside* threats while living inside 'gated communities', as pioneered in cities like Los Angeles. As Mike Davis (1992: 221–64) has shown, such a response to the problem of 'law and order' leads to a lot of middle-class talk about 'community' and to the development of strategies designed to keep the 'riff-raff' at bay.

Hogg and Brown (1998: 206) claim that crime prevention

> is not founded on a concern to prevent or remedy the problems of violence and predatory property crime so much as to insulate 'respectable' middle-class communities against them . . . in such strategies is a very clear idea of who are the potential victims worthy of protection. Crime is tolerable if it is confined to those who have no voice in political and civic affairs.

A hybrid neo-conservative–neo-liberal policy framework cannot help but produce some of these effects. If 'law and order' budgets are in an increasingly inverse relationship to welfare expenditures, then certain models of 'crime prevention' are bound to emerge. This may be achieved in part by increasingly partial forms of crime prevention which focus only on the crimes of the 'underclass' or the 'socially excluded'. We need to ask in what ways it is still possible to insist that criminologists pay attention to traditional forms of corporate crime or to new kinds of 'green crime'. ('Green crime' refers to everything from the deaths of over 6,000 victims of the release of deadly gases at the Union Carbide factory in Bhopal, India, through the illegal dumping of hazardous waste, to persistent large-scale pollution of air, soil and water. See Carrabine et al. 2004: 320–8.)

It is again a telling commentary on the complicity of some criminologists and the crime-prevention agenda in a world in which the authority of corporations is being enhanced, that crime-prevention programmes do not identify routine business practices like arson, tax evasion, or the illegal exploitation of low-paid workers as a central part of their concerns.

There are, in short, some very good reasons why criminologists may have to rethink their approach to 'crime' and the 'crime-prevention' project.

As Stan Cohen argues, we need to pay attention to what 'crime prevention' ought to mean in the context of increasingly polarized societies, and one where nation states and big corporations routinely engage in criminal acts as much as do the perpetrators of street crime. This is not about being more 'relevant'; nor is it being cynical, as Sutton (1996) has suggested. Rather it is all about thinking more critically and expansively about what crime and crime control could mean in our time. We will return to these issues in Chapters 10 and 11.

As our discussion of the new emphasis on 'victims' in Chapter 9 indicates, while there are substantial doubts about the objectivity of a category like 'the crime rate', there can be no doubting the reality of the experiences of victims. This is true of the countless millions of victims of state-sponsored genocide, torture or terror in the twentieth century. It is true also of the people whose economic well-being has been destroyed or compromised by the depredations of business and professional fraud associated with corporate collapses like Enron or Permalac, or the fraudulent auditing practices of global accounting companies like Arthur Andersen. It is true, too, of the people who have been the victims of criminal assault or petty property crime.

A morally sensitive appreciation of the status of victims will not seek to render identical the sufferings of the victims of state-sponsored genocide and the clichéd reaction to graffiti-covered walls that treats such vandalism as a symptom of the end of Western civilization. It will seek to respond appropriately to each kind of criminal activity. Perhaps, as Hughes argues (1998: 156), there is still time and an opportunity to promote a paradigmatic shift away from talking about crime prevention to an approach that talks about human rights and social justice. As Hughes (ibid.: 157) puts it, to reveal 'the subordination of questions of crime control to those of social justice and human rights may open up a new discourse of possibilities beyond the current one'.

Conclusion

This discussion of crime prevention has not engaged with the narrowly technical issues or concerns of conventional criminology, such as which form of crime prevention works or does not, which scheme, programme or initiative holds 'promise'. As Cohen has noted (1996), the history of crime prevention is replete with good intentions gone wrong and of hope turned to despair. Crime-prevention initiatives come and go, as do the ideas and philosophies that inform them.

The most recent focus on 'community safety' and 'risk management' is merely the latest in a long line of crime-prevention strategies designed to curb crime and restore social order. Criminologists have been centrally involved in promoting crime prevention – indeed as Grabosky and James illustrate (1995: xviii), they are self-consciously 'proud' of their successes in reducing crime. While not wishing to dismiss the benefits or achievements of these approaches, we have nonetheless suggested that criminology, with its continued focus on crime prevention, may have set an enduring intellectual and ethical trap for itself. Equally, the call for a 'relevant' discipline may also limit the capacity of criminology to think about the role played by crime prevention in our time and to consider other perspectives that talk instead of human rights and social justice. A narrowly and *practically* conceived preoccupation with crime prevention may merely stifle the imagination of a more reflexive criminology. If we are to make sense of the historical and contemporary nature of crime prevention in Western societies we need more critical analysis, and that is likely only to irritate the dedicated criminological problem-fixers of our time – or those whom Loader and Sparks (1993) call the practitioners of 'jobbing criminology'.

Review questions

Why has crime prevention become such a prominent part of contemporary criminology and of public policy-making?

Is crime prevention an inherently conservative project?

In what ways, if any, does crime prevention point to traditional preoccupations within contemporary criminology?

Further reading

Braithwaite, J., 1989a, *Crime, Shame and Reintegration*, Cambridge University Press, Cambridge.

Carrabine et al., 2004, *Criminology: A Sociological Introduction*, Routledge, Abingdon.

Christie, N., 1993, *Crime Control as Industry: Towards GULAGS Western Style?*, Routledge, London.

Walters, R., 2003, 'New Modes of Governance and the Commodification of Criminological Knowledge', *Social and Legal Studies*, Vol. 12, No. 1: 5–26.

White, R. and Sutton, A., 1995, 'Crime Prevention, Urban Space and Social Exclusion', *Australian and New Zealand Journal of Sociology*, Vol. 31, No. 2: 82–99.

9

VICTIMS AND VICTIMOLOGY

For most of the twentieth century criminologists paid much more attention to those defined as criminals and offenders than they did to the victims of criminal activity. In the 1970s that neglect ended. As Erez (1991) observed, one consequence of the debates that the 'new criminologists' sponsored in the 1970s was to remind us that the 'forgotten' and 'eliminated' victims of crime should be a legitimate object of enquiry for criminologists. The study of victims, or 'victimology', has now become a recognized theme in contemporary criminology. It has also become a central theme in much criminal justice policy-making as victims' rights groups, neo-conservative think-tanks and sections of the media promote campaigns for tougher sentencing of criminals. One result is that it has become unthinkable for any ambitious politician to come out against being 'tough' on law and order. In Britain in 2002 the Blair government's White Paper *Justice for All* (Home Office 2002: para. 3) pledged to 'rebalance the criminal justice system in favour of the victim and the community so as to reduce crime and bring more offenders to justice'.

In this chapter we address the origins of victimology and some of the problems and possibilities associated with it. We are not interested in the more technical issues like the credibility of victimization surveys (Hazlehurst 1996). Nor is there any assessment of the methodological and other difficulties associated with the study of victims, although we touch on these matters. As in Chapter 8, we ask why and how it has come about that criminologists and criminal justice policy-makers are now interested in victims and in victims' rights. Again we suggest that criminologists and all those who read criminology need to think past the sometimes narrow and limiting assumptions that have shaped the practice of criminology.

We begin by assessing the assumption that *the victim* is a self-evident category of enquiry in criminology. We turn then to the constructive schemes at work which position victimology in a criminal justice policy-making framework based on a set of unified assumptions about the victims of crime, and aimed at the prevention and/or reduction of crime and its victims among certain *targeted* populations. We look at the actual diversity of positions within criminology about the victims of crime, as well as the wider social and political concerns that have influenced the growing attention given to victims over recent years. How valid, for example, is Jackson's concern that '"rebalancing" a criminal justice system in favor of victims may risk injustice to defendants with little tangible benefit in terms of rights and remedies for the victims' (2003: 312)?

On violence and victims

If we begin by asking 'Who, then, is a victim?' we could say that it is what a criminal does when they commit a crime. Criminal activity, like the 'violence' of murder, rape or assault or even a house theft or street mugging, creates 'victims'. Surely this is all straightforward and common sense.

Yet it is odd that most criminology texts proceed without the most basic conceptual clarification or discussion of what is to count as 'violence'. As the criminologist Michael Levi (1994: 859) notes – and without doing anything himself to redress the problem – the 'conceptual issue of "what counts as violence" does not cause too many difficulties for criminologists in practice *because they usually ignore it*' (author's emphasis). It may be that the very obviousness of 'violence' has suggested to most criminologists that there is no need to clarify what is meant by it. This may have some implications for how we think about 'victims'.

If we start to think carefully about violence its self-evident status dissolves. Anthony Arblaster (1975: 81) urges us to approach violence as something eminently questionable, which means trying to take as little as possible for granted about it. Richard Gelles, an American expert on domestic violence, notes that violence 'has proven difficult to define . . . Attempts to clarify the concept of violence have demonstrated the difficulty of distinguishing between legitimate and illegitimate violence' (quoted in Cerulo 1998: 14).

There are several tendencies at work when people begin to think about criminal violence and the characteristics of being a victim. One is to emphasize the spectacular and physical qualities of 'violence'; another is to insist on the deviant, even criminal, nature of all violence. On this basis violence is recognized and measured by its visible effects, the spectacular blood of wounded bodies, the material destruction of objects, or by the visible damage done in the world of 'objects'.

Yet the self-evident status of violence – and of victims – rapidly dissolves when we start to think about it. The last thing we should do is assume that violence or becoming a victim is a case of the 'bleeding obvious'.

How, for example, should we respond to Ristow and Shallice's report on the interrogation in July–August 1971 of fourteen Irish Republican Army (IRA) 'suspects' in Northern Ireland? The interrogation was carried out by agents of the British Combined Services Intelligence Centre, operating as agents of the UK government:

> The men were hooded (black hoods, like pillow cases, were placed over their heads except during the actual interrogation); they were forced to stand at a wall in a search position supported only by their fingertips and wearing loose fitting boiler suits for periods of up to 16 hours continuously, and returned to position forcibly when they fell; they were subjected to a continuous loud 'white' noise of 85–87 decibels; they were deprived of sleep during at least the first several days of a week of interrogation and they were deprived of food except for a round of bread and a pint of water at six hour intervals . . . By inducing temporary psychosis they left most of the men permanently psychiatrically scarred.
>
> (1976: 271–3)

Such psychological torture was part of a larger pattern of torture used by UK police and military forces in Northern Ireland (Miller 1993: 123–7). Should we talk about violence and victims in this context? In turn the British use of torture in Northern Ireland is only a small and not especially violent example of the near-universal reliance on torture by governments and police in the twentieth century (Amnesty International 1993). Since 2001 the so-called 'war on terrorism' has legitimized the use by US military and police personnel of illegal techniques, including indefinite incarceration without charges being laid or trial, and torture of 'terrorist suspects', using euphemisms like 'rendition' to describe this practice.

Yet if we rely on the results of research about what *ordinary people* think violence is, it seems that many people do not regard torture carried out by police or security forces as *real* violence; nor do people think of those who get tortured as *victims*. People across a wide range of social and economic circumstances agree that 'crimes of violence' are very significant sources of social anxiety and that the seriousness of property and violent offences increases in parallel with the severity of the legal sanctions applied (Levi 1994). This points to the quite conventional distinction many people, including criminologists, make between 'criminal' violence and 'legitimate force'. As Archer and Gartner argued (1978: 220–1), if official violence is nearly invisible in most criminological research, this reflects 'the high order of legitimation official violence enjoys . . . Official killings therefore differ from illegal violence in that they result from governmental orders, are usually performed by several agents acting collectively and are justified as serving some higher purpose.'

Yet the conventional emphasis on violence as 'illegal activity' has some strange effects. As Miller writes:

> All historical work and most sociological work on societal violence focuses on public violence of private citizens: crime, riots, strikes, rebellion, and war. What escapes view is intra-household violence on the one hand – men beating wives, and parents beating children, various types of sexual exploitation – and on the other hand, the violence the state uses to keep order and maintain its position – prisons, police, the impoverishment effected by exploitative taxation and the violence of the law itself.
>
> (1993: 72–3)

Feminists for example have rightly argued that gender blindness has long obscured women's experience of violence like rape within marriage, the abduction of children by the state or welfare agencies, or the 'low key, aggressive and intimidating daily behaviours towards women [including] bullying and harassment done by other women as well as men and found in mainstream public and private settings . . .' (Bessant and Cook 1997: 11).

In short, reflection on violence and its victims indicates that they are far from being self-evident matters.

Miller (1993) has got the basic perspective on violence right when he suggests that it is essentially a form of social practice or action; that is, it is just like other kinds of social interactions; such as talking, using public transport or going to school. It is action because it is purposive and involves motives, ideas and feelings, and yet like all action it is never confined merely to whatever the perpetrator desired or intended. It is social because it involves a number of people. It is therefore perspectival because, like most other forms of social action, it involves three kinds of people: namely *perpetrators*, *victims* and *observers*. How violence is defined, experienced and known depends in part on how the roles of *perpetrators*, *victims* and *observers* are assigned.

Several clarifications are needed here before we proceed. Most violence involves face-to-face encounters and has an obvious immediacy. The rapist or murderer usually has to be in close physical proximity to the victim to commit the deed. Sometimes the perpetrator plans the violence, in which case it is a premeditated act, though murder, as Polk (1994) shows, is most often a spur of the moment act. Yet while a lot of violence involving perpetrators and victims takes place, as it were, in a 'face-to-face' way involving individuals who can see or touch each other, there are other possibilities. Violence can involve large groups of people and it can involve perpetrators whom the victims never see. As Mike Davis (2001: 23–60) demonstrates, Britain's official policy in India in 1876–78 was designed to starve vast numbers of Indians into submission. The result was at least 10 million deaths. This was a process in which the victims and the perpetrators rarely, if ever, met. As Burleigh and Wipperman (1992) point out, the killing of millions of Jews, gypsies and psychiatric patients by the Nazi racial state after 1939 involved real perpetrators who did the killing, but it also involved a very large bureaucracy and officials who directed the killing at a distance and whose organizers rarely saw the results of their planning.

Secondly, the role of *observer* goes to the question of how *we know* that an act of violence or a crime has taken place. Victims of assault, rape, theft, torture or genocide experience violence in the most direct and frightful ways possible. Yet it is also important that the violence be known and any claims that a rape, a murder or a genocide has taken place have to be tested. This is a difficult part of the criminal law in the case of rape. The victim, typically a woman, knows in truly terrible ways what has happened, but for the allegation to lead to a conviction it must be tested in any number of ways, including medical testing and cross-examination in a courtroom. In this way the *observer* can refer to a real person who witnesses a violent act as well as to a system of inquiry instigated by the criminal justice system itself. The observer role relates both to the evidence presented and to the practices of experts, lawyers, witnesses, documents, and so forth. The observer role, in short, relates to all the ways in which those other than the victim and the perpetrator can be said to 'know' that a violation of a victim has taken place.

The way violence is defined, experienced and *known* depends in part on how the roles of *victims*, *perpetrators* and *observers* are assigned. While these three roles are mostly stable and clearly distinguished, this is not to say that on occasion the roles can shift. Each of these 'roles' requires that those involved in the field of action entertain different points of view and therefore sustain any number of prospective evaluations. For example, the long-term victim of domestic violence can decide to 'take it no longer' and wreak a terrible revenge by killing her or his abuser. Since the 1990s there have been many trials of women who have killed their abusive partners: our judgements about who is 'victim' and who the 'perpetrator' may alter as we hear the unfolding story of a woman whose husband has systematically abused, harassed and hit her and who has now turned the tables and killed her oppressor. Journalists engaged in reporting the drug trade or a hostage-taking event can suddenly become victims themselves, as the case of Ireland's Veronica Guerin indicates. Groups who have themselves engaged in terrorism to achieve certain political ambitions, like the Jewish militants who made up the Stern Gang or the Hagganah in Palestine before 1948, can become the 'victims' of terrorism when Palestinian militants turned these tactics back on the state of Israel in the 1980s and 1990s. Anyone who has watched the sexually charged violence in David Lynch's *Blue Velvet* will recall the shifting roles within the film, as well as the possibility that some men and women in the audience will experience complex or transient reactions to what is taking place on the screen. Even more complicated will be our reactions to stories of women (who in a patriarchal society are invariably the 'victims') who rape or abuse the children in their care (FitzRoy 1997).

Violence is perspectival because it is something done *to* or *with* others, and so is always relational. Any or all of these relational 'roles' can produce or sustain any number of prospective evaluations which seek to establish and define both the signs of violence and the motives for violence. For criminology this has some interesting effects. It means that what gets to be counted as violence and who gets to be identified as a victim can be highly variable.

In many cases violence is very much a feature of intimate relationships. As feminists (Mirlees-Black 1999) have long understood, violence is normally part of a repertoire of behaviour within domestic relationships, and so involves people who know each other. Most violence takes place within either the family or other relationships. For many women up until the 1970s the weekly drunken sex act, and the slapping or beating meted out by their partners, were just part of a 'woman's lot', practices which were simply never spoken about or identified as a problem. Until quite recently it was accepted as both normal and desirable that children were beaten, slapped or punched, actions which if done to an adult would constitute an act of assault. Family members have always stood a far higher chance of being assaulted, raped or murdered in their own homes than on the street. And why was it accepted for so long that large numbers of children could be stripped away from working-class or ethnically 'third-class' parents, and relocated in 'better' family settings or even in institutional settings *for their own good*? It is not surprising therefore that the media in the UK, the USA or Australia have found it far easier to focus on 'street crime' than on crimes like these.

In part, what counts as violence and who comes to be known authoritatively as a victim depends on who is in a position to authoritatively define that some conduct is or is not violent. The tangled legal and social processes involved in South Africa's Truth and Reconciliation Commission indicate how complex are the relations between groups competing both for moral rectitude and political power where there are also competing claims about who the *real* victims are (Hayner 2001). The little-known case of American actions on the island of Okinawa involved the killing, in April 1945, of approximately one-third of the indigenous population, accounting for some 160,000 civilians, by US marines (Cameron 1994: 166–201). This was genocide directed at innocent people and 'justified' subsequently by reference to the nature of the military operations and the collapse of 'normal' marine discipline.

These examples simply remind us that violence is perspectival. As Miller (1993: 65) argues, 'our views of violence depend on so many variables of sight, sound, pain, on categories of law and morality, on levels of technology, on rules of group formation, on legitimacy and status'. Violence is perspectival also because it involves both historical and relational judgements. What was once defined as acceptable can over time become unacceptable or vice versa. Depending on particular social and cultural settings, violence can be visible and acknowledged or it can simply be made invisible. Rarely do victims, perhaps by definition, have the capacity to transform their experiences into an authoritative definition or exemplary statement that then gets some kind of social or official sanction. More often, and especially in the last 100 years, it is an observer, typically an 'expert', who by means of reclassification transforms a once-acceptable action into violence. As with so many other 'social problems', questions like 'what is violence?' and 'who is the victim?' point to the role played by our belief systems or discourses in revealing or obscuring the existence of a problem. If something is defined as a problem – or is not – then there are real consequences – or not. This reminds us that not all perspectives are equal.

Yet while we have insisted here on the need to think carefully about violence and victimhood, we also need to recall that in many situations there *are* clear-cut distinctions between victims and perpetrators, and that the experiences of victim and perpetrator are both different and discernible. Primo Levi (1993), one of the great witnesses to the Nazi policy of killing Europe's Jews after 1939, has argued forcefully that we should not be under any illusion that the characteristics that define the violator and victim are so interchangeable as to be entirely unclear:

> The oppressor remains what he is, and so does the victim. They are not inter-changeable . . .
>
> I do not know, and it does not much interest me to know, whether in my depths there lurks a murderer, but I do know that I was a guiltless victim, and I was not a murderer. I know that the murderers existed, not only in Germany and still exist, retired or on active duty, and that to confuse them with their victims is a moral disease or an aesthetic affectation or a sinister sign of complicity.
>
> (1993: 25, 48–9)

So how have mainstream criminologists dealt with the fact that there are *victims* of crimes? And how adequately has this discovery been thought out?

Inventing victimology

As Erez (1991) observed, most criminologists have tended to focus their attention on those defined as 'criminals' and 'offenders' as opposed to the 'forgotten' and 'eliminated' victims of crime. Von Hentig in the 1940s and later Mendelsohn (1974) were among the first criminologists to focus on victims and persistent patterns of victimization. Both authors pointed to the tendency of certain individuals to become 'victims of crime' as well as arguing the need for criminologists to record and catalogue patterns of victimization. Despite the ground-breaking nature of these studies, their point was blunted by being accommodated within the scientism of mainstream criminology that took for granted the self-evident status of both 'the victim' and 'crime'.

Other criminologists came to believe that the study of offenders was fatally compromised by the fact that the majority of crimes went unreported and undetected, such that a huge 'dark figure' of crime lay beyond the vision of criminologists and of governments (Young

1999). This problem has of course not gone away. In England and Wales in the first years of the twenty-first century, it seemed that police 'detected' only 23 per cent of recorded crime (Simmons and Dodd 2003).

If the number of offences, offenders and victims of crime proved elusive and not easily amenable to the rigours of *scientific* analysis, then clearly a different investigative strategy was required. A body of empirical research got under way in the early 1980s which focused on carrying out victim surveys and other empirical analyses of the nature and extent of criminal victimization in designated areas (Walklate 1998: 114).

Studying victims: three broad approaches

Sandra Walklate (1998) has argued that criminology has developed a diverse approach to the study of victims. Her work opens up the possibility of a more thoughtful appreciation of the ways in which victimology, victimization and victims can be thought about. Walklate (1998) points to three dominant approaches to the study of victimization: positivist victimology; radical victimology; and critical victimology.

Positivist victimology

According to Walklate (ibid.: 115) positivist victimology is concerned primarily with the patterns, trends and 'regularities' of victimization. The study of victimology by positivist criminologists emphasizes 'those patterns of behaviour, which can be identified, objectively and through a commitment to a traditional conception of "scientific" method' (Walklate 1988). Typically, researchers who begin with this assumption tend to carry out surveys of victims in order to establish the 'where, when and how' of victimization. In the early 1980s the *British Crime Survey*, conducted by what was then the Home Office Research Unit, demonstrated (at least to the authors' satisfaction) that fear of crime far outstripped its actual occurrence in any given community. Other research studies, such as the US *Task Force on Victims of Crime* (cited in ibid.: 115), have used similar surveys to highlight the risks of crime and the potential to create victims. A basic lack of reflexivity is a major characteristic of such surveys. There is a tendency to take the concept of *victim* for granted and to avoid any reference to the socio-political context in which the research is taking place. Walklate (ibid.: 116) concludes that

> positivist victimology, and the survey work emanating from it, may provide snapshots of regularities and criminal victimization but cannot provide an understanding of the social and historical reproduction of those regularities through time and space. Such a concern demands minimally a different theoretical understanding of the term 'victim', and maximally, a different theoretical starting point.

Indeed, without a more comprehensive discussion of such matters, victimology becomes a device fit mainly for the purposes of crime prevention or reduction without fully acknowledging that the state chooses to 'see' those whom it wants to see and ignores those not readily identified as 'victims' (Young 1999). As Crawford (1997) suggests, the distinction between 'deserving' and 'undeserving' victims raises some important questions about the way in which the category of *victim* has been constructed.

The contemporary politics of law and order reflects the way in which the concept of victim has been used to achieve certain neo-conservative objectives. Recent 'naming and shaming' campaigns mounted by sections of the British and Australian media against repeat sex offenders illustrate the way in which victims have been used to inflame public opinion and to bring about unsavoury practices in respect of certain categories of offenders. This adds weight to the argument that the term 'victim' should not be regarded as a scientifically neutral term, as often suggested by conventional criminologists.

Radical victimology

Although what can be called 'positivist victimology' provides the dominant perspective in mainstream criminology, an alternative is 'radical victimology'. Radical victimologists, like Cohen (1993), have argued for a broader conception of victims that takes account of criminal victimization as one element of a more general *social* victimization. According to Walklate (1998: 116), 'radical victimology' is best characterized by its emphasis on human rights and the idea of justice. It is interesting to reflect on the status of a discipline like criminology, where the words 'criminal justice' appear with great regularity, and to inquire how many of the classic works of the discipline, to say nothing of the standard texts in contemporary criminology, carry out any extended discussion of the principles of justice. (Carrabine et al. 2004: 259–66, for example, offer a modest and quite narrow discussion of 'justice'.)

Radical victimology focuses on those who are most affected by factors such as poverty, unemployment, racism, sexism and marginalization. Criminal offences are seen as contingent on and deeply embedded in these wider issues. Accordingly, a study of victims could be broadened to embrace those socio-economic and political factors that underpin criminal victimization. While radical victimology goes well beyond the assumptions of positivist victimology, it is nonetheless constrained by an overreliance on victim surveys. As Walklate (1998: 118–19) rightly points out, such a treatment dovetails, albeit inadvertently, with the narrow and taken-for-granted constructions of the status of 'victim' found in the works of positivist victimologists:

> [R]adical victimology tries to construct and work with a much more general notion of victimization and with a stable and nuanced understanding of the sources of such victimization. Its failure to break free of positivism at a fundamental level results in a political agenda not that dissimilar from that of a more conservative political persuasion.

Critical criminology

While recognizing the difficulties in defining the term 'critical', particularly since there are so many competing and sometimes contradictory perspectives under that umbrella,

Walklate identifies a 'critical' approach to victimology, noting (1998: 126) that 'a key concern for critical victimology . . . is to challenge the use of the term "victim" and the circumstances under which such a term may be applicable. In so doing it constitutes a fundamental challenge to the domain assumptions of victimology as a discipline.' Walklate suggests that 'correctionalist victimology' is little more than an attempt to legitimize various regulatory and disciplinary practices of government. It is apparent that by using the term 'victim' in an uncontested fashion, and by merely focusing on data collection to establish empirically certain patterns of victimization, criminologists are unlikely to recognize or address some other theoretical or interpretive possibilities, such as those raised by radical victimologists. By this we mean that the study of victims in itself needs to become the object of critical analysis, and we need a keener appreciation of how discourses on victims' rights connect to current debates around citizenship.

However, we cannot easily have it both ways. We cannot take *seriously* the plight of those regarded as 'victims' and then slip into yet another round of deconstructionist critique. To be sure, it is necessary to engage the narrow and partial positivist constructions of victimization, and to highlight the socio-political underpinnings of victim discourse. Yet it is also necessary to acknowledge some of the glaring realities associated with crime and its effects. Thus, while Walklate questions the positivist focus on the regularity of victimization, arguing correctly that it is far more difficult to explain 'one-off' victimization, she is reluctant to discuss specific evidence on the ways in which certain individuals and groups are repeatedly rendered victims. These cannot be analysed away or treated merely as abstract discursive effects. Indeed, if we were to take such a course then we would likely repeat the same mistake as the 'new criminologists' who, in their pursuit of a fully developed 'social theory of crime', forgot to acknowledge the actual experiences of those affected by criminal activities. Equally, as Stan Cohen (1997) argues, it needs to be acknowledged that a simple analytical retreat into victim surveys, as conducted by positivist and 'left-realist' criminologists, is likely to prove just as unrewarding.

Three interconnected factors have helped to consolidate the evolution of victimology and the focus on victims in contemporary criminal justice policy-making:

- the emergence of what has been termed 'post-social criminology';
- a revolt against radical criminology; and
- the emergence of victims' rights movements.

Post-social criminology

The emergence of what O'Malley (1996) has called 'post-social criminology' has paralleled the ascendancy of the radical blend of neo-liberal economics and neo-conservatism initiated by the Thatcher government in the UK (1979–89) and during the Reagan presidency in the USA (1980–88). As we argued in Chapter 8, Thatcherism and Reaganomics ushered in both radical, neo-liberal, economic policies and a neo-conservative emphasis on the notions of 'individual responsibility', the 'traditional family', 'traditional values' and the virtues of self-regulation and self-management. In criminology and in criminal justice policy-making, this encouraged the *discovery* of victims.

In this 'new' intellectual framework, crime was treated as a symptom of the breakdown of traditional authority, a result, it was said, of the 'anything-goes' permissiveness sponsored by social movements like Gay Lib and the Women's Movement of the 1960s and 1970s. It was also suggested that a generation of 'do-gooders', like social workers, left-wing politicians and liberal church leaders, had given too much emphasis to offenders and their rights, while victims were too often ignored and left in a state of despair. It was asserted that the justice system had gone 'soft' on crime and courts were 'too lenient' on offenders, making the plight of victims even worse. In short, the balance between victims and offenders, rights and responsibilities, morality and permissiveness, had apparently been tipped in favour of the criminal (Abbott and Wallace 1992; Brake and Hale 1993).

Neo-liberal and neo-conservative politicians and governments ran reform campaigns designed to reinstall 'traditional values' appropriate to a moral order rediscovering its roots. A new kind of 'blame' talk which caught offenders, families and indeed whole communities in its grasp began to be promoted by ambitious politicians and crusading tabloid journalists (Campbell 1993; Walklate 1998). Social policy and criminal justice policy increasingly targeted the 'enemies within', namely welfare-dependent 'scroungers', 'dole cheats', the long-term unemployed and various 'antisocial' elements, including 'delinquents' and repeat offenders. Governments gave increased funding to those criminologists who focused on the 'hard facts' of crime through studies on offending populations, situational crime prevention and, above all, the victims of crime.

'Post-social' criminology and a new breed of administrative criminologists set about undertaking numerous large-scale studies (mostly surveys) into the characteristics and antecedents of both offenders and the victims of crime. These studies were highly selective and conducted largely within the framework of a narrowly constituted positivist research project.

This observation leads us to the second factor, the collective state of mind of criminologists and the reactions to radical criminologists like the 'new criminologists' in the 1970s. As we argued in Chapter 4, *The New Criminology* (Taylor, Walton and Young 1973) marked some kind of high point for 'radical criminology'. By the end of the 1970s, however, criticism of the 'new criminology' had largely deflated what proved to be a somewhat fragile hot-air balloon (Sumner 1994). That Jock Young, one of the authors of the 'new criminology', had within two years rejected his earlier position was one indicator. Pavlich (2000) argued that a combination of disciplinary complacency and a significant number of affinities between mainstream criminology and the revival of the neo-conservative ethos also played its part in blunting the edge of 'radical criminology'. Those affinities lay in the very bedrock of *scientific* criminology which, as Steve Fuller suggests (2000: 38) of the larger positivist enterprise, in many social sciences has been at once 'foundational, authoritarian and risk averse'.

Criticism from more conservatively inclined criminologists was directed at the exclusion of victims of crime in Taylor, Walton and Young's work, along with the alleged tendency to elevate the offender to the status of hapless victim of the capitalist system. Inevitably, these views provided fertile ground for severe and lasting criticism of 'academic' criminology in general and of 'radical' criminology in particular. It did not help either that some of the criticism came from within the ranks of radical or progressive criminologists. Stan Cohen (1997) was to criticize radical criminology on several grounds, including its apparent ignoring of the reality of the experiences of the victims of street crime. He said (1997: 105–6) that it was not helpful if radical criminologists glossed over the significance of street crime. Instead of demystifying the crime problem as a product of media myths, 'moral panics', faulty categorization or 'false consciousness', Cohen insisted that crime had to be acknowledged as a real problem for the working class and other vulnerable groups:

> The weak and the powerless are the targets of crime. There is a rational core to their fear and insecurity. Victimization studies have rediscovered old victims (the working class, the elderly, ethnic minorities) and discovered some 'new' ones – notably women victims of sexualized violence. Indeed, it was the feminist critique of the 'romantic' strain . . . that presented [radical criminology] with its most serious anomalies. The result in any event, is that the damaging, brutalizing and demoralizing consequences of conventional crime must be confronted rather than glossed over.

The apparent myopia of the 'radical criminologist' in relation to victims, and the complex questions associated with such matters, left the door open for both those on the Right and those who called themselves 'left-realists' (Young 1988) to declare that they would 'take crime seriously'.

Both conservative and 'left-realist' criminologists eschewed what they called the 'idealism', or what may more simply be called the confusion, of the 'new criminologists'. They sought instead to demonstrate a newly acquired recognition of the 'reality' of crime by focusing on 'empirical' research into crime victims. It was always doubtful that any simple strategy of law enforcement would work on its own, largely because of the very low levels of police detection of offences. Given this, conventional criminologists seeking to demonstrate their 'relevance' argued that a focus on victims might provide a better way of identifying the nature and consequences of criminal behaviour.

Strategies of 'situational crime prevention' fitted neatly into this new paradigm. Criminologists had only to undertake the necessary victim surveys and to identify the circumstances surrounding criminal victimization and they could be seen as playing a front-line role in attacking the crime problem. So mainstream criminologists began to carry out elaborate surveys of victimization as part of the project of crime prevention and reduction. It was confidently expected that consideration of survey findings by politicians and policy-makers would result in a more targeted programme of prevention aimed at lessening the likelihood of persons becoming victims of crime. 'Left-realists' also got involved in this kind of research, though they concentrated more on the working-class victims of crime and the need for more 'democratized' forms of policing in the inner city (Zedner 1994).

There were other elements at work supportive of an interest in victims. There have been important shifts in the relations between governments, universities and academic criminologists over the past few decades, producing what Israel (2000) calls a 'criminology for profit'. This is a consequence of pressures on universities and academics to become more 'entrepreneurial', as university managers call on academic researchers to actively seek out research funding and provide services to clients. This has eroded any authority attached to the traditional idea of the academic as 'critic and conscience of society'. Criminologists and a whole new cadre of security and intelligence personnel devoted their considerable energies to developing and marketing technologies of research, surveillance and protection. Indeed, since the early 1990s there has been an extraordinary growth in the development, marketing and consumption of 'home security' (Karmen 1990; Hogg and Brown 1998). In other words, the assumption of a crime rate that was 'out of control' and the growing awareness of victimization have paralleled the development of an increasingly privatized sector offering security and intelligence services (Young 1999). This security market is of course used by and is receptive to some communities rather than others, the costs of installing or hiring the required levels of security restricting the use of such security by those residing in poorer areas.

Finally it mattered that the evolution of victimology was taking place in a context where victims were organizing themselves.

Victims' rights movements

The emergence in a number of Western countries of victims' rights organizations during the 1980s has not been well researched. On the face of it these victims' rights movements, like Parents for Megan's Law in the USA or Victim Support in the UK, represented themselves as movements aimed simply at adjusting a perceived imbalance between victims and offenders in the criminal justice system (Carrabine et al. 2004: 127). Whether there was simply an elective affinity operating or some deeper linkages, these movements arose in the context of a political mobilization by powerful and well-funded organizations.

Typically these organizations were disposed to a neo-conservative 'politics of resentment'. Many of the members of these groups were dismayed or outraged by the political successes and public visibility of feminism, the gay and lesbian movements, to say nothing of the decline of 'traditional' Christian and family values and institutions, factors all tending to the 'death of Western civilization'. These movements promoted 'tougher' law and order policies as their proponents spread doubt about the practices of the judicial system and the viability of 'welfare' approaches to criminal justice practice. It has also produced media-led vigilante campaigns designed to publicize the release of prisoners and the location of ex-prisoners, especially those with convictions for sex crimes. As Karmen (1990: 58) observes:

> Instead of arguing about the powers of the government versus the right of the individual, law and order advocates equate the rights of the victim with the rights of the criminal. They charge that the scales of justice are unfairly tilted in favor of the wrongdoer at the expense of the innocent injured party.

Karmen (ibid.: 30–8) also shows how a distinct but related move for further recognition of and advocacy on behalf of victims' rights arose as a consequence of social movements such as the civil rights movement, the Women's Movement, gay and lesbian campaigns and children's rights movements. What united these groups was an attempt to highlight both the harm experienced by certain vulnerable groups and the need for comprehensive systems of support that directed the resources of government more towards the victim than the offender.

Campaigns for a more 'victim-oriented' system of justice coincided with moves to make some fundamental changes to the philosophical underpinnings of the criminal justice system itself. Hudson (1987, 1993) argues that the ascendancy of the 'justice model' promoted persistent campaigns to change sentencing practices, with greater emphasis being placed on offender 'responsibility' and 'accountability' than on other 'extraneous' factors.

This has included the introduction of mandatory sentencing policies in countries with a long history of common law, like the USA and Australia. Mandatory sentencing undoes centuries of judicial practice based on the principle that 'the punishment should fit the crime' and of penal policies that had left a significant degree of discretion with judges and parole boards about the length of custodial sentences. In Australia two states, Western Australia and the Northern Territory, introduced mandatory sentencing in the early 1990s largely with the significant population of Aboriginal people as the target group. In the Western Australian case a series of high-speed police pursuits of young aboriginals driving stolen cars that resulted in a number of fatal collisions led a well-known neo-conservative talkback radio host to sponsor a 'Rally for Justice' promoting mandatory sentencing for repeat offenders. The Lawrence Labour government capitulated quickly. Courts in Western Australia and the Northern Territory were required to sentence teenage aboriginal boys who had stolen pencils or, in one case, a towel to prison sentences normally reserved for very serious criminal offences. The Northern Territory legislation, which was in clear breach of the UN Covenant on the Rights of the Child, was repealed in 2002.

As Crawford (1997) argues, such changes dovetailed with what was seen by victim organizations as the need for a system of justice that held offenders more accountable for their actions and which simultaneously shifted the burden of state support to the victim. This has seen the introduction of victim compensation schemes and the growth of numerous victims' support groups. It has led to the implementation in some countries of 'victim impact statements' in sentencing practice. It has enhanced the role played by victims in family conferencing forums. These shifts in policy and practice suggest the degree to which victims have been incorporated into the workings of Western systems of criminal justice.

Inevitably, victims' groups vary significantly in terms of what they see as the 'problem of crime'. Some have put more emphasis on 'tough' and punitive law and order measures, while others point to the need for institutional change. Naffine (1997) argues that women's groups have been among the most effective advocates of change with public campaigns against domestic violence and other sexualized offences against women. This has led to a significantly increased awareness of such matters and the introduction of specialized support and protective services, as well as fundamental changes to the legal system.

Victimization and fear of crime

What can we learn about victimization and the fear of crime from the available empirical studies? One simple point can be made: the fear of crime invariably has little to do with its actual occurrence. To put this another way: the fear of crime far outweighs the actual level of criminal activity. This disparity varies according to social groups. For instance, the elderly tend to be most fearful of crime but are among the least affected victims. Additionally, they appear to believe that young people, especially young males, are the main perpetrators of serious crime, usually directed against elderly people. This belief sits alongside the long-standing view that young people, especially young men, are the group most likely to engage in criminal conduct. Yet in a report undertaken by the Australian Bureau of Statistics entitled *The 1993 Australian Crime and Safety Survey* (cited in Roach-Anlue 1998), a large body of victimization data was published. As noted by Roach-Anlue (ibid.: 103), the study found that 8 per cent of people aged 15–24 were the victims of personal crime, including robbery, assault and sexual assault. Young men aged 15–24 years were most 'at risk' of being victims of crime. By comparison only 0.7 per cent of those aged 65 years and over experienced personal crimes. Generally, men are the main victims of crime (although this needs to be qualified according to type of crime and age category), just as they are also more likely to offend. This research also showed that 7.9 per cent of unemployed people were victims of crime compared to 3.9 per cent of employed persons. The research suggested that 8.3 per cent of households were victims of crime as opposed to 3.7 of actual persons. Married people were least vulnerable to victimization, while all-female households were significantly more prone to crime, as were single-female-headed households.

Given the fact that indigenous and coloured populations in Australia, the USA and the UK are frequently depicted as highly disposed to commit crime, it is important to also recognize their victimization. In Australia, as Cunneen's research (1990, 1991) has shown, young Aboriginals are prone to victimization on a number of levels, including repeated and often serious assaults at the hands of the police on the street and while in custody. Another group who regularly experience violence in the Australian context are indigenous women. (This is paralleled by the experience of Afro-American women in the USA and immigrant groups in the UK.) Thus, while indigenous people as a whole are nearly seven times more likely to experience crime than their non-indigenous counterparts, it is Aboriginal women who often come off the worst. High levels of domestic violence directed at women and children in remote and rural communities in Australia reflect the many problems facing indigenous communities, such as inadequate income, lack of economic infrastructure, poor welfare services, and persistent alcohol and substance abuse. Such findings are repeated time and again in other victimization studies, which reveal significant patterns of victimization affected by gender, age, ethnicity and other factors (for summary of such studies see Cook 1997: 118–31; Crawford 1997).

Yet, while victim surveys are undoubtedly a useful mechanism for identifying which groups are prone to certain offences, they are only ever partial and selective representations of the nature and extent of crime in any given area. As Roach-Anlue (1998: 105) concludes: 'Victim surveys are . . . an important source of information about crime and indicate that some crimes are more likely to be reported to the police than are others, thus attesting to the inaccuracies inherent in police data.'

Walklate and others have rightly noted that debates about victimization reliant on victim surveys can take us only so far. This raises important analytical and theoretical questions about the ways in which our knowledge of crime victims is constructed. Problems of selective reporting, under-reporting, cultural barriers to reporting, different ways of recording crimes across time and place, changing definitions of crime, and so forth, mean that (as with the concept of crime) it is difficult to make any firm or meaningful statements about the levels of victimization.

A more productive course may be to consider victimization using Garland's 1997 framing of criminology as a governmental discourse concerned primarily with the prevention and reduction of a socially constructed 'crime problem'. Such an analysis touches on the core questions of how we come to *know* about crime and victims, and what all this means for the practices of social surveillance, regulation and intervention in our time. We illustrate the potential for interesting analysis in this area by examining victimization and fear-of-crime ~~effects~~ discourses within the context of certain political imperatives.

The politics of victimization and fear of crime

Victim surveys have only limited usefulness in alerting us to the full range of crimes perpetrated against individuals and social groups. As Hogg and Brown (1998: 89–90) point out: 'While [victim surveys] . . . indicate that there are high rates of reporting of the more persistent forms of theft on the part of such victims, they are unable to provide us with information concerning a vast range of other economic crimes and their victims.' Victim surveys tell us little or nothing about 'victimless crimes' such as illicit drug-trafficking and corporate and state corruption (ibid.: 90). They tell us even less about the victims of corporate, or organizational, crime, many of whom either don't see themselves as victims or else are far removed from those who perpetrate these offences. The actions of multinational companies in, for instance, selling sub-standard or dangerous products to the Third World, exploiting child labour or breaching health and safety regulations by employing children and women to mine blue asbestos in Zambia, may produce victims who, once again, are geographically and socially far removed from the corporate or organizational perpetrator. It may be next to impossible in such cases for the victims to mount an effective case against a powerful or remote offender. In the case of 'green' crimes like pollution, the victims may not even understand themselves to be victims.

Such considerations are central to a broader understanding of victims. Victim surveys tend to reflect both the narrow range of knowledge and the methodologies on which they rest their credibility as well as the imperatives of certain political agendas. By this we refer both to the political use of the concept of *victim* (usually aimed at the introduction of 'tough law and order' measures) as well as to a range of specific research practices aimed at identifying the 'crime problem' and the 'solutions' to it.

A useful starting point is found in a recent essay dealing with 'fear of crime' (Lee 1999). Lee develops a 'genealogical' perspective drawing on the work of Foucault (1991) and Garland (1997) to highlight the way in which fear-of-crime discourses over the past two decades or so have merged with certain political responses to crime on the part of many governments. As Lee (1999: 243–4) concludes in response to the question 'Fear of crime – What is it?':

> The fear of crime in terms of governance, has emerged empirically in the nexus of various regimes of criminological knowledge, public beliefs, politics, and imperatives of government. This emergence, in terms of the broader political and criminological discursive terrain, has been contingent upon various historically specific regimes of disciplinary, political and cultural knowledge and utility. As

a result of the ongoing attempts at the objectification of the fear of crime combined with the neo-liberalism inherent in contemporary western political thought, there has been the putting into discourse of the individual as a *fearing subject*. The fear of crime now operates as an instrument of government in terms of the self-regulation of this fearing subject. By this I mean that the fear of crime has become part of the mentalities of modern liberal governance in terms of the regulation of individual subjects and therefore the wider population.

If we apply this analysis to the idea of victimization, then it becomes necessary to turn to the role of victimology in contemporary state policy. In terms of the processes of governance over others, it is apparent that victimization studies have been used explicitly to develop a 'politics of law and order' driving preventive programmes aimed at the lessening of 'risk' among certain victim-prone populations. These programmes have resulted in processes designed to identify those most 'at risk' of crime either as 'perpetrators' or as 'victims', and to develop ways of ensuring a greater sense of 'community safety'. Deborah Lupton (1999) argues that crime audits, safety audits and elaborate statistical surveys have become the hallmarks of a new social methodology aimed at calibrating the extent of risk in our midst. 'Predictive indicators' have thus been used as a justification for intervention strategies which focus on the psychological make-up of individuals, 'family functioning' (including such things as 'parenting skills', 'family therapy', to say nothing of the increasing resort to drugs like Rintolin to manage the behaviour of children and teenagers said to be difficult to control), school performance and increased 'community-based' resources. Many of these projects resemble the earlier moral discourses and interventions on the part of social reformers, child-savers, charity workers and others in the nineteenth and early twentieth centuries. These normalizing projects were characterized then by the 'neo-classical' view that the moral and behavioural traits of the working class and the urban and rural poor were undesirable and less virtuous than those displayed by the more 'respectable' classes (Hunt 1999). As Nikolaus Rose (1990, 2000) has shown, the logic of 'social control' has been characterized by a remarkable consistency over time insofar as certain forms of behaviour have been deemed more 'acceptable' and therefore normative than others. Normalizing projects of the eighteenth and nineteenth centuries bear a significant resemblance to many of those in our time that likewise serve to legitimize interventions into the families and communities of the 'lower classes'. Public awareness of victims' rights and political attempts to develop crime-prevention strategies have served in a number of ways. They both heighten the fear of 'crime' and foster anxiety about the 'risks' in our midst, while justifying the development of an expanding panoply of interventionist 'law'n order' projects (Cohen 1984; Rose 1990; Lee 1999).

Most recently the creation of the 'fearing subject' has legitimized all those projects aimed at facilitating greater 'self-protection' and 'responsibility' in the family household, neighbourhood and 'community' (Crawford 1997). This process of devolving responsibility back from governments to individuals, households and communities, has produced many innovations. Pat O'Malley (1997) points to the growth in domestic security, walled estates or gated communities, some with armed guards, the normalizing of video surveillance, including placing cameras in school toilets, and private security patrols. All these have become normal parts of a culture of 'risk' in which the 'citizen' is obliged to take greater responsibility for his or her own affairs. At another level, the creation of 'partnership' schemes, community policing, Adopt-a-Cop, 'Buddy' systems, school-based police liaison officers, and so forth, reflect a greater emphasis over recent years on 'self-management' in local areas. Victim-support groups, victims' rights associations and other such local organizations have worked closely with other community groups and the police under the rubric of 'community safety' and 'social defence'.

Mainstream criminology has buttressed an overly narrow concern with defining the crime problem and the apparent solutions. As Walklate (1998: 128) points out, we require a better understanding of the 'structural' context of victimization and also a more comprehensive insight into how this intersects with general patterns of social benefits and social suffering (Bourdieu et al. 2000).

Conclusion

Rather than focusing on the usual metrics associated with victim surveys, we have chosen instead to discuss this body of knowledge as a discourse produced in a particular kind of political space. In seeking to outline the criminological contribution to the study of victims we referred to three broad areas of inquiry: positivistic, radical and critical (Walklate 1998). We argued that these approaches reflect both the diversity of positions within criminology about the victims of crime as well as the wider social and political concerns that have influenced the growing attention given to victimization over recent years. Inevitably, any discussion of victimization takes us beyond the secure confines of criminological theory or empirical inquiry to an exploration of how this discourse *fits into* the wider scheme of things. Drawing on the feminist work of Sandra Walklate and others, we argued that much is to be gained through an analysis that focuses on how debates about victims are constructed and why it is that the state chooses to see victims in the way it does (Young 1996). This does not sustain any exercise in statistical compilations of objectively verifiable victim populations but rather how the various academic discourses on victimology take their particular character. It is, in turn, also an account of the practices of government and the mechanisms by which the problem of crime can be addressed by a more systematic identification of both the victim and perpetrator.

This, of course, is not to dismiss the importance of surveys and other studies in highlighting the experiences of victims, or to deny the role that victims might play in facilitating a more equitable and balanced approach to justice. However, criminologists need to take account of the constitutive nature of victimology and its use in the framework of modern governance. We need to pay more attention to the way talk of risk, victimology and fear of crime links to the changing nature of regulation and discipline. Neo-liberal policies are a serious challenge to criminology insofar as the pace of change in neo-liberal states has already produced significant and lasting transformations in social, economic and political relations. The regulatory intentions (Silbey 1996; Young 1999) of contemporary victimology require far more critical attention.

The point of this for a criminology able to reflect responsibly on the state of affairs in the world is pointed to by the problem of state crime and the numbers of victims of state-sponsored crime and terror in the twentieth century.

Review questions

Is the status of a victim always a simple objective matter?

Given the relatively recent discovery of victims, what social and political factors best explain the emergence of an interest in victimology among modern criminologists?

Identify certain groups of people who do not get to be identified as victims by current victimology surveys.

Further reading

Ericson, R., Baranek, P. and Chan, J., 1991, *Representing Order, Crime, Law and Justice in the News Media*, Open University Press, Buckingham.

Fattah, E., 1993, *Towards a Critical Victimology*, Macmillan, London.

Polk, K., 1994, *Why Men Kill: Scenarios of Masculine Violence*, Cambridge University Press, Cambridge.

Walklate, S., 1990, 'Researching Victims of Crime: Radical Victimology', *Social Justice*, Vol. 17, No. 3: 25–42.

Young, J., 1988, 'Risks of Crime and Fear of Crime: A Realist Critique of Survey-Based Assumptions', in Maguire, M. and Pointing, J. (eds), *Victims of Crime: A New Deal?*, Open University, Milton Keynes.

10

CRITICAL ABSENCES: CRIMINOLOGY AND CORPORATE CRIME

Conventional criminologists, journalists and whatever is meant by 'public opinion' are fixated on a very narrow idea of *crime* as something that low-income or working-class people do when they steal, behave violently, drink to excess or take drugs. This idea is unfortunate because the scale and the scope of crimes committed by powerful companies and high-income professionals are staggering, as are the terrible consequences for large numbers of people affected by white-collar, or corporate, crime. As a useful point of comparison we can start with the FBI's Uniform Crime Report for 2000. This revealed that there were 407,842 robberies in the USA, netting the perpetrators a total of $477 million or an average of $1,170 per robbery. Comparisons can be odious but they can also be telling. As Punch (1996) points out, just one broker employed by Drexel, Werner, Lambert in the 1980s, and working on take-over deals, relied on insider trading, created dummy companies and engaged in secret, offshore operations, fraudulently netting himself hundreds of millions of dollars. That broker successfully 'plea-bargained' his case while agreeing to pay back $600 million in return for the dropping of the 90 criminal charges he was facing!

In 1949 US criminologist Edwin Sutherland published his *White-Collar Crime*, a book that rapidly achieved the status of a classic in criminology. His collaborator Donald Cressey argued that this book forced all those involved in the study and administration of criminal justice to 're-examine the ground on which they have traditionally made generalizations about crime and criminals' (1961: ii). In the 1980s Stuart Henry (1985: 70), too, was effusive in his praise of Sutherland's classic study, saying that it had

> turned the subject matter of criminology on its head. Instead of being the tools of the powerful serving to measure and motivate the largely pathetic crimes of the poor, criminologists have turned people's evidence, blowing the whistle on the far more lethally potent, socially pernicious and economically draining crimes of the powerful.

Perhaps so. We are more inclined to think that both Cressey and Henry were engaging in wishful thinking. Henry's celebration of a criminology fully alive to the 'lethally potent, socially pernicious and economically draining crimes of the powerful' is somewhat overstated. Echoing Gandhi's quip about 'Western civilization' after hearing that British troops had massacred hundreds of Indians at Amritsar in 1921, we too might say 'Ah, critical criminology . . . what a good idea that would have been'.

In this chapter we continue our exploration of modern criminology by paying attention to the way criminologists have dealt with white-collar crime, or crimes committed by middle-class professionals, business people and sometimes by whole corporations. (In Chapter 11 we look at the case of crimes of the state about which criminologists have had almost nothing to say across the twentieth century.)

In each case we outline and think carefully about the activities in question as well as the 'constructive schemes' used by criminologists to make their discipline what it is. The cases of white-collar crime and state crime suggest that the constructive schemes at work in mainstream criminology are *partial*, in both senses of the word: having an interest in or preference for something, as well as telling only part of a larger story.

Certainly some criminologists have understood that the significance of white-collar crime extends well beyond the study of corporate or 'economic crime' *per se* to encompass the very ways in which all kinds of crimes and criminal behaviour are thought about. Radical and critical criminologists have often used the idea of white-collar crime to argue that mainstream criminology reveals certain deeply entrenched social and political prejudices. Our concern is captured by Dirkis and Nichol (1996) when they argued that conventional criminologists have preferred to focus on working-class crime and crimes of the poor rather than make corporate crime or the crimes committed by economic and professional elites a central feature of criminological theory and research.

We begin by outlining Sutherland's original arguments about white-collar crime and looking at the variety of critical evaluations of Sutherland's work before turning to some of the varieties of corporate crime that continue to matter. We then argue that as a discipline mainstream criminology to date has only been *partially* committed to studying criminal conduct. In its preoccupation with street crime or petty crimes against property, mainstream criminology appears to be constrained by existing 'popular', 'political' and disciplinary definitions of what constitutes crime and the crime problem.

Edwin Sutherland and white-collar crime

Written at some risk to his career and reputation, Sutherland's famous book has long been regarded as one of the most important interventions in criminology in the second half of the twentieth century. Equally its influence on what conventional criminologists *actually do* has been patchy at best.

Sutherland's study of white-collar crime was a development of his theory of 'differential association' which he had outlined in the late 1920s (Sutherland and Cressey 1978). The theory of differential association argued that criminal behaviour was *learned* in specific socio-cultural contexts that were 'favorably disposed towards law violation'. According to Sutherland crime could not be explained in terms of an individual's predisposition to such behaviour, but was much more a consequence of relationships with other people for whom crime was an acceptable activity. This account, however, led Sutherland to different conclusions from those to which many other criminologists have come.

Sutherland argued that a distorted picture of crime in the USA had been created such that offending behaviour was identified exclusively with low-income, low-status people.

He reached this conclusion after a major review of criminological theories, including Sheldon and Eleanor Glueck's 1950 work which stressed the role played by 'social pathologies' like poverty and 'broken families'. In the course of that review he explicitly rejected these social–pathological explanations of crime because they focused too narrowly on low-income, migrant or black populations in US cities. Sutherland's point was that crime could be committed by *anyone*, from *any* background. Crime was far from being something only the 'lower orders' did.

In effect Sutherland pointed to a fundamental social prejudice which complacently accepted that 'crime' was what only the 'lower orders' or 'working-class people' did. The result, as Taylor, Walton and Young (1973: 91–138) and Garland (1997) have argued, was a body of criminological knowledge grounded in the belief that the crimes that mattered were committed by low-income, low-status or working-class people. This feature has indeed characterized many strands of criminology, from neo-classical criminology, through the ecological theory of the Chicago School and later formulations of 'social dis-organization' theory to the sociological forays into 'street-corner' crime and delinquency. Thus, robbery, burglary, theft, criminal damage and assault became synonymous with the core idea of 'crime'. This preoccupation with working-class people and 'the poor' (or the 'underclass') continues to underpin modern actuarial criminology and contemporary research into 'risk factors' (Bessant, Hil and Watts 2005).

Sutherland put his objection to this long-standing prejudice when he boldly stated that

> persons of the upper socio-economic class engage in much criminal behavior . . . this criminal behavior differs from the criminal behavior of the lower socio-economic class principally in the administrative procedures which are used in dealing with the offenders . . . [these] variations in administrative procedures are not significant from the point of view of causation of crime.
>
> (1983: 9)

Sutherland thought that crime could be committed by a corporate financier or a leading politician as easily as by a young, working-class man mixing with the 'wrong' crowd. Sutherland wanted to discomfort common-sense criminological accounts of crime. Sutherland suggested, with considerable understatement, that what he called 'white-collar' crime was employed 'merely to call attention to crimes that are not ordinarily included within the scope of criminology' (ibid.: 9).

Corporate crime

In 1940 Sutherland identified the types of offence that he thought should be included in the category of 'white-collar' crime. These included

> misrepresentation in financial statements of corporations, manipulations on the stock exchange, commercial bribery, bribery of public officials directly or indirectly to secure favorable contracts and legislation, misrepresentation in advertising and salesmanship, embezzlement and misapplication of funds, short

weights and measures and misgrading of commodities, tax frauds, misapplication of funds in receivership and bankruptcies.

(1994: 67–8)

In effect white-collar crime referred to 'crime committed by a person of respectability and high social status in the course of his occupation' (1983: 9).

Using these criteria Sutherland claimed that the earliest white-collar criminals included many of the great nineteenth-century American entrepreneurs (or 'robber barons') like the Pierpont Morgans, the Rockefellers and the Fiskes, who engaged in large-scale and often blatantly fraudulent and corrupt business practices as part of their *normal* business practices. According to Sutherland, white-collar crime was widespread and occurred regularly in the 1930s and 1940s in the US 'land offices, insurance, munitions, banking, public utilities, stock exchanges, the production industry, the real estate industry, receiverships, bankruptcies, and politics' (1983: 10). In order to make this case Sutherland devoted the bulk of his book to a well-documented analysis of 70 of America's largest non-financial corporations and 15 public utilities (that is, electrical generation and light corporations). Sutherland identified evidence of dubious systematic trade practices (especially illegal restraints of trade such as price-fixing), manipulation of patents, trademarks and copyrights (often issued exclusively to a small number of powerful corporations), misrepresentation in advertising and unfair labour practices on the part of these corporations.

In relation to the public utilities, Sutherland described forty-four cases in which state and federal laws had been violated, including unauthorized extensions and cessations to services, foreclosures and security issues. Sutherland pointed out that despite widespread violations of laws, few if any of the utility corporations had been successfully prosecuted. Anticipating the many subsequent studies of corporate crime, Sutherland (ibid.: 210–13) outlined a number of reasons for the virtual immunity of corporations and their most senior managers to prosecution. These included official ignorance of corporate activities, self-protecting 'propaganda' on the part of corporate managers, strong legal representation of corporate bodies in Federal Trade Commission inquiries and, finally, the use of illegal 'slush funds' to support elections of politicians favourable to the interests of these corporations. In this way, Sutherland pointed to the fact that wealthy individuals and powerful organizations regularly commit criminal offences.

As Sutherland showed, white-collar crimes are as common as crimes by the powerless and are usually far more harmful in their effects, yet they rarely get to be recognized as a serious problem. Sutherland's account offers numerous insights into the preoccupation of both the media and the police with the often numerous, but largely petty, crimes committed by low-income and powerless people. He shows how the preoccupation with *ordinary* crime in a number of ways renders invisible the incidence and severity of major crimes committed by rich and powerful people. This means the crimes of the powerful are often unnoticed while governments seem unable or unwilling to frame laws to deal effectively with these crimes. He argued that white-collar criminals do not always get prosecuted and were more likely to escape conviction; the penalty was more likely to be a warning or a fine rather than prison while the consequences and severity of the effects of their crimes were simply not noticed.

Using official data Sutherland showed that for 70 of the biggest US corporations, 980 judicial judgments had been made against them for a wide range of offences in just over

20 years. He documented how some 75 per cent of US banks had violated banking laws in the 1930s and 1940s. Sutherland also showed that the scale and costs of white-collar crimes were far greater than those of ordinary working-class crimes. While individual burglaries or thefts might net the thief thousands of dollars and impact on several people, the typical white-collar crime nets millions and harms many people. This argument would be validated in the USA in the collapse of hundreds of trust and loans institutions in the late 1980s, with billions of dollars stolen from numerous American families. It was repeated in the USA by the collapse of Emron and the criminal collapse of the Italian multinational Permalac with debts of $10 billion, both in 2003. We can see here, too, the way language works to cover up what is happening, when we recall that economic liberals benignly called these spectacular instances of white-collar crime instances of 'market failure'.

Evaluating Sutherland and white-collar crime

Sutherland's original account of white-collar crime has been subjected to extensive evaluation, development, criticism and rebuttal since the mid-1980s, the responses to his work taking several forms.

The reception given to Sutherland's account of white-collar crime by his peers is an example of how genuinely critical thought too often gets dealt with. As is well known, although Sutherland's 1949 'classic' was one of the publishing highlights of the 1940s, Sutherland was not permitted to publish the actual text he wrote because he had named hundreds of major corporations found guilty of criminal activity. The full and unexpurgated text was finally published only in 1983!

Mainstream criminologists still routinely recognize and pay homage to the work of original and critical writers like Sutherland, and then pay them the supreme compliment due to their dangerously critical ideas by forgetting all about them so that they can continue doing more conventional criminology.

One response has been to accept the general thrust of Sutherland's work both as unproblematic and as a call to criminologists to do more and better (Friedrichs 1996). As Box (1983: 32–4) asks:

> On which type of crime should we be concentrating? Surely, the deleterious consequences that street crime has on our sense of community pales besides the way in which corporate crime fractures the economic and political system . . . Concern should focus first on understanding 'how it is possible for corporate crime to be endemic in our "law and order" society', and second, and hopefully flowing from this understanding, 'how can it be contained and regulated?'

Sutherland's insight was ignored by most of his colleagues. So it is that in every decade since, other criminologists, like Clinard and Yeager (1980), Waldman (1990), Friedrichs (1996) or Braithwaite (1984, 2000), remind their colleagues of the need to rediscover white-collar crime.

Other criminologists, working from the premiss that white-collar crime is an unproblematic concept, have added to Sutherland's account by identifying new kinds of corporate crimes that he could not have identified because they did not exist in the 1940s. Dirkis and Nichol (1996: 258), for instance, point to new crimes such as computer hacking. Subsequently we have seen how the release of computer viruses, such as the Love Virus, on to the Internet has crippled corporate computer systems globally. Similarly, breaches of intellectual property rights have increased as the Internet has become more accessible. Most recently law-enforcement agencies have had to deal with 'identity theft' as thieves use credit card information or Internet-based banking facilities to 'hack' into people's bank and credit charge accounts, using these personal details to their own advantage. Carrabine et al. (2004) point to 'green' crimes or gross environmental violations like the *Exxon Valdez* oil spill in Alaska, or Union Carbide's release of deadly toxic fumes in Bhopal, India. Naturally, none of these activities could have been foreseen by Sutherland.

Other criminologists, however, have remained sceptical about the value of Sutherland's contribution, leading to more critical scrutiny of the very idea of white-collar crime. Critics have argued that Sutherland failed to distinguish clearly between the size, structure and operations of corporate organizations and the way these factors can shape corporate crime. Some have argued that these considerations are important in understanding the specific contexts in which corporate crime takes place. John Braithwaite, who has contributed to major studies of corporate crime over the past few decades, points out that

> the distribution of crime depends on the viability of legitimate and illegitimate opportunities to achieve organizational goals and the extent to which sub-cultural realities of regulated organizations and the state foster sub-cultures of resistance to law and the extent to which these organizations have internal controls which expose offending to shaming.
>
> (1989a: 353)

These critics suggest that the internal operations of corporate organizations are shaped – and constrained – both by their size and by the kinds of management processes that have been put in place. These factors will have a direct bearing on the emergence of corporate criminal activity. Jamieson (1994: 93) claims, though not with much evidence to substantiate his case, that 'large, poor performing companies in profitable industries and with few managers are most prone to criminal activity'. Blankenship (1993: xx–xxvi) argues that while such findings can point to the type of corporate enterprise that may exhibit signs of criminal activity, far more data are needed on differences in organizational opportunities and power in corporate organizations before such claims can be tested or confirmed. It remains the case that little is known about the motivations that lead corporate managers to engage in illegal activities. As Nelken (1994a: 367 and 1994b) argues: 'Far more research is needed on the modus operandi – the "how" of "white-collar" crime (motivation, meaning, actions, decisions, alliances, escape routes, "techniques of neutralization" etc.' The relative dearth of this kind of research is, of course, partly a consequence of the way mainstream criminologists continue to be preoccupied with 'ordinary crime', based on the premiss as Braithwaite (1989a: 100) observes, with tongue firmly in cheek, that 'crime is what the working class commit'.

That a relatively small band of criminologists who research white-collar crime, like Braithwaite (1984, 2000), Grabosky and Braithwaite (1986), Erman and Rabe (1997),

Simon (1999) and Ruggiero (2000), are preoccupied with organizational factors and characteristics has one strange effect. It leads to a blanking out of the role played in economic crime by personal dispositions and motives. This tendency possibly reflects the way mainstream sociology and criminology has tended to over-emphasize social 'structural' factors, like the collective characteristics of organizations, because of a perceived need to establish and defend disciplinary boundaries, and to keep the lines between disciplines like sociology and psychology clear and well defined. Alaheto suggests, in one recent attempt to insert the personal motivations and personality of economic criminals back into the picture, that Sutherland's refusal to acknowledge the role of personal factors rests on a confusion between personality *per se* and the idea of psychic health. Sutherland appears to believe that

> sick criminals show character disturbances because of a misdirected primary socialisation that shapes their personality; healthy criminals do not show any character disturbances and thereby no personality! Economic criminals may not as a rule show [the] psychic or social defects . . . seen in murderers, or burglars, but it is a serious misapprehension to maintain that the personality of economic criminals does not matter . . .
>
> (Alaheto 2003: 336)

As Alaheto indicates, it is an empirical matter to determine whether it is possible that anyone could carry out an economic crime if he or she faces the same organizational possibilities given his or her position in a company, have the same capacity to carry out the activity and are given the same opportunity. Or is it the case, as he suggests, that some people are more inclined to carry out economic crimes than others? He goes on to report on a small research project he carried out in Sweden involving 128 interviews with business people, some of them implicated in business crime and others who were not. His modest conclusion (ibid.: 351) is that some personality traits, like the level of regard for moral and legal norms, play a part in people's disposition to engage in corporate crime and that 'personality does matter in economic crime . . . but . . . how much it matters is hard to say'.

This discussion suggests that the idea of white-collar crime is not without its problems. Sutherland's own account of white-collar crime remained, as he admitted, 'undeveloped'. There can be little doubt that the extension of criminological analysis to actions beyond conduct not formally defined as constituting a breach of criminal (or commercial or civil) law is a direct challenge to criminologists who are preoccupied with such breaches. Yet, as McBarnett argued (1991: 341), it is well known that 'the definition of crime is "manipulated" not only by law enforcement agencies but also by those subject to the law and the label themselves'.

For these criminologists there is considerable ground for concern about the kind of activities we are invited to include under the heading of 'white-collar' crime, and related issues like the role played by collective processes versus more personal issues like intent and motive.

For instance, it has long been known that many industries through the twentieth century have sustained levels of injury and even deaths found otherwise only on battlefields. As Goodwin (1996: 441) shows, in the US mining industry in 1941 alone, 64,764 men were killed or injured in accidents. Carson (1981) too showed how in the 1970s the UK's oil industry sustained a very high level of avoidable injury and death. Criminologists, for instance Clarke (1990), who do not dispute the completely unacceptable nature of work practices leading to consequences like these, nonetheless insist that it is a moot point whether such practices deserve to be equated with illegal activities such as deliberate fraud and deception practised by stockbrokers, lawyers or bank employees. Perhaps so. Yet British criminal law has long recognized that unlawful deaths can be a consequence either of homicidal intent, or murder, or unintended but negligent activities better defined as manslaughter.

Clarke (ibid.: 16) writes of his own approach to business crime, which

> covers a much wider range of misconduct, which may be none the less damaging and otherwise undesirable resulting from duress, incompetence, negligence, lack of training, lack of clarity in the rules, opportunism, technical infraction, or sheer muddle headedness rather than calculated deceit motivated by greed.

Given the interplay between the inherent complexity of large-scale attempts to cover up or deflect responsibility and the sheer pain and horror of some examples of 'corporate misbehaviour', such a distinction (and the mitigation it implies) may not always be warranted. Can we, or should we, distinguish between terrible deeds deliberately pre-meditated and terrible deeds which responsible people, with the capacity and the knowledge to act responsibly, nonetheless did nothing to avoid?

Baxi (1986) asks us, in effect, how should we think about the case of Union Carbide's plant at Bhopal, in India? On one day in 1986, the plant inadvertently released deadly gas into the air killing thousands of Bhopal's residents. How should we respond to the Soviet Union's attempt to cover up the events leading to the release of deadly radiation by a dangerously broken down nuclear reactor at Chernobyl in 1987? Such cases might suggest that it is not at all clear that the deceit or lying which went on at the highest levels in either case warrants a less serious reaction than, say, the 'usual' response to a premeditated murder of another citizen by a 'criminal'. Should 'inaction' of this kind mitigate our ethical or legal response to such problems and their consequences?

How have conventional criminologists dealt with the thrust of Sutherland's account of white-collar crime? How did they deal with his claim that the 'crimes' committed by corporations brought into sharp relief the need to widen the scope of criminological inquiry from 'street crime' to crimes that included the activities of respectable people and elite groups and organizations?

Some of Sutherland's conventional criminological critics have been concerned that his inclusion of a wide range of corporate 'offences', including those that breach both criminal and civil laws, threatens the very boundaries of criminological analysis. Conventional criminologists critical of the category of 'white-collar' crime have simply dismissed it, as James Q. Wilson did when he said that 'predatory street crime is a far more serious matter than consumer fraud, or anti-trust violations . . . because predatory street crime . . . makes difficult or impossible the maintenance of meaningful human communities' (1975: xix). Others have argued that any attempt to investigate white-collar crime will run immediately into severe conceptual or definitional problems. Hirschi and Gottfredson (1987: 958) claimed that Sutherland tended to ignore those people of low status who commit 'white-collar' crimes: 'the assumption that "white-collar" criminals differ from other criminals is simply an assumption for which there is no good evidence'.

In this way it is argued that Sutherland's use of the term 'white-collar' is not all that different from the category of 'lower-class crime' to which he appears so opposed. Nelken (1994a: 366), for one, argues that the drift away from a focus on criminal law violation poses a danger of eroding 'the boundaries of the discipline'. Nelken (1997: 895–7) claims that the whole category of 'white-collar' crime (and the literature on it) needs to recognize at least 'seven kinds of ambiguity' about the very idea. Perhaps his response depends on the entirely unexceptionable proposition that human conduct is very complex, though he does not supply any reasons why he might say this. Perhaps it is a consequence of his desire to pursue a certain kind of conceptual essentialism (and being disappointed when he cannot). Either way, the grounds of his concerns are never made entirely clear. That this criticism ignores the way 'ordinary crime' or 'violence' is treated as an 'obvious' or 'common-sense' idea nonetheless points to some of the very fundamental prejudices at the heart of the constructive schemes of conventional criminology, prejudices that Sutherland was trying to acknowledge and move beyond.

Problems of definition

It is important to note that Sutherland's approach to white-collar crime focused specifically on misleading advertising, unfair and exploitative labour practices, and illegal financial manipulations, while excluding crimes committed by the rich and powerful such as murder, drunk-driving, assault or rape. Sutherland made this distinction because he believed that these latter actions were not typically organizational or 'occupational procedures'. Sutherland's definition also excluded organized crime, or 'mob' activities, since the perpetrators possessed 'neither respectability nor high status' (1983: 9). As Alaheto (2003: 335–6) has noted, Sutherland's approach to white-collar crime rests on the basic assumption that this kind of crime does not reflect individual, personal dispositions so much as the social relations and dynamics at work in a profit-seeking organization and its field of operations. Alaheto (2003: 335) stresses that the 'act of economic crime was seen as a collective act (the complexity of the organization) and not as an act caused by one single agent's personality characteristics'. Many criminologists who have studied white-collar crime, for example Erman and Rabe (1997) and Ruggiero (2000), have agreed with Sutherland.

Others, however, have insisted, as Sharyn Roach-Anlue (1996: 225) does, on distinguishing between *white-collar* crime and *occupational* crime. On this account white-collar crime refers to crimes like fraud and embezzlement of a company's funds or those of its clients, false advertising, insider trading, and the like; occupational crime, on the other hand, involves crimes committed by individuals during the course of their jobs, such as a teacher who rapes a student or a doctor who murders a patient. Thorn (1996: 285) agrees, adding yet another category – *organized* crime, which he argues should be treated as a discrete category of offending involving persistent and planned 'gangsterism' and 'mob' activities such as large-scale unregulated gambling, prostitution, drug-dealing or extortion. Organized crime and occupational misdemeanours, in turn, are distinguished from *corporate* crime in which criminal or harmful activities arise out of the pursuit of corporate objectives and are designed, presumably, to benefit the corporate goals of profit, exclude corporate competitors or promote other organizational goals.

While this attempt to establish some clear definitional boundaries is perhaps worthwhile, some of these distinctions can be difficult to sustain. What Roach-Anleu (1996) refers to as 'occupational crime' occurs sometimes in organizations that encourage or at least fail to prevent the illegal actions of its employees. This was the case in the Roman Catholic diocese of Boston whose leaders, as well as a number of Cardinals, allowed decades of systematic sexual and physical abuse of children and young people in schools and welfare institutions under their care. There is even evidence in this case of a 'generational transmission' of the criminal activity as the young victims of paedophile priests were 'groomed' by them to join the priesthood and in turn become predatory abusers of children and teenagers (Burkett and Bruni 1995).

Likewise the idea that there are clear-cut boundaries between respectable, high-status businessmen and people engaged in 'organized' crime may be harder to sustain than Sutherland allowed. The systematic hiring by legitimate businessmen and major companies like Ford of thugs, supplied by the Chicago mobster Al Capone in the late 1920s, to break up lawful union activities seems to muddy this boundary-defining attempt quite quickly. So too does the extensive record of links between legitimately wealthy US businessmen and politicians, like Joseph Kennedy (and his sons, including President John F. Kennedy), and organized crime figures like Sam Gianccana in the 1950s and 1960s. (While he was President, John Kennedy 'dated' the girlfriend of Giancanna, a leading 'mob' boss.)

We need to recall here the point made by Alfred Kinsey, one of the greatest of America's empirical social scientists and author of two monumental studies of American sexual behaviour. Kinsey (1948: 238) observed that nature itself neither produces nor recognizes clear-cut conceptual definitions: only humans pursue and value taxonomic pigeon-holes and often at the cost of ignoring the actual mess of reality. Because none of us is exempt from this urge to construct and defend conceptual pigeon-holes, we think there is some point to David Nelken's observation that Sutherland's approach to white-collar crime conflated a number of different concerns, being 'built on an overlap of (at least) three different types of behaviour: crimes by high status people, crimes for organizations and crimes against organizations' (1994a: 358). However, Nelken does not help matters when he goes on to suggest that making these conceptual points are matters amenable to simple empirical investigation. This leads Nelken (ibid.: 361) to somewhat confusingly claim that the 'term "white-collar" . . . combines definition and explanation . . . a [combination that] makes it impossible to investigate the empirical correlation between high status and criminality'.

Nelken has drawn attention to some important distinctions, leading us to focus on his last two cases, namely 'crimes for organizations' and 'crimes against organizations'. We think this makes for a useful, simple distinction.

Crimes *against* organizations and crimes *for* organizations

Crimes *against* organizations are those that take place inside major companies, usually at the behest of a lone individual or a small number of people.

Possibly the most spectacular example of this is the case of Nick Leeson, a Singapore-based trader who 'lost' £1.9 billion and brought the British bank Barings to its knees in the mid-1990s. (This had the consequence of bringing Lloyds, the British insurance underwriter, to its knees as well.) Barings in this case may have been 'culpable', but only because its senior executives failed to ensure that there was effective internal monitoring of what its agents were doing. What that lone broker committed was, in effect, a crime against both Barings and Lloyds and all their customers. More common are cases like that involving Victoria University in Australia where a small number of managers knowingly conspired with 'legitimate' businessmen over many years to defraud that university by constructing false invoices for non-existent cleaning services, netting themselves at least $AU27 million. Less common, and arguably less a case of crime than mindless irresponsibility, was that involving the National Australia Bank which 'lost' $AU180 million because of the activities of four of its currency traders. It seems that the traders, who were engaged in normal currency, lost a lot of the bank's money as the global currency market went through one of its periodic down-turns. Rather than inform their managers of the losses, the four traders decided to try illicitly to invest their way out of trouble, a gamble that failed. The bank's normal risk-management mechanisms failed to detect the irregularities and it took a 'whistle-blower' to alert the bank and the police to what had happened.

On the other hand, crimes *for* organizations involve collective intent knowingly to engage in illegal activity by a significant number of players, including high-ranking executives, as a matter of policy and calculation. Disclosures of spectacular forms of negligence, fraud and embezzlement have afforded criminologists opportunities to inquire into the malpractices of individuals at the very heart of the corporate world (Grabosky and Sutton 1989).

The scale and diversity of the forms that this kind of corporate malfeasance can take makes it difficult to render these occurrences amenable to simple generalizations. The following 'spectacular' cases going back over a half-century make this point. They also point to the social impact of such instances of corporate crime, namely the widespread human pain and suffering in the form of unemployment, the destruction of whole communities as older people lose their lifetime savings and superannuation entitlements, and the visceral pain of bodily disfigurement and birth defects.

The Thalidomide case

The costs of producing a new therapeutic drug (conservatively estimated on average to be $AU160–200 million) and the potential profits (often running into billions) put enormous pressure on pharmaceutical companies to come up with new products while minimizing costs, often achieved by cutting corners on risk management. Such was the case with the major German pharmaceutical company Grünenthal which during the 1950s produced and promoted a drug called 'Thalidomide'. Thalidomide was developed as a tranquilliser. The drug was advertised as completely safe, non-poisonous and non-toxic. It was widely marketed as being safe enough to be taken by pregnant women. This advertising and the advice given to doctors prescribing the drug occurred despite the fact that early clinical trials of the drug had identified some worrying side-effects, such as nausea, constipation and giddiness. These results were, however, either suppressed or ignored by Grünenthal.

In the UK, the distribution of Thalidomide began in 1958. In the early 1960s, however, evidence began to emerge of gross congenital or birth defects associated with the use of the drug by women during pregnancy. Doctors began to come across cases of babies born without legs, arms, feet or hands, or at best with vestigial limbs. Grünenthal mounted a fierce campaign against its accusers while repeatedly ignoring negative evidence emerging from its own clinical trials. William McBride, an Australian doctor, carried out extensive tests after 1961 to establish beyond reasonable doubt that Thalidomide was the cause of gross birth defects. McBride's work led to a prolonged publicity campaign against the company.

Finally in 1968, a civil case was brought against Grünenthal. After two-and-a-half years of legal argument the company agreed to settle out of court. This meant, in effect, that the company escaped criminal prosecution. It was not until the 1970s, however, in the UK that a settlement was offered by the company to its victims. The courts found against the company and $54,000 was awarded to each family adversely affected by the drug. By this time, of course, many of the 'Thalidomide babies' were young teenagers. The company used every means available to protect its position in the face of sustained criticism and expert opinion over a twenty-year period. Maurice Punch has noted that its strategies included 'denial, secrecy, discrediting opponents, employing extensive legal powers, and grudgingly minimizing compensation' (1996: 165).

In an ironic postscript, William McBride, the doctor who first revealed the problem with Thalidomide, had his own career brought to an ignominious end in the late 1990s when it was discovered he had been faking some of his own research.

The Dalkon Shield

The Dalkon Shield was an intra-uterine contraceptive device (IUD) made by the US-based company A.H. Robins. Made largely of plastic and metal, the device was physically implanted inside the uterus of women seeking to prevent unwanted pregnancy. It was widely promoted as a safe alternative to the contraceptive pill, which in the late 1960s was itself beginning to attract increasing criticism and concern. However, complaints about the Dalkon Shield began to surface in the early 1970s when significant numbers of women reported both high pregnancy rates and spontaneous abortions. Eighteen women were said to have died from spontaneous abortions in the USA alone.

The company claimed publicly that the evidence about the negative side-effects of using their IUD was 'inconclusive'. Crucial submissions from medical researchers critical of the device were ignored. These researchers had pointed to the way that the small cord trailing from the device acted as a conduit for bacterial infection to enter the uterus. The spurs used to hold the device in place against the uterine lining were also carrying infections. Despite this evidence the company continued to manufacture its product. Some ten years later the company yielded to growing public pressure and advised doctors to remove the Shields from women still wearing them. More than 15,000 women have since sued the company, resulting in settlements by the mid-1980s of over $US200 million. As Albanese (1995: 159–61) shows, the manufacturing company engaged in denial, secrecy, the discrediting of critics and opponents, and employed extensive legal resources to block its detractors' and victims' claims for restitution, and only grudgingly offering minimal compensation.

In 1985, A.H. Robins, the company responsible for the continued production of the IUD, was declared bankrupt.

The Guinness affair

During the early 1980s, the City of London, which housed some of the most powerful financial institutions in the UK, experienced something of a sea-change in the economic and policy context in which it operated. The 1980s, presided over by the 'free market', neo-liberal, economic policies promoted vigorously by the Thatcher government, was the decade of revitalized 'economic liberalism', the 'casino economy' and the 'go-getter' society. Greed was pronounced 'good'. The new hot-house climate of unfettered competition permeated every aspect of the day-to-day practices of highly paid corporate 'buccaneers'. Conditions were ripe for the limits of the 'corporate game' to be well and truly exceeded. One of the most infamous cases of illegal and unethical corporate practice occurred in the course of the take-over of Scottish whisky producer Distillers by the prestigious and highly respected brewing company, Guinness.

A senior manager of Guinness, Ernest Saunders, orchestrated the take-over of Distillers, which finally occurred in April 1986. However, it soon became clear that the take-over was effected in ways that did not seem entirely legal. The Department of Trade and Industry, the Bank of England and both major political parties became aware of a number of unsavoury practices which occurred during the take-over, including suspected bugging of the offices of Distillers' directors, attempted bribery, leaks of confidential information and a systematic campaign of misinformation. This was all co-ordinated by Ernest Saunders who demonstrated a remarkable capacity to present himself as a charming, yet aggressive business executive bent on maximizing his company's market position. While many of his practices seemed somewhat 'ungentlemanly' and perhaps even 'not quite British', Saunders fell foul of the law by encouraging an illegal share-support scheme aimed at bolstering Guinness's position during the period of the take-over. Saunders and his associates were eventually found guilty of breaching some key corporate laws. Saunders was given a five-year prison sentence and the others received shorter prison terms plus fines. The punitive fine of one defendant ran into millions of pounds and was the highest ever awarded by a court in such a case. Equally the trial itself cost the British taxpayers a staggering £20 million (Punch 1996: 165–80).

Wall Street insider trading scandal

As in the UK, the 1980s in the USA was a decade of deregulation, corporate take-overs, acquisitions, 'merger mania' and cut-throat competition. The new ethos of aggressive entrepreneurship, fuelled in part by the neo-liberalism of Reaganomics, generated a climate in which companies sought to gain market advantage, often using unethical and illegal practices. The early 1980s produced a 'bull market' characterized by big increases in share values on Wall Street. The impulse to buy shares consumed brokers, institutions and investors alike. Some share-brokers proved unable to resist the temptation to trade information that privileged them during the process of negotiating and bidding for shares. The phenomenon of 'insider trading', in which dealing/trading involving the sharing of confidential information denied to the ordinary investor, became widespread in the mid-1980s.

The exposure of insider trading and other illegal practices of three brokers working for the firm of Drexel, Burnham, Lambert (DBL) shook Wall Street out of its complacency. Suspicious of an impressive number of DBL take-over deals, the US Securities and Exchange Commission found extensive evidence of insider trading as well as other dubious practices (such as the creation of dummy companies and secret offshore holdings). The extent of the brokers' illegal dealings was revealed in the massive fines and amounts of restitution involved in judgments on the case. One of the brokers agreed to pay $US50 million in 'restitution' for illegally earned profits, while another broker paid back a further $US11 million. The third broker 'plea-bargained' his case and agreed to pay back $US600 million in return for the dropping of nearly 90 charges. The company for which the brokers worked also agreed to pay $US650 million partly as a fine and partly towards a fund for investors to claim compensation for losses incurred.

Maurice Punch's analysis of the DBL case concludes with the vexed question: 'Why do some managers seem to leave their consciences behind when they enter the doors of the corporation?' (1996: 154). The answer to this question, as Punch points out, may have to do with the economic environment of trading/dealing during the 1980s, the lack of effective regulation and the seductive excitement and emotional highs that can be part of any transgressive behaviour. As Jack Katz (1988) points out, there are common emotional seductions at work in a wide variety of criminal behaviour from what he calls righteous homicide to violent rape or a vicious physical assault. As one of Drexel, Burnham, Lambert's brokers pointed out in an introspective account on his illegal practices: 'It was only in time that I came to view myself as an insider-trading junkie. I was addicted to the excitement, the sense of victory. Some spouses use drugs, others have extra-marital affairs, I secretly traded stocks' (quoted in Punch 1996: 48).

The Enron collapse

At the start of the twenty-first century there have been multi-billion-dollar corporate collapses, such as Enron in the USA and HIH Insurance in Australia, that involved major criminal practices, including the falsifying of corporate accounts, asset-stripping by senior executives and illicit auditing practices by highly respected accounting companies. In 2002 the multinational accounting house of Arthur Andersen, responsible for auditing company activities like Enron's, was implicated in fraudulent practices designed to cover up these criminal activities.

The collapse of Enron, a major US energy company, late in 2001 with billions of dollars of debts is one such case. (A core group of executives including its finance manager, Andrew Plastow, had systematically appropriated hundreds of millions of dollars for their personal use. Plastow, who admitted to fraudulently manipulating Enron's publicly reported financial results, alone stole $US58 million. He agreed early in 2004 to repay $30 million and accept a ten-year prison sentence in return for giving evidence against other, more senior, executives.)

Cases like this illustrate, if only in a certain abstracted way, the general characteristics of corporate crime.

Firstly, corporate crime on these scales is possible only because of the unequal distribution of power and resources that define contemporary market-based, capital-intensive, economic systems. Modern market-based economies are characterized by, and indeed depend on, quite major power imbalances between (i) companies and their employees and (ii) companies and the consumers of their goods and services. These imbalances are grounded in the access that corporations have to enormous financial resources, and thereby to formidable legal resources and unequal knowledge (Pearce 1976). When, as increasingly they do, corporations become multinational corporates, they do so to further protect themselves from the effects of national legal, regulatory and taxation systems. However, as Pearce and Tombs (1991: 415) point out,

> there is an inherent contradiction, on the one hand, between the profit-making goal of business enterprise within competitive capitalism, the modes of calculation and the forms of organization developed by the executives to achieve this goal and, on the other hand, the taking of [a] socially responsible attitude to the consequences of these activities . . .

Yet, as McGahey (1976) pointed out decades ago, the quest for profit by itself does not account for unethical or illegal corporate practices.

Most of the normal business activities of major companies like these are protected by thick layers of legal protection of commercial confidentiality and laws of defamation, while bedrock laws guaranteeing basic property rights to these companies provide a secure, lawful basis for their operations. Only slowly and painfully have regimes of legal rights pertaining to workers (and their unions) and to consumers (and their rights) been established over the past century. These regulatory regimes have only partially redressed the fundamental power imbalance. Curiously, this movement has often been most pronounced in the USA, the heartland of aggressive pro-capitalist rhetoric, which has a rich tradition of law-making designed to prevent the excessive concentration of corporate power. While it is possible to be cynical about some of this, the US system still has teeth, as the case brought against Microsoft in 2001 suggests.

The need for strong regulatory regimes is apparent given the human and economic costs of corporate crime. The numbers of victims and the costs to the community of corporate malfeasance, or fraud and corruption, leading to corporate collapses, are staggering. Thousands of workers have been laid off with wages still owing, and shareholders, insurance holders or customers have lost huge sums, often involving lifetime savings or pension funds. In Australia the collapse of HIH led to a nationwide increase in insurance premiums, forcing many providers out of business and closing down hundreds of community organizations no longer able to pay the increased premiums for public liability insurance. The pain and physical suffering following on malfeasance by pharmaceutical and medical companies are likewise very serious and are often extended over decades. One case involving the manufacture of silicone breast implants that led to serious infection took decades of class action, resolved only in 2004.

It seems clear that the 'acquisitive excesses' of business organizations have been ignored or often treated leniently by regulatory authorities (Stitt and Giacopassi 1993: 77). The privatized, even secretive, culture of the corporate world, with its ability to often screen-off and protect its executives from close scrutiny by governments and regulators, is reflective of the residual power of big companies.

This is suggested by a summary of a decade of corporate malfeasance in the UK. Carrabine et al. (2004: 200–01), using annual reports produced by the Serious Fraud Office (1991–2003), tabulate nine major cases of corporate fraud, deception and corruption involving an aggregate of £2,570 billion. The company collapses, and the financial losses involved, directly affected tens of thousands of shareholders, employees, pension-holders and people with bank savings. Yet the response of the criminal justice system seems muted in contrast to the scale of these crimes. In some cases the perpetrators, like Robert Maxwell, who seems to have committed suicide before he could be arrested, were never brought to justice. Those company directors who were brought before the courts typically received prison sentences of no more than three years or else got away with suspended sentences and derisory fines.

On constructive schemes

It seems plain that Sutherland's work has not led to a major paradigm shift in the assumptions underpinning conventional criminology. It is true that some high-profile criminologists like John Braithwaite have been enthusiastic practitioners and advocates of more research and theory on corporate crime. Small numbers of contemporary criminologists continue to be interested in white-collar crime and to report on cases of crimes by corporations and the numerous obstacles to investigation and successful prosecution in cases of suspected corporate crime (Clinard and Yeager 1983; Braithwaite 1984, 2000; Brown and Chiang 1993; Albanese 1995; Cohen and Simpson 1997; Ruggiero 2000).

Blankenship (1993: 51) claims that the task still facing conventional criminologists is 'to continue debate over the definition of the crime that will facilitate expanded study of avoidance harms that plague society'. Such an analysis, according to Blankenship, should lead us to think much harder about the activities of multinational tobacco and pharmaceutical companies in Third World countries, dumping unsafe products like cigarettes with tar levels that are now legally prohibited in Western societies. What should we think about the actions of pharmaceutical companies which, in order to test drugs for use in treating HIV/AIDS, avoid the ethical restraints normal in Western societies by selecting AIDS-ravaged populations in Africa as 'guinea-pigs' for clinical trials? As part of normal clinical trial practice, the scientific personnel of these companies offer placebos – or substances with no clinical value – to terminally ill patients who believe they are getting drugs that will treat their illness.

Blankenship (ibid.: 53) argues that any definition of 'crime' should be expanded to include actions on the part of individuals, companies and governments that impact negatively on the quality of life of persons or the community. Stitt and Giacopassi (1993: 57–8) state that we must consider the extent of 'corporate harm' visited on countless victims as a result of corporate malpractice – for example, the thousands of deaths resulting from vehicle defects, cigarette-induced disease, asbestosis-related cancers, coal-dust and pollution-related disease, and so forth.

Generally, however, white-collar, or corporate, crime continues to lead a fugitive existence in modern criminology in comparison to the crimes of the poor and the working class.

There are many reasons for this comparative neglect. The complexity of the cases and the fact that regulatory bodies find it difficult to penetrate the legal smokescreens thrown up by expensive lawyers partly explains why there are still so few criminological studies of corporate crime. The readiness of companies to take legal action against investigatory journalists and academic researchers is another. For instance, in Australia, Wackenhutt, a US-based company with subsidiaries (such as Group Four in the UK), and Australian Correctional Management owns and operates an increasing number of privatized prisons. This company has made it plain that it will act to protect its activities by robust legal action against the small number of criminologists interested in evaluating its corporate activities. (A more 'subtle' intervention involves the same company deciding in the late 1990s to fund the establishment of a Professorial Chair in Criminology in the University of Melbourne's criminology department in Victoria, a state which then had the highest ratio – 48 per cent – of privatized prisons in the world.)

For a number of reasons (such as self-protection, interest and research complexity) ordinary corporate crimes (other than those of the most spectacular kind involving massive fraud or mass destruction) have always been less interesting to criminologists than the more readily identifiable crimes of the urban poor and working class. Perhaps it is the cloak of respectability so readily claimed by the corporate world that has served to deflect the sustained attentions of criminologists and others. Indeed, even when studies of corporate crime are conducted they tend to concentrate on its more readily identifiable and 'sensational' manifestations. The mundane, routinized aspects of corporate deviance – often those more difficult to detect – have tended to receive less scholarly attention. As Albanese (1995: 186) points out,

> white-collar crime draws most attention when it mimics street crime – especially when bodies and traumatized victims can be gazed upon. A consequence of this is that 'fear of crime' continues to be associated with street crime, rather than with the criminal behavior of 'respectable' corporate companies.

Despite evidence that public awareness of corporate crime has increased, as have calls for harsher penalties (Evans et al. 1993), it seems that such behaviour continues to be seen as an aberration, involving excessive risk-taking or personal oddities that do not reflect on the corporate world as a whole. Shapiro (1990: 362–3) argues that Sutherland's 'painstaking work has in part had the opposite effect (of broadening the scope of the discipline), segregating the rich and poor and removing intensive critiques about those of privilege from mainstream criminology'. According to Shapiro, this failure to focus on the crimes of the powerful and the privileged is a consequence of Sutherland's attempt to develop a theory that explained all forms of crime. Rather than constructing a theoretical framework that acknowledged the influence of specific social interests (including those conventionally represented in terms of the *structures* of class and gender) or the impact of organizational power vested in the state or in business corporations which control considerable economic and intellectual resources devoted to protecting their interests, criminologists who follow Sutherland have given vent to their 'muck-raking instincts' by dwelling on the 'individual's wardrobe' (ibid.: 362). Shapiro might be right in suggesting that too many of the studies of corporate crime have adopted a muck-raking approach which reinforced the simple idea that a few bad apples spoiled the economic barrel rather than suggesting that there were some serious design problems in the barrel itself.

The corporate world may have its 'rotten apples', its swindlers, hustlers and thieves, but it is not lumped together in the same *totalizing* way as the supposedly criminogenic 'underclass' or the urban poor and working-class communities (Bessant 1995).

McBarnett suggests that some criminologists, fearful of being accused of engaging in 'mere polemics' or being 'ideologically motivated', have opted for the safe ground of doing research on conduct that constitutes 'out-and-out crime'. Behaviours such as the partial disclosure of taxable income, which McBarnett nicely refers to as 'non-disclosing disclosure', is according to some criminologists *marginal* to the interests of the discipline. McBarnett (1991: 341) adds that criminology has tacitly colluded with corporate actors who mount elaborate moral justifications of their so-called marginal actions. The attempt to expand the definition of 'crime' is, of course, not without its problems. But it does pose a challenge to the way in which crime is normally conceptualized in mainstream criminology.

Much of the conceptual to-ing and fro-ing by contemporary criminologists about corporate crime assumes that there is a range of behaviours that require further close empirical inquiry. This claim assumes that the conduct manifesting itself as 'white-collar' crime has a certain objective status. This relies on the idea, which has underpinned the constructive scheme of mainstream criminology, that an essential meaning can and/or should be determined for the category being researched, thereby rendering the concept useful for the kind of empirical research they wish to pursue.

When the 'crime problem' is thought about, and when official statistics are used to inform accounts of 'increasing crime', the idea of crime is invariably associated with the *traditional* offences of the urban working class and poor: robbery, theft, burglary, assault, drunkenness, and so forth (Garland 1996). Rarely is crime equated in the public mind with companies that engage in systematic and deadly pollution or breaches of health and safety regulations, or with the lengthy careers of businessmen like Alan Bond or Christopher Skase in Australia and Robert Maxwell in the UK.

Indeed, early on in the twenty-first century, as we discussed in Chapters 8 and 9, it seems that the gaze of mainstream criminology has turned once more to the crimes of the urban poor. The renaissance of a criminology dedicated to the study of a narrowly conceived 'crime problem', the renewed interest in identifying *risk* factors and an interest in crime prevention suggest that contemporary criminology has maintained its age-old concerns.

In short, the prospects of a sustained criminological analysis of corporate crime seems for the time being rather remote. As Shover and Bryant point out (1993: 167), because 'the ranks of social scientists exploring corporate crime shows no sign of impending increase, we are unlikely to see a significant increase in the number of investigations'. This lament, as familiar now as it was during the 1940s, reveals the general orientations of conventional criminology.

Given such an enduring tradition in the criminological literature, a fruitful way forward may be to examine the way in which criminological knowledge has been organized in relation to the question of crime. The fact that corporate crime produces untold damage and harm to millions of people has not (in a lasting way) altered many of the usual concerns of conventional criminology. The discipline has, through its selection of research topics and its collective methodological effort, produced bodies of knowledge that contribute to certain imaginings of the 'crime problem' (Young 1996). Despite the burst of enthusiasm, for example in the late 1980s when the crimes of corporate organizations received considerable attention, the focus of criminological inquiry and public consciousness of crime remains wedded to the illegal behaviours of the lower classes.

This clearly gives rise to large questions about corporate crime and the modern economy in democratic capitalist nation states. Box (1983: 16) may well be right that corporate crime is inextricably linked to both the destructive and the supportive processes of a capitalist economy. How will criminology adequately explain the sources and contexts of modern corporate crime, especially in a context marked by relentless globalizing trends?

Conclusion

In this chapter we have focused on corporate crime and its place in criminology. Sutherland's 1949 crucial intervention provided a much-needed stimulus to the discipline in terms of contesting long-standing preoccupations with the crimes of the working class. His work, while flawed, opened up the possibility of a somewhat different reading of crime from that which has traditionally preoccupied many criminologists. However, Sutherland's actual legacy has been patchy. As Box (1983: 18) puts it, 'Sutherland's study did, at the time, constitute a rich legacy to bequeath to criminology . . . [but] sadly, it is a legacy scorned by its putative beneficiaries.'

As we have argued in previous chapters, criminologists since the 1980s have sponsored a striking return to the study of traditionally defined 'crime'. Criminology has reaffirmed its commitment to the traditional concerns of the discipline, confirming its interest in the *practical* concerns of mainstream criminologists in situational crime prevention, in the rise of victimology and in the surveys of inner-city crime conducted by the 'new realists'.

Goethe's idea of an 'elective affinity' captures the way in which the current *public* preoccupation with working-class and underclass criminality is connected to the dramatic social and economic polarization in societies like the USA, the UK and Australia. Large numbers of low-paid and middle-income groups have lost a significant share of national income while the well-to-do increase their share of national income. That 'the rich are getting richer' and everyone else is getting poorer is a direct consequence of the undermining of the public sphere, the erosion of social liberal welfare interventions and the assaults on jobs and wages – facilitated by attacks on trade unions. Yet, just as the impact of globalization and continuing evidence of corporate crimes, such as the Baring Bank collapse (Rawnsley 1994), will not go away (Brown and Chiang 1993), nor does the need for a critical and reflexive criminology.

A critical or sceptical criminology begins, not with the apparently simple and/or objective violation of the criminal law, but rather with the processes by which notions of *crime* and *criminality* are first constructed and then operationalized by powerful or authoritative legal and policing agencies. As Nelken (1994a: 366) argues, it highlights 'the possibility of divergence between legal, social and political dynamics of criminality – but in so doing it reminds us of the artificiality of all definitions of crime'. The study of corporate crime alerts us to the diversity of modern crime. It raises important questions about the way crime and the crime problem are thought about both by criminologists and others.

Review questions

Why does Sutherland's insistence on looking at white-collar crime challenge mainstream criminology so much?

How well does Sutherland's approach to occupational crime deal with issues like systemic sexual abuse of children in institutional care or a corporate decision in, say, a major drugs company to take short cuts on clinical trials for a new drug?

How should collective, or organizational, responsibility and individual responsibility be determined and allocated when a large corporation like Union Carbide is responsible for a major environmental disaster such as happened in Bhopal?

Further reading

Braithwaite, J., 1989b, 'Criminological Theory and Organizational Crime', *Justice Quarterly*, Vol. 6, No. 3: 333–58.

Evans, T.D., Cullen, F. and Dubeck, P.J., 1993, 'Public Perceptions of Corporate Crime', in Blankenship, M.B. (ed.), *Understanding Corporate Criminality*, Garland, New York.

Grabosky, P. and Sutton, A. (eds), 1989, *Stains on a White Collar: Fourteen Studies in Corporate Crime or Corporate Harm*, Hutchinson, Sydney.

Ruggiero, V., 2000, *Organized and Corporate Crime*, Dartmouth, Ashgate.

Swaaningen, R. van, 1997, *Critical Criminology*, Sage, London.

11

CRITICAL ABSENCES: CRIMINOLOGY AND CRIMES OF THE STATE

When Russian armies occupied Berlin in May 1945 they brought defeat to the Third Reich and an end to the war in Europe. The world then discovered the enormity of one of the greatest of the 'crimes against humanity' of the twentieth century. This was what the German Nazi state under Adolf Hitler between 1941 and 1945 called the *Endlösung* (or Final Solution; see Roseman 2002 and Browning 2004). This 'final solution' of the 'Jewish problem' saw more than 3 million Jews gathered up after 1941 from all over occupied Europe and killed in four purpose-built 'death camps'. Millions more had already been liquidated, especially in Poland and Russia, by mass shootings carried out in the wake of invading German armies. Yet the 'final solution' was only part of a larger policy exercise designed to create a 'racially hygienic' society in Germany. Children and adults with physical and mental disabilities, psychiatric patients, Russians, Poles and Sinti, homosexuals and people with 'antisocial tendencies' had all been swept up into camps or clinics and killed (Burleigh 1994). The Nazis' policy used all of the resources of modern government, including scientific research, universities, modern industrial technology and the resources of a large bureaucracy. For some it is an inexplicable event defying rational explanation. For others it is just one instance of a much larger problem of crimes by states committed against humanity (Robertson 1999).

The twentieth century saw repeated highly organized and systematic criminal violence perpetrated by states against their own citizens. There is a vast research literature produced by historians, legal scholars, philosophers and political scientists documenting the history of state crime. Yet conventional criminology has largely ignored the problem of crimes by the state.

Given the mountains of research and theory on the smaller, indeed comparatively insignificant, quantity of 'ordinary' street crime, when compared to the scale of the violence and atrocities committed by governments, it is extremely odd that criminologists should have lapsed into near-complete silence about this matter.

While it is impossible to document an absence, or what Green and Ward (2004: vii) refer to as a 'paucity of relevant material within criminology', Myrtle's exemplary annotated bibliography (*Violence in Australia*, 1991) tells us that sociologists and criminologists construe criminal violence as something done by just about everyone except governments (ibid.: 303–20). In Britain the most recent edition of the mammoth and authoritative *Oxford Handbook of Criminology* (Maguire, Morgan and Reiner 2002) allocated just one paragraph of its 1,200-plus pages to the issue of state crime and violence – as it had done in the 1997 edition.

This is not to say that criminologists have completely ignored the problem. In 1998 David Friedrichs published a benchmark two-volume collection of articles on the theme of 'state crime' as part of an International Library of Criminology series. As Friedrichs (1998: i) noted, this work was being published at the end of the twentieth century, yet it 'is dismaying to confront the general neglect of the topic of state crime in the criminological literature. State crime as a major focus of criminological attention has yet to be realized.' That is to put the case fairly mildly. (It is entirely characteristic that there are very few criminologists included in Friedrichs's collection.)

For that reason it is also important to record that criminologists like Schwendinger and Schwendinger (1975), Chambliss (1989), Grabosky (1989), Barak (1991), Miller (1992), Simon (1996, 1999), Jamieson (1998), Cohen (2001), McLaughlin (2001) and Green and Ward (2004) have addressed the problem of crimes by governments. Several general texts, like Beirne and Messerschmidt (1995), Fattah (1997) and Carrabine et al. (2004), have also fully acknowledged state crime. Yet it is noteworthy that some of this work (Bayart et al. 1999; Kang 2002) deals with the wrongdoings of state officials where government illegality is largely understood as an extension of white-collar crime, chiefly involving corruption and frequently relying on corporate and government collusion. This tendency is also somewhat on display in the first large-scale efforts by criminologists to encompass the generality of state crime, such as Barak (1991) and Green and Ward (2004). To our knowledge, no criminologist has addressed 'stand-out' cases like Stalin's Terror, 1930–39 (Medvedev 1989), the Nazi genocide or the other state-sponsored genocides of the twentieth century.

This leads us to ask why so many criminologists have completely overlooked state crime. What does this tell us about the constructive schemes at work in mainstream criminology? Of necessity, this chapter differs from the rest of the book in that we are not able to report on a large body of criminological research and theory on state crime. Rather state crime can be identified here only as a field with considerable intellectual potential for the discipline. That such a case has to be made at all is reflective of a discipline that continues to be preoccupied with an overly narrow band of concerns.

Thinking about state crime

Mainstream criminological 'common sense' is well summed up by J.Q. Wilson (1975: xix) in a book called *Thinking About Crime.* There Wilson asserts that 'predatory street crime is a far more serious matter than consumer fraud, anti-trust violations . . . because predatory street crime . . . makes difficult or impossible the maintenance of meaningful human communities'. Leaving aside the denial of the damage caused by corporate and white-collar crime, to say nothing of crimes by the state, Wilson's preoccupation with street crime reflects a familiar preoccupation in criminology. Wilson makes no effort to recognize state crime or to think about it. This is a problem, because Wilson is profoundly mistaken about the actual effects of predatory street crime in comparison to the effects of state crime.

It is a simple empirical proposition that most of the serious crime, and the most serious crimes, in the modern world are those committed by states (Green and Ward 2004: vii). This is true whether we think of crimes of violence, including homicide, sexual assault, serious assault, kidnapping and torture, or economic crime, including embezzlement, bribery and other forms of corrupt practice. The scale of these crimes is often so great that ordinary language categories like 'murder' fail to be adequate and words like 'genocide' have to be used.

However, the essential problem is that most of this activity goes on invisibly because so much of it is never named as 'crime'. This is a consequence of the intersection of political and conceptual issues that accompany any attempt to talk about crimes of the state.

Criminology and the invisibility of state crime

Fattah (1997: 67) vigorously criticized criminology's 'traditional and persistent bias' in favour of 'focusing on crimes by the powerless, not the powerful . . . [and] on crime by individuals, not crime by governments and corporations'. Why is this so? There are several factors at work in the absence of state crime from criminology.

It is not surprising that conventional criminology has had a problem recognizing state crime. After all most criminologists in practice define 'crime' in terms of whatever it is that their governments define legally as criminal. This is true even though many criminologists, especially those promoting conventional criminology as an *empirical science*, as Wilson and Herrnstein (1985: 22) do, insist that crime is an *objective* reality and a *universal* category.

Governments rarely if ever identify the bad things they do as 'crimes', especially when they descend into 'radical evil'. Perhaps this is why it is unsurprising that most criminologists have some difficulty recognizing, let alone thinking about, crimes of the state. Friedrichs (1998: xvi) insists for example that

> the conceptual, definitional and methodological issues in the realm of state crime are especially daunting . . . [though] any systematic treatment of state crime must grapple with these issues. State crime, political crime, human rights issues and 'legitimate' military, diplomatic and domestic initiatives are entangled in complex ways and must be disentangled.

We get some insight into the 'daunting problem' state crime presents when a very sophisticated and sceptical criminologist like Stan Cohen (1993: 97–100; 2001) tries to talk about what is properly 'criminal' about 'crimes of the powerful', including states.

Cohen (ibid.) began by reviewing the work of Schwendinger and Schwendinger (1975), who had tried to develop an account of state crime by drawing on an expanded notion of 'white-collar' crime and focusing on the idea of *social injury*. Invoking this ethical idea, the Schwendingers ended up equating cases of genocide and cases of economic exploitation.

Cohen (1993: 98) properly objects that equating genocide with economic exploitation is mistaken:

> Now besides the point that [genocide and economic exploitation] are hardly morally equivalent categories . . . genocide is crucially different from economic exploitation [because] it is recognized in current political discourse as crime by

the state [and] it is clearly illegal by internal state laws and . . . the 1948 UN Convention Against Genocide.

Cohen (ibid.: 98) claims:

> By any known criteria, genocide is more self-evidently criminal than economic exploitation. The Schwendingers make no such distinction, nor try to establish the criminality of human rights violations. Instead they launch into a moral crusade against imperialistic war, racism, sexism and economic exploitation.

Cohen, to his credit, wants to take the idea of crime seriously without getting into 'definitional quibbles', while simultaneously avoiding the 'error' that the Schwendingers have fallen into. Their error was to expand the object of study, namely 'crimes of the state', into 'everything we do not like at the time'. Cohen (ibid.: 99) objects to this, arguing that 'early attempts to define the concept of state crime and link it to human rights violations failed because they were too woolly and polemical'.

Cohen wishes to avoid both moral revulsion and ethical criteria in formulating a definition, insisting that in many cases there is an 'objective reality' about 'crimes of the state'. He contends that the Schwendingers (1975) are wrong and are not entitled to expand the idea of crime beyond the parameters which states themselves employ in defining conduct as criminal. His solution is that state crime should map closely the usual state definitions of crime while reflecting the discourse of human rights as embedded in the UN Charter of Human Rights of 1948 or in Britain's Human Rights Act of 1998. In other words, Cohen (1993) argues that the discourse of human rights and international law runs 'parallel' to the discourse of the criminal law, and provides us with an objective basis for saying what state crime is – and is not.

Yet Cohen's argument has its own problems. Firstly he is right to make the common-sense point that most of the bad things governments do involve activities like murder, rape, espionage, kidnapping, wrongful imprisonment and assault, and that these actions are already identified as crimes by law. Yet it is a different matter to then observe, as Cohen does, that the criminal activities carried out by states are 'objective', because they are 'legally defined offences' and so subject to the normal legal processes of discovery, investigation and punishment by the state. If this were so, then there would never have been any need to worry about conceptualizing or defining state crime. Crimes of the state are the crimes that states dare not name.

Secondly, and to develop this point, what Cohen includes *and* excludes from his 1993 account of state crimes are worthy of note. He includes, for instance, torture, which he understands as the systematic use of physical and psychological violence by police, security and judicial personnel, even though he knows that many governments continue to permit and to practise torture. On the other hand, Cohen excludes the 'welfarist' practise of stealing poor and indigenous children from their families, a policy which for most of the twentieth century has been accepted as a normal, desirable and lawful practice by many states. In effect, and without falling into the trap of assuming that things are only 'real' when they are spoken about or conceptualized, there is a problem about what gets to be named as a criminal activity. Cohen fails to fully acknowledge this problem because he is worried about becoming a 'relativist'. Cohen rightly rejects any relativist framing of the problem of state crime produced by an excessive preoccupation with 'discourse' on the part of some post-modernist writers. Megill (in McLaren 1995: 64) makes Cohen's point for him when he insists that

> all too easy is the neglect or even dismissal of a natural and historical reality that ought not to be neglected or dismissed . . . For if one adopts in a cavalier and single minded fashion the view that everything is discourse or text or fiction, the *realia* are trivialised. Real people who really died in the gas chambers at Auschwitz or Treblinka become so much discourse.

Yet Cohen's lurch into a kind of 'conceptual objectivism' is neither warranted nor helpful. For one thing, a good deal of state crime is not *obvious* or easy to detect. State crimes do not possess either a legal status or an *obvious* material objectivity, given the secrecy with which some state activities are surrounded. There is also an irreducibly political and contested character to any definition of activity as criminal.

Any attempt to discuss or define crimes of the state and state violence is an irreducibly political activity. As Isaiah Berlin said during a debate about the historical 'uniqueness' of the Nazis' 'final solution': 'There must be a good deal more to the question of uniqueness – the placing in "context" of this event – than a mere historical assessment of an objective kind. It has a conspicuously political motive' (quoted in Thomas 1990: 19).

The myopia of criminologists on the question of state crime reflects a long-standing attempt by liberal political theorists in English-speaking countries to legitimize certain kinds of state activities by distinguishing between legitimate 'force' and illegitimate 'violence'.

As Pierre Manent (1996) points out, this distinction goes back to the very origins of political liberalism. Recalling the primal 'state of nature' as a time of universal violence, a 'war of all, against all', Hobbes's indelible contribution to the liberal tradition of the seventeenth century was his argument that the state was established to regulate the human tendency to violence, and if necessary to do so by coercive means (Arblaster 1987). One result is that liberal theorists have rarely acknowledged the actual record of state crime and violence. And, when they have done so, it is invariably something for which only the 'other side', that is, fascists, communists, 'radicals' and most recently 'terrorists', are responsible.

In this account the liberal state is represented as a moral and legal exemplar. Within the liberal tradition, government *legality* is always assumed to be the norm. A government can do no wrong because it is the guarantor of the rights and freedoms inscribed in the constitution that lays out the rule of law. Accordingly, the state 'provides the minimum and neutral ground rules for any social living' (Reiman 1989: 154). Working within this tradition the criminologist Grabosky allows that while agents of the state sometimes 'go feral' (1989: 11–17), states do not 'normally' pursue violent or criminal policies. This assumption underpins his theory of 'government illegality' which rests on the proposition that 'organizational pathologies' are the basis of state crimes. A 'normal', well-run state works to constrain illegality. Only when aberrant factors like 'poor leadership', 'inadequate recruitment', poor training or failure to supervise officials occurs does 'government illegality' become a possibility. Here the state itself is not the problem, just poor frail human nature as individual officials or police 'become corrupt' or 'abuse' their legitimate power.

Such a liberal account collapses before the evidence of persistent state-sponsored terror, genocide and the systematic abuse of human rights in the twentieth century, even in the seemingly most liberal and 'progressive' countries (see Rummel 1994; Robertson 1999). It is worth noting that Grabosky was writing in Australia – a liberal democratic society, where the rule of law has long provided a stable point of reference. Yet Grabosky was writing barely a decade after the report of a Royal Commission into New South Wales prisons was released in 1978. That Royal Commission uncovered evidence 'of systematic and calculated brutality . . . perpetrated against prisoners . . . by some officers'. Apropos one prison, in Grafton, Royal Commissioner Nagle reported that it was one of 'the most sordid and shameful episodes in NSW penal history' (Royal Commission 1978: 134). Nagle found that it had been a long-standing practice that all new prisoners admitted to the 'Intractable Section' would be stripped naked while still wearing a security belt and handcuffs, and were then punched, kicked and clubbed with rubber batons, often until the prisoner was semi-conscious. The prison officers' union in evidence to the Royal Commission argued that this systematic 'flogging' of prisoners was 'official departmental policy' (Vinson 1982: 11). As Commissioner Nagle observed, that 'defence did not work at the Nuremberg trials [and] it does not succeed here' (Royal Commission 1978: 77).

The effects of the liberal blanking-out of the possibility of state crime may be one reason why many people, including criminologists, seem all too prepared to accept the legitimacy of their governments' policies, whatever they may be. A small body of research suggests that most 'ordinary people' either do not regard state violence as criminal violence or are prepared to define it as legitimate. Archer and Gartner (1978: 220–1) argued that official violence was nearly invisible in most discussions of murder and aggression. At the height of the US war in Vietnam in 1969, one American survey found that 50 per cent of the sample said that when police shot 'race rioters' or 'looters' this was not 'violence' (cited in Archer and Gartner 1978: 221). A 1968 survey found that 57 per cent of a US sample agreed that 'Any man who roughs up a policeman has no complaint if he gets roughed up in return' (quoted in ibid.: 220). Most criminologists appear more than willing to follow popular sentiment in this regard.

Criminologists are hardly likely to take the lead where angels and most ordinary citizens fear to tread. As Stohl and Lopez (1984: 3; see Stohl and Lopez 1986) observe, it has long been customary for mainstream criminologists to denounce an interest in state crime, seeing such an interest to be 'skewed', 'biased', 'ideological', 'not in the mainstream of the literature' and 'out of touch with real political events'. Friedrichs (1998: xv) considers that fear of flouting convention adds to certain anxieties criminologists have about their professional standing:

> A focus on state crime cannot be recommended as a particularly efficient approach to academic and professional success. Furthermore it is hardly surprising that it has typically been more difficult to obtain research funding for state crime from state entities (in some cases raising the prospect of biting the hand that you hope will feed you). And for those who surmount the hurdles just described, the challenges of obtaining access to research venues and credible data tend to exceed those facing the researcher of more conventional criminological and criminal justice topics.

Green and Ward (2004: 1) point out that if states define what is criminal then a state can be criminal only 'on those rare occasions when it denounces itself for breaking its own laws'. It is plain that among the many resources governments can bring to bear on the problem is their capacity to render acceptable, politically and even legally, policies or activities which only later are identified or understood to be 'criminal'. While Hitler circumvented key legal guarantees of civic rights embodied in the Weimar constitution, he did so with strong popular support from the German electorate (Gellately 2002: 13–27). And, as Macfarlane-Icke (1999) points out, many of the German nurses who were involved in the killing of 150,000–200,000 psychiatric patients after 1939 did so because they understood the policy to be lawful. Equally Stalin's political terror of the 1930s, in which millions of Russians were killed and millions more jailed in the Gulag camp system, was carried out within a framework of constitutional and legal processes, albeit perfunctorily (Applebaum 2003: 127–8).

States can easily mobilize the resources of the law and the criminal justice system, as well as engage in the management of public opinion through the mass media, to render both *normal* and *acceptable* conduct that is criminal. The mobilization of these resources can blind many decent citizens to what is going on around them. For example, in Australia the abduction from their parents of tens of thousands of 'half-caste' babies and children for placement with 'white families' was carried out into the 1960s as a 'welfare practice' within a larger, racist, 'White Australia' policy. Only in the 1990s were these 'welfare policies' recognized for the genocidal tendency they actually endorsed – as defined by the criteria set out by the 1948 UN Convention Against Genocide (Manne 2002). Yet the problem remains that until the idea of genocide is taken seriously no justice can be done. This problem was on display in Australia in 1999–2000 when two Aboriginal people from the 'stolen generations' tried to sue the Australian government. They found their claim to reparation for their injuries blocked by a judgment in the Federal Court in 2000 that the enabling legislation that was in place when they were abducted was 'lawful' and 'normal practice'.

In large measure, then, it seems that, as with white-collar and corporate crime, the very idea of state crime challenges head-on the central preoccupations and the assumptions that make up the constructive schemes of conventional criminology. This discussion suggests some of the reasons why crimes of the state have not been acknowledged or dealt with by conventional criminology. We turn now to consider crimes of the state more directly.

Crimes of the state

Green and Ward (2004: 1–2) offer a useful starting point when thinking about state crime: namely, to recognize that there are certain norms of conduct in international law, many of them embodied in UN covenants or charters that states cannot violate with complete impunity, to say nothing of states that have their own Bills or Charters of Human Rights, like the UK (1998) and Australian states and territories like Victoria in 2006. This provides a basis for saying that states engage in practices which violate legal norms and that these norms, especially those defining universal human rights, 'reflect, however imperfectly, principles of justice that criminologists ought to support'. State crime involves the violation of these human rights. We would add that not all infringements of human rights are equally serious so as to merit the use of the label 'crime': many of the human rights spelt out in various covenants, like those dealing with children or women, involve 'positive freedoms', such as the right to good education, healthcare and privacy. The idea of state crime is best applied to harmful or illegal acts carried out by officials on behalf of the state which infringe fundamental rights, like the right to be protected from murder, torture, compulsory sterilization or illegal detention. These kinds of conduct clearly impose harm to and hurt through cruel and inhumane treatment. In this light Friedrichs (1998: x) suggests that 'governmental crime encompasses harmful acts carried out on behalf of the state as well as harmful or illegal acts carried out by state officials for their own benefit or the benefit of their party'.

A second starting point is to acknowledge that the failure of some criminologists to recognize crimes of the state, possibly in order to defend their discipline's *objectivity*, rests on a basic confusion. To accept that there are social and/or political processes at work in criminalizing certain activities but not others does not entail accepting a kind of mindless relativism. If activities like genocide, state-sponsored famines, and the use of arbitrary arrest, detention, torture or rape as instruments of terror are real, then judgments to define these things as criminal are real, as will be the consequences of detecting and punishing such crimes.

In talking about state crime here we include as instances those cases where states have as a deliberate policy engaged in homicidal violence, systematic terrorism, organized disruption of families (including the abduction of children) and the systematic detention, harassment and surveillance of their citizens. Much of this activity has been a product of formal policy processes – some of it covert and secretive, much of it not.

The most obvious and chilling face of the 'radical evil' wrought by governments is state-sponsored mass-murder or genocide (Chalk and Jonasson 1990). John Ralston Saul (1997: 11) estimates that since 1945 some 40 million people have been killed – at the rate of 5,000 civilians a day, every day. At its most extreme this can take the form of genocide perpetrated by states using police, military, para-military and special personnel in which millions of citizens are killed. In places like Afghanistan, Chad, Ethiopia, Eritrea, Iraq and Zimbabwe mass-graves uncovered in one year (1992) revealed the remains of thousands of victims of political terror (Amnesty International 1993: 5).

In the last thirty years of the twentieth century we have seen:

- the CIA-backed killing of at least 600,000 ethnic Chinese and 'communists' in Indonesia in 1965–67;
- the 'disappearance' of more than 2,000 'leftists' after General Pinochet seized power in Chile in 1973, again with the blessing of American officials;
- the killing of 1.3 million people in Pol Pot's Cambodia in 1975–79;
- the politically inspired 'disappearance' of 90,000 Argentinians in the late 1970s;
- the killing of over 250,000 Ugandans by Idi Amin's government;
- the murder of tens of thousands of Kurds by Iraqi forces during the 1980s, including the use of poison gas supplied, ironically, by the US government;
- the deaths of 250,000 East Timorese at the hands of Indonesian military forces in 1978;
- the deaths of at least 10,000 South Africans prior to the ending of apartheid;

- the murder of over 1 million Hutus in Burundi (now Rwanda) in two waves of genocidal violence (1988 and 1994); in the latter instance 900,000 Hutus were murdered in less than 3 months, even as UN troops in Rwanda watched helplessly (Dallaire 2004); and
- the widespread process of 'ethnic cleansing', involving the systematic rape, torture, starvation and murder by Serbian security forces of Muslim Bosnians after 1992 and of Albanians in Kosovo in 1998–99.

The use of famine as an instrument of state violence has been another regrettable aspect of great crimes against humanity. Sen (1981) argues that while these events may start naturally with a drought, it is official action – or inaction – that turns them into famines. As Becker (1996) reminds us, the single greatest state crime of the twentieth century was the Chinese famine of 1961–63 that killed 20–30 million people, mostly peasant farmers. This was a policy-driven exercise undertaken purposively by the leadership of the Chinese Communist Party to impel Chinese agriculture down the path to socialist modernity. It bears an awful similarity to the Bolshevik famines of the early 1930s that killed millions of Ukrainian peasant farmers as part of Stalin's attempt to introduce 'socialism in one country' (Conquest 1968). These great crimes sit alongside a larger pattern of state-sponsored famine in many so-called 'developing' societies where governments engage in military campaigns, encourage social dislocation and breakdown and carry out war crimes while managing the food supply or even international emergency aid to crush resistance. De Waal (1997) shows that the Ethiopian famine of 1983–85 was a war crime carried out by the Ethiopian government to crush independence movements in Tigray and northern Wollo. In 2006–7 the UN and the rest of the world have watched as millions of people in Darfur in southern Sudan face extinction.

At a more mundane level, policy-driven murder, involving the 'disappearance' of political opponents, is a practice at which governments in Chile in the 1970s and Argentina in the 1980s became adept. While far from genocidal, the death toll from these activities is still shocking and qualifies as 'radical evil'.

Political terror stands as another defining feature of state policy-making in the twentieth century. It was a century that saw persistent campaigns of political terror and harassment waged against citizens deemed to be a problem to the security of the state, or an affront to 'racial' purity or a threat to the 'community'. This has included unjust imprisonment, often involving forced labour, exposure to inclement environments (for example, extreme heat or cold) and insufficient amounts of food and water, as in the Armenian genocide (1916–18), the Nazi death camps and the Soviet Gulags. The numbers of those injured, imprisoned, raped, physically relocated, abused, tortured and psychiatrized by states are at least as large as those who have fallen victim to genocidal violence.

Few if any nation states have been exempt from one or more versions of state violence throughout the twentieth century. Since late 2001 the world has been asked by the USA to join in its 'War on Terrorism'. Without for a minute condoning the events of 11 September 2001, it is sobering to re-read William Chambliss's presidential address to the American Society of Criminology in 1988 (Chambliss in Friedrichs 1998: 183–208).

Chambliss recites a long list of official, albeit covert, US involvement in bloody coups and political assassinations in Indonesia, Guatemala, Nicaragua, Chile, the Dominican

Republic and Vietnam. This involvement says Chambliss was 'never legally authorized . . . the murders, assassinations and terrorist acts that accompany coups are criminal acts by law in both the United States and in the country in which they take place'. Among the many crimes committed he notes the work of one Ricardo Morales, working for both the FBI and the CIA, who planted a bomb on a flight into Venezuela which killed 73 people and was active in the cocaine running carried out by the CIA. Chambliss recalls the official role of the CIA in the 1980s in managing parts of the Colombian drug cartel to supply it with funds for its work in Iran, a role that included money laundering and murder. He refers too to 'the deaths of 80 people in Beirut, Lebanon when a car bomb was exploded on May 8 1985 . . . the bomb was set by a Lebanese counter terrorist unit working with the Central Intelligence Agency'. Chambliss (in ibid.: 198) notes rather benignly: 'Assassination plots and political murders are usually associated in people's minds with military dictatorships and European monarchies . . . Assassination however has become a tool of international politics that involves modern nation-states of many different types.'

Draper (1991: 23) reminds us that in 1987 the Nicaraguan government took the US Government to the International Court of Justice in The Hague. At issue was Nicaragua's claim that the CIA had carried out acts of terrorism by mining Nicaraguan harbours, bringing about the deaths of numerous citizens. The International Court of Justice agreed and found the US government guilty, fining it millions of dollars. The US government firmly declined to recognize the court's jurisdiction.

We should recall that in this way the USA has been consistent: government has persistently refused to sign the UN Convention on Genocide. This, as Piotrowicz and Kaye (2000: 189–93) recall, has been paralleled by the UK government's refusal to legally proceed against General Augusto Pinochet, the former President of Chile, in 1999. (Pinochet stood accused by the Spanish government of torture and hostage-taking. His death late in 2006 pre-empted the trial he was facing.) This perhaps indicates the hypocrisy, which normally attends many governmental expressions of respect for international law.

Even more routine has been the use of campaigns of terror involving systematic political surveillance, psychological harassment and intrusive surveillance of citizens. States everywhere, including liberal democracies, have used espionage, harassment and torture against their citizens. These kinds of state crime have all happened or are happening now. While authoritarian and one-party states have been particularly adept at these practices, we need to recall that liberal-democratic states have engaged in some of these forms of state crime. The use of imprisonment and torture has long been a routine method of dealing with political dissent or for simply maintaining law and order. Few governments or their police agencies, whatever their kind or political disposition, have chosen not to use torture at some point in the twentieth century, including policing and penal agencies in the UK, Australia and the USA. Ristow and Shallice (1976: 271–3) reported on the interrogation in July–August 1971 of fourteen Northern Irish IRA 'suspects' by agents of the British Combined Services Intelligence Centre and how the UK government relied on the use of torture. Such psychological torture was part of a larger practice of physical torture used by UK police and military forces in Northern Ireland (Miller 1993: 123–7). Yet the UK's use of torture at the end of the twentieth century was a small and not unusual instance of the near-universal use of torture by various states around the world (Amnesty International 1993). The founding director of the US FBI, J. Edgar Hoover, used sexual blackmail to harass and control generations of American politicians and activists. After the 11 September 2001 attacks on Washington and New York, the Bush administration sought and received legal advice sanctioning the use of carefully calibrated torture against 'suspected terrorists' from officials like Alberto Gomez, who subsequently became the US Attorney-General (2006–7).

Finally there have been the unremitting campaigns by states and their welfare and policing bureaucracies to strip the children of working-class and/or indigenous families away from their families 'for their own good'. This is not to say that if it is difficult to understand genocidal violence, it may be hard also to understand why it is that states have, in the name of 'welfare' and in an apparent spirit of benevolence, stripped large numbers of children away from their parents. This was done, as we indicate shortly, in ways that led the children to believe that their parents were dead, while leaving the parents to believe their children would be 'better off' elsewhere (Van Krieken 1998). Because it has not received the attention we think it deserves and because of constraints on space, we focus on this instance of crimes by the state.

The case of the disappearing children

Nothing catches the Janus-faced nature of modern *welfare-state* policies as does the history of child abduction carried out in the name of welfare by governments. Nothing catches the breath as does the refusal to acknowledge the potential for abuse, violence and sexual exploitation on the part of state agencies, or to address these problems when evidence begins to surface (Van Krieken 1998).

Since the mid-1980s, Canadians (Bagnell 1987), Australians (Bean and Melville 1987; Gill 1998), Americans (Berry 1992; Burkett and Bruni 1995) and Britons (Humphreys 1994) have been rocked by revelations of systematic violence and abuse perpetrated against 'their' children and young people. What was especially shocking was the revelation that the perpetrators worked in institutions like churches, community- and state-run welfare agencies, including the police, the judicial system, immigration departments, and individual priests, teachers and welfare workers functioning as parents (*in loco parentis*). The abuse and violence involved a range of activities, including:

- the removal of countless children from their mostly low-income and/or working-class families and their re-location in training institutions or with foster and adoptive parents, which included the removal of tens of thousands of British children as part of 'Imperial Child Migration' schemes (Humphreys 1994; Palmer 1997; Gill 1998) to Australia, Canada and Southern Africa, where many were subjected to violence and sexual abuse by their institutional or private care-givers;
- the removal by police and welfare agencies of hundreds of thousands of indigenous children from their families in 'regions of recent settlement', like Canada, New Zealand, the USA and Australia, and their relocation as state wards to placements with 'white families' until well into the 1960s (Human Rights and Equal Opportunity Commission 1997; Bird 1998);

- the unwarranted use of state wards and orphans as subjects in medical experiments in several Australian states in the 1950s;
- the systematic sexual exploitation in schools, orphanages and welfare centres of young children and teenagers by religious and secular teachers and welfare workers; and
- regimes in state-run youth-training centres of physical abuse, economic exploitation and inappropriate punishments (Commission of Inquiry into Abuse of Children in Queensland Institutions 1999).

Rationalizing child-stealing

If we ask why governments have removed children from their parents and families, the answer is that governments constituted a series of 'problems' to which 'solutions' involving the forced separation of children from their parents became desirable. Certain discourses sanctioned solutions like incarceration, detention and training of children and young people, practices which continue to this day.

In the first half of the twentieth century, the development of these programmes had an international character that crossed political boundaries which appeared to otherwise distinguish liberal from non-liberal regimes. Invariably the targets of these 'bio-political policies' were relatively powerless or excluded people deemed marginal, antagonistic or 'antisocial' elements, in contrast to what was considered to be 'normal', or 'healthy', people.

Racially defined groups have generally attracted stringent attention from their governments: European Jews, Sinti Roma, Slavs, black Africans, 'First Nation' people in North America and Aboriginal people in Australia, Canada and New Zealand have experienced the force of this attention. Similarly, many working-class and poor people have also been targets of the attention of governments and community organizations variously identified as religious, charitable, middle-class and, more recently, as professional welfare groups.

In this process certain ideas played a leading role and in ways which directly implicate criminology as well as other social sciences. We have already indicated how the amalgam of modernist, scientific and racial discourses referred to as 'eugenics' played a leading role in conventional criminological research and theory in the first half of the twentieth century. The history of eugenics illustrates the way the discursive constitution of problems and solutions in respect of children and families occurred. It was a discourse that was significant in shaping many of the programmes that produced generations of 'lost children'.

Child welfare and the role of ideas

Donzelot (1979) observes that from the mid-nineteenth century, children were identified as a part of the population that required systematic state intervention, a process in which *childhood* became a central animating idea. A favourite theme for earnest concern throughout the nineteenth century was the idea that each child should be given the opportunity to enjoy a period in which their natural innocence, plasticity, dependence and spiritual growth could flourish by being protected from adult activities while guided towards maturity (Aries 1969).

Everywhere governments were cajoled by politicians, philanthropists and educators, into 'saving' children from vice and poverty. 'Child-saving' in the USA had a certain Yankee strength of character. One New York scheme, established by C.L. Bruce of the Children's Aid Society in 1853, involved 'child-savers' taking children off the streets and from 'vicious families', holding them in lodging houses and then placing them with families (Smith 1911: 319).

In the early twentieth century a more scientific approach called 'child studies' began to develop, alongside the 'child-saving' movement, which attempted to chart the 'normal' development of the child and 'his [sic]' childhood (Griffin 1993: 1–26).

The identification of 'racially unhygienic' elements drew sustenance and inspiration from the respectable, progressive body of social and biological scientific thought manifest in the international movement of racial hygienists and eugenicists, with adherents in every modern society who were respectable scientists, doctors, architects, civil servants, judges, town-planners, teachers and social workers (Friedan 1963; Kamin 1974). Eugenics (as we saw in Chapter 2) began as a combination of technical analysis of 'individual differences' (including intelligence) with elements of late-nineteenth-century popular racism, class prejudice and imperialism. Its founder, Sir Francis Galton, developed the statistical techniques enabling the analysis and measurement of co-variance to demonstrate his claim that intelligence – 'racial fitness' – was a factor spread genetically through the population. Galton and fellow eugenicists like Burt (1965), Pearson and Spearman argued that states could and should discourage the 'racially unfit' from breeding while encouraging 'racial hygiene' by education, welfare, child migration and other measures. In the first four decades of the twentieth century these prejudices evolved into scientized categories and practices involving measurement and a range of medical, educational and criminological interventions (Graham 1977; Kevles 1985).

In each case the eugenic discourse was modified to take account of local circumstances. In Germany the evolution of racial policies central to the constitution of the Nazi state after 1933 as a racial state can be explained by reference to the production of specifically German eugenic discourses (Weiss 1987). These discourses constituted the problem as one of 'racial degeneracy' requiring 'racial hygienic' policies designed to control and eventually eliminate 'racial degenerates', discourses that gained increasing credibility in Germany after 1918 (Weindling 1989).

The USA also led the world in passing 'racial hygiene' legislation to sterilize the 'unfit' – mostly black and poor people (Dickens 1968). By the 1930s more than thirty US states had passed such legislation. In Australia eugenic arguments co-mingled no less easily with liberal-democratic, labourist and white supremacist ideas and categories (Roe 1984). This eugenic discourse informed the policy framework that led to the separation of 'half-caste' children from their parents from the beginning of the twentieth century under 'native' welfare laws (Kidd 1997: 80–152).

Eugenicists were implicated in these movements in two ways.

1   Key figures in the 'child studies' movement, like G. Stanley-Hall (1904), contributed to the modern common-sense thinking about 'childhood' and 'adolescence' as two phases in the 'life-cycle', understood as a series of phases which each individual had to advance through in the course of her or his life. This conception of an inevitable and

natural developmental process depended on specific notions about what 'childhood' and 'adolescence' were and how the necessary adjustments ought to be negotiated (McCallum 1990). Particularly important was the notion that adolescence was a specially difficult, even 'agonistic', phase with many threats and temptations that might lead the young person astray. Other key figures, for example Burt (1965), developed a model of moral and social development within which an account of delinquency became possible.

2   Eugenicists contributed to a 'scientific' redefinition of the child problem, and the solutions proposed were deemed central to public policy. A complaint of many in the early 'child-saving' movement was that it lacked scientific method. A range of eugenicist human-service professionals (doctors, public-health specialists, teachers and educators, social workers, criminologists and sociologists, psychologists and urban planners) who saw themselves at the forefront of 'modern' scientific and progressive movements dominated their policy communities into the 1930s. Eugenicists identified many social problems in terms of 'racial fitness' which allegedly determined the survival of 'society' or, more specifically, the ruling groups and/or dominant *white* race. The threats to survival were said to have stemmed from inter- and intra-breeding, and the over-breeding of some sections of the population.

From the 1920s on, eugenicist ideas ran wide and deep, whether in relation to child welfare, juvenile delinquency, family planning, public health or the identification and measurement of everything from human nutritional needs, the intellectual capabilities of a given population or the best use of urban and natural resources.

Child abduction policies

Child abduction policies came to be a normal part of welfare-state regimes in many countries, including Australia, the USA, the UK and Germany, variously, from 1900 through to the 1960s (Read 1982, 1984; Bagnell 1987; Read and Edwards 1989; Cunneen 1990; Wicks 1995; Human Rights and Equal Opportunity Commission 1997). Imperial Child Migration schemes were one expression of this general impulse. These migration schemes frequently functioned with a degree of coercion, secrecy and abusive violence (Gill 1998: 593). The children of 'unsuitable parents', including single mothers and 'racially unfit' persons, especially involving working-class or poor people, were subject to these actions.

The most extreme forms of child abduction were practised in the Third Reich. Under the cover of war and in pursuit of 'racial hygienic' (*Rassenhygiene*) policies, the Third Reich after 1941 pursued a policy of child abduction, the main agent of the programme being the National Socialist People's Welfare (or NSV). Founded in 1931 to provide food relief for Berlin's unemployed Nazi Party members, Hitler mandated the NSV in 1933 to address 'all questions of charity and the people's welfare' in Germany (Burleigh and Wipperman 1992). With some 16 million members, the NSV was the second largest of the party organizations. Germany soon had a vast network of relief schemes operating to address a range of issues (for example, 'winter relief', 'tuberculosis relief', 'mother and child relief').

In the pre-war years and in ways consonant with the Nazi regime's preoccupations, the NSV began stamping out 'antisocial elements' like 'promiscuous women', 'homosexuals', Jews, and 'juvenile delinquents'. In 1935 the NSV took over the German Adoption Service and in 1936 the adoption services of the German Red Cross. By 1937 the NSV Reich Adoption Service was advertising the fact that it made available only 'healthy children'. It established around ninety-two youth hostels to deal with 'difficult' and 'juvenile delinquents' as part of its 'youth relief' scheme.

As Burleigh and Wipperman (ibid.: 72–3) argue, the NSV's 'child welfare' programme involved relocating approximately 200,000 children in Eastern Europe. Orphans were removed from children's homes or from their foster parents, while other children were taken from kindergartens, schools or off the streets. Young children were placed in NSV kindergartens and those who successfully passed a 'racial selection' process were sent to 'Germanization' centres in the Old Reich, given new papers, names and forbidden to use their native language. After the war fewer than 20 per cent were reunited with their parents. In like fashion and after 1942, children of Polish and Soviet forced labourers working in the Third Reich were subject to a racial selection process: those who passed were farmed out for adoption; those who failed were retained as slave labour, starved to death or subsequently gassed.

In Britain there is an equivalent though less violent history of coercive, secretive child abduction undertaken in a partenership between the state and philanthropic agencies. Here the motivations also assumed a racial rationale (spreading 'British stock' across the Empire), complemented by anxiety about the 'dangerous classes'. Philanthropists and evangelically minded religious groups used child migration as an element in a project designed to reform the moral and social practices of the 'perishing classes', paupers and slum-dwellers.

Building on a history of imperial 'child-saving' migration schemes in the nineteenth century, organizations like the Salvation Army, Barnardos, the Fairbridge Farm School movement and the Christian Brothers entered into 'clearing' the streets and orphanages of England of unwanted children and sending them to various parts of the British Empire (Gill 1998). The inter-war years saw child-migration schemes commence, while the war years (1939–45) saw many young children enter Australia, South Africa and Canada as evacuees, and many more came as part of post-war migration schemes.

Gill (ibid.: 86–7) estimates that at least 30,000 children were brought into Australia in the twentieth century. It is estimated that one in ten Canadians alive now are descendants of the migrant 'children of the Empire'.

Most of these schemes until the 1940s articulated imperial themes allied to a strong sense of the need to remedy the defects of poverty and working-class family life. Kingsley Fairbridge, a Rhodesian who started the Empire Settlement Scheme in 1905, identified loyalty to God, King and Empire as the basis of his work. He established one school at Pinjarra, 85 kilometres south of Perth, Western Australia, where between 1913 and 1981 some 1,500 child migrants were settled (ibid.: 158). The Barnardos scheme was committed to eugenicist ideas, using IQ testing and insisting on the physical fitness of the children they selected for settlement. Until the 1960s, it was also insisted that the children's skin met the 'whiter than white' test (ibid.: 129).

Isolation, fierce disciplinary regimes, often involving sadistic sexual, physical and emotional abuse, characterized many of the settlement schemes. Organizations like the Christian Brothers school at Bindoon (founded in 1936) under the rule of brutal principals (like Brother Francis Keeney) became notorious for such abuses.

Abuse of a different kind characterized welfare practices directed at the children of Aboriginal people in Australia and at indigenous families in other 'regions of recent settlement' (Read 1984). Church and welfare agencies and police officers made applications for court orders under the various welfare laws operating in state and territory jurisdictions to remove children from families where there was 'evidence' of neglect and/or abuse (Goodall 1990). The denial of Aboriginality, deceit about the status of parents and children by authorities when relatives sought information about the children's whereabouts, and the economic exploitation and physical and sexual abuse all have a familiar ring to them (Cuneen 1990).

According to recent Australian inquiries possibly as many as 40,000 Aboriginal children were taken from their families between the 1880s and the 1960s and placed with white families (Manne 2002). Between 1903 and 1930 one in three Aboriginal children was taken from her or his parents in NSW alone. Inside their white foster homes many young Aboriginal people performed domestic labour and in some cases experienced sexual abuse. In the light of clearly articulated government statements, especially in the 1930s, there is little doubt that this policy was genocidal in nature.

In 1930 it was conventionally accepted in the Northern Territory that 'half-castes almost without exception are more degraded than the blacks for they have the evil tendencies of both black and white intermingled and intensified' (Austin 1993: 21). At a Conference of Commonwealth and State Aboriginal Authorities in 1937, J.B. Cleland, Professor of Pathology at Adelaide University (Australian Archives 1993: 10), argued that the half-castes were not dying out but were increasing, and so 'becoming a problem for the future'. In 1938–39 Norman Tindale (1941: 124) undertook a study of 'half castes' in all states – except the Northern Territory. He found that there was a 'phenomenal rate of multiplication'. These half-castes were 'a mediocre type, often but little inferior to the inhabitants of small white communities which have, through force of circumstances, remained in poverty, ignorance and isolation'. Tindale accepted the prevailing view that the growth of the half-caste population was a problem best solved by 'their complete biological assimilation'.

Biological assimilation became the dominant idea among the key Aboriginal agencies which served as Aboriginal Protectorates. In 1929 W.J. Bleakley, Queensland's long-serving Chief Protector, believed (Australian Archives 1993: 23) that the half-castes were a difficult problem because 'what they inherited from the superior intelligence and taste of whites was always going to be nullified by the retarding instincts of the blacks'. Among Bleakley's recommendations in 1929 to the Commonwealth, were proposals for 'the complete separation of the half-caste from the Aborigines with a view to their absorption by the white race' by placing them in white missions like Hermannsburg (1929: 26–7). As he put it: 'Their blood entitles them to be given a chance to take their place in the white community . . . That this may be successfully accomplished, the children should be removed from aboriginal associations at the earliest possible age . . .' (ibid.: 29).

Dr Cecil Cook, Chief Protector of Aboriginals (1927–39) and Chief Medical Officer of the Northern Territory, was no less committed to the maintenance of a 'white Australia': 'the native has actually become an intruder in a white man's country. Politically the Northern Territory must always be governed as a white man's country, by the white man for the white man' (quoted in Markus 1990: 90). Cook accepted that the 'pure blood aboriginal' was doomed to extinction and was therefore no problem for White Australia (ibid.: 91). The 'half-castes' were another, and more serious, problem. For Cook they represented a large and ever-increasing underclass. (In 1938–39 they comprised about 13 per cent of the 6,700 non-Aboriginal population of the Northern Territory.) He believed they were a source of social instability, lacking a settled place in either Aboriginal or white societies. Their 'racial vigour', evidenced by their fertility rate, was such that he contemplated 'with growing anxiety' the prospect that within 15 or 20 years the 'half-castes' would outnumber the white population of the Territory. As Cook put it, in terms that Himmler, another racial utopian, might well have applauded: 'In the Territory . . . the preponderance of colored races, the prominence of colored alien blood and the scarcity of white females to mate with the white male population, creates a position of incalculable future menace to purity of race in tropical Australia' (quoted in Austin 1993: 134).

Cook's solution in his own words was to 'breed out' the problem population by stripping half-caste children from their families, relocating them with white families. As Cook observed: 'In the Territory . . . every endeavor is being made to breed out the color by elevating female half-castes to white standards with a view to their absorption by mating into the white population' (quoted in ibid.: 146). Assuming the inevitable disappearance of the 'pure blood Aboriginal' courtesy of his own programme of 'breeding him white', Cook envisaged the complete eradication of the black population within 'five or six generations'. In the 1930s Cook was not alone. In 1937 a 'national approach' to the 'half-caste problem' was proposed at the Conference of Commonwealth and State Aboriginal Authorities, which resolved that

> this conference believes that the destiny of the natives of Aboriginal origin lies in their ultimate absorption by the people of the Commonwealth . . . and that efforts of all state authorities should be directed towards the education of children of mixed aboriginal blood at white standards, and their subsequent employment under the same conditions as with a view to their taking their place in the white community on an equal footing with the whites.
>
> (quoted in Choo 1989: 6)

Though the Australian High Court thought otherwise (see Storey 1998), any reading of the very plain statement of the UN Convention on Genocide (1948), Article II, clauses (d) and (e), makes very clear the implications for understanding the policy of child welfare as it was applied to Australia's Aboriginal and 'half-caste' children: 'genocide means any of the following acts committed with intent to destroy, in whole or part, a national, ethnical, racial or religious group, such as: (d) imposing measures intended to prevent births within the group; (e) forcibly transferring children of the group to another group'.

Conclusion

In this chapter we have not explored the violent end of the spectrum of state crime where 'radical evil' has stamped itself indelibly on the lives of hundreds of millions of people; rather, we have considered the ambivalent face of child 'welfare' where coercion, secrecy, insensitivity and violence paralleled good intentions, racial and class prejudices, and scientific chauvinism.

We have not sought to locate this case study within any overarching theory of the state, nor to emulate efforts by Collins (1974) or Bauman (1992) who, following Weber (1947), see in the distinctive features of state crime and violence the potential of impersonal, amoral, rational bureaucracies. Against the tendencies to 'theoretism' we need to remain faithful to elucidating what is existentially concrete (Arendt 1963: xvii).

Our treatment here of crimes of the state insists on acknowledging the enormous scale of the criminal activity involved. Faced with the scale and intensity of these activities, Hannah Arendt (1958) observed that they so far outreach the normal comprehension of criminality as to render dubious the very framework of law and morality itself. The crimes against humanity briefly canvassed here are an example of what Immanuel Kant (1724–1804) called 'radical evil'. By this Kant meant affronts to human dignity so widespread, so insistent, persistent and organized that our ordinary moral assessments and responses seem to dwindle into irrelevance. Indeed the scale of state crime can sometimes have a numbing effect.

Too often government policies assume a taken-for-granted status that can inhibit the perpetrators from 'thinking what they are doing'; something Arendt (1963) asserted was central to the 'banality of evil'. State crime depends not on 'evil' motives or 'pathological' monsters of depravity but rather on good intentions, the taken-for-granted invocation of appeals to 'national security' or 'social solidarity', the pursuit of some utopian project and, above all, an inability, as Arendt (ibid.: 4) put it, to 'think what we are doing'.

We can in principle show why each case of state crime happened without making any particular assumption either that these patterns of conduct and processes are either unique, one-off events, or that they are mundane, repetitive, predictable events. States have engaged in these activities for reasons we can elucidate. There were – or are – deliberate intentions and desires which link policy-makers and the actual perpetrators of state crime and violence.

What are the implications of all this for criminology? This is a challenging question, given that conventional criminology has managed to avoid the issue. Stan Cohen's 1993 discussion of the treatment of Palestinians at the hands of the Israeli government is a notable exception to an otherwise obdurate discipline. Indeed, state crime and violence have been subjects largely reserved for the analyses of political scientists, historians and philosophers. Why has criminology been so myopic in relation to such issues? We indicated earlier why this might be the case: namely, that many criminologists have been traditionally drawn to the accepted wisdom that the 'crime problem' is synonymous with 'street crime' or the 'underclass'. Criminological attention has been drawn in some quarters to corporate, organized and white-collar crime, even though the discipline has retreated back to the sanctuary of its more traditional concerns.

The death toll, the physical harm and the suffering produced by state crime outweighs any of the crime rates researched by criminologists. It also far outstrips any of the consequences to date of the terrorist activities which since 11 September 2001 have become the focus of the so-called 'War on Terrorism'. That the US State Department has moved to make any actions by governments fall within its definition of terrorism says a great deal about what is at stake. We need to remind ourselves constantly how important it is that we continue to be thoughtful about the things that matter.

Review questions

Why are crimes of the state so difficult for conventional criminology to deal with?

Why do crimes against the citizens of one state, either by that state or by another, constitute such a major problem?

Should the practice of child welfare against indigenous peoples in Australia, Canada, the USA and South Africa be regarded as genocide or as an example of state crime?

Further reading

Arendt, H., 1963, *Eichmann in Jerusalem: A Study in the Banality of Evil*, Harcourt-Brace-Jovanovich, New York.

Barak, G. (ed.), 1991, *Crimes by the Capitalist State: An Introduction to State Criminality*, SUNY Press, Albany, NY.

Cohen, S., 2001, *States of Denial*, Polity Press, Cambridge.

Friedrichs, D.O. (ed.), 1998, *State Crime*, Ashgate, Aldershot, 2 vols.

Green, P. and Ward, T., 2004, *State Crime: Governments, Violence and Corruption*, Pluto Press, London.

Ross, J.I. (ed.), 1995, *Controlling State Crime*, Garland, New York.

Rummel, R., 1994, *Death by Government*, Transaction Press, New Brunswick, NJ.

Simon, D., 1999, *Elite Deviance* (6th edition), Allyn & Bacon, Boston, MA.

Stohl, M. and Lopez, G. (eds), 1986, *Governmental Violence and Repression: An Agenda for Research*, Greenwood Press, Westport, CT.

CONCLUSION: TOWARDS A REFLEXIVE CRIMINOLOGY

Criminology as a discipline at the start of the twenty-first century seems to be in as robust a shape as it has ever been. In contrast to some of the other social sciences – like sociology and economics – there are no obvious signs of crisis in the form of the closure of university departments or a loss of intellectual confidence. Popular interest in crime, the newsworthiness of crime and a persistent political preoccupation with issues of 'law and order' point to a context in which criminology will doubtless continue to thrive. Whether this is a good thing or not will be determined by many other people and over the coming decades.

We have tried in this book to say why conventional criminology is not in quite the good shape some of its promoters might imagine it to be. We have used a combination of historical inquiry and critical analysis of some themes and issues in contemporary criminology to point to some persistent problems with the discipline.

The historical inquiry suggests that many of the ways criminologists think about and do criminology today have their origins in a period when the intellectual foundations of modern criminology were being laid down. This historical inquiry began with scepticism about the long-standing tendency by many to treat the history of criminology as a story of progressive advances in knowledge marked by clearly defined *stages*. This history of disciplinary progress typically tells a story about the origins of modern criminology that are to be found in 'classical criminology' created by philosophers like Beccaria and Bentham in the eighteenth century. This was followed by the 'positivist criminology' of Lombroso in the 1870s, succeeded by a 'neo-classical criminology' that, in turn, set the stage for 'modern criminology'. Yet there seems to be more messiness, repetition and recycling of old ideas than this *stadial* story of historical progress allows for. While it is hardly surprising that many things have changed or moved on intellectually, an examination of contemporary criminology suggests that some core ideas, arguments and assumptions are proving remarkably long-lived.

Having taken our history of criminology into the 1970s we then turned to modern criminology. We did not attempt an exhaustive overview of all the theoretical and research themes that preoccupy contemporary criminologists. We could not provide a detailed account of all the research issues or theoretical approaches to be found in modern criminology in one short book. We adopted a more selective approach which enabled us to identify some of the characteristic arguments criminologists advance when they set out to explain criminal activity, by linking it to unemployment or poverty or to 'dysfunctional families'. We then moved on to look at some of the current policy issues that criminologists who aspire to be both *practical* and *relevant* have promoted, like crime prevention and the relatively recent discovery of the special status of victims in the criminal justice system.

In our account of the way criminologists approached these themes and questions, we have emphasized the special role played by an array of assumptions, or what Holton (1988) has called 'themata', in any kind of human knowledge or belief system. These are fundamental beliefs about things like the nature of reality, the characteristics of human action, the way credible knowledge of reality is acquired and, in the case of criminologists, the nature of crime and related concepts. These assumptions are in turn assembled into a variety of 'constructive schemes' that inform the discourses used by practising criminologists. These 'constructive schemes' include the metaphors and key concepts that constitute a discipline's vocabulary, the kinds of questions that criminologists address, the preferred methods that make credible knowledge possible, and the theoretical, or explanatory, frameworks presumed to already possess credibility.

To insist that there is a single or dominant consensus within mainstream criminology is not warranted, even if we looked to the work done by criminologists who conform to the conventions of what Loader and Sparks (1993) call 'jobbing criminology'. Equally, as writers like O'Malley (1992, 1996) have suggested, criminological research that measures and assesses specific criminal justice issues and objectives has become increasingly important in 'risk' societies shaped by neo-liberal and neo-conservative policy agendas. This contemporary context means that certain forms of administrative and scientific criminology find favour with governments, the mass media, and with public and private funding bodies.

All of this has certain intellectual consequences. More critically oriented criminologists, for example, may find that neither their colleagues nor the funding bodies are all that eager to fund their kind of criminology. This makes sense of Wright's 2000 analysis of introductory criminology textbooks published between 1990 and 1999, which suggests that contemporary critical–radical perspectives are all too often left out of such books. This is what we mean in saying that, while there is hardly a single consensus within criminology, there is a conventional kind of criminology defined by a cluster of constructive schemes having certain common assumptions. The nature of those constructive schemes and the problems with them are on display in the way conventional criminologists discuss the unemployment–crime link or the way crime is explained by reference to 'dysfunctional families' or 'inadequate parenting'.

The problematic effects of these constructive schemes are even more sharply illuminated when we turn to examine what criminologists have to say about white-collar, or corporate, crime and the crimes against humanity committed by states through the twentieth century. Conventional criminology has treated white-collar crime in what can only be called an ambivalent fashion, while it has essentially ignored state crime. The essential problem here is that both corporate crime and crimes of the state generate patterns of violence, suffering and loss that are truly staggering in comparison to the consequences of what, for want of a more elegant phrase, we might call 'normal crime'.

It is this state of affairs that surely merits the recovery of Alfred Schutz's damning judgement of the quality of US social science when he arrived in North America as one of the European émigrés fleeing Nazi terror in 1940: he said simply that they were 'intellectually vacuous and morally nihilist' (Schutz 1986: 59). Though this is a harsh judgement, and has some element of exaggeration, it comes close to capturing our concerns with contemporary criminology.

Some problems with conventional criminology

Our concerns about conventional criminology can be enumerated in six points. Firstly, there is an excessive and, in our view, unwarranted preoccupation with 'ordinary', 'predatory' or 'street' crime. Needless to say, we are not suggesting that it is irrelevant or wrong to worry about homicide, robbery, rape or assault. These activities involve hurt, injury and loss for those people who become their victims. Yet this preoccupation seems to have blinded too many criminologists to the ways in which state crime and corporate crime can involve even more alarming and widespread experiences of pain, hurt and injury.

Secondly, this preoccupation with 'ordinary crime' goes hand in glove with a disposition to research only population groups who are economically, socially and politically relatively weak and/or vulnerable. Research of 'normal' people, middle- or upper-class families, elite groups, corporations or states is rarely if ever done. Instead the focus is on unemployed people, working-class people, low-income and low-status people, people under 18, 'people of colour' and immigrants, who are massively over-represented in the research archives of criminology. The typical rejoinder is that these groups and institutions are those which do the crime. This is true enough, but only partially true. We need to recall that while there are mountains of research on juveniles, people under the age of 18 are not the key players in US serious crime statistics. Recall, too, that just one high-status, high-income stock-broker stole $US600 million and wreaked financial havoc on hundreds of thousands of citizens in the 1980s. Compare this to the total value of all the robberies committed in America – calculated at $US447million in 2000 (FBI 2001), and our point can be seen for what it is: a call for some rebalancing of the research focus. Such a rebalancing would acknowledge the force of Sutherland's observation that

> persons of the upper socio-economic class engage in much criminal behavior . . . this criminal behavior differs from the criminal behavior of the lower socio-economic class principally in the administrative procedures which are used in dealing with the offenders . . . [these] variations in administrative procedures are not significant from the point of view of causation of crime.
>
> (1983: 9)

Some criminologists who claim to be 'progressive', 'critical' or 'radical' would go on to argue that the failure of conventional criminology to take Sutherland seriously points to a conservative disposition manifest in an undue regard for the way things are. Yet this is to make a different point from the one we are making: as we have suggested, at various points it too often seems that 'critical', 'left-realist' or 'progressive' criminologists end up researching the same problems and population groups, and their work, while using a different political vocabulary, actually reinforces the tendencies we have referred to.

For example, it seems that writers across the entire political spectrum, represented by Polk (1993), Eckersley (1988, 1992), White (1994), Grover and Soothill (1996: 398–415), Murray (1990, 1994), Mann and Roseneil (1994), have all been able to talk about an unemployed 'underclass' engaging in self-destructive, criminal and 'antisocial behaviours'. Macnicol (1987: 295) made our point for us when he pointed out the 'odd bedfellows' the *discovery* of 'an underclass' permitted: 'The ideological thrust of this rediscovery [of the underclass] was a curious combination of reformist social engineering ... and a conservative "social pathology" perspective which emphasize[s] cultural deprivation.' The 'odd bedfellows' effect has also been explicated by George Pavlich (2000: 118), who argues that 'radical' and 'conservative', or 'administrative', criminologies have in fact 'partially sustained' each other. This is because the work of 'critical criminologists' has relied on 'traces of administrative concepts in formulating their radical images at any given moment'. As Schwartz (1997) and Pepinsky (1997) both observe, 'critical criminology' has become a kind of umbrella-term to describe a very wide range of *alternative* ways of thinking. However, when Pavlich (2000) examined the way 'critique', or 'critical thinking', is understood, he concluded that it had been constrained by being framed within a narrow idea of disciplinary proprieties that centres on 'positivist assumptions and the lure of scientific absolutes'.

This leads to our third point, which is that often both 'left-wing' and 'conservative' criminologists demonstrate an excessive regard for the authority associated with the *objectivity* and scientism that define the research methods used in conventional practice. Here we see the effect of certain *epistemological* assumptions that reside within the constructive schemes of conventional criminology. ('Epistemology' is the term philo-sophers use to name the ideas and debates entertained about how to make knowledge credible or 'truthful'.) One of the key assumptions here is that language is representational and that it is only a matter of aligning 'brute' reality with our language categories for us to achieve reliable knowledge. That is to say, the postulate of 'realism' holds that we have only to refer to reality to check that our language categories are doing the job of representing reality effectively or truthfully.

Our fourth point is that too many practising criminologists maintain a steadfast commitment to a range of orthodox assumptions about the correct methods and practices needed to do criminology. For in spite of the apparent diversity that is said to define modern criminology, if we look across the agenda of conventional criminology, two mantras are consistently heard, both easily traced back to the regard conventional criminology has displayed for a certain idea about 'proper science'. The first is a call for 'more research ... more information' (Ashworthy 1994: 854). From this perspective, criminologists always seem to be confronted by a 'deficit' of empirical data or information. This is accompanied by a persistent stress on *rigorous*, *empirical* measurement and the testing of hypotheses and theories (Zedner 1994: 1209). 'Empirical' here actually means a privileging of numbers and a variety of descriptive and analytic statistical techniques. As Maguire (1994: 226–7) has noted, the 'numerology of criminology' is obsessive:

> A salient feature of almost all modern forms of discourse about crime is the emphasis placed upon terms associated with quantification and measurement: 'volume', 'extent', 'growth', 'prevalence', 'trends', and so on ... Criminologists

... are aware of the power of the 'language of numbers', and even those oriented
to qualitative research methods routinely produce quantitative data to reinforce and
'legitimate' their findings.

This is the clearest clue to the continued preference of many criminologists for a broad-
church kind of 'positivism' when framing their work. This preference is evident in the
pursuit of 'theory construction', understood as the production of explanatory-cum-
predictive statements. Expecting that highly sophisticated statistical techniques of data
collection and analysis can deliver the long-sought 'Holy Grail' of criminology, a 'general
theory of crime' (Weatherburn 1993), which has bewitched some contemporary
criminologists like Gottfredson and Hirschi (1990) and Braithwaite (1989a), is another.

Fifthly, there are substantial problems associated with the assumption that crime is an
objective, even timeless and universal, category, and that all conduct is *caused* by *objective*
factors that can be scientifically elucidated, measured and predicted. This represents one
of the ways in which a certain kind of sociological determinism has had an unhelpful impact
on criminology. It is simply assumed in conventional criminology that the qualities defining
certain patterns of conduct as 'pro-social' or 'antisocial' are inherent in those forms of
conduct or behaviour themselves. It is not, for instance, a product of the relation between
the behaviour and some normative system. That is, social behaviours are somehow
observable, fixed and determinate markers of the conduct itself because the alleged social
order is such that deviations are in fact breaches of a dominant, single, unitary and coherent
moral code. 'The assumption that there is a single, "objective" social and moral reality
called "society" against which social problems like "poverty", "unemployment" or
transgressive behaviors, or "violence" or more generally "deviance" and "crime" can be
approached.' Criminologists have long assumed that social conduct, whether law-abiding
or 'antisocial', is a stable, objective or observable matter. This assumption makes these
phenomena amenable both to study and to conceptualization by those social sciences using
properly *scientific* methods of research. (This is part of the postulate of phenomenalism,
central to empiricism.) Durkheim (in Giddens 1984: 351) argued strongly at the end of the
nineteenth century for the 'thingness' of his 'social facts' when he asserted that 'a thing is
any object of knowledge which is not naturally controlled by the intellect, which cannot be
adequately grasped by a simple process of mental activity'.

Jack Katz (1988: 3) points out crisply why the resultant determinism will not do:

> Firstly, many of those people who fall into the supposed causal categories do not
> commit the crimes that the research predicts they will. Secondly, many of those
> who do commit crimes do not fit the designated causal categories. Finally, many
> who do match the predictive indicators of criminality, and who do eventually
> commit the crime it has been predicted they will commit, go for long periods
> without engaging in the predicted criminal activity.

Any one of these problems should give reason for alarm. Taken together, they constitute a
devastating critique of explanatory-cum-predictive theories of crime causation, like that
offered by Gottfredson and Hirschi (1990) or Braithwaite (1989a).

There are several issues at stake here. The narrow preoccupation with certain kinds of 'normal' crime leads to a blanking-out of other kinds of crime that are at least as serious, if not more so. The insistence on certain theoretical explanations then fails to *explain* the normal kinds of crime, let alone the full range of problematic human conduct that an adequate and inclusive idea of crime demands. The preferred kinds of *causal* explanations in turn fail to adequately understand the motivational and ethical components of human action. This point has been explored in detail in two remarkable yet widely ignored books by Lonnie Athens (1992, 1997) who, like Jack Katz (1988), has set about persuading his peers of the fundamental insight that we humans act on the basis of what we think, feel and believe to be desirable and that we are *responsible* both ethically and motivationally for what we do. It hardly needs to be added that this idea is fundamental to the operations of the criminal law.

As Athens (1997: 117–18) points out, the conventional criminologist treats the criminal as a passive agent 'whose criminal acts are products solely of causal factors that may be internal, external or both'. Athens's preference is to treat criminals as 'actors' who do what they do 'based on their past experiences in handling situations similar to the one at hand'. The result is an intellectually more rigorous and ethically more sensitive approach to criminal activity:

> Since human beings are normally aware of at least some of the contingencies that confront them in any situation, they can always exercise some control over their conduct . . . A human being's decision to commit a criminal act is therefore elevated from the status of epiphenomenon to that of real decision.
>
> (ibid.: 117–18)

Finally these characteristic assumptions, preferences and exclusions add up to a number of overlapping constructive schemes that help to define conventional criminology. We have reflected at various points throughout this book why this state of affairs should be so in terms of the role played by ordinary social prejudices that none of us are immune to. It matters that most academic criminologists tend to be from the middle classes and to work in institutions that enjoy considerable social status and which reward academics with a comfortable lifestyle. The broader social and political context matters too because all social research has a political dimension that needs to be taken into account by criminologists.

> Irrespective of the content of criminological research, when released it enters a political arena that reaches many audiences. Therefore the political dimensions involved in conducting criminological research should be foreseen by criminologists and recognized as part and parcel of a process that has the potential to confront governing authorities and influence the policies and practices of the state crime control apparatus.
>
> (Walters 2003: 16)

It may be a truism that a discipline like criminology and its practitioners interact with its social, economic and political context. Acknowledging that, however, matters, and conventional criminologists do not always do so as much as they might. This is a key aspect of what we mean by 'reflexivity'. Our very modest suggestion is that some more reflexivity could embellish the practice of criminology.

We mean by reflexivity more than is usually meant by calls to embrace a certain kind of 'critical criminology'. Criminologists like De Haan (1990), Henry and Milovanovic (1991), Hunt (1991), Young (1994) and Carrington (1993, 1997) have explored the implications of what in Chapter 4 we called 'post-modernism' for renovating modern criminology. Fattah (1997), for example, offers a critique of 'modernist' criminology combining a 'post-modernist' scepticism allied to a humanist ethic. Post-modernist ideas have also made themselves felt in related areas like socio-legal studies, feminist theory and the sociology of deviance.

Yet conventional criminology keeps sailing on, undisturbed by the critics and post-modern sceptics. This may mean one of two things: that critics and sceptics influenced by post-modernism are profoundly wrong and so should go unheeded; or, as we suspect, that the persistence of old habits of mind in mainstream criminology is testimony to the profound capacity of many of us to keep on believing what we want to believe in spite of what anyone else says.

We are not convinced that this is a good thing. At the very least we think that this self-confidence is misplaced. There is a case for criminologists to practise more critical thinking than they usually do. Yet we are not urging the adoption of a post-modernist framework by criminologists. Promoting such a position is problematic, given that the very use of words like 'post-modernist' implies that all of the ideas being criticized can be lumped together and called 'modernist'. This rather overstates the coherence of the old 'modernist' ideas and the coherence of the new 'post-modernist' ideas.

We do think, however, that a more thoughtful criminology is possible and desirable. We suggest below how a higher order of critical thinking might yield more insight into the complex interplay between the practices that constitute a social science like criminology and its social context. To do this we call on the idea of reflexivity.

On reflexivity

The work of Pierre Bourdieu offers a very persuasive account of what reflexivity involves and why it matters.

Reflexivity of course can be vacuous and an excuse for being simply 'self-referential', something which many 'post-modernists' engage in, often to a tedious extent. What makes Bourdieu's call (2001) for greater reflexivity worth heeding is not only its unsparing character; more significantly, Bourdieu wants to bolster the possibilities of sustaining a rational practice of 'science' where that word takes on a larger meaning than is normal. Bourdieu is no relativist, because he operates with a strong view of science as a rational practice. For this reason Bourdieu did not have much patience with 'post-modern' deconstructionists like Derrida or Lyotard whom he considered 'anti-scientistic'. As Bourdieu (Bourdieu and Wacquant 1992: 47) says: 'One does not have to choose between obscurantism and scientism. "Of two ills", said Karl Kraus, "I refuse to choose the lesser".' Bourdieu (2001) offers an appropriate antidote to both 'post-modernist' relativism and conventional ideas about *objective* social sciences via what Wacquant (ibid.: 36) called his 'signature obsession with reflexivity'. As Loic Wacquant (ibid.: 37) points out, Bourdieu starts off from where Giddens (1984, 1990) left off when he identified three different yet related ideas of reflexivity set against three points of reference: namely, 'agency', 'science' and 'society'.

In terms of *agency*, we humans are said to be 'reflexive' inasmuch as we are conceptual and symbolic creatures who possess the capacity to turn back on ourselves and engage in self-monitoring and self-transforming activities. Secondly, as a source of practice that is *scientific*, the social sciences like criminology are 'reflexive', because the knowledge they generate is sent out into the societal context and produces what Giddens calls a 'double hermeneutic' effect by describing the social context in ways that help, in turn, to transform that reality. For example, a given piece of research on drug-use or drink-driving can inform policy that sets out to change the behaviour of people. Finally, in an abstract sense *society* itself can be said to be reflexive insofar as it is within the total space which we call 'society' that a capacity evolves to control and programme 'its' own development, a quality or capacity that is properly speaking historical.

Without negating these closely related ideas about reflexivity, Bourdieu adds the truly distinctive idea that reflexivity itself is a requirement and a form of social-scientific work. Take the standard injunction of one of the earliest advocates of reflexivity in sociology–criminology found in the work of Alvin Gouldner (1971). Gouldner argues for the idea that as an 'I', the sociologist–criminologist needs to engage in a practice of 'conscious self-reflection', by applying the basic insight of Marx that everything we think is shaped by the lives we lead and by our position, be it in terms of class, gender or ethnicity, in the world. Bourdieu does not disparage this kind of critical reflection; he insists, however, on some distinctive 'add-ons'.

There are, says Bourdieu, three ways that social scientists develop 'blind spots'. The social co-ordinates of class, gender and ethnicity may well help to blur our sense of self and help close down reflection on why we think what we think. The second problem lies in an inability to understand how the position we occupy within a given academic or disciplinary field may affect our thinking. This is especially likely, given especially that a discipline like criminology may also be shaped by the larger dispositions of social power, like the way a given market-based practice to do with research investment may impinge on our scientific work. Social scientists are typically always situated near what Bourdieu calls 'the dominated field of power' and are therefore 'under the sway of the forces of attraction and repulsion that bear on all symbolic producers'. The final problem, and this is Bourdieu's most insistent emphasis, is that the way people engage in their intellectual life itself may seduce them into treating the world, as Manent suggests, as a *spectacle* to which they are simply *spectators*.

The kind of reflexivity proposed by Bourdieu rejects what Manent has called the 'spectator model' of social science. The 'spectator model' at work in the social sciences is a consequence of social scientists hoping to emulate the physical sciences. Since their origin 200 years ago, the dominant trend in the social sciences has been to stress, in Pierre Manent's words, 'the effect of necessity acting in history and society' (1998: 51). With crystal clarity, Manent (ibid.: 54) shows that many of the social sciences attempt to *know* reality via a 'viewpoint' which 'adopts the viewpoint of the spectator. The viewpoint of the spectator is all the more pure and scientific in that it accords no real initiative whatever to the agent or agents, but considers their actions or their works as the necessary effect of necessary causes.'

Among the many effects of this viewpoint, as William James (1906) understood all too well, has been a persistent flight from experience and action. As Giddens observed famously of Talcott Parsons's rather grand 'theory of social action', there was 'not a lot of action in Parsons'. The same can be said with equivalent force of the many statistically oriented and 'empirical' research projects carried out by criminologists. To amend the point Manent (1998: 54) makes about sociology, we can say that the pursuit of a 'science of crime' has seen criminologists in particular adopt a 'forceful and deliberate distancing from any familiarity with what is real in order to achieve the distance and height of Science'. The consequence, adds Bauman, is to privilege structure over human agency and choice. This in turn leads to researchers taking what are really only intellectual constructs, like 'structures', 'social disorganisation', and turning them into things that seem to be real, because: 'Position implies structure, structure implies system, system implies boundaries: that is the possibility of saying what belongs and what does not belong to the system . . .'(Bauman 1992: 71). Adopting the spectator point of view can encourage us to treat the world as 'a space full of significations to be interpreted rather than as concrete problems to be solved practically'. This is a problem because it may lead us to entirely miss the defining features of a given field of practice like criminology and its relation to the practices of crime detection and crime control. That is, engaging in theoretical work may lead us to miss the point of why we do the research or construct the theory. As Bourdieu (1992: 38) puts it: 'Whenever we fail to subject to systematic critique the presuppositions inscribed in the fact of thinking the world, of retiring from the world, and from action in the world in order to think that action, we risk collapsing practical logic into theoretical logic.'

The only antidote to this is to subject all of our research and theoretical work to persistent and relentless reflexive critique. We should do this, he says, whether we are using questionnaires, statistical techniques, Foucauldian genealogy, coding techniques or ethno-methodology. Reflexivity means and requires a 'systematic sociological critique' of these techniques and assumptions. It requires a rigorous, scientific, reflective practice that makes the fundamental shaping of thought itself, as a social activity determined by objective factors, including both conscious and unconscious aspects, into its central object of research and thought. This is required, since it involves, as Bourdieu (1990: 10) puts it, 'thinking out the unconscious or un-thought categories of thought which delimit the thinkable and predetermine the thought'.

This requires far more than attention being paid to the inner life of sociologists by means of some kind of 'diary-keeping'. It is not something best done by thinking about 'the ego at work' on the research, as Garfinkel and Giddens seem to imply, rendering reflexivity an 'ego-logical' process. Reflexivity calls for rigorous scientific research into the organizational forms in which academics work, like universities and their disciplines, their journals and research-grant practices, as well as the cognitive structure of the discipline, addressing both its conscious and unconscious aspects (see Bourdieu 1988).

This will involve paying attention to the deployment of the categories and the metaphors, for example, of criminology, especially within a given *national* framework, in ways that take account of the theories, the assumptions, the paradigms, problems and the scholarly judgements at work within that academic field. That is, the subject of scientific reflexivity must be the entire field of social science itself. As Bourdieu (1990: 14) puts it, this requires 'subjecting the position of the observer to the same critical analysis as that of the constructed object at hand', i.e. the topic of social scientific research. This further entails that what 'has to be done is not to magically abolish this distance by a spurious primitivist participation but to objectivize this objectivizing distance and the social conditions that make it possible such as the externality of the observer, the techniques of objectivation he uses, etc.' (ibid.: 14).

In effect, the kinds of reflexivity proposed by Bourdieu require that we embed a 'theory of theoretical practice' at the heart of our scientific practice. What this gives rise to is on show in his book on Heidegger where Bourdieu 'calls out' Heidegger and his infamous Rector's Address of May 1933 ('The Defence of the University'), in which this very famous German philosopher attacked the welfare state before proclaiming his anti-Semitism *and* his enthusiastic support of Nazism. Bourdieu (1991: 3) insists that we need to engage in a 'dual reading' of Heidegger:

> We must abandon the opposition between a political reading and a philosophical reading, and undertake a simultaneously political and philosophical dual reading of writings which are defined by their fundamental ambiguity . . . His discourse from beginning to end has a rare ambiguity for it manages to subordinate existential and ontological categories to the historical moment so that they create the illusion that their philosophical intentions have an a priori applicability to the political situation as when he relates 'freedom of research' to 'State coercion' and makes 'labour service' and 'armed service' coincide with 'knowledge service', so that by the end of the lecture, the listener does not know whether to turn to read Diels on the 'pre-Socratics' or to join the SA.
>
> (ibid.: 5)

We see here precisely why Bourdieu proposes that the chief obstacle to engaging in the kind of reflexivity he speaks of is not epistemological but rather social and political. This kind of reflexivity cannot help but raise other people's hackles, beginning with those intellectuals and academics who cling to their idea of academic freedom and their *objectivity*. For Bourdieu, reflexivity helps us escape the delusions of such ideas.

Towards a reflexive criminology

What are the implications of the idea of reflexivity for criminology? We are not alone in thinking that it challenges modern criminology to be more thoughtful. The work of criminologists like De Haan (1990), Hunt (1991), Henry and Milovanovic (1994) and Carrington (1997) has pointed to the importance of modern criminology becoming more thoughtful in this sense.

Criminologists need to be more reflexive about their activities in any given social and intellectual context. This simply means paying attention to the kind of society of which they are a part. In such a context it matters that we are able to think well about crime and the social-scientific work done by contemporary criminologists. Well-established, objectified categories like *crime* and the *crime problem* need to be subjected to thoughtful analysis along with their contributions to particular bodies of criminological theory and research. That is, rather than being treated as a conceptual conduit to an objective reality, the concepts and ideas that constitute the body of knowledge (about crime and related matters), or what Young (1996) calls 'imaginings', need to become the focus of inquiry *in themselves.*

Contemporary criminologists have claimed their discipline to be a bona fide social science. Though they operate from apparently diverse *theoretical* perspectives – like 'strain theory', 'urban ecology' or 'biological determinism' – most criminologists have, we have shown, more or less consciously, sustained an overlapping series of cognate 'constructive schemes'. In doing this they have mostly assumed that their research protocols, their data and their conclusions, along with their theoretical frameworks, all represent the way *the world actually is.* (The major exceptions to this generalization have been those criminologists who have worked within a broadly defined 'symbolic interactionist' or 'interpretivist' constructive scheme or, as we could now say, 'discourse'.)

Crime has for too long been conventionally understood as a problem solved and governed by institutions and processes in the criminal justice system the history of which is best understood *empirically.*

The narrow preoccupation with what constitutes proper research methods has hampered thinking about the processes of constituting and researching crime and criminality historically. This can mean that criminologists fail to understand how their use of categories like *crime* or *the criminal* can beg all sorts of questions, such as how such categories came into existence in the first place, who produced them and why.

There is clearly some value in asking empirically minded social scientists to be more reflexive. As Agger (1991: 121) argues, this is a request for criminologists to think about their own role in the '"discovery" of social problems. It asks for criminologists to reflect on the ways . . . their own analytical and literary practices encode and conceal value positions . . .'.

Secondly we are critical of those modern criminologists who think of crime as a reality that is discoverable via the 'empirical' research techniques produced by social scientists. We think that rather more empirical work would improve the capacity of criminologists to inform their communities. Too many criminologists fail to actually get out into the streets of the great cities or explore the activities of states and corporations, preferring instead to operationalize their concepts or apply rigorous statistical tests of goodness to their data. That is, empirical criminologists are often *insufficiently* empirical. By that we mean that there is in too much 'empirical' criminological research an unwillingness to pay attention to what is actually happening.

'Left-realist' criminologists like Stan Cohen (1997) have worried endlessly about falling into the swamp of relativism. Richard Rorty (1999: 23) points out that to think reflexively about the social use of language does *not* mean a retreat into 'mindless relativism':

> Insofar as 'post-modern' philosophical thinking is identified with a mindless and stupid cultural relativism – with the idea that any fool thing that calls itself culture is worthy of respect – then I have no use for such thinking. Philosophical pluralism does not entail such stupidity. The reason to try persuasion rather than force, to do our best to come to terms with people whose convictions are archaic or

degenerate, is simply that using force, or mockery, or insult is likely to decrease human happiness.

(1999: 276)

Finally, as Jack Katz (1988) has argued, criminologists need to be able to pose the core questions in ways that do not rely on *structural* or *causal* mechanisms. We cannot establish why some people engage in criminal action by referring in an almost magical way to 'structural factors' (like unemployment, poverty, low level of education or social exclusion). It is simply not the case that most people who are unemployed, or who are in the lowest income brackets or did not complete secondary schooling, are the people who commit most of the crime.

A criminology adequate to its task needs to ask why men and women engage in that wide range of human conduct to which words like 'crime' and 'criminal' might sensibly be applied. It needs to be able to do this while being sensitive to the difficult implications of our insistence that we cannot assume any secure foundations underpinning the relation between actuality and language.

Further reading

Anderson, W.T. (ed.), 1995, *The Truth About the Truth: De-Confusing and Re-Constructing the Postmodern World*, G.P. Putnam, New York.

Henry, S. and Milovanovic, D., 1994, 'The Constitution of Constitutive Criminology: A Post-modern Approach to Criminological Theory', in Nelken, D. (ed.), *The Futures of Criminology*, Sage, London.

Pavlich, G., 2000, *Critique and Radical Discourses on Crime*, Ashgate, London.

Rose, N., 1990, *Governing the Soul: The Shaping of the Private Self*, Routledge, London.

Wright, R., 2000, 'Left Out? The Coverage of Critical Perspectives in Introductory Textbooks, 1990–1999', *Critical Criminology*, Vol. 9, No. 1: 101–22.

BIBLIOGRAPHY

Abadinsky, H. and Winfree, L., 1992, *Crime and Justice: An Introduction*, Nelson-Hall, New York.

Abbott, P. and Wallace, C., 1992, *The Family and the New Right*, Pluto Press, London.

Agger, B., 1991, 'Critical Theory, Post-Structuralism, Post-Modernism: Their Sociological Relevance', in Scott, W. and Blake, J. (eds), *Annual Review of Sociology*, Vol. 17, Annual Reviews, Palo Alto, CA.

Ainsworth-Darnell, J. and Roscigno, V., 2001, 'Stratification, School-Work Linkages and Vocational Education', Paper presented at Annual Meeting of the American Sociological Association, Anaheim, CA.

Alaheto, T., 2003, 'Economic Crime: Does Personality Matter?', *International Journal of Offender Therapy and Comparative Criminology*, Vol. 47, No. 3: 335–55.

Albanese, J., 1995, *White-Collar Crime in America,* Prentice-Hall, Englewood-Cliffs, NJ.

Alder, C., 1986, '"Unemployed Women Have Got It Heaps Worse": Exploring the Implications of Female Youth Unemployment', *Australia and New Zealand Journal of Criminology*, Vol. 19: 210–40.

Alexander, J., 1987, *Twenty Lectures: Sociological Theory since World War II*, Columbia University Press, New York.

Allen, E. and Steffensmeier, D., 1989, 'Youth Underemployment and Property Crime: Differential Effects of Job Availability and Job Quality on Juvenile and Adult Arrest Rates', *American Sociological Review*, Vol. 50: 317–32.

Altatt, P. and Yeandle, J., 1992, *Youth Unemployment and the Family*, Routledge, London.

Amnesty International, 1993, *Getting Away with Murder: Political Killings and Disappearances in the 1990s*, Amnesty International, London.

Anderson, T., Magnusson, D. and Wennburg, P., 1997, 'Early Aggressiveness and Hyperactivity as Indicators of Adult Alcohol Problems and Criminality: A Prospective Longitudinal Study of Male Subjects', *Studies on Crime and Crime Prevention*, Vol. 6, No. 1: 7–20.

Anderson, W.T. (ed.), 1995, *The Truth About the Truth: De-Confusing and Re-Constructing the Postmodern World*, G.P. Putnam, New York.

Applebaum, A., 2003, *GULAG: A History of the Soviet Camps*, Allen Lane, London.

Arblaster, A., 1975, 'What Is Violence?', in Milliband, R. and Saville, J. (eds), *The Socialist Register 1975*, Merlin Press, London.

Arblaster, A., 1987, *The Rise and Fall of Western Liberalism*, Oxford University Press, Oxford.

Archer, D. and Gartner, R., 1978, 'Legal Homicide and its Consequences', in Kutash, I., Kutash, S. and Auchinloss, L. (eds), *Violence: Perspectives on Murder and Aggression,* Jossey-Bass, San Francisco, CA.

Arendt, H., 1958, *The Human Condition*, University of Chicago Press, Chicago, IL.

Arendt, H., 1963, *Eichmann in Jerusalem: A Study in the Banality of Evil*, Harcourt-Brace-Jovanovich, New York.

Aries, P., 1969, *Centuries of Childhood*, Penguin, Harmondsworth.

Aristotle, 1976, *Ethics* (trans. Thompson, J. and Introduction by Barnes, J.), Penguin, Harmonds-worth.

Ashworth, A., 1994, *The Criminal Process: An evaluative study,* Clarendon Press, Oxford.

Athens, L., 1992, *The Creation of Dangerous Violent Criminals*, University of Illinois Press, Urbana.

Athens, L., 1997, *Violent Criminal Acts and Actors Revisited*, University of Illinois Press, Urbana.

Aune, J.A., 2001, *Selling the Free Market*, Guilford Press, New York.

Austin, T., 1993, *I Can Picture the Old Home and So Clearly: The Commonwealth and Half-Caste Youth in the Northern Territory 1911–1939*, Aboriginal Studies Press, Canberra.

Australian Archives, 1993, *Between Two Worlds*, AGPS, Canberra.

Ayer, A.J., 1959, *Language, Truth and Logic*, Penguin, Harmondsworth.

Bagguley, P. and Mann, K., 1992, 'Idle Thieving Bastards? Scholarly Representations of the Underclass', *Work, Employment and Society*, Vol. 6, No. 1 : 112–26.

Bagnell, K., 1987, *The Little Immigrants: The Orphans Who Came to Canada*, Macmillan, Toronto.

Bannister, R., 1987, *Sociology and Scientism: The American Quest for Objectivity 1880–1949*, University of North Carolina Press, Chapel Hill.

Barak, G. (ed.), 1991, *Crimes by the Capitalist State: An Introduction to State Criminality*, SUNY Press, New York.

Bauman, Z., 1978, *Hermeneutics and Social Science*, Columbia University Press, New York.

Bauman, Z., 1990, 'Philosophical Intimations of Postmodern Sociology', *Sociological Review*, Vol. 38, No. 3: 411–44.

Bauman, Z., 1991, *Intimations of Postmodernity*, Routledge, London.

Bauman, Z., 1992, *Modernity and the Holocaust*, Cornell University Press, Ithaca, NY.

Baxi, U., 1986, *Mass Disasters and Multinational Liability: The Bhopal Case*, Indian Law Institute, Delhi.

Bayart, J.F., Ellis, S. and Hibou, B., 1999, *The Criminalization of the State in Africa*, James Currey, Oxford.

Bean, P. and Melville, J., 1989, *Lost Children of the Empire*, Unwin-Hyman, London.

Beccaria, C., 1963, *On Crimes and Punishments* (trans. Paolucci, H.), Bobbs Merrill, New York.

Beck, U., 1992, *Risk Society*, Sage, London.

Becker, G., 1968, 'Crime and Punishment: An Economic Approach', *Journal of Political Economy*, Vol. 76, No. 2: 169–217.

Becker, G., 1978, *The Economic Approach to Human Behavior*, University of Chicago Press, Chicago, IL.

Becker, H., 1963, *Outsiders: Studies in the Sociology of Deviance*, Free Press, New York.

Becker, H., 1964, *The Other Side: Perspectives on Deviance*, Free Press, New York.

Becker, J., 1996, *Hungry Ghosts: China's Secret Famine*, John Murray, London.

Beirne, P., 1993, *Inventing Criminology: Essays on the Rise of 'Homo Criminalis'*, SUNY Press, New York.

Beirne, P. and Messerschmidt, J., 1995, *Criminology* (2nd edition), Harcourt Brace College Publishers, New York.

Bellair, P., Roscigno, V. and McNulty, T., 2003, 'Linking Local Labour Market Opportunity to Violent Adolescent Delinquency', *Journal of Research in Crime and Delinquency*, Vol. 40, No. 1: 6–33.

Berger, P. and Luckmann, T., 1969, *The Social Construction of Reality*, Anchor Books, New York.

Berry, J., 1992, *Lead Us Not into Temptation*, Doubleday, New York.

Bessant, J., 1995, 'The Discovery of an Australian "Juvenile Underclass"', *Australian and New Zealand Journal of Sociology*, Vol. 31, No. 1: 13–27.

Bessant, J., 1996, *Youth Unemployment and Crime: Policy, Work and the 'Risk Society'*, Youth Research Centre, University of Melbourne, Melbourne.

Bessant, J. and Cook, S. (eds), 1997, *Women and Violence*, Sage, London.

Bessant, J. and Watts, R., 1993, 'Young People and Violence: A Focus on Schools', in Chappell, D. and Lincoln, R. (eds), *Violence II*, Australian Institute of Criminology, Canberra.

Bessant, J., Hil, R. and Watts, R., 2005, *Discovering Risk*, Peter Lang, New York.

Bessant, J., Watts, R., Dalton, T. and Rowe, J., 2003, *Homelessness and Heroin Use*, AHURI, Melbourne.

Bessant, J., Watts, R., Dalton, T. and Smyth, P., 2006, *Talking Policy*, Allen & Unwin, Sydney.

Bird, C. (ed.), 1998, *The Stolen Children: Their Stories*, Random House, Sydney.

Black, D., 1970, 'The Production of Crime Rates', *American Sociological Review*, Vol. 35. No. 4: 733–48.

Black, D., 1980, *The Manners and Customs of Police*, Academic Press, New York.

Blalock, H., 1960, *Social Statistics*, McGraw-Hill, New York.

Blankenship, M., 1993, 'Understanding Corporate Criminality: Challenges and Issues', in Blankenship, M.B. (ed.), *Understanding Corporate Criminality*, Garland, New York.

Bleakley, J.W., 1929, *The Aboriginal and Half-Castes of Central Australia and North Australia*, Government Printer, Canberra.

Bledstein, B., 1976, *The Culture of Professionalism*, W.W. Norton, New York.

Block, M. and Heineke, M., 1975, 'A Labor Theoretical Analysis of Criminal Choice', *American Economic Review*, Vol. 65: 314–25.

Blumer, H., 1969, *Symbolic Interactionism*, Prentice-Hall, Englewood-Cliffs, NJ.

Bohme, G., 1975, 'The Social Function of Cognitive Structures: A Concept of the Scientific Community within a Theory of Action', in Knorr, D., Strasser, H. and Zillian, H. (eds), *Determinants and Controls of Scientific Development*, Reidel, Dordrecht.

Boswell, J., 1994, *The Marriage of Likeness: Same Sex Unions in Pre-Modern Europe*, Harper-Collins, London.

Bottomley, K. and Coleman, C., 1986, *Understanding Crime Rates*, Saxon House, Farnborough.

Bottomley, K., Johnstone, G. and Penn, J. (eds), 1998, *New Directions in Labour's Crime Policy Examined*, Pluto Press, London.

Bourdieu, P., 1988, *Homo Academicus*, Polity Press, Cambridge.

Bourdieu, P., 1990, *The Logic of Practice*, Polity Press, Cambridge.

Bourdieu, P., 1991, *The Craft of Sociology: Epistemological Preliminaries*, De Gruyter, New York.

Bourdieu, P., et al., 2000, *The Weight of the World: Social Suffering in Contemporary Society*, Polity Press, Cambridge.

Bourdieu, P., 2001, *In Other Words: Essays Towards a Reflexive Sociology*, Polity Press, Cambridge.

Bourdieu, P. and Waquant, L., 1992, *Towards a Reflexive Sociology*, UCLA Press, Los Angeles, CA.

Bowlby, J., 1940, 'The Influence of Early Environment', *International Journal of Psychoanalysis*, Vol. 21: 154–78.

Bowlby, J., 1953a, *Attachment and Loss*, Hogarth Press, London, Vol. 1.

Bowlby, J., 1953b, 'Some Pathological Processes Set in Train by Early Mother–Child Separation', *Journal of Mental Science*, Vol. 99: 265–72.

Bowlby, J., 1965, *Child Care and the Growth of Love*, Penguin, Baltimore, MD.

Box, S., 1983, *Power, Crime and Mystification*, Tavistock, London.

Box, S., 1987, *Recession, Crime and Punishment*, Macmillan, London.

Box, S. and Hale, C., 1982, 'Economic Crisis and the Rising Prisoner Population in England and Wales', *Crime and Social Justice*, Vol. 17: 20–35.

Boyd, E., Berk, R. and Hamner, K., 1996, 'Motivated by Hate or Prejudice? Categorization of Hate-Motivated Crimes in Two Police Divisions', *Law & Society Review*, Vol. 30: 819–50.

Braithwaite, J., 1984, *Corporate Crime in the Pharmaceutical Industry*, Routledge & Kegan Paul, Boston, MA.

Braithwaite, J., 1988, 'Crime', in Najman, J. and Western, J. (eds), *A Sociology of Australian Society*, Macmillan, Melbourne.

Braithwaite, J., 1989a, *Crime, Shame and Reintegration*, Cambridge University Press, Cambridge.

Braithwaite, J., 1989b, 'Criminological Theory and Organizational Crime', *Justice Quarterly*, Vol. 6, No. 3: 333–58.

Braithwaite, J., 1996, Introduction to Hazlehurst, K. (ed.), *Crime and Justice: An Australian Textbook in Criminology*, Law Book Company, Sydney.

Braithwaite, J., 2000, *Regulation, Crime, Freedom*, Ashgate, Aldershot.

Brake, M. and Hale, C., 1993, *Public Order and Private Lives*, Routledge, London.

Breitman, R., 1991, *The Architect of Genocide: Himmler and the Final Solution*, Brandeis University Press, Hanover.

Brenner, H., 1977, 'Health Costs and Benefits of Economic Policy', *International Journal of Health Services*, Vol. 7: 581–623.

Brenner, W. and Harvey, M., 1978, 'Economic Crises and Crime', in Savitz, L. and Johnson, N. (eds), *Crime and Society*, Wiley, New York.

Britt, C., 1994, 'Crime and Unemployment Among Youths in the United States, 1958–1990', *American Journal of Economics and Sociology*, Vol. 53, No. 1, January: 99–108.

Brown, S.E. and Chiang, C.-P., 1993, 'Defining Corporate Crime: A Critique of Traditional Parameters', in Blankenship, M.B. (ed.), *Understanding Corporate Criminality*, Garland, New York.

Browning, C., 2004, *The Origins of the Final Solution: The Evolution of Nazi Jewish Policy, September 1939–March 1942*, University of Nebraska Press, Lincoln, Yad Vashem, Jerusalem.

Brownstein, H., 2000, 'The Social Production of Crime Statistics', *Justice Research & Policy*, Vol. 2, No. 2: 73–89.

Burchell, G., 1993, 'Liberal Government and Techniques of the Self', *Economy & Society*, Vol. 2, No. 3: 13–39.

Burkett, E. and Bruni, F., 1995, *A Gospel of Shame: Children, Sexual Abuse and the Catholic Church*, Viking, New York.

Burleigh, M., 1994, *Death and Deliverance: 'Euthanasia' in Germany c.1900–1945*, Oxford University Press, Oxford.

Burleigh, M. and Wipperman, F., 1992, *The Racial State: Germany 1933–1945*, Cambridge University Press, Cambridge.

Burt, C., 1965, *The Young Delinquent* ([1925] 3rd edition), University of London, London.

Cain, M. (ed.), 1989a, *Growing Up Good: Policing the Behaviour of Girls in Europe*, Sage, London.

Cain, M., 1989b, 'Realism, Feminism, Methodology, and Law', *International Journal of the Sociology of Law*, Vol. 14: 255–67.

Cain, M., 1990, 'Towards Transgression: New Directions in Feminist Criminology.', *International Journal of the Sociology of Law*, Vol. 18, No. 1: 1–18.

Cameron, C.M., 1994, *American Samurai: Myth, Imagination and the Conduct of Battle in the First Marine Division, 1941–1951*, Cambridge University Press, New York.

Camic, C. (ed.), 1991, *Talcott Parsons: The Early Essays*, University of Chicago Press, Chicago, IL.

Campbell, A., 1987, 'Self-Reported Delinquency and Home Life: Evidence from a Sample of British Girls', *Journal of Youth and Adolescence*, Vol. 16, No. 2: 13–34.

Campbell, B., 1993, *Goliath: Britain's Most Dangerous Places*, Macmillan, London.

Canguilhem, G., 1990, *The Normal and the Pathological*, Zone Books, New York.

Carrabine, E., Iganski, P., Lee, M., Plummer, K. and South, N., 2004, *Criminology: A Sociological Introduction*, Routledge, Abingdon.

Carrington, K., 1989, 'Manufacturing Female Delinquency: A Study of Juvenile Justice', Unpublished Ph.D. Thesis, Macquarie University.

Carrington, K., 1992, 'Policing Families and Controlling the Young', in White, R. and Wilson, B. (eds), *For Your Own Good*, La Trobe University Press, Bundoora.

Carrington, K., 1993, *Offending Girls: Sex, Youth and Justice*, Allen & Unwin, Sydney.

Carrington, K., 1997, 'Postmodernism and Feminist Criminologies: Fragmenting the Criminological Subject', in Walton, P. and Young, J. (eds), *The New Criminology Revisited*, Macmillan, London.

Carson, W.G., 1981, *The Other Price of Britain's Oil*, Martin Robertson, Oxford.

Caspi, A., Henry, B., McGee, R., Moffitt, T. and Silva, P., 1995, 'Temperamental Origins of Child and Adolescent Behaviour Problems', *Child Development*, Vol. 57: 357–406.

Castells, M., 1998, *End of Millennium*, Blackwell, Oxford.

Cernkovich, S., Giordano, P. and Rudolph, J., 2000, 'Race, Crime and the American Dream', *Journal of Research in Crime and Delinquency*, Vol. 37: 131–70.

Cerulo, K., 1998, *Representations of Violence*, Spectrum, New York.

Chalk, G. and Jonasson, S., 1990, *Genocide: A Historical and Sociological Perspective*, CUNY Press, New York.

Chambliss, W., 1989, 'State-Organised Crime - The American Society of Criminology, 1988 Presidential Address', *Criminology*, Vol. 27:183–208.

Chan, J., 1996, 'Crime Prevention and the Lure of Relevance: A Response to Adam Sutton', *Australian and New Zealand Journal of Criminology*, Vol. 27, No. 1: 13–120.

Chiricos, T., 1987, 'Rates of Crime and Unemployment: An Analysis of Aggregate Research Evidence', *Social Problems*, Vol. 34: 187–212.

Chomsky, N., 1986, *Pirates and Emperors*, Black Rose, Montreal.

Chomsky, N., 1996, *Class War*, South End Press, Boston, MA.

Choo, C., 1989, 'Black Must Go White', Unpublished M.Phil. Thesis, University of Western Australia, Perth.

Christie, N., 1993, *Crime Control as Industry: Towards GULAGS Western Style?*, Routledge, London.

Chung, L.J., Hill, K., Hawkins, J., Gilchrist, L. and Nagin, D., 2002, 'Childhood Predictors of Offense Trajectories', *Journal of Research in Crime and Delinquency*, Vol. 39: 60–90.

Cicourel, A., 1968, *The Social Organisation of Juvenile Justice*, Heinemann, London.

Clarke, M., 1990, *Business Crime: Its Nature*, Polity Press, Cambridge.

Clinard, M.B. and Yeager, P., 1980, *Corporate Crime*, Free Press, New York.

Cohen, L., Felson, M. and Land, K., 1980, 'Poverty Crime Rates in the United States: A Macro-Dynamic Analysis, 1947–1977, with Ex-Ante Forecasts for the Mid-1980s', *American Journal of Sociology*, Vol. 86: 90–118.

Cohen, M. and Simpson, J., 1997, 'The Origins of Corporate Criminality: Rational Individual and Organisational Actors', in Lofquist, W., Cohen, M. and Rabe, G. (eds), *Debating Corporate Crime*, ACJS–Anderson, Cincinnati, OH.

Cohen, S., 1973, *Folk Devils and Moral Panics*, Paladin, St Albans.

Cohen, S., 1974, 'Criminology and the Sociology of Deviance in Britain', in Rock, P. and McIntosh, M. (eds), *Deviance and Social Control*, Tavistock, London.

Cohen, S., 1984, 'The Deeper Structures of the Law or "Beware of the Rulers Bearing Justice"', *Contemporary Crisis*, Vol. 8: 54–79.

Cohen, S., 1992, 'Footprints in the Sand: A Further Report on Criminology and the Sociology of Deviance in Britain', in Cohen, S., *Against Criminology*, Transaction, New Brunswick, NJ.

Cohen, S., 1993, 'Human Rights and Crimes of the State: The Culture of Denial', *Australian and New Zealand Journal of Criminology*, Vol. 26: 97–115.

Cohen, S., 1996, 'If Nothing Works, What is Our Work?', *Australian and New Zealand Journal of Criminology*, Vol. 27, No. 1: 2–18.

Cohen, S., 1997, 'Intellectual Scepticism and Political Commitment: The Case of Radical Criminology', in Walton, P. and Young, J. (eds), *The New Criminology Revisited*, Macmillan, London.

Cohen, S., 2001, *States of Denial*, Polity Press, Cambridge.

Coleman, C. and Moynihan, J., 1996, *Understanding Crime Statistics*, Oxford University Press, Oxford.

Coleman, J., 1961, *The Adolescent Society*, Free Press, Glencoe, IL.

Collins, R., 1974, 'Three Faces of Cruelty: Towards a Comparative Sociology of Violence', *Theory & Society*, Vol. 1: 415–40.

Commission of Inquiry into Abuse of Children in Queensland Institutions, 1999, *Report*, Government Printers, Brisbane.

Comte, A., 1877, *System of Positive Philosophy*, Longmans, Green, London.

Connolly, W., 1983, *The Terms of Political Discourse* (2nd edition), Princeton University Press, Princeton, NJ.

Conquest, R., 1968, *The Great Terror*, Macmillan, London.

Cook, D., 1997, *Crime, Poverty and Disadvantage*, Child Poverty Action Group, London.

Coventry, G., 1993, 'The Ascendancy of Crime and the Demise of Social Justice', *Transitions: Journal of the Youth Affairs Network of Queensland*, Vol.3, No. 3, December: 9–23.

Crawford, A., 1997, *The Local Governance of Crime*, Clarendon Press, Oxford.

Crawford, A., Kones, T., Woodhouse, T. and Young, J., 1990, *Second Islington Crime Survey*, University of Middlesex, Middlesex.

Cressey, D., 1961, Preface, in Sutherland, E. and Cressey, D., *White-Collar Crime* (2nd edition), Holt, Rhinehart & Winston, Newport, RI.

Crutchfield, R. and Pitchford, S., 1997, 'Work and Crime: The Effects of Labour Market Stratification', *Social Forces*, Vol. 76: 93–118.

Cunneen, C., 1990, 'A Study of Juvenile Detention in Australia', Report Commissioned by the National Inquiry into Racist Violence, Human Rights Commission, Sydney.

Cunneen, C., 1991, 'Law and Order and Inequality', Social Justice Collective (eds), *Inequality in Australia*, Macmillan, Melbourne.

Cunneen, C., 1994, 'Enforcing Genocide? Aboriginal Young People and the Police', in Alder, C. and White, R. (eds), *The Police and Young People*, Cambridge University Press, Melbourne.

Currie, E., 1985, *Confronting Crime: An American Challenge*, Pantheon Books, New York.

Dallaire, R., 2004, *Shake Hands with the Devil: The Failure of Humanity in Rwanda*, Carroll & Graf, New York.

Danziger, K., 1990, *Constructing the Subject: Historical Origins of Psychological Research*, Cambridge University Press, Cambridge.

Davis, M., 1992, *City of Quartz*, Verso, London.

Davis, M., 2001, *Late Victorian Genocide*, Verso, London.

Dean, M., 1990, *The Constitution of Poverty*, Routledge, London.

Dembo, R. and Schmeidler, J., 2003a, 'A Classification of High-Risk Youths', *Crime & Delinquency*, Vol. 49, No. 2: 201–30.

Dembo, R. and Schmeidler, J., 2003b, *Family Empowerment Intervention: An Innovative Service for High-Risk Youths and Their Families*, Haworth, Binghampton.

Developmental Crime Prevention Consortium, 1999, *Pathways to Prevention, Developmental and Early Intervention Approaches to Crime*, Commonwealth Attorney-General's Department, Canberra.

Devery, C., 1991, 'Disadvantage and Crime in New South Wales', New South Wales Bureau of Crime Statistics and Research, Sydney.

Devine, F., 1989, 'Privatised Families and their Homes', in Garland, A. and Crow, G. (eds), *Home and the Family: Creating the Domestic Sphere*, Macmillan, London.

Dewey, J., 1956, *Experience and Education* (1938), University of Chicago Press, Chicago, IL.

Dewey, J., 1980, *The Public and its Problems*, University of Chicago Press, Chicago, IL.

Diamond, J., 1998, *Guns, Germs and Steel,* Basic Books, New York.

Dickens, D., 1968, *Eugenics and the Progressives*, University of Kentucky, Nashville.

Dickinson, D., 1994, *Crime and Unemployment*, Department of Applied Economics, Cambridge University, Cambridge.

Dirkis, M. and Nichol, G., 1996, 'Corporate and White-Collar Crime', in Hazlehurst, K. (ed.), *Crime and Justice: An Australian Textbook in Criminology*, LBC Information Services, Melbourne.

Donaldson, M., 1991, *Time of Our Lives: Labour and Love in the Working Class*, Sydney, Allen & Unwin.

Donzelot, F., 1979, *Policing the Family*, Pantheon, New York.

Downes, D., 1966, *The Delinquent Solution*, Routledge & Kegan Paul, London.

Draper, T., 1991, *A Very Thin Line: The Iran Contra Affairs*, Hill & Wang, New York.

Dreyfus, H. and Rabinow, P., 1990, *Michel Foucault: Beyond Structuralism and Hermeneutics*, Hutchinson, London.

Dugdale, R., 1877, *The Jukes: A Study in Crime, Pauperism and Heredity*, Putnam, New York.

Dunlop, R., 1995, 'Family Processes. Towards a Theoretical Framework', in Funder, K. (ed.), *Images of Australian Families*, Longman Australia, Melbourne.

Durkheim, E., 1951, *Suicide: A Study in Sociology* (1897), Free Press, New York

Durkheim, E., 1982, *The Rules of Sociological Method* ([1894] trans. Halls, W.), Macmillan, London.

Duster, T., 1987, 'Crime, Youth Unemployment and the Black Urban Underclass', *Crime and Delinquency*, Vol.33, No. 2, April: 47–63.

Eckersley, R., 1988, *Casualties of Change: The Predicament of Young People in Australia: A Report on the Social and Psychological Problems Faced by Young People in Australia*, Commission for the Future, Carlton.

Eckersley, R., 1992, *Youth and the Challenge to Change*, Commission for the Future, Carlton.

Ellis, H., 1914, *The Criminal* (3rd edition), Walter Scott, London.

Erez, E., 1991, *Victim Impact Statements*, Australian Institute of Criminology, Canberra.

Ericson, R., Baranek, P. and Chan, J., 1991, *Representing Order, Crime, Law and Justice in the News Media*, Open University Press, Buckingham.

Erlich, I., 1975, 'The Deterrent Effect of Capital Punishment', *American Economic Review*, Vol. 65: 397–417.

Erman, M.D. and Lundamn, R., 1992, Introduction, in Erman, M.D. and Lundamn, R. (eds), *Corporate and Governmental Deviance: Problems of Organisational Behaviour in Contemporary Society*, Oxford University Press, New York.

Ermann, M. and Rabe, G., 1997, 'Organisational Processes (Not Rational Choice) Produce Most Corporate Crime', in Lofquist, W., Cohen, M. and Rabe, G. (eds), *Debating Corporate Crime*, ACVJS–Anderson, Cincinnati.

Eubank, E., 1937, 'Errors of Sociology', *Social Forces*, Vol. 16, No. 2: 178–202.

Evans, T.D., Cullen, F. and Dubeck, P.J., 1993, 'Public Perceptions of Corporate Crime', in Blankenship, M.B. (ed.), *Understanding Corporate Criminality*, Garland, New York.

Farrington, D., 1978, 'The Family Backgrounds of Aggressive Youths', in Hersov, L., Berger, M. and Schaffer, S. (eds), *Aggression and Anti-Social Behaviour in Childhood and Adolescence*, Pergamon, Oxford.

Farrington, D., 1987, 'Implications of Biological Findings for Criminological Research', in Mednick, S., Moffit, T. and Stack, A. (eds), *The Causes of Crime: New Biological Approaches*, Cambridge University Press, Cambridge.

Farrington, D., 1994, *The Influence of the Family on Delinquent Development*, in Henderson, C. (ed.), *Crime and the Family*, Family Policy Studies Centre, London.

Farrington, D., 1997, 'Human Development and Criminal Careers', in Maguire, M., Morgan, R. and Reiner, R. (eds) *The Oxford Handbook of Criminology*, Oxford University Press, Oxford.

Farrington, D., Gallagher, B., Morley, L., Ledger, R. and West, D., 1986, 'Unemployment, School Leaving and Crime', *British Journal of Sociology*, Vol. 26, No. 4: 35–51.

Fattah, A., 1997, *Criminology: Past, Present and Future: A Critical Overview*, Macmillan, London.

Fattah, E., 1993, *Towards a Critical Victimology*, Macmillan, London.

FBI, 2001, *Crime in the United States 2000*, Federal Bureau of Investigation, Washington, DC.

FBI, 2002, *Crime in the United States 2001*, Federal Bureau of Investigation, Washington, DC.

Felson, M., 1994, *Crime and Everyday Life: Insight and Implications for Society*, Pine Forge Press, San Francisco, CA.

Field, S., 1991, *Trends in Crime and Their Interpretation: A Study of Recorded Crime in Post-War England and Wales*, Home Office Research Study No. 119, HMSO, London.

Finnis, J., 2005, *Natural Law and Natural Rights*, Clarendon Press, Oxford.

FitzRoy, L., 1997, 'Women's Violence', in Bessant, J. and Cook, S. (eds), *Women and Violence*, Sage, London.

Foster, J., 1990, *Villains, Crime and Community in the Inner City*, Routledge, London.

Foucault, M., 1977, *Discipline and Punish*, Penguin, Harmondsworth.

Foucault, M., 1980, *Power/Knowledge: Selected Interviews and Other Writings, 1972–1977*, Pantheon, New York.

Foucault, M., 1981, 'Questions of Method: An Interview with Michel Foucault', *Ideology and Consciousness*, Vol. 8: 7–26.

Foucault, M., 1991, 'Governmentality', in Burchell, G., Gordon, C. and Miller, P. (eds), *The Foucault Effect: Studies in Governmentality*, Harvester-Wheatsheaf, London.

Fox, J., 1978, *Forecasting Crime Data*, Lexington Books, Lexington, KY.

Freeman, C. and Soete, L., 1994, *Work for All or Mass Unemployment*, Pinter, London.

Friedan, B., 1963, *The Feminine Mystique*, Norton, New York.

Friedrichs, D., 1996, *Trusted Criminals: White-Collar Crime in Contemporary Society*, ITP–Wadsworth, Belmont, CA.

Friedrichs, D.O. (ed.), 1998, *State Crime*, Ashgate, Aldershot, 2 vols.

Frost, N. and Stein, M., 1989, *The Politics of Child Welfare: Inequality, Power and Conflict*, Harvester-Wheatsheaf, London.

Frow, J., 1989, 'Discourse and Power', in Gane, M. (ed.), *Ideological Representation and Power in Social Relations: Literary and Social Theory*, Routledge, London.

Fuller, S., 2000, *Thomas Kuhn: A Philosophical History of Our Times*, University of Chicago Press, Chicago, IL.

Funder, K., 1995, 'Family: An Overview', in Funder, K. (ed.), *Images of Australian Families*, Institute of Family Studies, Melbourne.

Gadamer, H.-G., 1977, *Philosophical Hermeneutics* (trans. Linge, D.), University of California Press, Berkeley.

Gadamer, H.-G., 1994, *Truth and Method* (4th edition), Plenum, New York.

Garfinkel, H., 1967, *Studies in Ethnomethodology*, Prentice-Hall, Englewood Cliffs, NJ.

Garland, D., 1985, *Punishment and Welfare: A History of Penal Strategies*, Gower, Aldershot.

Garland, D., 1990, *Punishment and Modern Society: A Study in Social Theory*, Oxford University Press, Oxford.

Garland, D., 1992, 'Criminological Knowledge and its Relation to Power', *British Journal of Criminology*, Vol. 32, No. 4: 403–22.

Garland, D., 1994, 'Of Crimes and Criminals: The Development of Criminology in Britain', in Maguire, M., Morgan, R. and Reiner, R. (eds), *The Oxford Handbook of Criminology*, Clarendon Press, Oxford.

Garland, D., 1996, 'The Limits of the Sovereign State', *British Journal of Criminology*, Vol. 36, No. 4: 445–71.

Garland, D., 1997, 'Of Crimes and Criminals: The Development of Criminology in Britain', in Maguire, M., Morgan, R. and Reiner, R. (eds), *The Oxford Handbook of Criminology* (2nd edition), Oxford University Press, Oxford.

Garland, D., 2001, *The Culture of Control*, Cambridge University Press, Cambridge.

Garratty, J., 1984, *Unemployment in History*, Harper & Row, New York.

Geertz, C., 1974, *The Interpretation of Culture*, Hutchinson, London.

Gellately, R., 2002, *Backing Hitler: Consent and Coercion in Nazi Germany*, Oxford University Press, Oxford.

Gelsthorpe, L., 1989, *Sexism and the Female Offender: An Organisational Analysis*, Gower, Aldershot.

Genn, H., 1988, 'Multiple Victimisation', in Maguire, M. and Pointing, J. (eds), *Victims of Crime: A New Deal?*, Open University, Milton Keynes.

Giddens, A., 1984, *The Constitution of Society*, Polity Press, Cambridge.

Giddens, A., 1990, *The Consequences of Modernity*, Polity Press, Cambridge.

Giddens, A., 1999, *Runaway World: How Globalisation Is Reshaping Our Lives*, Profile Books, London.

Gill, A., 1998, *Orphans of the Empire*, Vintage, Sydney.

Gilling, D., 1997, *Crime Prevention: Theory, Policy and Politics*, UCL Press, London.

Gluckmann, M., 1976, *Structuralist Thought in Contemporary Social Theory*, Routledge & Kegan Paul, London.

Glueck, S. and Glueck, E., 1950, *Unravelling Juvenile Delinquency*, Harper & Row, New York.

Goffman, E., 1959, *The Presentation of Self in Everyday Life*, Anchor Books, New York.

Goffman, E., 1968a, *Asylums*, Penguin, Harmondsworth.

Goffman, E., 1968b, *Stigma*, Penguin, Harmondsworth.

Goodall, H., 1990, 'Saving the Children: Gender and the Colonisation of Aboriginal Children in NSW, 1788 to 1900', *Aboriginal Law Bulletin*, Vol.2, No. 44, June: 6–9.

Goode, W.J. and Hatt, P., 1952, *Methods in Social Research*, McGraw-Hill, New York.

Goodwin, D., 1996, *No Ordinary Time*, Simon & Schuster, New York.

Goring, C., 1913, *The English Convict: A Statistical Study*, HMSO, London.

Gottfredson, M. and Hirschi, T., 1990, *A General Theory of Crime*, Stanford University Press, Stanford, CA.

Gould, S.J., 1989, *The Mismeasure of Man*, Penguin, Harmondsworth.

Gouldner, A., 1971, *The Coming Crisis of Western Sociology*, Avon, New York.

Grabosky, P., 1989, *Wayward Governance*, Community Relations Council, Canberra.

Grabosky, P. and Braithwaite, J., 1986, *Of Matters Gentle: Enforcement Strategies of Australian Business Regulatory Agencies*, Oxford University Press, Melbourne.

Grabosky, P. and James, M. (eds), 1995, *The Promise of Crime Prevention: Leading Crime Prevention Programs*, Australian Institute of Criminology, Canberra.

Grabosky, P. and Sutton, A. (eds), 1989 (eds), *Stains on a White Collar: Fourteen Studies in Corporate Crime or Corporate Harm*, Hutchinson, Sydney.

Graham, J. and Bowling, B., 1996, *Young People and Crime*, Home Office Research Unit, London.

Graham, L., 1977, 'Science and Values: The Eugenics Movement in Germany and Russia in the 1920s', *American Historical Review*, Vol. 82: 1133–64.

Green, P. and Ward, T., 2004, *State Crime: Governments, Violence and Corruption*, Pluto Press, London.

Greenberg, D., 1977, 'The Dynamics of Oscillatory Punishment Processes', *Journal of Criminal Law and Criminology*, Vol. 68: 643–51.

Greenblatt, S., 1992, *Marvellous Possessions*, Clarendon Press, Oxford.

Greer, G., 1967, *The Female Eunuch*, Angus & Robertson, Sydney.

Grieve, N. and Burns, A. (eds), 1994, *Australian Women's Contemporary Feminist Thought*, Oxford University Press, Melbourne.

Griffin, C., 1993, *Representations of Youth*, Polity Press, Cambridge.

Grover, C. and Soothill, K., 1996, 'A Murderous "Underclass"? The Press Reporting of Sexually Motivated Murder', *Sociological Review*, Vol. 4, No. 3, August: 398–415.

Haan, W. de, 1990, *The Politics of Redress: Crime, Punishment and the Penal Abolition*, Unwin-Hyman, Boston, MA.

Habermas, J., 1983, 'Modernity – An Unfinished Project', in Foster, H. (ed.), *The Anti-Aesthetic*, Bay Press, Batsford.

Hacking, I., 1983, *Representing and Intervening*, Cambridge University Press, Cambridge.

Hacking, I., 1990, *The Taming of Chance*, Cambridge University Press, Cambridge.

Hacking, I., 2000, *The Social Construction of What?*, Harvard University Press, Cambridge, MA.

Hagedorn, J., 1990, 'Back in the Field Again: Gang Research in the 1990s', in Huff, C. (ed.), *Gangs in America*, Sage, Newbury Park, CA.

Haggerty, R., Sherrod, L., Garmezy, J. and Rutter, M., 1996, *Stress, Risk and Resilience in Children and Adolescents*, Cambridge University Press, New York.

Hale, C. and Sabbagh, D., 1991, 'Testing the Relationship between Unemployment and Crime: A Methodological Comment on Empirical Analysis Using Time Series Data from England and Wales', *Journal of Research and Crime and Delinquency*, Vol. 28: 400–17.

Hall, S., 1974, 'Deviance, Politics and the Media', in Rock, P., and McIntosh, M. (eds), *Deviance and Social Control*, Tavistock, London.

Hall, S. and Jacques, M. (eds), 1989, *New Times: The Changing Face of Politics in the 1990s*, Lawrence & Wishart, London.

Hall, S. and Jefferson, T. (eds), 1976, *Resistance Through Rituals*, Hutchinson, London.

Halliday, M.A.K., 1978, *Language as Social Semiotic*, Edward Arnold, London.

Hammersley, M., Ramazanoglu, C. and Gelsthorpe, L., 1992, 'Debate: Feminist Methodology, Reason and Empowerment', *Sociology*, Vol. 26, No. 2: 187–218.

Hartley, R. and Wolcott, I., 1994, *The Position of Young People in Relation to the Family*, National Clearing House for Youth Studies, Hobart.

Harvey, D., 1990, *The Condition of Postmodernity*, Blackwell, Oxford.

Hayner, P., 2001, *Unspeakable Crimes: Confronting State Terror and Atrocity*, Routledge, London.

Hazlehurst, K. (ed.), 1996, *Crime and Justice: An Australian Textbook in Criminology*, Law Book Co., Sydney.

Healy, W.J., 1915, *The Individual Delinquent*, University of Chicago Press, Chicago.

Heidensohn, F., 1986, *Women and Crime*, Macmillan, London.

Heidensohn, F., 1989, *Crime and Society*, Macmillan, London.

Hempel, C., 1965, 'The Function of General Laws in History', in Hempel, C., *Aspects of Scientific Explanation* (1942), Free Press, New York.

Hempel, C., 1966, *Philosophy of Natural Science*, Prentice-Hall, Englewood Cliffs, NJ.

Henry, S., 1985, Book Review, *British Journal of Criminology*, Vol. 25, No. 1: 70–3.

Henry, S. and Milovanovic, D., 1991, 'Constitutive Criminology: The Maturation of Critical Criminology', *Criminology*, Vol. 29: 293–315.

Henry, S., and Milovanovic, D., 1994, 'The Constitution of Constitutive Criminology: A Postmodern Approach to Criminological Theory', in Nelken, D. (ed.), *The Futures of Criminology*, Sage, London.

Hil, R. and McMahon, A., 1995, 'In the Shadows: The Silence and Silenced Family in Juvenile Justice Research', *Children Australia*, Vol. 20, No. 4: 4–8.

Hil, R. and McMahon, T., 2004, *Families and Juvenile Crime*, Peter Lang, New York.

Hil, R., McMahon, T. and Buckley, A., 1996, *Another Hole in the Wall: A Progress Report on a Study of Young People, Crime and Families in North Queensland*, Youth Research Centre, Melbourne.

Hirschi, T., 1969, *Causes of Delinquency*, University of California Press, Berkeley.

Hirschi, T. and Gottfredson, M., 1987, 'Causes of White-Collar Crime', *Criminology*, Vol. 25: 949–74.

Hitchens, C., 1989, *Prepared for the Worst: Selected Essays and Minority Reports*, Chatto & Windus, London.

Hoare, J. and Robb, P., 2006, *Crime in England and Wales Update to June 2006, Home Office Statistical Bulletin 16/06*, online: www.homeoffice.gov.uk/ids.

Hobsbawm, E., 1975, *The Age of Revolution, 1815–1848*, Collins, London.

Hogg, R. and Brown, D., 1998, *Rethinking Law and Order*, Pluto Press, Armadale.

Holman, B., 1995, *Children and Crime*, Lion Press, Oxford.

Holton, G., 1988, *Thematic Origins of Scientific Thought: Kepler to Einstein* (2nd edition), Harvard University Press, Cambridge, MA.

Home Office, 2002, *Justice for All*, Cmd 5563, Home Office, London.

Hood, R. and Sparks, R., 1971, *Key Issues in Criminology*, Hutchinson, London.

Hudson, B., 1984, 'Femininity and Adolescence', in McRobbie, A. and Nava, M. (eds), *Gender and Generation*, Macmillan, London.

Hudson, B., 1987, *Justice Through Punishment*, Routledge & Kegan Paul, London.

Hudson, B., 1993, *Penal Policy and Social Justice*, Macmillan, London.

Hughes, G., 1998, *Understanding Crime Prevention: Social Control, Risk and Late Modernity*, Buckingham: Open University Press.

Human Rights and Equal Opportunity Commission, 1997, *Bringing Them Home: The 'Stolen Children' Enquiry*, Human Rights and Equal Opportunity Commission, Sydney.

Hume, L.J., 1981, *Bentham and Bureaucracy*, Cambridge University Press, Cambridge.

Humphreys, M., 1994, *Empty Cradles*, Doubleday, London.

Hunt, A., 1991, 'Postmodernism and Critical Criminology', in MacLean, B. and Milovanovic, D. (eds), *New Directions in Critical Criminology*, Collective Press, Vancouver.

Hunt, A., 1999, *Governing Morals: A Social History of Moral Regulation*, Cambridge University Press, Cambridge.

Hunter, I., 1994, *The Rise of the School*, Allen & Unwin, Sydney.

Husserl, E., 1981, *The Coming Crisis of European Science*, North Western University, Urbana, IL.

Hyman, H.H., 1955, *Survey Design and Analysis*, Free Press, Glencoe, IL.

International Centre for the Prevention of Crime, 1997, *Worldwide Best Practice in Crime Prevention*, online: www.crime-prevention-int.org.

Israel, M., 2000, 'The Commercialisation of Australian University-Based Criminology', *Australian and New Zealand Journal of Criminology*, Vol. 33, No. 1: 1–20.

Jackson, J., 2003, 'Justice for All: Putting Victims at the Heart of Criminal Justice?', *Journal of Law and Society*, Vol. 30, No. 2: 309–26.

Jacobs, J., 1962, *The Life and Death of Great American Cities*, Vintage Books, New York.

Jacoby, R., 1974, *Social Amnesia*, Basic Books, New York.

James, W., 1994, *Pragmatism* (1906), Dover, New York.

Jamieson, K., 1994, *The Organization of Corporate Crime: Dynamics of Antitrust Violation*, Sage, Thousand Oaks, CA.

Jamieson, R., 1998, 'Towards a Criminology of War in Europe', in Ruggiero, V., South, N. and Taylor, I. (eds), *The New European Criminology: Crime and Social Order in Europe*, Routledge, London.

Jankovic, I., 1977, 'Labour Markets and Imprisonment', *Crime and Social Justice*, Vol. 9: 17–31.

Jeffrey, C., 1972, 'The Historical Development of Criminology', in Mannheim, H. (ed.), *Pioneers in Criminology* (2nd edition), Patterson Smith, Montclair, NJ.

Jeffs, T. and Smith, M., 1990, 'Demography, Location and Young People', in Jeffs, T. and Smith, M. (eds), *Young People Inequality and Youth Crime*, Macmillan, London.

Jones, H., 1965, *Crime and the Penal System*, University Tutorial Press, London.

Kafka, M., 2003, 'Sex Offending and Sexual Appetite: The Clinical and Theoretical Relevance of Hypersexual Desire', *International Journal of Offender Therapy and Comparative Criminology*, Vol. 47, No. 4: 439–51.

Kamin, L.J., 1974, *The Science and Politics of IQ*, Penguin, Harmondsworth.

Kang, C., 2002, 'Crony Capitalism: Corruption and Development in a Culture of Denial', *Australian and New Zealand Journal of Criminology*, Vol. 26: 97–115.

Karmen, A., 1990, *Crime Victims: An Introduction to Victimology*, Brooks–Cole, Pacific Grove, CA.

Katz, C., 2003, 'Issues in the Production and Dissemination of Gang Statistics: An Ethnographic Study of a Large Midwestern Police Gang Unit', *Crime & Delinquency*, Vol. 49, No. 3: 485–516.

Katz, J., 1988, *Seductions of Crime: Moral and Sensual Attractions of Doing Evil*, Basic Books, New York.

Kevles, D., 1985, *In the Name of Eugenics*, University of California Press, Berkeley.

Kidd, R., 1997, *The Way We Civilise*, University of Queensland Press, Brisbane.

Kinsey, A., 1948, *The Sexual Behavior of the Human Male*, Saunders & Co., Boston, MA.

Klamer, A. and Leonard, T., 1994, 'So What's an Economic Metaphor?', in Mirowski, P. (ed.), *Natural Images in Economic Thought: Markets Read in Tooth and Claw*, Cambridge University Press, New York.

Kracaeur, J., 2003, *Under the Banner of God*, Doubleday, New York.

Krieken, R. van, 1998, 'The Stolen Generations: On the Removal of Australian Indigenous Children from Their Families and Its Implications for the Sociology of Childhood', paper delivered at the ISA Congress, July, Montreal.

Kuhn, T.S., 1970, *The Origins of Scientific Revolutions* (2nd edition), University of Chicago Press, Chicago, IL.

Lakoff, G. and Johnson, M., 2003, *Metaphors We Live By* (2nd edition), University of Chicago Press, Chicago, IL.

Laub, J. and Sampson, R., 1988, 'Unraveling Families and Delinquency: A Re-Analysis of the Gluecks' Data', *Criminology*, Vol. 26, No. 3: 355–79.

Lauretis, T. de, 1989, 'The Violence of Rhetoric: Considerations on Gender and Representation', in Armstrong, N. and Tennenhouse, L. (eds), *The Violence of Representation: Literature and the Violence of Literature*, Routledge, London.

Lee, M., 1999, 'The Fear of Crime and Self-Governance: Towards a Genealogy', *Australian and New Zealand Journal of Criminology*, Vol. 32, No. 3: 227–46.

Leflore, L., 1988, 'Delinquent Youths and Family', *Adolescence*, Vol. 23, No. 91: 47–59.

Lemert, E., 1951, *Social Pathology*, McGraw-Hill, New York.

Levi, M., 1994, 'Violent Crime', in Maguire, M., Morgan, R. and Reiner, R. (eds), *The Oxford Handbook of Criminology*, Oxford University Press, Oxford.

Levi, P., 1993, *Survival in Auschwitz* (1947), Collier, New York.

Leys, S., 1999, *The Angel & The Octopus: Collected Essays 1983–1998*, Duffy & Snellgrove, Sydney.

Little, D., 1991, *Varieties of Social Explanation*, Westview Press, Boulder, CO.

Loader, I. and Sparks, R., 1993, 'Ask the Experts', *Times Higher Education Supplement*, 16 April.

Loeber, R. and Stouthamer-Loeber, M., 1986, 'Family Factors as Predictors of Juvenile Conduct Problems and Delinquency', in Tonry, M. and Morris, N. (eds), *Crime and Justice*, University of Chicago Press, Chicago, IL.

Lombroso, C., 1911, *Criminal Man: According to the Classification of Cesare Lombroso* (1876), Putnam, New York.

Lovry, G., 1994, 'The Family as a Context for Delinquency Prevention', in Wilson, J.Q. and Lowry, G. (eds), *Families, Schools and Delinquency Prevention*, Springer-Verlag, New York.

Lupton, D., 1999, *Risk*, Routledge, London.

Lynn, P. and Elliott, D., 2000, *The British Crime Survey: A Review of Methodology*, National Centre for Social Research, London.

McBarnett, D., 1991, 'Whiter than White Collar: Tax Fraud, Insurance and the Management of Stigma', *British Journal of Sociology*, Vol. 42: 323–44.

McCallum, D., 1990, *The Social Production of Merit*, Falmer Press, London.

McCloskey, D., 1998, *The Rhetoric of Economics* (2nd edition), University of Chicago Press, Chicago, IL.

McFarland-Icke, B., 1999, *Nurses in Nazi Germany*, Yale University Press, New Haven.

Macfarlane, L., 1974, *Violence and the State*, Nelson, London.

McGahey, C., 1976, *Deviant Behavior: Conflict and Interest Groups*, Macmillan, New York.

MacIntyre, A., 1988, *Whose Justice? Which Rationality?*, Duckworth, London.

McKenna, K., 1999, 'The Brain Is the Master Organ in Sexual Function: Central Nervous System Control of Male and Female Functions', *International Journal of Impotence Research*, Vol. 11, Supplement: 48–55.

McLaren, P., 1995, *Critical Pedagogy and Predatory Culture*, Routledge, London.

McLaughlin, E., 2001, 'Political Violence, Terrorism and States of Fear', in Muncie, J. and Mclaughlin, E. (eds), *The Problem of Crime* (2nd edition), Sage–Open University, London.

Macnicol, J., 1987, 'In pursuit of the underclass', *Journal of Social Policy,* No. 16: 293–318.

McRobbie, A., 1991, *Feminism and Youth Culture*, Macmillan, London.

Maguire, M., 1994, 'Crime Statistics, Patterns and Trends', in Maguire, M., Morgan, R. and Reiner, R. (eds), *The Oxford Handbook of Criminology*, Oxford University Press, Oxford.

Maguire, M., 1997, 'Crime Statistics, Patterns and Trends', in Maguire, M., Morgan, R. and Reiner, R. (eds), *The Oxford Handbook of Criminology* (2nd edition), Oxford University Press, Oxford.

Maguire, M., 2002, 'Crime Statistics, Patterns and Trends', in Maguire, M., Morgan, R. and Reiner, R. (eds), *The Oxford Handbook of Criminology* (3rd edition), Oxford University Press, Oxford.

Maguire, M., Morgan, R. and Reiner, R. (eds), 1994, *The Oxford Handbook of Criminology*, Oxford University Press, Oxford.

Maguire, M., Morgan, R. and Reiner, R. (eds), 1997, *The Oxford Handbook of Criminology* (2nd edition), Oxford University Press, Oxford.

Maguire, M., Morgan, R. and Reiner, R. (eds), 2002, *The Oxford Handbook of Criminology* (3rd edition), Oxford University Press, Oxford.

Manent, P., 1996, *An Intellectual History of Liberalism* (trans. Balinski, R.), Princeton University Press, Princeton, NJ.

Manent, P., 1998, *The City of Man* (trans. LePain, M.), Princeton University Press, Princeton, NJ.

Mann, K. and Roseneil, S., 1994, '"Some Mothers Do Have 'Em": Backlash and the Gender Politics of the Underclass Debate', *Journal of Gender Studies*, Vol. 3, No. 3: 317–31.

Manne, R., 2002, *The Stolen Generations*, Quarterly Essay, Melbourne.

Mannheim, H., 1955, *Group Problems in Crime and Punishment*, Routledge & Kegan Paul, London.

Mannheim, H., 1957, 'Report on the Teaching of Criminology in the United Kingdom', in UNESCO, *The University Teaching of Social Science: Criminology*, UNESCO, Lausanne.

Mannheim, H. (ed.), 1960, *Pioneers in Criminology*, Stevens, London.

Mannheim, H., 1965, *Comparative Criminology*, Routledge & Kegan Paul, London.

Markus, A., 1990, *Governing Savages*, Allen & Unwin, Sydney.

Martin, H. and Schuman, H., 1997, *The Global Trap: Globalisation and the Assault on Democracy and Prosperity*, Pluto Press, Armadale.

Marvin, W., Sellin, T. and Figlio, R., 1972, *Delinquency in a Birth Cohort*, University of Chicago Press, Chicago, IL.

Mason, B., 1996, 'From Shamans to Shaming: A History of Criminological Thought', in Hazlehurst, K. (ed.), *Crime and Justice: An Australian Textbook in Criminology*, Law Book Co., Sydney.

Mathers, C. and Schofield, D., 1998, 'The Health Consequences of Unemployment: Evidence', *Medical Journal of Australia*, Vol. 168: 178–82.

Matza, D., 1960, *Becoming Deviant*, Prentice-Hall, Englewood Cliffs, NJ.

Medvedev, R., 1989, *Let History Judge: The Origins and Consequences of Stalinism*, Harper & Row, New York.

Mendelsohn, B., 1974, *Victimology*, D.C. Heath, Lexington, KY.

Merton, R.K., 1969a, 'Social Structure and Anomie' (1938), in Cressey, D. and Ward, M. (eds), *Delinquency, Crime and Social Process*, Harper & Row, New York.

Merton, R.K., 1969b, *On Theoretical Sociology*, Free Press, New York.

Messner, S. and Rosenffeld, R., 1997, *Crime and the American Dream* (2nd edition), Wadsworth, Belmont, CA.

Mestrovic, S., 1997, *Anthony Giddens: The Last Modernist*, Routledge, London.

Michael, J. and Adler, M., 1933, *Crime, Law and Social Science*, Patterson Smith, Montclair, CA.

Midgley, M., 2001, *Wickedness: A Philosophical Essay* (2nd edition), Routledge, London.

Miller, N., 1992, *Stealing from America*, Paragon House, New York.

Miller, P. and Rose, N., 1990, 'Governing Economic Life', *Economy and Society*, Vol. 19:1–31.

Miller, W.I., 1993, *Humiliation and Other Essays on Honor, Social Discomfort and Violence*, Cornell University Press, Ithaca, NY.

Millett, K., 1971, *Sexual Politics*, Sphere, London.

Mills, C. Wright, 1963, *The Sociological Imagination* (2nd edition), Oxford University Press, New York.

Mirlees-Black, C., 1999, *Domestic Violence: Findings from a New British Crime Self-Completion Survey*, Home Office Research Study 191, Home Office, London.

Mishra, R., 1984, *The Crisis of the Welfare State*, Harvester-Wheatsheaf, Brighton.

Morgan, P., 1978, *Delinquent Fantasies*, Temple Smith, London.

Moser, C.A., 1958, *Methods in Survey Research*, Duckworth, London.

Mukherjee, S., 1996, 'Measuring Crime: The Magnitude of the Crime Problem', in Hazlehurst, K. (ed.), *Crime and Justice: An Australian Textbook in Criminology*, Law Book Co., Sydney.

Muncie, J., 1998, 'Reassessing Competing Paradigms in Criminological Theory', in Walton, P. and Young, J. (eds), *The New Criminology Revisited*, Macmillan, London.

Murray, C., 1990, *The Emerging British Underclass*, Institute of Economic Affairs Health and Welfare Unit, London.

Murray, C., 1994, *Underclass: The Crisis Deepens*, London, Institute of Economic Affairs Health and Welfare Unit, London.

Myrtle, R., 1991, *Violence in Australia: An Annotated Bibliography*, Australian Institute of Criminology, Canberra.

Naffine, N., 1997, *Feminism and Criminology*, Polity Press, Oxford.

National Council for the International Year of the Family, 1994, *Creating the Links: Families and Social Responsibility*, AGPS, Canberra.

Nelken, D., 1994a, 'White-Collar Crime', in Maguire, M., Morgan, R. and Reiner, R. (eds) *The Oxford Handbook of Criminology*, Oxford University Press, Oxford.

Nelken, D., 1994b, 'Introduction', in Nelken, D. (ed.), *White-Collar Crime,* Dartmouth, Sydney.

Nelken, D., 1997, 'White-Collar Crime', in Maguire, M., Morgan, R. and Reiner, R. (eds), *The Oxford Handbook of Criminology* (2nd edition), Oxford University Press, Oxford.

Nelson, J., Megill, A. and McCloskey, D. (eds), 1991, *The Rhetoric of the Human Sciences*, University of Wisconsin Press, Madison.

Newburn, T., 2003, 'The Future of Policing', in Newburn, T. (ed.), *The Handbook of Policing*, Willan, Cullompton.

Newman, O., 1972, *Defensible Space: People and Design in the Violent City*, Architectural Press, London.

Nietzsche, F., 1956, *The Genealogy of Morals* (trans. Kaufman, W.), Vintage, New York.

Nino, C., 1996, *Radical Evil on Trial*, Yale University Press, New Haven, CT.

Nisbet, R., 1974, *The Sociological Tradition*, Open University, Milton Keynes.

Novak, M., 1994, 'Beyond the Welfare State', *IPA Review*, April–May.

Nussbaum, M., 2001, *The Fragility of Goodness* (2nd edition), Cambridge University Press, Cambridge.

O'Connor, I., 1992, *Youth, Crime and Justice in Queensland*, Criminal Justice Commission, Brisbane.

O'Grady, C., 1992, 'A Rising Star in the Prosecution of Juveniles in Victoria', *Youth Studies Australia*, Vol. 11, No. 4 :13–27.

O'Malley, P., 1992, 'Risk, Power and Crime Prevention', *Economy and Society*, Vol. 21, No. 3: 252–75.

O'Malley, P., 1996, 'Post-Social Criminologies: Some Implications of Current Political Trends for Criminology Theory and Practice', *Current Issues in Criminal Justice*, Vol. 8, No. 1: 68–81.

O'Malley, P., 1997, 'The Politics of Crime Prevention', in O'Malley, P. and Sutton, A. (eds), *Crime Prevention in Australia: Issues in Policy and Research*, Federation Press, Sydney.

Osborne, D. and Gaebler, T., 1993, *Reinventing Government: How the Entrepreneurial Spirit Is Transforming the Public Sector*, Plume Publications, New York.

Painter, K., 1991, *Wife Rape, Marriage and the Law: A Survey Report*, Faculty of Social Science, Manchester University Press, Manchester.

Palmer, B., 1990, *Descent into Discourse: The Reification of Language and the Writing of Social History*, Temple University Press, Philadelphia, PA.

Palmer, G., 1997, *Reluctant Refugee: Unaccompanied Refugee and Evacuee Children, 1933–45*, Simon & Schuster, Sydney.

Park, R., 1915, 'The City: Suggestions for the Investigation of Human Behavior in the City', *American Journal of Sociology*, Vol. 20, No. 5: 577–612.

Parr, J., 1980, *Laboring Children: British Immigrant Apprentices to Canada, 1869–1924*, University of Toronto Press, Toronto.

Parsons, T., 1971, *The System of Modern Societies*, Prentice-Hall, Englewood Cliffs, NJ.

Parton, N., 1991, *Governing the Family: Childcare, Child Protection and the State*, Macmillan, London.

Pascal, B., 1962, *Pensées*, Editions du Seuil, Paris.

Paul, D., 1998, *The Politics of Heredity*, SUNY Press, New York.

Pavlich, G., 2000, *Critique and Radical Discourses on Crime*, Ashgate, London.

Payne, J. and Payne, C., 1994, 'Recession, Restructuring and the Fate of the Unemployed: Evidence of the Underclass Debate', *Sociology*, Vol. 28, No.1, February: 1–20.

Pearce, F., 1976, *Crimes of the Powerful: Marxism, Crime and Deviance*, Pluto Press, London.

Pearce, F. and Tombs, S., 1991, 'Policing Corporate Skid Rows: A Reply to Keith Hawkins', *British Journal of Criminology*, Vol. 31, No. 4: 415–26.

Pearson, G., 1975, *The Deviant Imagination*, Macmillan, London.

Pease, K., 1997, 'Crime Prevention', in Maguire, M., Morgan, R. and Reiner, R. (eds), *The Oxford Handbook of Criminology* (2nd edition), Oxford University Press, Oxford.

Pepinsky, H., 1997, 'Crime, Criticism, Compassion and Community', *The Critical Criminologist*, Vol. 7, No. 3.

Perelman, C. and Olbrecchts-Tyteca, M., 1969, *The New Rhetoric*, D. Reidel, Dordrecht.

Pfohl, S., 1985, *Images of Deviance and Social Control*, McGraw-Hill, New York.

Piotrowicz, R. and Kaye, S., 2000, *Human Rights: International and Australian Law*, Butterworths, Sydney.

Polk, K., 1993, 'Reflections on Youth Subcultures', in White, R. (ed.), *Youth Subcultures: Theory, History and the Australian Experience*, National Clearing House for Youth Studies, Hobart.

Polk, K., 1994, *Why Men Kill: Scenarios of Masculine Violence*, Cambridge University Press, Cambridge.

Polk, K. and Tait, D., 1990, 'Changing Youth Labour Markets and Youth Life Styles', *Youth Studies*, Vol. 9, No. 1, February.

Popper, K., 1974, *Conjectures and Refutations*, Routledge & Kegan Paul, London.

Potas, I., Vining, J. and Wilson, P. (eds), 1990, *Young People and Crime: Costs and Prevention*, Australian Institute of Criminology, Canberra.

Proctor, R., 1988, *Race Hygiene: Medicine Under the Nazis*, Harvard University Press, Cambridge, MA.

Punch, M., 1996, *Dirty Business: Exploring Corporate Misconduct*, Sage, London.

Queensland Criminal Justice Commission, 1992, *Youth, Crime and Justice in Queensland*, Queensland Criminal Justice Commission, Brisbane.

Quételet, A., 1842, *A Treatise on Man* (trans. Knox, R. and Smibert, T.), Chambers, Edinburgh, online: www.cimm.jcu.edu.au/hist/stats.quet/qbkfour5.htm.

Quinney, R., 1974, *Criminal Justice in America*, Little, Brown, Boston, MA.

Quinney, R., 1979, *Criminology*, Little, Brown, Boston, MA.

Radzinowicz, L., 1966, *Ideology and Crime*, Stevens, London.

Ralston Saul, J., 1997, *The Unconscious Civilisation*, Penguin, Ringwood.

Rankin, J.H., 1983, 'The Family Context of Delinquency', *Social Problems*, Vol. 30, No. 4: 34–48.

Rawnsley, J., 1994, *Going for Broke: Nick Leeson and the Collapse of Barings Bank*, Harper-Collins, London.

Read, P., 1982, *The Stolen Generations: The Removal of Aboriginal Children in NSW 1883–1969*, NSW Department of Aboriginal Affairs, Sydney.

Read, P., 1984, *The Stolen Generations*, University of Queensland Press, Brisbane.

Read, P. and Edwards, A. (eds), 1989, *The Lost Children*, Doubleday, Sydney.

Regoli, R.M. and Hewitt, J., 1991, *Delinquency and Society: A Child-Centered Approach*, McGraw-Hill, New York.

Reiman, J., 1989, 'A Radical Perspective on Deviance', in Kelly, D.H. (ed.), *Deviant Behavior: A Text Reader in the Sociology of Deviance*, Plenum, New York.

Reiman, J., 2001, *The Rich Get Richer and the Poor Get Prison* (6th edition), Allyn & Bacon, Boston, MA.

Rhoads, J.K., 1991, *Critical Issues in Social Theory*, Pennsylvania State University Press, Philadelphia, PA.

Rieff, P., 1978, *The Triumph of the Therapeutic: Uses of Faith After Freud*, Penguin, Harmondsworth.

Ristow, W. and Shallice, T., 1976, 'Taking the Hood Off British Torture', *New Scientist*, Vol. 71, Nos. 10–12: 271–3.

Roach-Anlue, S., 1991, *Deviance, Conformity and Social Control*, Longman, Melbourne.

Roach-Anlue, S., 1996, *Deviance, Conformity and Social Control* (2nd edition), Addison Wesley Longman, Melbourne.

Roach-Anleu, S., 1998, *Deviance, Control and Conformity* (3rd edition), Allen and Unwin, Sydney.

Robertson, G., 1999, *Crimes Against Humanity*, Penguin, London.

Robertson, R., 1992, *Globalisation*, Sage, London.

Rock, P., 1973, *Deviant Behaviour*, Hutchinson, London.

Rock, P. (ed.), 1988, *A History of British Criminology*, Oxford University Press, Oxford.

Rock, P., 1994, 'The Social Organisation of British Criminology', in Maguire, M., Morgan, R. and Reiner, R. (eds), *The Oxford Handbook of Criminology*, Oxford University Press, Oxford.

Roe, M., 1984, *Nine Australian Progressives: Vitalism in Bourgeois Social Thought 1890–1960*, University of Queensland Press, Brisbane.

Rorty, R., 1979, *Philosophy and the Mirror of Nature*, Princeton University Press, Princeton, NJ.

Rorty, R., 1999, *Philosophy and Social Hope*, Penguin, Harmondsworth.

Rose, N., 1990, *Governing the Soul: The Shaping of the Private Self*, Routledge, London.

Rose, N., 2000, *Powers of Freedom: Reframing Political Thought*, Cambridge University Press, Cambridge.

Roseman, M., 2002, *The Villa, the Lake, the Meeting: Wannsee and the Final Solution*, Penguin, London.

Ross, J.I. (ed.), 1995, *Controlling State Crime*, Garland, New York.

Royal Commission, 1978, *Report of the Royal Commission into New South Wales Prisons* (Justice J. F. Nagle, Royal Commissioner), Government Printer, Sydney (NSW Parliamentary Papers 1976–77–78, No. 322).

Rubington, E. and Weinberg, M. (eds), 1968, *Deviance: The Interactionist Perspective*, Macmillan, London.

Rubinstein, W., 2004, *Genocide*, Pearson Longman, Harlow.

Ruggiero, V., 2000, *Organized and Corporate Crime*, Dartmouth, Ashgate.

Rummel, R., 1994, *Death by Government*, Transaction Press, New Brunswick, NJ.

Rusche, G. and Kirschheimer, K.R., 1939, *Punishment and Social Structure*, Russell & Russell, New York.

Rutter, M., 1972, *Maternal Deprivation Reassessed*, Penguin, Harmondsworth.

Rutter, M. and Giller, H. (1983), *Juvenile Delinquency: Trends and Perspectives*, Penguin, Harmondsworth.

Sack, F., 1994, 'Conflicts and Convergences of Theoretical and Methodological Perspectives in Criminology', in Ewald, U. (ed.), *New Definitions of Crime in Societies in Transition to Democracy*, Forum Verlag Godesberg, Bonn.

Scarry, E., 1985, *The Body in Pain*, Harper & Row, New York.

Scheper-Hughes, N. and Wacqant, L. (eds), 2002, *Commodifying Bodies*, Sage, London.

Schneewind, J.B., 1998, *The Invention of Moral Autonomy*, Cambridge University Press, New York.

Schon, D., 1980, 'Generative Metaphor: A Perspective on Problem-Setting in Social Policy', in Ortony, A. (ed.), *Metaphor and Thought*, Cambridge University Press, Cambridge.

Schur, E., 1974, *Crimes Without Victims: Deviant behaviour* (2nd edition), Prentice Hall, New York.

Schutz, A., 1972, *The Phenomenology of the Social World* (1932), Heinemann, London.

Schutz, A., 1986, *The Correspondence of Alfred Schutz and Aron Gurwisch*, University of Indiana Press, Bloomington.

Schwartz, M., 1997, 'Does Critical Crime Have a Core or Just Splinters?', *The Critical Criminologist*, Vol. 7, No. 3.

Schwartz, M. and Friedrichs, D., 1994, 'Postmodern Thought and Criminological Discontent: New Metaphors for Understanding Violence', *Criminology*, Vol. 32, No. 2: 221–46.

Schwendinger, H. and Schwendinger, J., 1975, 'Defenders of Order or Guardians of Human Rights?', in Taylor, I., Walton, P. and Young, J. (eds), *Critical Criminology*, Routledge & Kegan Paul, London.

Sen, A., 1981, *Poverty and Famines: An Essay on Entitlement and Deprivation*, Oxford University Press, Oxford.

Sercombe, H., 1995, 'The Face of the Criminal Is Aboriginal: Representations of Aboriginal Young People in the *West Australian* Newspaper', in Bessant, J., Carrington, K. and Cook, S. (eds), *Cultures of Crime and Violence: The Australian Experience*, La Trobe University Press, Melbourne.

Sereny, G., 1997, *Albert Speer: His Battle for the Truth*, Viking, New York.

Seyd, P., 1987, *The Rise and Fall of the Labour Left*, Macmillan, London.

Shapiro, S.P., 1990, 'Collaring the Crime, Not the Criminal: Reconsidering the Concept of White-Collar Crime', *American Sociological Review*, Vol. 55, No. 3: 346–65.

Shaw, C. and McKay, H., 1942, *Juvenile Delinquency in Urban Areas*, University of Chicago Press, Chicago, IL.

Schur, E., 1974, *Radical Non-Intervention*, Harper & Row, New York.

Sherman, L. and Glick, B., 1984, *The Quality of Police Arrest Statistics*, Police Foundation, Washington, DC.

Shihadeh, E. and Ousey, G., 1998, 'Industrial Restructuring and Violence: The Link between Entry-Level Jobs, Economic Deprivation and White Homicide', *Social Forces*, Vol. 77: 185–206.

Shover, N., 1998, 'White-Collar Crime', in Tonry, M. (ed.), *The Handbook of Crime and Punishment*, Oxford University Press, New York.

Shover, N. and Bryant, K., 1993, 'Theoretical Explanations of Corporate Crime', in Blankenship, M.B. (ed.), *Understanding Corporate Criminality*, Garland, New York.

Silbey, D., 1996, *Geographies of Exclusion*, Routledge, London.

Simmons, J. and Dodd, T. (eds), 2002, *Crime in England and Wales 2001–2002*, Office of National Statistics, London.

Simmons, J. and Dodd, T. (eds), 2003, *Crime in England and Wales 2002–2003*, Office of National Statistics, London.

Simon, D., 1996, *Elite Deviance* (5th edition), Allyn & Bacon, Boston.

Simon, D., 1999, *Elite Deviance* (6th edition), Allyn & Bacon, Boston, MA.

Simpson, S., Harris, A.R. and Mattson, B.A., 1993, 'Measuring Corporate Crime', in Blankenship, M.B. (ed.), *Understanding Corporate Criminality*, Garland, New York.

Smart, C., 1975, *Women, Crime and Criminology*, Routledge & Kegan Paul, London.

Smart, C., 1997, *Women, Crime and Criminology* (2nd edition), Routledge, London.

Smith, S.G., 1911, *Social Pathology*, Macmillan, New York.

Sparks, R., 2000, 'Perspectives on Risk and Penal Politics', in Hope, T. and Sparks, R. (eds), *Crime, Risk and Insecurity*, Routledge, London.

Spencer, H., 1965, *The Study of Sociology*, Free Press, New York.

Stanley, I. and Wise, S., 1983, *Breaking Out: Feminist Consciousness and Feminist Research*, Routledge & Kegan Paul, London.

Stanley-Hall, G., 1904, *Adolescence*, Appleton, Philadelphia, PA, 2 vols.

Stattin, H., Romelsjö, A. and Stenbacka, M., 1997, 'Personal resources as modifiers of the risk for future criminality', *British Journal of Criminology*, Vol. 37: 198–223.

Steedman, C., 1990, *Childhood, Culture and Class in Britain: Margaret Macmillan 1860–1931*, Rutgers University Press, New Brunswick, NJ.

Stern, J., 1982, 'Does Unemployment Really Kill?', *New Society*, 10 June: 421–2.

Stigler, S., 1987, *The History of Statistics*, Belknap Press at Harvard, Cambridge, MA.

Stitt, B. and Giacopassi, D.J., 1993, 'Assessing Victimization from Corporate Harms', in Blankenship, M.B. (ed.), *Understanding Corporate Criminality*, Garland, New York.

Stohl, M. and Lopez, G. (eds), 1984, *The State as Terrorist*, Aldwych Press, London.

Stohl, M. and Lopez, G. (eds), 1986, *Governmental Violence and Repression: An Agenda for Research*, Greenwood Press, Westport, CT.

Storey, M., 1998, '*Kruger vs The Commonwealth*: Does Genocide Require Malice?', *UNSW Law Journal*, Vol. 21, No. 1: 224–37.

Sumner, C. (ed.), 1990, *Censure, Politics and Criminal Justice*, Open University, Milton Keynes.

Sumner, C., 1994, *The Sociology of Deviance: An Obituary*, Open University, Buckingham.

Sumner, C., 1997, 'Censure, Crime and State', in Maguire, M., Morgan, R. and Reiner, R. (eds), *The Oxford Handbook of Criminology* (2nd edition), Oxford University Press, Oxford.

Sutherland, E., 1924, *Criminology*, J.B. Lippincott, Philadelphia, PA.

Sutherland, E., 1947, *Criminology*, J.B. Lippincott, Philadelphia, PA.

Sutherland, E., 1983, *White-Collar Crime* (1949), Yale University Press, New Haven.

Sutherland, E., 1994, 'White-Collar Criminality' (1940), in Jacoby, J. (ed.), *Classics of Criminology*, Waveland, Illinois.

Sutherland, E. and Cressey, D., 1970, *Criminology*, J.B. Lippincott, PA.

Sutherland, E. and Cressey, D., 1978, *Criminology* (10th edition), Lippincott, New York.

Sutton, A., 1996, 'Crime Prevention: Promise or Threat?', *Australian and New Zealand Journal of Criminology*, Vol. 27, No. 1: 52–69.

Sutton, A. and O'Malley, P. (eds), 1997, *Crime Prevention in Australia: Issues in Policy and Research*, Federation Press, Armadale.

Sutton, A. and White, R., 1995, 'Crime Prevention, Urban Space and Social Exclusion', *Australian and New Zealand Journal of Sociology*, Vol. 34, No. 2: 82–99.

Swaaningen, R. van, 1997, *Critical Criminology*, Sage, London.

Tait, D., 1994, 'Cautions and Appearances: Statistics about Youth and Police', in White, R. and Alder, C. (eds), *The Police and Young People in Australia*, Cambridge University Press, Cambridge.

Tarde, G., 1886, *La criminalité comparée*, Alcan, Paris.

Tarde, G., 1890, *Penal Philosophy*, Green & Co, London.

Task Force on Crime Prevention, 1999, *Getting Tough on Crime*, Queensland Government, Brisbane.

Taylor, C., 1977, 'Interpretation and the Sciences of Man', in Dallmayr, F. and McCarthy, T. (eds), *Understanding and Social Enquiry*, University of Notre Dame Press, Notre Dame, IN.

Taylor, I., 1983, *Crime, Capitalism and Community: Three Essays in Socialist Criminology*, Butterworth & Co., Toronto.

Taylor, I., 1997, 'The Political Economy of Crime', in Maguire, M., Morgan, R. and Reiner, R. (eds), *The Oxford Handbook of Criminology* (2nd edition), Oxford University Press, Oxford.

Taylor, I. and Taylor, L., 1973, *Politics and Deviance*, Penguin, Harmondsworth.

Taylor, I., Walton, P. and Young, J., 1973, *The New Criminology: For a Social Theory of Deviance*, Routledge & Kegan Paul, London.

Taylor, I., Walton, P. and Young, J. (eds), 1975, *Critical Criminology*, Routledge & Kegan Paul, London.

Thomas, G. (ed.), 1990, *The Unresolved Past: A Debate in German History*, St Martin's Press, New York.

Thomas, W.I., 1923, *The Unadjusted Girl: With Cases and Standpoint Analysis*, Little Brown, Boston, MA.

Thompson, K., 1998, *Moral Panics*, Routledge, London.

Thorn, C., 1996, 'Big Business – Organised Crime', in Hazlehurst, K. (ed.), *Crime and Justice: An Australian Textbook in Criminology*, LBC Information Services, Melbourne.

Thrasher, F., 1927, *The Gang: A Study of 1313 Gangs in Chicago*, University of Chicago Press, Chicago, IL.

Tindale, N., 1941, 'Survey of the Half-Caste Problem in South Australia', *Proceedings of the Royal Geographical Society of South Australia*, Vol. 42.

Todorov, T., 1996, *Facing the Extreme: Moral Life in the Concentration Camps*, Owl Books, London.

Tomasic, R., 1991, *Casino Capitalism: Insider Trading in Australia*, Australian Institute of Criminology, Canberra.

Tong, R., 1989, *Feminist Thought: A Comprehensive Introduction*, Allen & Unwin, Sydney.

Toulmin, S., 1961, *The Uses of Argument*, Cambridge University Press, Cambridge.

Touraine, A., 1986, *The Return of the Actor*, University of Minnesota Press, Minnesota.

Turner, B.S. (ed.), 1990, *Theories of Modernity and Postmodernity*, Sage, Newbury Park, CA.

Tygart, C.E., 1991, 'Juvenile Delinquency and Number of Children in a Family', *Youth and Society*, Vol. 22, No. 2: 525–36.

Unger, R.M., 2005, *What Should the Left Propose?*, Verso, London.

Utting, D., 1994, 'Family Factors and the Rise in Crime', in Coote, A. (ed.), *Families, Children and Crime*, Institute of Public Policy Research, London.

Utting, D., 1995, 'When the Talking Has to Stop', *Guardian*, February 22.

Utting, D., Bright, J. and Henricson, C., 1993, 'Crime and the Family: Improving Child-Rearing and Preventing Delinquency', Family Policy Studies Centre, London.

Vinson, T., 1982, *Prison Reform*, Penguin, Ringwood.

Vold, G., 1958, *Theoretical Criminology*, Oxford University Press, New York.

Vold, G., Bernard, T. and Snipes, J., 2002, *Theoretical Criminology* (5th edition), Oxford University Press, New York.

Waal, A. de, 1997, *Famine Crimes: Politics and the Disaster Relief Industry in Africa*, James Currey, Oxford.

Walby, S., 1992, 'Post-Post-Modernism? Theorizing Social Complexity', in Barratt, M. and Phillips, A. (eds), *Destabilizing Theory: Contemporary Feminist Debates*, Polity Press, Cambridge.

Waldman, M., 1990, *Who Robbed America?*, Random House, New York.

Walker, A., Kershaw, C. and Nicholas, J.M., 2006, *Crime in England and Wales 2005/06*, online: www.homeoffice.gov.uk/rds/index.htm.

Walker, M. (ed.), 1995, *Interpreting Crime Statistics*, Oxford University Press, Oxford.

Walker, N., 1965, *Crime and Punishment*, Edinburgh University Press, Edinburgh.

Walklate, S., 1990, 'Researching Victims of Crime: Radical Victimology', *Social Justice*, Vol. 17, No. 3: 25–42.

Walklate, S., 1998, *Understanding Criminology*, Open University Press, Milton Keynes.

Walklate, S., 2003, *Gender, Crime and Criminal Justice* (2nd edition), Willan Publishing, Devon.

Walklate, S., 2004, 'The Protective Society? Seeking Safety in an Insecure World', *Community Safety*, Vol. 3, No. 1: 38–48.

Walklate, S., 2006, *Criminology: The Basics*, Routledge, Abingdon.

Wallerstein, I., 1974, *The Modern World System*, Academic Press, New York.

Walters, R., 2003, 'New Modes of Governance and the Commodification of Criminological Knowledge', *Social and Legal Studies*, Vol. 12, No. 1: 5–26.

Walton, P. and Young, J. (eds), 1998, *The New Criminology Revisited*, Macmillan, London.

Watts, R., 1996, 'Unemployment, the Underclass and Crime in Australia: A Critique', *Australian and New Zealand Journal of Criminology*, Vol. 29, No. 1: 1–19.

Watts, R., 2006, 'The Politics of Discourse: Academic Responses to the Dawkins Reform of Higher Education 1945–1991', in *Fifty Years of Melbourne Studies in Education*, La Trobe University, Bundoora.

Weatherburn, D., 1992, 'Economic Adversity and Crime', *Trends and Issues*, No. 40, Australian Institute of Criminology, August.

Weatherburn, D., 1993, 'On the Quest for a General Theory of Crime', *Australian and New Zealand Journal of Criminology*, Vol. 26, No. 1: 35–46.

Weber, M., 1947, 'Social Action and its Types', in Weber, M., *The Theory of Social and Economic Organisation* (trans. Henderson, A. and Parsons, T.), Free Press, Glencoe, IL.

Weindling, P., 1989, *Health, Race and German Politics between National Unification and Nazism, 1870–1945*, Cambridge University Press, Cambridge.

Weinrich, H., 2004, *Lethe: The Art and Critique of Forgetting*, Cornell University Press, Ithaca, NY.

Weiss, S., 1987, 'The Race Hygiene Movement in Germany', *Osiris*, No. 3: 193–236.

Wells, L. and Rankin, J., 1986, 'The Broken Homes Model of Delinquency: Analytical Issues', *Journal of Researching Crime and Delinquency*, Vol. 23, No. 1: 13–29.

Wells, L. and Rankin, J., 1991, 'Families and Delinquency: A Meta-Analysis of the Impact of Broken Homes', *Social Problems*, Vol. 38, No. 1: 33–49.

West, D.J., 1967, *The Young Offender*, Penguin, Harmondsworth.

West, D.J., 1969, *Present Conduct and Future Delinquency: First Report of the Cambridge Study in Delinquent Development*, Heinemann, London.

West, D.J., 1972, *The Future of Parole,* Duckworth, London.

West, D J., 1982, *Delinquency: Its Roots, Causes and Prospects*, Harvard University Press, Cambridge, MA.

West, D. and Farrington, D., 1977, *The Delinquent Way of Life*, Heinemann, London.

White, R., 1989, 'Making Ends Meet: Young People, Work and the Criminal Economy', *Australian and New Zealand Journal of Criminology*, Vol. 22, No. 2: 22–34.

White, R., 1994, 'The Making of a Youth Underclass', *Youth Studies Australia*, Vol. 13, No. 1: 18–24.

White, R., 1995, 'The Poverty of the Welfare State: Managing the Underclass', in Emy, H.V. and James, P. (eds), *The State in Question*, Macmillan, Melbourne.

White, R., 1997, 'The Business of Youth Crime Prevention', in Sutton, A. and O'Malley, P. (eds), *Crime Prevention in Australia: Issues in Policy and Research*, Federation Press, Armadale.

White, R. and Haines, F., 1996, *Crime and Criminology: An Introduction*, Oxford University Press, Melbourne.

White, R. and Sutton, A., 1995, 'Crime Prevention, Urban Space and Social Exclusion', *Australian and New Zealand Journal of Sociology*, Vol. 31, No. 2: 82–99.

Wickham, G., 1992, 'Knowing Law, Knowing Politics', *International Journal of the Sociology of Law*, Vol. 11, No. 2: 137–47.

Wicks, B., 1995, *The Day They Took the Children*, Stoddart, Toronto.

Wiers, P., 1945, 'Wartime Increases in Michigan Delinquency', *American Sociological Review*, Vol. 10: 515–23.

Wiesner, M. and Capaldi, D.M., 2003, 'Relations of childhood and adolescent factors to offending trajectories of young men', *Journal of Research in Crime and Delinquency*, Vol. 40: 231–62.

Wilkins, L., 1965, *Social Deviance*, Tavistock, London.

Williams, K., 1981, *From Pauperism to Poverty*, Routledge & Kegan Paul, London.

Wilson, J.Q., 1975, *Thinking About Crime*, Basic Books, New York.

Wilson, J.Q. and Herrnstein, R.J., 1985, *Crime and Human Nature*, Simon and Schuster, New York.

Wilson, P., 1988, 'Beyond the Rhetoric on "Law and Order"', *Legal Services Bulletin*, Vol. 13, No. 2, April.

Wilson, P. and Arnold, J., 1986, *Street Kids*, Collins Dove, Blackburn.

Wilson, W.J., 1987, *The Truly Disadvantaged: The Inner City, the Underclass and Public Policy*, University of Chicago, Chicago, IL.

Wilson, W.J., 1996, *When Work Disappears: The World of the New Urban Poor*, Alfred Knopf, New York.

Winch, P., 1958, *The Idea of a Social Science*, Routledge, London.

Winfield, R., 1989, *Overcoming Foundations: Studies in Systematic Philosophy*, Columbia University Press, New York.

Winnicott, D., 1964, *The Child, the Family and the Outside World*, Penguin, Harmondsworth.

Winnicott, D., 1968, *The Family and Individual Development*, Social Science Paperbacks, London.

Winnicott, D., 1971, *Play and Reality*, Basic Books, New York.

Winnicott, D., 1984, *Deprivation and Delinquency*, Penguin, Harmondsworth.

Wittgenstein, L., 1953, *Philosophical Investigations*, Blackwell, Oxford.

Woodiwiss, A., 1990, *Social Theory after Postmodernism: Rethinking Production, Law and Class*, Unwin & Hyman, Winchester.

Wright, R., 2000, 'Left Out? The Coverage of Critical Perspectives in Introductory Textbooks, 1990–1999', *Critical Criminology*, Vol. 9, No. 1: 101–22.

Wundersitz, J., 1993, 'Some Statistics on Youth Offending: An Inter-Jurisdictional Comparison', in Gale, F., Naffine, N. and Wundersitz, J. (eds), *Juvenile Justice: Debating the Issues*, Allen & Unwin, Sydney.

Young, A., 1996, *Imagining Crime: Textual Outlaws and Criminal Conversations*, Sage, London.

Young, J., 1971, *The Drugtakers: The Social Meaning of Drug Use*, Paladin, London.

Young, J., 1988, 'Risks of Crime and Fear of Crime: A Realist Critique of Survey-Based Assumptions', in Maguire, M. and Pointing, J. (eds), *Victims of Crime: A New Deal?*, Open University, Milton Keynes.

Young, J., 1994, *Policing the Streets*, London Borough of Islington, London.

Young, J., 1997, 'Breaking Windows: Situating the New Criminology', in Walton, P. and Young, J. (eds), *The New Criminology Revisited*, Macmillan, London.

Young, J., 1999, *The Exclusive Society: Social Exclusion, Crime and Difference in Late Modernity*, Routledge, London.

Zedner, L., 1994, 'Victims', in Maguire, M., Morgan, R. and Reiner, R. (eds), *The Oxford Handbook of Criminology*, Oxford University Press, Oxford.

INDEX

Abadinsky, H., 2
Abbott, P., 146, 156, 178
Aboriginals in Australia, 159, 213, 217–23
Agger, B., 237
Ainsworth-Darnell, J., 115
Alaheto, T., 123, 193, 195
Albanese, J., 198, 203
Alder, C., 117
Alexander, J., 61
Allen, E., 118
Altatt, P., 146
American criminology, 53–4, 62–9
American dream, 64–5
Amnesty International, 171
Anderson, T., 88, 160
anomie, 61, 64–6
'anti-social' behaviour, 133, 141–5, 158–61,
    230; idea of, 17, 61–6
apartheidt, 173
Applebaum, A., 213
Arblaster, A., 170, 211
Archer, D., 171, 212
Arendt, H., 5, 224
argument structure in criminology, 97–103
Aries, P., 218
Aristotle, 8, 83
Ashworthy, T, 230
assumptions,101–3, 118–19, 230; about crime
    prevention, 158–62; epistemic, 102; ethical,
    102; ontological, 102
Athens, L., 75, 127, 232
Aune, J., 155
Auschwitz, 76
Austin, T., 222
Ayer, A.J., 41

Bagguley, P., 115
Bagnell, K., 217, 220
Barak, G., 208

Bauman, Z., 89, 224, 235
Baxi, U., 194
Bayart, J., 208
Bean, P., 217
Beccaria, G., 36–8, 227
Beck, U., 150
Becker, G., 38, 156
Becker, H., 71, 72–3, 75–6, 103
Becker, J., 215
Behaviour, 60
behaviourism, 60
Beirne, P., 2, 6, 23, 57, 60, 208
Bellair, P., 115
Bentham, J., 32, 36–8, 43, 151, 227
Berger, P., 72
Berlin, I., 211
Berry, J., 217
Bessant, J., 115, 128, 156, 158, 160, 171,
    203
bio-politics, 152
Bird, C., 217
Black, T., 22
Blair, T., 18, 112, 149, 155, 169
Blalock, H., 68
Blankenship, D., 192, 203
Bleakly, W., 222
Bledstein, B., 56
Block, M., 115
Blumer, H., 72
Bohme, G., 90, 118
Bosswell, J., 14
Bottomley, K., 149
Bourdieu, P., 8, 185, 233, 234, 235, 236
Bowlby, J., 132–5, 153
Box, S., 112. 117, 118, 190, 205
Boyd, E., 21
Braithwaite, J., 156, 191, 192, 203, 231
Brake, M., 77, 148, 178
Brenner, W., 115